INSIDERS'GUIDE® to
Williamsburg and Virginia's Historic Triangle

18TH EDITION

SUSAN CORBETT

Globe Pequot

GUILFORD, CONNECTICUT

All the information in this guidebook is subject to change. We recommend that you call ahead to obtain current information before traveling.

Globe Pequot

An imprint of The Rowman & Littlefield Publishing Group, Inc.
4501 Forbes Blvd., Suite 200
Lanham, MD 20706
www.rowman.com

Distributed by NATIONAL BOOK NETWORK

Copyright © 2021 by The Rowman & Littlefield Publishing Group, Inc.
This Globe Pequot edition 2021
Cover photo by KenWiedemann/GettyImages
Maps by Melissa Baker, copyright © by The Rowman
& Littlefield Publishing Group, Inc.
Title page photo © The Nico Studio/Shutterstock.com

British Library Cataloguing in Publication Information available

Library of Congress Cataloging-in-Publication Data available

ISBN 978-1-4930-4531-0 (paper : alk. paper)
ISBN 978-1-4930-4532-7 (electronic)

∞™ The paper used in this publication meets the minimum requirements of American National Standard for Information Sciences—Permanence of Paper for Printed Library Materials, ANSI/NISO Z39.48-1992.

Contents

About the Author

Susan Corbett has been a journalist for more than 30 years. She is also the author of several novels for young readers, including *The Last Newspaper Boy in America* and *Free Baseball*. She lives in Williamsburg, Virginia.

HALF HOLLOW HILLS COMMUNITY LIBRARY

Great News! Our temporary location,
Chestnut Hill Elementary School
in Dix Hills, is now open!

Chestnut Hill	Melville Branch
600 S. Service Rd	510 Sweet Hollow Rd
Dix Hills, NY 11746	Melville, NY 11747
(631)-421-4530	(631) 421-4535

08/17/2021

Items checked out to:
p17481612

Title: **The insiders' guide to Williamsburg : and**
Barcode: 30614003746361
Call #: 917.5542 WILLIAMSBURG
Due: **09-07-21**

Total items checked out: 1

'ou just saved an estimated $15 by
using the Library today.

Thank you for visiting!

How to Use This Book

The Williamsburg area is nothing if not resilient. Two wars were fought and ended here—bringing America its first taste of independence and, nearly a century later, ending the divisive war that nearly split the country in two.

What's a little pandemic compared to that?

Well, a lot it turns out. Like other communities, adjusting to the demands necessitated by the coronavirus stressed the area to its breaking point for a while.

And yet, what a testament to creativity the Historic Triangle's response has been. Can't eat inside? Restaurants moved their tables outside, masked up their servers, converted menus to disposable paper options and reduced hours so more time could be spent keeping their businesses clean. Retail outlets offered curbside pickup. The attractions opened with temperature checks and by temporarily capping the number of visitors allowed inside.

As a result, there have been some big changes. Certain roads closed to vehicular traffic so they could be used for al fresco dining instead. Many businesses closed altogether, although hopefully not permanently. If you had a favorite buffet-style restaurant, it has likely changed its business model. Free breakfasts at area hotels went into grab-and-go brown bags.

Nonetheless, Williamsburg still offers a lot to do, even if some of it has to be done for a while with social distancing rules in place. History, roller coasters, an outlet shopping mall that might take two days to get through.

And there is more to see here than just the sites in Williamsburg. No visit to the Virginia's Historic Triangle is complete without imagining the end of the Revolutionary War on Yorktown's battlefields or stepping aboard a replica of the (tiny!) ships that brought Captain John Smith and his crew from England to Jamestown.

This book lays out the best sites to see, things to do, and places to eat and stay. Recognizing that families are always on the lookout for adventures that will broaden their children's horizons, we've added more activities that can be enjoyed in the great outdoors to our Kidstuff and Parks and Recreation chapters. Likewise, Colonial Williamsburg offers a long list of programs designed to entertain and enlighten the entire family. It's a selection you can review with your children as you sit down and plan your vacation.

To help you decide where to rest your weary head, our Accommodations chapter gives you plenty of choices, from familiar chain hotels to unique bed and breakfasts, with an easy pricing key. Entries are organized by category, in alphabetical order. In our Dining chapter, eateries are listed in alphabetical order.

We've included information about the best places in town to shop, grouped by location or type of merchandise.

Our chapter on Attractions highlights the two major theme parks, Colonial Williamsburg, and lesser-known places, like beautiful plantation houses and historic churches.

If there's a duffer in your party, peruse our Parks and Recreation chapter for the lowdown on local courses. Other outdoor pursuits are also explored in that chapter, which directs you to places where you can hike, bike, swim, or drop that hook, line, and sinker in and around the Williamsburg area. Our Day Trips chapter can tell you how to get to points of interest outside the Historic Triangle and what to do once you reach them.

As in previous editions, we have dedicated considerable attention and space to Newport News and Hampton, adjacent cities on the Virginia Peninsula that are just a short jaunt east of Williamsburg on I-64. This in-depth chapter includes information on attractions, restaurants, accommodations, and shopping. In essence, it's a microcosm of the information we give you on Williamsburg and shares enough data for planning a separate visit to this area, dubbed the Lower Peninsula.

Moving to Virginia or already residing here? The Living Here appendix offers information on relocation, retirement, education, health care, and local media.

Williamsburg and Virginia's Historic Triangle

Williamsburg claims a long and fascinating history. In its three centuries, Virginia's former capital enjoyed both periods of great fortune and dramatic decline before reinventing itself through an unprecedented restoration process that began in the mid-1920s.

This successful effort at re-creating Williamsburg's past in a way that it can be enjoyed in the present is what draws visitors to the 18th-century buildings and brick-paved streets of the city. Most find themselves moved and inspired by seeing this re-creation of early American life spread out in front of them. In town to discuss his documentary on Thomas Jefferson, filmmaker and historian Ken Burns called his visit to Williamsburg "the highlight of my professional life."

Speaking at a convention at the College of William & Mary several years ago, Pulitzer Prize–winning historian David McCullough said exploring the past is "an antidote to self-pity" because no matter how bad off we might think ourselves now, "others have had it worse."

Of course, we don't think for one minute that you're here in Williamsburg to gloat over your forefathers' misfortunes. We do believe, however, that if you have come to town to seek a little perspective—or maybe just a thrilling loop-de-loop on a roller coaster—you're in the right place.

WHY WILLIAMSBURG?

Did you ever wonder why the early colonists chose Williamsburg as the seat of government for Virginia? Believe it or not, you can thank the lowly mosquito for getting Williamsburg off the ground. When English settlers set foot on New World soil in 1607, they made their homes in Jamestown, which became the center of the Virginia Colony's government. But Jamestown lay on a low, marshy island that was also home to a well-established (and quite nasty) population of stinging and biting insects. Some settlers, fearing island conditions could lead to epidemics and finding the current site not grand enough for the capital city of America's largest colony, lobbied for relocation to a place called Middle Plantation, 5 miles inland. This settlement, which had grown up around a 17th-century palisade built as a defense against Indian attack, was a small village composed of stores, mills, a tavern, a church, and an assortment of homes by 1690. In reality, there was nothing grand about it, but it sat on relatively high ground and had access to both the James and York Rivers via navigable creeks.

For those who advocated moving inland, serendipity struck in the form of fire, when the Jamestown Statehouse burned for the fourth time in 1698. Thus, the basically unformed village of Middle Plantation became the locus for colonists who envisioned a capital city equal to their aspirations. The name Middle Plantation, more rural than regal, was changed to Williamsburg in honor of William III, king of England, and building began.

The new capital was laid out in a distinctly geometrical fashion, dictated by the colonists' current ideas about proper urban planning. The Market Square, or town commons, and a main street stretching from the Capitol building to the newly established College of William & Mary were the key structural elements of the plan. The Capitol and the college, along with Bruton Parish Church, represented stability and continuity to early settlers.

By the mid-18th century, Williamsburg was a thriving center of commerce and government. Close to 2,000 people, half of them slaves, called the city home on the eve of the American Revolution. Tailors, carpenters, bakers, gunsmiths, wheelwrights, merchants, clerks, and slaves all worked to form the support system for the capital city's growing number of—what else—politicians and lawyers. While the latter two professions wielded power and enjoyed considerable prestige, there are those who would argue that the most important persons in town were the tavern keepers. Taverns were not just for drinking, after all; they were the political, social, and cultural heart of colonial life. If the walls of the Raleigh Tavern could speak, surely they would tell of the clandestine sessions held there by Virginia's burgesses. They could also tell tales of a more scandalous and less heroic sort. Thomas Jefferson didn't brand the town "Devilsburg" for no reason.

The prominent role Williamsburg played in events leading to the Revolutionary War is well known. In 1765 Patrick Henry delivered his rousing (some said treasonous) Stamp Act speech at the House of Burgesses here. The First Continental Congress was called from here in 1774. And, for all intents and purposes, the Revolution ended a dozen miles away, with the surrender of Cornwallis to Washington on the fields of Yorktown in 1781.

FROM RICHES TO RAGS

But as the Revolutionary War wound down, Williamsburg's days as a center of government were over. In 1780, shortly after Jefferson was elected to succeed Patrick Henry as Virginia's governor, the capital was moved to Richmond.

Jefferson had long advocated moving the capital west to reduce traveling distances for officials coming from the far reaches of the colony (then stretching as far west as present-day Illinois). Richmond also was judged a safer site, in terms of both climate and military defense.

As Richmond moved into the spotlight, Williamsburg suffered through a decline and loss of prestige and vitality. Taverns closed; public buildings fell into ruin. The number of residents dwindled to about 1,400. Shortly after the Revolution, the empty Governor's Palace and Capitol burned. Only two institutions of note remained: the college, with enrollment greatly diminished, and the Public Hospital for the Insane. (Town wags liked to say that the only difference between the two was that the latter required some proof of improvement before letting you leave.)

The Civil War did little to enhance Williamsburg's fortunes. Though most of the 18th-century buildings survived, federal troops occupied the town for three years, and the college was forced to close after the Wren Building burned. In 1862, McClellan's Union forces battled through in their attempt to reach Richmond, the Confederate capital.

The arrival of the railroad in 1880 inspired a revival. The C&O's Fast Flying Virginian, also called the Cannonball Express, ran daily from its southern terminus in Newport News, through Williamsburg and on to Toledo, Ohio. (Dinner in the dining car cost less than a dollar, and that included whiskey.) New houses sprang up near the C&O depot, roads were paved, and William & Mary added dorms, a library, and a gymnasium. But Williamsburg remained a quiet college burg, rather insulated, until the mid-1920s, when a Rockefeller came to town.

> **i** In Virginia, if you are looking for the experience of living history, you'll find nearly every era represented at numerous special events and destinations year-round. For free brochures on African American, Native American, and Hispanic heritage, or for information on Civil War battlefields and sites, call the Virginia tourism hotline at (800) VISITVA (847-4882).

BACK TO RICHES AGAIN

Luckily for Williamsburg, Dr. W. A. R. Goodwin, rector of Bruton Parish Church, was a man of vast imagination. He saw past the shabby exteriors of the many old buildings and dreamed of restoring the town's faded heritage. Goodwin was also a persuasive fellow and was able to interest philanthropist John D. Rockefeller Jr. in his vision of a vibrant Williamsburg. The two men teamed up and, in 1926, work on the restoration of the colonial capital began. Rockefeller not only provided funds but also personally devoted himself to the ambitious project by directing the measurements of buildings and spearheading research efforts.

Fittingly, the Raleigh Tavern was the first restored building opened to the public, in 1932. Soon the Governor's Palace and reconstructed Capitol were ready for viewing as well. Colonial Williamsburg, repository of the American past, was well on its way to becoming the re-created village it is today. Tourists arrived in small numbers at first, but after Queen Elizabeth's visit to the Historic Area in 1957, the public began coming in droves. Hotels, motels, restaurants, and shopping centers sprang up to serve them.

Benefiting from the ready audience Colonial Williamsburg provided, a number of nearby Historic Triangle attractions decided to put on the ritz. National Park Service properties at Jamestown and Yorktown were improved. Jamestown Settlement, adjacent to Jamestown Island, opened in 1957. Yorktown Victory Center opened in 1976 (and was renamed the American Revolution Museum in 2015 as part of a $50 million renovation). In 2014, paid attendance at the two attractions totaled nearly 550,000.

Anheuser-Busch arrived in the area, first with a brewery and then with the enormously popular Busch Gardens theme park, which celebrated its 45th anniversary in 2020. The Williamsburg Pottery Factory grew from a roadside stand into a vast and somewhat indescribable retail complex that has drawn millions of shoppers annually. By the time Water Country USA opened its doors in 1984, Williamsburg had reinvented itself again—this time as a vacation destination with something for everyone to enjoy, not just the history buffs.

ABOUT THE ECONOMY

Attracting tourists isn't the only business of the Historic Triangle, though it is the major driver. The other is education, with two world-class institutions, the

College of William & Mary and the Colonial Williamsburg Foundation, at its core. That said, industry, commerce, and professional services have also grown dramatically. Regionally, the economy has long hosted military and related contractors—shipbuilding historically, but increasingly such high-technology fields as remote sensing and computer-driven simulations.

In and around Williamsburg proper, the Anheuser-Busch name remains although on properties the St. Louis-based beer company no longer owns. The brewery, bought by the Belgian-based beer conglomerate InBev in 2008 is a major employer, producing millions of barrels of beer a year. The former Busch theme parks—Busch Gardens and Water Country USA—were sold to the private equity group in 2009 and are now operated as units of Seaworld Parks and Entertainment. Busch's luxury resort, Kingsmill, located adjacent to Busch Gardens and the brewery, was sold to Escalante Golf for $31 million in 2017, which revived the resort's sponsorship of the Ladies Professional Golf Association (LPGA) Pure Silk Open, which is held annually on the links at Kingsmill in May. The event is highly popular with fans and draws a competitive field of the sport's top athletes.

Other major local employers in and around Williamsburg include hotels and time-share resorts. The majority of the business establishments within the city limits fall into the retail trade or accommodation/food services category. Williamsburg has also become a magnet for medicine. In addition to the oldest mental health facility in the country, Eastern State Hospital, the city and adjacent James City County are home to the campuses of Sentara Williamsburg Regional Medical Center and Riverside Doctor's Hospital.

> **i** When you begin thinking about a trip to Williamsburg and its historic sister cities, check the VisitWilliamsburg.com website, run by the Greater Williamsburg Chamber & Tourism Alliance, for ideas and resources. Got a specific question? Give them a call at (757) 229-6511.

The region's population growth has also been a critical economic factor, especially in the areas immediately surrounding the city of Williamsburg. James City County, for example, almost tripled in population between 1990 and 2019, to more than 76,000, and is projected to top 110,000 by 2040. That has meant significant spending and jobs in construction, both of homes and commercial facilities. The region rebounded from the 2008 recession, and until the pandemic, unemployment had remained below the national average, largely because of the cushioning effect of military spending and other government programs.

Williamsburg Facts

Original inhabitants: Powhatan tribe

Founding of English settlement: 1631

Original name: Middle Plantation

Area: 9.2 square miles

Williamsburg population: 14,954 including nearly 9,000 students at the College of William & Mary (2019)

Total population of area including Williamsburg, York, and James City Counties: 159,683

Oldest educational institution: College of William & Mary, founded 1693 (second oldest in the US, behind Harvard)

Number of alumni who served as US president: 3

Year first psychiatric hospital in North America was founded in Williamsburg: 1770, original name: Public Hospital for Lunaticks, current name: Eastern State Hospital

Number of tourists who visit the area per year: 6 to 8 million

Principal employers: Tourism, education

Unemployment rate: 4.3 (2020)

Average rainfall: 48 inches

Average snowfall: 5 inches

Average temperature January high: 52°F

January low: 33°F

July high: 91°F

July low: 71°F

Median home sale price: $355,000

Percentage of population 25 or older with a bachelor's degree or higher: 57 percent

Those programs stretch far beyond building ships and maintaining military bases. For instance, the region has one of the highest concentrations of scientists and engineers in the country—and they don't just work at shipyards. They're also at places like NASA's Langley Research Center in Hampton, which specializes in aeronautics, and the US Department of Energy's Jefferson Lab in Newport News, where particle accelerators and high-energy lasers give scientists insight into the basic nature of atoms.

If you need to know more about the area's economy, there are a number of useful resources. Both the *Virginia Gazette* and the *Daily Press* cover regional economic news. More broadly, the Virginia Economic Commission (virginia works.com) maintains economic data for the city and state, and the University of Virginia's Weldon Cooper Center for Public Service (coopercenter.org) is a one-stop directory for all types of in-depth private and government statistics and trends.

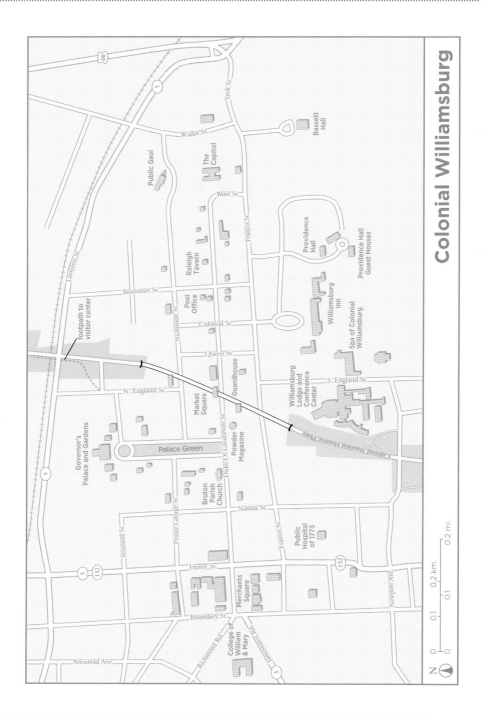

Colonial Williamsburg

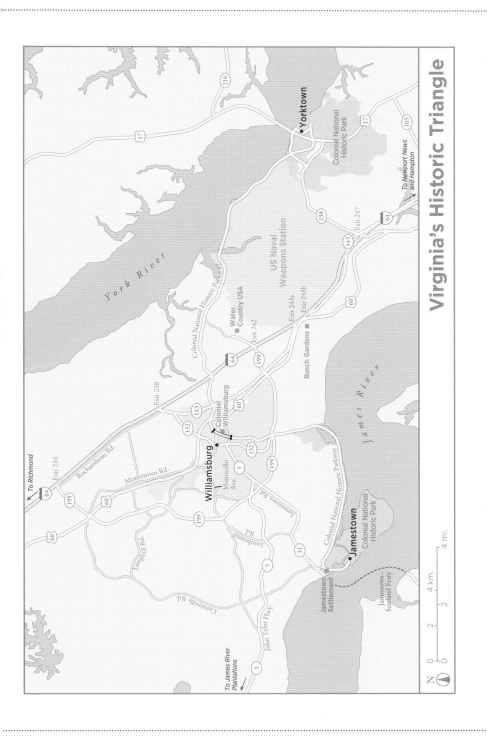

Virginia's Historic Triangle

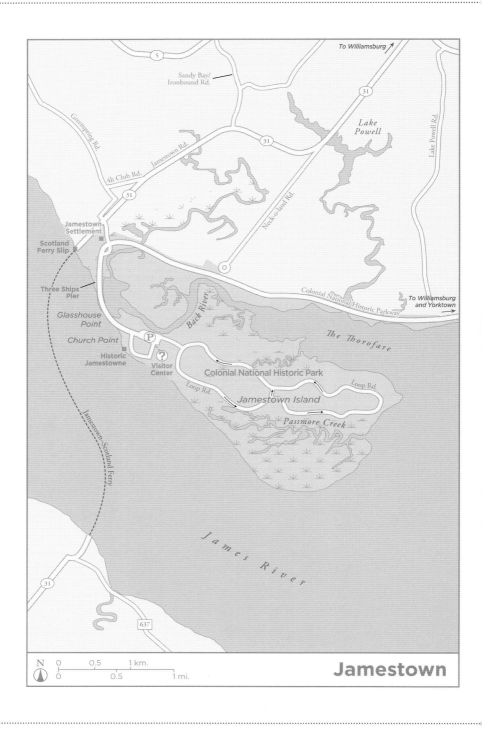

Jamestown

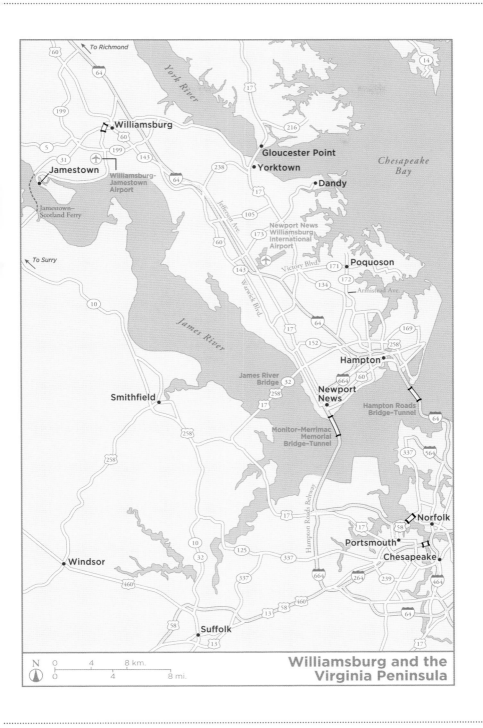

Williamsburg and the
Virginia Peninsula

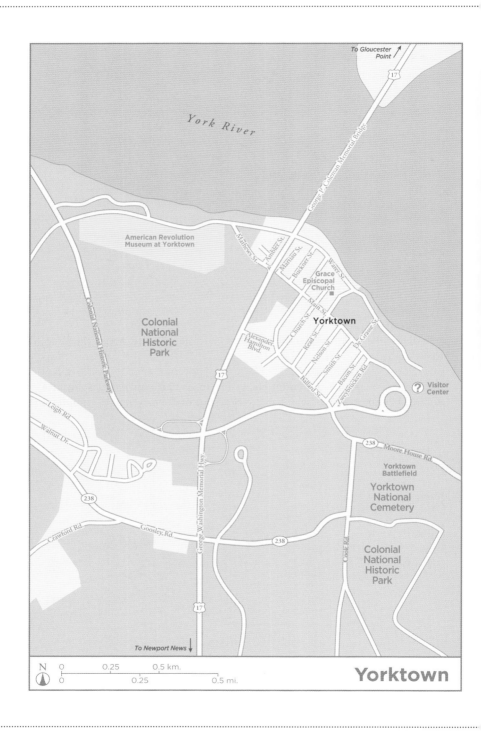

Getting Here, Getting Around

One thing to always remember around Williamsburg and most of Virginia: Very few roads run compass straight. The hilly, river-crossed terrain doesn't lend itself to it. Williamsburg, Jamestown, and Yorktown are small, and roads in the heart of the localities are paved versions of the early paths of the colonists: quaint, sometimes narrow, and often congested. This is a town where the major intersection of the Historic Area is known locally as "Confusion Corner." Give yourself plenty of time to make it to your destination at the desired hour.

Before you can hope to find your way around, it's essential you get a brief geography lesson.

Williamsburg is the northwesternmost city on the Virginia Peninsula which also includes the cities of Hampton, Newport News, Poquoson, and the counties of James City and York.

Across the York River to the north is Gloucester County. Across the James River to the south is South Hampton Roads, or Southside—the cities of Norfolk, Portsmouth, Chesapeake, Suffolk, and Virginia Beach. Taken together, the Virginia Peninsula and South Hampton Roads make up a geographic area dubbed Hampton Roads, which is also the name of the harbor at the mouth of the James River around which most of these cities are located.

With a population of almost 1.8 million, Hampton Roads is the nation's 37th-largest metropolitan statistical area, about the same size as Charlotte, North Carolina, or Austin, Texas.

GETTING HERE

By Automobile

The Virginia Peninsula is sometimes called the world's largest cul-de-sac. People driving to the area have a limited number of routes to choose from.

From the north or south, most visitors arrive via I-64, which connects with I-95 near Richmond. I-64 runs like a spine down the peninsula, then crosses over to the Norfolk area via a tunnel at the wide harbor where the James River meets the Chesapeake Bay.

If you're of a mind to ditch the interstates, there are two scenic alternatives: From the Washington, D.C., area, take US 301 to US 17 across Virginia's Northern Neck and Middle Peninsula. You'll cross the York River at Gloucester Point (there's a $2 toll, but it's collected only from northbound vehicles). You'll pass right by the historic Yorktown Battlefield and can connect to Williamsburg via the Colonial National Historic Parkway, a three-lane road made of river gravel set in concrete.

Another alternative from farther north: Ditch I-95 at Philadelphia and use the Delaware Turnpike and US 13 to the Chesapeake Bay Bridge-Tunnel (touted as an engineering wonder, a series of causeways, bridges, and two tunnels that span more than 17 miles at the mouth of the bay). There's a $18 ($14 off peak) toll each way—expensive, but often less than the aggravation of gridlock on the Washington Beltway or I-95.

From the Richmond area, one scenic alternative to I-64 is US 60, which intersects with I-295 east of Richmond. It's two lanes in each direction, divided in most places, but with frequent turnoffs and occasional traffic lights. The other choice is VA 5, the old plantation route between Williamsburg and Richmond. Protected as a Scenic Byway, VA 5 is a two—lane road through pretty countryside. It is especially picturesque during autumn and provides a cooler, tree-shaded—if slower—option during the heat of summer.

Traveling at legal speed on any of these three highways, you are within an hour of Williamsburg from downtown Richmond. One note about speeding: Besides authorities' usual vigilance, radar detectors are illegal in Virginia. Get caught with one and you'll get *another* ticket in addition to the one for speeding.

From the south—including the Norfolk area and North Carolina's Outer Banks—the main route to the peninsula is I-64 West through the Hampton Roads Bridge-Tunnel, one of the most frustrating water crossings you'll find anywhere. It's free—although the toll it extracts in time can be incalculable. Commuter rush hours (both directions, morning and afternoon, especially in and around the exits to the Naval Station Norfolk) are almost guaranteed to clog. Friday and Sunday afternoons in summer are usually congested, too, as weekend travelers to the Outer Banks add to the flow. But the tunnel can also jam up for no apparent reason at just about any time of day or night—all it takes is for one of the two lanes in either direction to shut down because of a vehicle breakdown, accident, truck turnaround (due to height restrictions), or road maintenance. In 2020, construction began on a $3.9 billion expansion project which will add twin two-lane tunnels west of the existing eastbound tunnel but completion is not expected until late 2025.

The alternatives: The Monitor-Merrimac Bridge-Tunnel (yes, it runs roughly at the place where the famous ironclad battle occurred) is an extension of I-664, the western leg of the Hampton Roads Beltway. Once on the peninsula, stay on I-664 until it connects with I-64, then continue northwest to Williamsburg.

The second alternate is the James River Bridge: Hop over to US 17 (either from the beltway, or from US 58 in Suffolk). Once across the bridge, continue up Mercury Boulevard to I-64.

Perhaps the most leisurely—and memorable—route is the (free) Jamestown-Scotland Ferry from Surry County. Approach Surry on VA 31 until it ends at the James River. Ferries run roughly every half hour during the day and evening, hourly overnight. The trip takes about 15 minutes and deposits you at the foot of Jamestown Road. (The ferry and its fleet of four vessels is an attraction in itself. For more, see our entry in the Day Trips chapter.)

> **i** VA 199 helps motorists circumvent traffic in central Williamsburg and make the trip from **Busch Gardens, Colonial Williamsburg,** or **Water Country USA** to **Premium Outlets** or **Pierce's Pitt Bar-B-Que** in record time. The northwestern two-thirds is a limited-access highway, so drivers can exit at any number of points en route.

By Plane

Three commercial airports and one small, privately owned public-use airport provide service to the area. All offer a choice of major airlines.

NEWPORT NEWS/WILLIAMSBURG INTERNATIONAL AIRPORT, 900 Bland Blvd., Newport News, VA 23602; (757) 877-0221; flyphf.com. The Newport News/Williamsburg International Airport (formerly Patrick Henry Field, hence the airport code "PHF)" is only 17 miles from the heart of Williamsburg.

Depending on your departure point, this can be a quick, cheap entry point to the area, although the loss of AirTran (after its 2011 merger with Southwest Airlines) has greatly reduced the number of flights into and out of this facility. Service is provided by **American Airways** (800) 428-4322 and **Delta** (800) 221-1212. There is direct service to Atlanta, Charlotte, and Philadelphia. All other service is via connections.

Once you're on the ground, you can catch a taxi. Fares vary wildly among cab companies so ask ahead. A full list of cab companies and shared shuttle services (advance reservations recommended) can be found on the airport's website (flyphf.com) under "Airport Information/Ground Transportation."

Car rental companies at the airport are **Avis** (800) 331-1212; **Budget** (800) 527-0700; **Enterprise** (800) 261-7331; **Hertz** (800) 654-3131; **National** (800) 227-7368; and **Zipcar** (866) 494-7227.

NORFOLK INTERNATIONAL AIRPORT, 2200 Norview Ave. (exit 279 off I-64), Norfolk, VA 23518; (757) 857-3351; norfolkairport.com. Norfolk International Airport lies 40 miles southeast of Williamsburg. Commercial air service is provided by **Allegiant** (702) 505-8888, **American** (800) 433-7300, **Delta** (800) 221-1212, **Frontier** (801) 401-9000, **Southwest** (800) 435-9792, and **United** (800) 241-6522.

Rental car companies have desks on Level 1 of the arrivals terminal near baggage claim. On-site rental companies are **Alamo** (800) 462-5266; **Avis** (800) 831-2847; **Budget** (800) 527-0700; **Dollar** (800) 800-4000; **Enterprise** (800) 736-8227; **Hertz** (800) 654-3131; **National** (800) 227-7368; and **Thrifty** (800) 367-2277.

Ground transportation is available 24 hours a day by taxi, Lyft, or Uber. See the full list of providers at norfolkairport.com/ground-transportation/taxi-cabs/.

WILLIAMSBURG JAMESTOWN AIRPORT, 100 Marclay Rd., Williamsburg, VA 23185; (757) 229-9256. This privately owned, public-use general aviation airport celebrated its 50th anniversary in 2020. The airport averages about 17,000 arrivals annually and houses 60 privately owned aircraft. The Williamsburg Flight Center operates on airport property, providing flight training with a fleet of six jet aircraft, plane maintenance, and air tours. A popular restaurant, Charly's Airport Café, serves lunch Tues through Sun and dinner (Fri night only) in the terminal with a patio and a view of the runway.

RICHMOND INTERNATIONAL AIRPORT, 1 Richard E. Byrd Terminal Dr., Richmond, VA 23250; (804) 226-3000; flyrichmond.com. Richmond International Airport, exit 197A off I-64, is about 45 miles west of Williamsburg and offers nonstop flights to 22 destinations and connecting flights to worldwide destinations.

Over the past two decades, the airport terminal and parking garages have undergone a $300 million overhaul, adding gates and, as a result, a lot more flying options and lower fares. Airlines operating out of Richmond International include **AirTran** (800) 247-8726; **American** (800) 433-7300; **Delta** (800) 221-1212; **JetBlue** (800) 538-2583; **Southwest** (800) 435-9792; **United** (800) 241-6522; and **USAir** (800) 428-4322.

You'll find the rental car companies adjacent to the baggage claim area. Companies that serve this airport include **Alamo** (877) 222-9075; **Avis** (800) 831-2847; **Budget** (800) 527-0700; **Dollar** (800) 800-3665; **Enterprise** (800) 261-7331; **Hertz** (800) 654-3131; **National** (800) 227-7368; **Payless** (800) 729-5377; and **Thrifty** (800) 367-2277.

Ground transportation to Williamsburg from the Richmond airport includes several taxi services (located curbside, in the center section of the lower level) and a sedan service provided by James River Transportation, which staffs a customer service counter in the terminal. You can email for specific pricing at sales@jamesrivertrans.com or call (804) 249-1052.

Close-up

The Williamsburg Trolley

Parking in the Historic Area is tight, and traffic during high season can be very congested. For years, one of the best amenities of staying in Colonial Williamsburg (CW) lodging was being able to leave your car behind for the day and hop on a CW bus, which circulates through and around the Historic Area, stopping at major points of interest. (Ticket holders may board at any stop.)

In 2009, the city added trolley service to expand the public transportation options outside the Historic Area. The red-and-green trolleys look traditional but have modern features like bicycle racks, air-conditioning, and full wheelchair accessibility.

Trolleys run from Merchants Square, along Richmond Road to Midtown Row, the new mixed-use development that replaced the old Williamsburg Shopping Center, then west on Monticello Avenue to the New Town area). Service is available from 9 a.m. to 9 p.m. every day except Fri, when the trolleys run until 11 p.m.

A complete loop takes about 30 minutes and costs $1.50 (exact fare only, cash accepted). An all-day pass for unlimited rides is $3 and can be purchased at the WATA ticket window at the Amtrak station, 468 N. Boundary St. Seniors ride for 50 cents. Kids 12 and under ride free with an adult. The trolley does not operate on Thanksgiving, Christmas, or New Year's Day.

Look for the round Williamsburg Trolley signs at locations in New Town, High Street, along Richmond Road, and in and around Merchants Square. Or just look for the trolley—it's hard to miss!

More information is available online at gowata.org (the Williamsburg Area Transit Authority) or by calling (757) 220-5493.

By Rail

AMTRAK, The Williamsburg Transportation Center, 468 N. Boundary St., Williamsburg, VA 23185; (757) 229-8750, (800) 872-7245; amtrak .com. Amtrak's Northeast Regional service generally halts in Richmond, but two trains a day stretch on to (and depart westward from) Williamsburg. The Amtrak terminal, a charming brick building built in 1935, is just 4 blocks from the Historic Area. The Amtrak offices and waiting room are located on the east side of the building. There is a vending area where travelers can grab a snack or pick up visitor information brochures.

Colonial National Historic Parkway

A visit to the Historic Triangle wouldn't be complete without a leisurely drive along Colonial National Historic Parkway, a 23-mile corridor specifically built to link the beginning and the end of the British colonial experience in America, with beautiful views of the James and York Rivers, and the rolling, wooded land between them.

The Colonial Parkway has limited exits and no amenities, commercial advertising, or trucks. But there is wildlife—deer, squirrels, muskrats, and possums may wander across the road. The waterways you encounter are home to fish, crabs, egrets, and waterfowl. Think of it as a "linear park," shielded from development. The drive is especially enchanting in spring, when the dogwood and redbud are blooming, and in the fall, when the hardwoods' leaves turn color.

A warning to the lead-footed: This is a federal road, and the speed limits, which range from 25 mph to 45 mph, are strictly enforced. Getting a ticket means appearing in federal court, where few beat the offense. Moreover, the road is made of river gravel set in concrete. Driving much faster than 45 mph gets noisy.

Points of interest are marked by numerous turnouts with informative signs. These often give historical information not covered by visits to individual sites, so the drive will complement tours of Jamestown, Williamsburg, or Yorktown. Above all, it demonstrates how history and the prosperity of the Historic Triangle are intertwined with the waterways, from colonial times to today.

Leaving Jamestown, you'll pass through woodlands of silver maples, river birches, pine, and spruce. The James River runs along your right. You'll note dozens of duck blinds in the marshes and creeks. The river is a flyway for many ducks as well as Canada geese.

Each turnout contains a historical marker. One on the Jamestown end notes the site of an early community called **Archer's Hope.** All five inhabitants were among the one-quarter of Virginia's colonists killed during a massacre on March 22, 1622. A little farther down the road toward Williamsburg, a marker notes the site of an early attempted settlement that actually predated Jamestown. In September 1570 a group of Spanish Jesuits landed along College Creek. They crossed the peninsula to the York River, where they established a mission. But six months later all of them, except one young boy, were wiped out during an attack. The young boy survived in the woods until he was rescued by a relief expedition in 1572.

The road then turns inland (and the speed limit drops to 35) as you enter Williamsburg. Just beyond a short tunnel (you'll pass under Duke of Gloucester Street in the heart of the Historic Area), there's a turnoff to Colonial Williamsburg; to stay on the Colonial Parkway, bear to your right.

Yorktown is 13 miles away, but there's plenty to see before you get there. Among the historical markers: the site of a Union Army advance on Williamsburg during the Civil War; Jones Mill Pond, a favorite local fishing hole; and the sites of Ringfield and Bellfield Plantations. Once you pass over King's Creek, the banks of the majestic York River open up before you. On the left side of the river is Gloucester County, a place full of a history all its own.

On this side of the river, a long dock stretching into the river is the loading pier of **Cheatham Annex,** an ammunition supply depot for the Naval Station Norfolk. Nearby a marker points out Werewocomoco, Powhatan's "chiefest habitation" and the place where Captain John Smith was held captive in 1607.

The **York River,** known as the Pamunkey by native inhabitants, flows over the deepest natural channel of any in the Chesapeake Bay tributary. That's why a little farther downriver you'll come across another pier. This one is located adjacent to the Yorktown Naval Weapons Station, established in 1918 to support the Atlantic Fleet, homeported in Norfolk. If you pull over into the Bracken's Pond turnout, you may see large naval ships taking on supplies. If you see armed guards along the parkway, red lights on the pier, or a ship flying a red flag, you'll know that's the business at hand.

Within minutes you'll come upon a left-hand exit for **Yorktown Waterfront,** the commercial district. Continue straight to reach Yorktown Battlefield, site of the British surrender to the American Continental Army in 1781, when the American Revolution came to a close.

The best way to enjoy the parkway is to set aside a few hours to explore. Ingredients for a picnic can be gathered at **The Cheese Shop** in Williamsburg, or the **Jamestown Pie Company** closer to the road's southern end. You'll find plenty of places to pull over and enjoy a waterside vista.

Close-up

Pronunciation Guide

English has been spoken here longer than anywhere else in North America, but visitors may be unfamiliar with some of these popular names, many of which date to the first meetings of Native Americans and the colonials.

Botetourt: BOT-a-tot. Lord Botetourt was the Virginia Colony's governor from 1768 to 1770. You'll see his name on area streets and the occasional room or hall of a public building.

Chickahominy River: chick-a-HOM-i-nee. This Indian word means "land of much grain." The river is in New Kent County and meets the James just west of Williamsburg.

DoG Street: Students and locals use this acronym for Duke of Gloucester Street, Colonial Williamsburg's central pedestrian thoroughfare.

Fort Eustis: fort YOU-stess. See our Newport News chapter for more information on this military facility and its transportation museum.

Gaol: jail. At the Public Gaol behind the Capitol on Nicholson Street in Colonial Williamsburg, visitors can see the small, dank cells where 18th-century criminals and debtors were incarcerated. Credit the British with the funny spelling.

Gloucester: GLOSS-ter. This county north of the York River is named after an English city.

Isle of Wight: ile-of-wite. Named after an English island, this county lies south of the James River.

Taxi service, provided by several companies, is available, but the major car rental companies' offices are some distance from the station. The closest is a locally owned company, **Colonial Rent-A-Car** at 4039 Ironbound Rd. Call (757) 220-3399 or (888) 220-9941 for specifics or visit the website at colonial rentacar.co.

By Bus

GREYHOUND, The Williamsburg Transportation Center, 468 N. Boundary St., Williamsburg, VA 23185; (800) 231-2222; greyhound.com. Greyhound offers nationwide service to and from the Williamsburg area. Arrivals

Mattaponi River: mat-ta-pa-NI. The name of this York River tributary is derived from an Indian language.

Norfolk: NAW-fok. Even natives sometimes disagree about the right way to say this city's name. The best advice probably is to say it quickly.

Pamunkey: puh-MUN-key. This Indian tribe's reservation is in King William County.

Poquoson: puh-KO-sen. Derived from the Indian for "low ground" or "swamp," this peninsula city (next to York County) is a popular suburb with the scientists and air crew from nearby Langley Air Force base and NASA Langley Research Center.

Powhatan: POW-a-tan. This famous Indian chief, father of Pocahontas, might be surprised to see his moniker used not only on streets but also as a name for a time-share development.

Rochambeau: row-sham-BOW. This French general was Washington's ally at Yorktown during the Revolutionary War.

Taliaferro: TOL-liv-er. This old Virginia family, originally Italian, had their name Anglicized. General William Booth Taliaferro was a wealthy planter and greatly aided the devastated College of William & Mary after the Civil War.

Toano: toe-AN-oh. This town in western James City County takes its name from an Indian believed to have been a member of Powhatan's tribe.

Wythe: with. George Wythe signed the Declaration of Independence, was William & Mary's first professor of law, and eventually became chancellor of Virginia. The Wythe House in Colonial Williamsburg was once his property.

and departures are from the Williamsburg Transportation Center, the same 1930s-era building that houses the Amtrak station but there is no on-site ticket window. Purchase a ticket online in advance.

Once You're Here

Here's an easy trick: Think of the region as a cross, with Colonial Williamsburg at the center. The Colonial Parkway, the upright portion of the cross, has Yorktown at the top and Jamestown at the bottom. US 60, the crossing arm, has Toano, Lightfoot, and the outlets to the left, and Busch Gardens and Water Country USA to the right.

> **i** When asking for directions, don't even try to figure out the compass directions (most locals don't bother). Because so few roads run by the compass (and not many more actually stay *straight* for very long), it's easier to have a destination in mind when you ask a local for directions: "Is that US 60 toward Premium Outlets (on the western edge of town), or US 60 toward Busch Gardens? (in James City County, on Williamsburg's eastern border)" or "Are you looking for I-64 toward Richmond or toward Norfolk?"

For getting around Williamsburg on your own, it might help to orient yourself by thinking of US 60 as the spine of the city. Toward the north and west from downtown Williamsburg, US 60 is named Richmond Road, the major commercial artery. From the William & Mary campus eastward, it travels Francis Street to York Street, where it turns east and is the route to Busch Gardens.

The fastest way to go *around* town is the U-shaped VA 199, which will get you from I-64 near Busch Gardens to I-64 near Lightfoot, bypassing the Historic Area altogether. Most of the route is limited access, restricting the number of stoplights.

History

Williamsburg served as the English colonial capital from 1699 to 1780 and, during that time, grew from a small settlement to a thriving, sophisticated urban center, reflecting the city's prominent role. By the mid-18th century, the population was nearing 2,000, half of which was enslaved. When court was in session, Williamsburg's population more than doubled, with citizens from the far reaches of the vast Virginia Colony arriving to participate in the fairs, festivities, and fancy dress balls of "publick times."

American ideals of democracy and liberty took root here in the 1700s, as colonists began to question, and finally repudiate, British rule. Patrick Henry inveighed against taxation without representation in the House of Burgesses in 1765. The First Continental Congress was called from Williamsburg in 1774. The Declaration of Rights, soon to become the foundation for the first 10 amendments to the Constitution, was penned here by George Mason. Thousands of Continental Army soldiers were billeted in Williamsburg, which bustled with revolutionary fervor. In 1780, however, Thomas Jefferson (William & Mary, Class of '62—1762, that is) succeeded in getting the capital moved to Richmond, and Williamsburg, no longer the heart of social, political, and economic life in Virginia, entered an era of sleepy decline. Its population waned, and businesses were forced to close. While it continued to function as the county seat, 19th-century Williamsburg was mostly a market town for area farmers, disturbed only by Union general George McClellan's 1862 Peninsula Campaign during the Civil War.

The College of William & Mary and the Publick Hospital remained the only institutions of much size or importance. Some buildings fell into neglect and burned (the Governor's Palace in 1781), but most of the 18th-century homes and structures continued to be used simply because there was little reason for new construction. While interim uses were at times less than noble (the Prentis Store survived in the early 20th century as a gas station and the Powder Magazine once served as a stable), the structures were saved from destruction.

Two Men and a Dream

Williamsburg might still be a sedate spot on the map if not for the actions of two men who conceived of a grander future for the once-great city. The Reverend W. A. R. Goodwin, rector of Bruton Parish Church, dreamed of reviving Virginia's colonial capital. He was successful in raising enough money to restore his own church, but in 1908 he left Williamsburg to become rector of a church in Rochester, New York. Then in 1923 he returned to become a professor of religion at the College of William & Mary. As luck would have it, the college chose Goodwin as its representative at a 1924 Phi Beta Kappa dinner in New York. Also attending the dinner was John D. Rockefeller Jr., heir to the Standard Oil fortune.

This meeting led to the Rockefellers' 1926 visit to Williamsburg, during which negotiations for the restoration of certain 18th-century buildings began. Planning was carried out in a highly secretive manner. Measurements of buildings were taken under cover of darkness. Rockefeller insisted on signing documents pseudonymously as "Mr. David." Town residents felt understandably apprehensive and mystified as they watched their rector buying up land. Rumors spread, and real estate values took off. Soon it was necessary to reveal to Williamsburg citizens the nature of the restoration plan. Initially, not all were pleased; some balked at the idea of their town being "sold." Others were skeptical about the practicality of such a scheme. As the restoration process began, however, the economic benefits of the project became clear. Tenancy agreements allowed most residents of 18th-century buildings to occupy their homes for life.

A Reconstruction Frenzy

Though Rockefeller at first intended to subsidize the restoration of a small number of structures, his enthusiasm and ambitions grew as research turned up more and more pertinent data. Drawings, maps, and records culled from libraries and museums in Europe and America revealed a trove of historical details. Teams of architects, led by William Graves Perry, restored original 18th-century sites and reconstructed others on original foundations. Hundreds of more modern buildings were razed or removed. Eighteenth-century building and brick-making techniques were painstakingly researched so that restorations and reconstructions would resemble the originals as closely as possible.

The success of Goodwin's and Rockefeller's grand vision is well documented today. More than half a million tour Colonial Williamsburg (CW, for short) each year. The Historic Area contains hundreds of restored public buildings, residences, outbuildings, dependencies, shops, and hostelries, plus acres of formal and informal gardens, pastures, and lanes.

While in one sense the restoration Goodwin and Rockefeller envisioned is complete, the vision of Colonial Williamsburg Foundation continues to evolve. In recent years, CW has redirected its focus somewhat. Previously, programs concentrated on the lives of an elite group—colonial governors, revolutionary leaders, and prominent citizens. There was critical backlash, perhaps most notably from the scholar Ada Louise Huxtable, whose 1997 book, *The Unreal America*, condemned historical restorations like Williamsburg as a "prettification of pioneer life." Today you will find more space given to the messier side of the

18th-century community, including frank acknowledgment of the inhumane treatment of Africans and other slaves, and of the second-class status of women. Slaves, indentured servants, women, tradespeople, and other "middling" folk are increasingly featured in interpretive programs that more accurately reflect the complexities of 18th-century history.

Modern Realities

In recent years the winds of change have begun blowing a little more forcefully down the dusty streets of Williamsburg. The bid for tourists' time and money is a competitive business, and paid admissions, which regularly hit the 1.2 million mark in the 1980s, dipped to 533,700 in 2019, a 50-year low.

New marketing campaigns, and an emphasis on retooling programs to make them kid-friendly, are part of the strategy to bring visitors back. Youngsters have more opportunities to see, touch, smell, and hear about the 18th century. Children are able to make stitch books, play hoops, master a colonial ball-and-cup game, polish silver with the silversmiths, and tread mud with the brick makers. Street theater that allows visitors to eavesdrop on the imagined conversations of military leaders, merchants, and other townspeople on the eve of war with England is scheduled throughout the day.

In 2010, CW opened its first "new" building on Duke of Gloucester Street in more than 50 years, R. Charlton's Coffeehouse, hoping to capitalize on America's specialty-coffee addiction. In 2015, CW retooled **Chowning's Tavern** as a Colonial-era alehouse, with a brighter decor and beers created by the local craft brewery, **Alewerks,** using authentic 18th-century recipes. On select dates, Chowning's hosts "Beers in the 'Burg," from 4 to 7 p.m., a ticketed ($25) beer tasting event with live music. In 2020, the foundation completed a $42 million "face-lift" of its art museums, which includes a new entrance, parking lot, the addition of an elegant cupola and another 65,000 square feet of exhibition space, and a new restaurant and retail space.

THE TRIANGLE

In a sense, America was born twice on this narrow peninsula bordered by the James and York Rivers—once, in 1607, when Captain Christopher Newport and his men stepped ashore on the banks of the river they named for their king and founded James Towne; again, in 1781, when the Continental Army defeated the British at **Yorktown** in the decisive battle of the American Revolution. That's a lot of history to pack into one 23-mile stretch. Thanks to forward-thinking preservationists who marked these sites as off-limits to development centuries ago, you can get a real sense of what happened here even if you only have a few days to visit.

Jamestown marked its quadricentennial in 2007—400 years since English colonists first debarked from their three wooden ships after a four month journey across the Atlantic and struggled, mightily, to establish a life here. Though largely abandoned as a settlement by 1750, this marshy island is thoroughly enmeshed in the American historical imagination, entangled with the legend of Pocahontas and John Smith, two figures who have come to represent the meeting of minds and clash of cultures that followed between the colonists and the Virginia Indians who inhabited this region first.

To mark the anniversary, both of Jamestown's major attractions—the Jamestown Settlement, which re-creates life in 17th-century America, and Historic Jamestowne, run by the US Park Service (and using the Old English spelling with the extra *e* on *town*), underwent major makeovers. Even Yorktown, where the National Park Service maintains the battlefields, got an overhaul, in anticipation of the surge of visitors. The result is that both areas look better than ever and, though devoted to the past, bring it to life in thoroughly modern ways. In Yorktown, new county administration buildings, including an eye-catching courthouse, have spruced up Ballard Street near the waterfront, which itself has been thoroughly spiffed up and renamed Riverwalk Landing, with a brick-paved path that connects the American Revolution Museum (formerly the Yorktown Victory Center) to the restaurants and shops along Water Street. (See our close-up on Riverwalk Landing.)

Jamestown and Yorktown—two of the Historic Triangle's crown jewels—continue to reinvent themselves while making strides to enhance the authenticity of each visitor's journey back in time. Read on for details about two towns that are such an integral part of American history.

Jamestown

Imagine leaving your home with little more than the possessions you could carry in a small chest, boarding a vessel powered only by breezes (or gales for the less fortunate) to cross the wild Atlantic Ocean. Imagine months at sea with no privacy, little fresh food, no heat or comfort of any kind, all to reach a land where previous attempts at settlement had ended in disaster. Who would undertake such a journey?

But imagine, too, dreaming of fertile land and of being free—from debt, from lack of opportunity, from city squalor, from whatever mistakes or burdens were part of your past. Hold the alternating hopes and forebodings of such an enterprise in your mind and you can begin to fathom the experience of the Jamestown settlement.

In December 1606 three wooden ships sailed from London for the New World. Southerly winds blew the 144 members of the expedition to the Caribbean. Here they obtained fresh provisions before voyaging again, this time up North America's eastern coast. Some four months and 6,000 miles after their departure from England, they found a swampy wilderness on the banks of the James River and pronounced it fit for putting down stakes. Thus, began our country.

The early years were difficult for the settlers of Jamestown, the New World's first permanent English-speaking colony. The climate proved hot and humid, the land marshy and mosquito ridden. Several of the colonists' attempts at industry, including glassmaking, failed to create a solid economy. And the large native population, ruled by Chief Powhatan, was understandably distrustful of these invaders from across the seas. The winter of 1609–1610, known as the "starving time," was especially terrible for the colony. Only about 90 gaunt settlers were still alive when supplies and reinforcements finally arrived. Indeed, more than half of the colonists who came to Virginia in the colony's first seven years died.

Ultimately, tobacco cultivation succeeded where all else had failed, ensuring (ironically, in retrospect) survival. More and more settlers arrived, attracted by cash-crop opportunities as well as the desire for a better life than that afforded by the rigidly hierarchical societies of Europe. Soon the Virginia Colony was flourishing; plantation society took firm root in its rich, sandy soils and lush woodlands.

In recent decades, Spanish documents have been uncovered that discuss the arrival of 20 or so Africans in Virginia in the summer of 1619. These written accounts suggest that the Africans first reached Virginia aboard the Portuguese ship *San Juan Bautista*, which had sailed from Luanda, Angola, bound for Mexico. Further research suggests that most of the Africans who came to Virginia during the first half of the 17th century hailed from Angola. These men and women more than likely knew how to farm and had been acquainted with both Europeans and Christianity. About a third of these early arrivals and their children were or became free, and some acquired their own land. The number of Africans in Virginia remained relatively small throughout the 17th century, accounting for only 2 to 3 percent of the non-Indian population in 1650, and about 10 percent by the turn of the century.

On July 30, 1619, the first representative legislative assembly in British America met at Jamestown. The community continued to thrive as the Virginia Colony's first capital until 1699, when, after fire destroyed the statehouse, the seat of government was moved inland to Williamsburg for reasons that also involved health problems caused by insects in Jamestown's low-lying marshland location. No longer a political or economic hub, by 1750 Jamestown ceased to exist as an actual community. Fortunately, much of the Jamestown story has been restored. Some genuine remnants of the famous settlement survive, including the bell tower of the church the colonists built and foundations of their simple homes. Archaeological discoveries (the highly acclaimed Jamestown Rediscovery Project, an ongoing archaeological dig, which began in 1994), scholarly research, and a number of organizations' dedication to understanding our nation's past have combined to produce the Jamestown historic experience today.

A First for the Free Ferry

Tiny Emmaleigh Cline made her second trip across the James River on the **Jamestown-Scotland Ferry** when she was just three days old. The first trip, in June 2015, was even more memorable: With the help of four crew members, she became the first baby ever born on the ferry.

A free service operated by the Virginia Department of Transportation, the ferry is the most picturesque way to cross the river. On the northeast end, the ferry deposits cars onto Jamestown Road for a straight shot to the historic attractions there, or the western terminus of the Colonial Parkway, the scenic route into CW or all the way to its eastern terminus in Yorktown. On the south side, cars arrive in rural Surry County. A 20-mile trip along VA 10 takes you into historic Smithfield, a charming small town of shops and restaurants, best known, of course, for its famous ham. (See more about this in our Day Trips chapter.)

There are four ferries in operation, departing at least once an hour, 24 hours a day, 365 days a year. Capacity varies between 28 and 70 cars. (Visit virginiadot.org/travel/ferry-jamestown.asp for vehicle restrictions and schedules.) Drivers and passengers are allowed to exit their vehicles for the 15-minute trip. It's a lovely stretch of water—look for the replica ships docked just south of the wharf at Jamestowne Settlement, bald eagles soaring in the sky above, and massive nests built by various species of hawks on pylons in the channels. Those are the more typical sights; a newborn baby is so rare that the four VDOT employees who sped the ferry across the water while arranging for an ambulance to be at the dock upon arrival in Jamestown, were all named honorary godfathers by Emmaleigh's parents.

There are two separate experiences for tourists and students in Jamestown: Historic Jamestowne, coadministered by the National Park Service and Preservation Virginia, and Jamestown Settlement, operated by the Jamestown-Yorktown Foundation. While these two attractions operate separately, they are just a mile apart and can be easily visited in the course of the same day.

After the 1699 fire that devastated Jamestown and forced the colonial capital to move inland to Williamsburg, Jamestown went into a ghostly decline. By 1750, it ceased to exist as a town. It wasn't until the late 19th century, and Preservation Virginia's 1889 purchase of a portion of Jamestown Island, that redevelopment—designed to protect the historic site—began in earnest.

Jamestown Settlement
Bobby Talley

Housing subdivisions line either side of Jamestown Road, which ends at the dock for the Scotland-Jamestown Ferry, a free service that takes cars (and their drivers and passengers) across the James River to Scotland in Surry County. But there is not much commerce in the area. The exceptions are worth noting because once you get to Jamestown proper, the only places to eat or shop are at the two major attractions—the national park site and Jamestown Settlement.

In our Dining chapter, see our complete descriptions of **La Casona** and the **Jamestown Pie Company.** Both of these establishments are located close to the Jamestown attractions. The Jamestown Pie Company is takeout only, although there are a few picnic tables in a stand of shady trees. It's a good place to stop for picnic fixings if you plan to tour the Colonial Parkway beginning at its western terminus.

Getting There

To get to Jamestown from I-64, take exit 242A, VA 199, which brings you to the Colonial National Historic Parkway, where signs will lead you to Jamestown. If you're coming from Williamsburg, simply take Jamestown Road (VA 31) and follow signs from there. Visitors arriving from the south on VA 31 will cross the James River on the Jamestown-Scotland Ferry, a pleasant (and free) excursion. Jamestown Settlement lies at the intersection of VA 31 and the Colonial Parkway, just up from the ferry docks.

A note on the Colonial Parkway: This scenic, 23-mile roadway was built specifically to connect Jamestown and Yorktown, marking the beginning and the end of the British colonial experience in America. There are no gas stations or amenities, but leave time to stop at the many roadside historical markers. (See our Close-up in the Getting Here, Getting Around chapter.)

Yorktown

For all the historic markers labeled 1600-something, Yorktown's history dates back even farther. The original settlers along this stretch of the York River were members of the Kiskiack tribe (part of the Powhatan Confederacy), who called the water the "Pamunkey."

Captain John Smith explored the area in 1607, but it was nearly 20 years before any large numbers of English settlers began to cultivate the rich land. The town itself was founded in 1691 by the Act for Ports and Towns passed by the Virginia General Assembly for the transport of the colony's lucrative tobacco crop to Europe via England. This was also, in part, an attempt to force urban growth in the colony and centralize the water traffic among the numerous plantations spreading up the Chesapeake Bay. Taking advantage of the deep channel of the York, British ships could pull far enough upriver for shelter from the storms of the Atlantic Ocean and the Chesapeake Bay. The network of creeks that crisscrosses the Virginia peninsula allowed access from the James River side as well.

The town takes its name from surrounding York County and the York River, which were renamed around 1643 to honor the Duke of York, later King James II. (Before that, the river was called the Charles in honor of James's father, the first Duke of York and later King Charles I. He lost his crown—not to mention his head—in the English Civil War.) Fifty acres of land on the plantation belonging to Benjamin Read—including a wharf, ferry, store, and well—were set aside for a county seat that was intended to grow and prosper in commerce. Sheltered by a bluff, with a wide beach to hold the storehouses and other businesses of the sea trade, the site became busy and flourished throughout the colonial period.

The oldest house in the town is the Sessions House, built in 1692 by Thomas Sessions, which survived the siege of 1781 and later the Civil War. A courthouse has stood on the same site since 1697, and a new church for York Parish was built in the same year. After their construction, the town's growth accelerated. By the mid-18th century, as many as 50 large trading ships would be in the vicinity of Yorktown at any given time, and the town had grown relatively prosperous.

In the latter half of the 1700s, however, the tobacco trade had shifted to the inland Piedmont region, and the shipping patterns changed accordingly. A slow process of decline began, and by 1776 the port was less important in commonwealth affairs. The Battle of Yorktown hastened the decline of the

Where the World Turned Upside Down

Every October 19, Yorktown throws a parade and sets off fireworks, all the sorts of things that most places break out for the Fourth of July.

The reason, of course, is that was the day the Battle of Yorktown was won, the day the Revolutionary Army of George Washington and the French army under Comte de Rochambeau defeated the British, or as Lin-Manuel Miranda phrased it in his musical, Hamilton, the day the "world turned upside down."

Of course, in 1781, the locals didn't celebrate much. Their town had just been almost obliterated by a six-week siege and eight-day bombardment, in which more than 15,000 shells were fired. Moreover, at the time no one really knew the war was over. While the surrender of Cornwallis's army was a major loss, the British still held New York and several important ports.

But politically, the British parliament had seen enough. The British had been fighting (and paying for) wars in America off and on since the French and Indian War began in 1754. On the continent and throughout the West Indies, they were skirmishing with the French and Spanish.

Faced with too many enemies and not enough cash, the British government chose to negotiate peace and grant independence to the colonies (which took almost two more years).

All that complexity isn't easily condensed into a fireworks show. The beauty of Yorktown, from a visitor's perspective, is that you can take in as much as you want—the pomp of simple "victory," or the minutiae of history, right down to walking the very grounds where that victory was won. Don't throw away your shot!

Close-up

"Hamilton" Happened Here

The phrase **"Battle of Yorktown"** conjures images of climatic pitched combat between closely packed ground troops. There were moments of that at Yorktown, of course—but the confrontation is more accurately described as a siege, stretching out over weeks, conducted by troops largely hidden from each other by giant earthen walls. Some of the most critical moments happened miles away, at the mouth of the Chesapeake Bay and at British headquarters in New York.

The war in the summer of 1781 was at a stalemate. The British held New York and other strategic points in the north, but they had no hope of seizing control of the countryside. In the South, a British army commanded by General Charles Lord Cornwallis had won key victories throughout the Carolinas and Virginia (nearly capturing Virginia governor Thomas Jefferson in the process). But by the late summer, Cornwallis's troops were badly in need of rest and reinforcements. He marched them toward Yorktown.

It seemed a perfect stronghold: port facilities on the York River, barely a mile from the Chesapeake Bay, and only 30 miles from the bay's entrance to the Atlantic. Marshes, creeks, and dense hardwood forests made a close approach to Yorktown difficult. Cornwallis immediately constructed earthen barriers to provide a defensive line for his nearly 10,000 men.

In reality, however, what Cornwallis built was a perfect trap—for himself.

His commander, General Henry Clinton, sent word that the British fleet would sail from New York to resupply and replenish Cornwallis's tired troops. But French spies had spotted Cornwallis's work and sent word themselves to the Marquis de Lafayette and General George Washington. The French fleet hurried to blockade the Chesapeake; Washington and the Comte de Rochambeau led their 7,000 troops on a four-week, largely secret, march from their base in Rhode Island to Virginia.

On September 5, the British fleet arrived at the bay—only to discover the French blockade. The two fleets pounded each other for 3 hours, neither able to win decisively. But the French didn't need to win—they simply needed to keep the British from reaching Cornwallis. The British, their ships badly damaged, withdrew to New York.

A week later, Washington and Rochambeau arrived in Williamsburg. Within the month, they were joined by thousands more French, who brought artillery and siege tools. Washington and his allied army, now more than 19,000 strong, headed to Yorktown.

Cornwallis, still confident that reinforcements were on the way, pulled his troops back from their outer line of defenses so he could concentrate them more tightly to repulse an attack. Washington and Rochambeau didn't attack directly, though—they seized the British outer defenses and set up to batter and starve the British into submission.

On October 6, in just a few hours, the allied troops built an earthen siege line—essentially a mile—long trench and berm. It allowed them to bombard the town while being protected from British fire. The cannon and mortar steadily pounded the town and wore down the supplies and morale of the British. Clinton, from New York, promised to arrive soon to break the siege—but Cornwallis was starting to worry that help wouldn't come in time.

On October 11, Washington ordered the digging of a second siege line, a quarter of a mile closer. From there, they could dominate the British position with fire from three sides. All that prevented the completion of that line was two forward British strongholds, the earthen forts known as Redoubts 9 and 10.

On the moonless night of October 14, two groups of French and Americans (commanded by none other than Alexander Hamilton) sneaked toward those forts. They carried their muskets—but left the weapons unloaded, lest an accidental shot alert the British to their approach. (*Hamilton* fans will recognize this from the lyric, "We cannot let a stray gunshot give us away.")

Standing inside **Redoubt 9,** you can vividly imagine the chaos and carnage of more than 400 men—British, Scots, German mercenaries, French, and Americans—clashing. With little time to reload their guns, the fights devolved to hand combat with bayonets and axes. The defenders were forced to give up in less than a half hour.

Now the allies could rain down shells at near—point—blank range. On October 16–17, Cornwallis, still hoping for reinforcements, tried a bold counterattack to buy time. It failed. That night, he began to retreat across the York River in a desperate attempt to flee northward. His first flotilla of small boats made it—but when they returned for another load, a sudden squall churned the river so violently that escape was impossible.

The British fate was sealed. Out of food and suffering terrible casualties, Cornwallis sent out an officer holding a white flag. After a day and a half of negotiations, Cornwallis's army—fully one-third of the British forces in colonial America—surrendered.

At the surrender ceremony on October 19, however, Cornwallis was not to be found. Humiliated, he complained of illness and remained in his quarters. His second-in-command led the 8,000 British troops to the place now called **Surrender Field.**

community. The intense barrage of cannon fire from the Allied siege line during the battle destroyed more than half of the town, and it never fully recovered.

Although there is little evidence remaining, the Civil War brought renewed activity to the town. During the Peninsula Campaign of that conflict, Yorktown was one anchor of the Confederate defenses crossing the peninsula to block Union progress toward Williamsburg; the fortifications of the Revolutionary War were renovated for that purpose.

Celebrations

Each year Yorktown observes two major celebrations related to its military history. Independence Day is celebrated with the rest of the nation, and crowds of people gather in and about the town to enjoy the traditional Fourth of July parade and the individual observations, entertainments, and celebrations at the museums, homes, and centers. The day culminates in a spectacular fireworks display on the York River, visible for miles around. On October 19 Yorktown again pulls out all the stops with exhibits, reenactments of military life, "tall ship" visits, naval reenactments, music, and other celebrations as Virginians and visitors celebrate Washington's United States' victory with appropriate enthusiasm. (For more on yearly events in and around Yorktown, turn to our Annual Events chapter.)

Yorktown Today

In many ways, Yorktown today remains as it has been for hundreds of years—a small village oriented toward the river from which it takes its name. The waters are still heavily used by commercial traffic—upstream to the naval weapons station and the paper mill at West Point 30 miles away, or to the Western Refining oil distribution terminal just downstream from the town.

Downtown Yorktown today makes concessions to the modern world—it's still the seat of government for York County; largely a suburb of Newport News, Hampton, and even Williamsburg; and home to 68,000. But other than those working in government offices, most of Yorktown is devoted to the area's history.

The waterfront is dominated by the results of a $25 million renovation completed in 2005—a riverwalk, improved beach facilities (yes, the river has a beach—a bow in the channel has deposited a deep bank of sand), and a shopping area.

Rent a segway to tour the Yorktown Riverwalk.
Michael Ventura Photography

Getting There

By far the most scenic way to Yorktown from Williamsburg is along the Colonial Parkway, a 23-mile roadway that bisects the peninsula from Jamestown to Yorktown, figuratively tracing the history of British colonial rule in America. (See our Close-up in the Getting Here, Getting Around chapter.)

Turnouts on both sides of the three-lane road (the middle lane is for passing) provide stopping places to read historical markers or simply view the scenery. Along the Yorktown end of the parkway, that scenery can occasionally include close-up views of today's military: The roadway passes through the Yorktown Naval Weapons Station, the depot for all ammunition used by the US Navy's Atlantic Fleet, headquartered at Norfolk.

If the parkway isn't your speed (literally: 45 mph), the next best approach from Williamsburg is eastbound I-64. Take the Yorktown Naval Weapons Station exit (exit 247); turn left on Jefferson Avenue (VA 143), then left again on Yorktown Road (VA 238).

From Norfolk or Newport News, exit I-64 at Fort Eustis Boulevard (exit 250). At the traffic light at the bottom of the ramp, turn left onto Jefferson Avenue (VA 143), and then quickly right at the next light onto Fort Eustis Boulevard (Route 105). Travel 3 miles to US 17, turn left. Watch carefully for signs as you near Yorktown. To get to the park service visitor center, take the Colonial Parkway exit to the right. For direct access to the downtown waterfront and the American Revolution Museum, you can either turn left, across oncoming traffic, to approach the town from the river bottoms—or from the uphill side by turning right onto Alexander Hamilton Boulevard at the York

County government center. Miss your turn and you'll end up crossing the York River on the Coleman (toll) Bridge.

VIRGINIA PENINSULA

Want to take in all the rich history and diversity the Virginia Peninsula has to offer while you're visiting Williamsburg? Head southeast on I-64 and check out Newport News and Hampton. Sailors might want submerge themselves in the exhibits at the Mariners' Museum in Newport News, one of the largest and most comprehensive maritime museums in the world. If you have your sights on the skies, you might choose the Virginia Air and Space Science Center in Hampton instead.

Because Hampton and Newport News are next door neighbors—and you pretty much get to each city the same way—we've combined information about them here. For convenience and ease of planning, however, we've kept listings of the attractions, restaurants, accommodations, shopping, and recreation in each city separate.

Newport News

Nowhere is the old adage "geography is destiny" truer than in Newport News. The long, narrow city hugs the James River for 18 miles but is barely a mile wide at its narrowest point. The vast stretches of waterfront made it a perfect place to build ships. Industrialist Collis P. Huntington brought the Chesapeake & Ohio railroad to a terminus at Newport News in 1882, and a few years later he established the Newport News Shipbuilding and Drydock Company along the waterfront. The company—and the city's fortunes—took off.

Today, that firm is called Huntington Ingalls Industries, and it builds nuclear-powered aircraft carriers and submarines, but the economy has diversified from its roots in shipbuilding. The Oyster Point business park in the center of the city is home to a number of manufacturers and service firms, including Canon, a branch of the Japanese copier and printer company, and the Thomas Jefferson National Accelerator Facility, a cutting-edge high-energy physics research lab that has made Newport News a familiar name in scientific circles. In recent years, Christopher Newport University (CNU) has transformed the landscape along Warwick Boulevard (US 60) by adding a magnificent performing arts center, a multipurpose sports complex, and several majestic buildings, each crowned with a cupola. Once a "commuter school," it's getting tougher to gain admission to CNU.

Progress has its price. Continued residential growth and the influx of new industry have further burdened the city's major highways, already hampered by having to serve the needs of a population spread out over this long, thin city. Rush hour can be chaotic, especially on I-64 and J. Clyde Morris Boulevard, the local name for US 17. The congestion starts earlier than most places because of the shipyard's schedule (roughly dawn until midafternoon; precise hours of the first shift vary seasonally).

Hampton

Neighboring Hampton prides itself on being a city of firsts. Settled in 1610, it is the oldest continuous English-speaking settlement in America (because Jamestown moved). Our nation's first free education has its roots in the city, which was also the site of America's first Christmas. The city also was the site of the nation's first formal trading post, and the first site for the National Advisory Committee for Aeronautics, the precursor of the National Aeronautics and Space Administration (NASA). Hampton's NASA Langley Research Center actually was established in 1917 to advance the nation's airplane research. Proponents of the center say the work done there in the 1930s on the design of advanced airplane wings gave the US and its allies the advantage that made them victorious in World War II. It wasn't until the late 1950s that NASA established the Space Task Group and located its office at Langley. Engineers and scientists in that group worked on America's original manned space program.

Hampton may have been "first to the stars," as city promoters like to say, but it also boasts a rich—and rather bloody—seafaring history. It was in

Hampton in 1718 that the freshly severed head of Blackbeard the pirate was stuck on a stick at the harbor entrance. During the Civil War, the ironclads *Merrimac* (CSS *Virginia*) and *Monitor* battled it out in the harbor, as the Confederates tried to break the Union's naval blockade with the hope of seizing Union-held Fort Monroe.

Throughout the centuries Hampton has endured, having survived shelling during the Revolutionary War and twice rebuilding from devastating fires—first during the War of 1812 and then during the Civil War, when Hampton citizens set fire to their homes rather than see the city fall to Union forces. Today Hampton is a vibrant city where commercial fishing, military installations, and aeronautic enterprises sustain a population of about 137,000. The downtown has at its nucleus the Virginia Air and Space Science Center and the restaurants and bars along narrow, cobblestoned Queen's Way.

Hampton also is home to Hampton University, the nation's largest historically Black private university. Each June the college, together with the city, sponsors the renowned Hampton Jazz Festival (despite the name, it's more about rhythm and blues than traditional jazz), which brings popular entertainers such as B. B. King, Aretha Franklin, and Kenny G. and thousands of jazz fans to the city. (For more on the Hampton Jazz Festival, turn to our Annual Events chapter.)

The festival—and other concerts and events—are held at the Hampton Coliseum, a late '60s-era arena that bears a startling resemblance to a flying saucer. The Coliseum Central area just northwest of the arena is the de facto commercial center of the city—home to the Hampton Roads Convention Center and the revitalized Peninsula Town Center mixed-use development, which opened in 2010 on the site of the bulldozed former Coliseum Mall.

Getting There

Both cities are a straight shot from Williamsburg east on I-64. The interstate runs through the northern half of Newport News before bisecting Hampton and crossing over and under the water to Norfolk via the Hampton Roads Bridge-Tunnel. While traffic congestion can be troublesome both during morning and afternoon rush hours, if the interstate is clear, it should take you about 20 to 25 minutes to get to Newport News, 30 to 40 minutes to Hampton.

In planning your trip to the Middle and Lower Peninsula, there are a few logical places to start.

HAMPTON VISITORS CENTER, Hampton History Museum, 120 Old Hampton Ln., Hampton, VA 23669; (800) 800-2202; visithampton.com. Stop here for brochures on everything from restaurants and accommodations to walking tours and citywide attractions. This also is the place to purchase tickets for a Hampton waterfront cruise, which departs from docks right at the center. Open daily 9 a.m. to 5 p.m.

NEWPORT NEWS VISITOR CENTER, 13560 Jefferson Ave. (inside Newport News Park, exit 250B off I-64), Newport News, VA 23603; (757) 886-7777, (888) 493-7386; newport-news.org. As you motor down I-64 from Williamsburg, stop here for brochures, directions, and general information about any city attraction. It's open 9 a.m. to 5 p.m. daily except Thanksgiving Day, Christmas Eve, Christmas Day, and New Year's Day. Brochures and information may also be obtained at the city's tourism development office, located in City Center mixed-use development: 700 Town Center Dr. (off Jefferson Boulevard), Ste. 320. Open 8 a.m. to 5 p.m., Mon through Fri.

Accommodations

The pineapple was the colonial symbol of hospitality, and it still signifies gracious accommodation. Today you'll have a much easier time finding welcome here than did the British, French, and Continental armies, and later the Civil War's Yankee soldiers. They boarded at the colonial inns and taverns in the Historic Area, the true antecedents of today's hotels, motels, and inns. Your stay should be much more comfortable.

The Williamsburg area offers more than 8,500 hotel and motel rooms in a wide range of prices, so you should have no difficulty finding something that suits you. All the major chains are here, but properties swap affiliations regularly: The Days Inn you stayed at last year may be a La Quinta this year. Because the advantage of a chain hotel is that you have a good idea of what you are getting before you even arrive, we only listed chain properties below if they offered some special advantage, like proximity to a particular attraction, a quiet setting, or an especially good restaurant nearby.

While we give you up-to-date details on amenities at the time of publication, some things can change abruptly. To ensure your satisfaction, we strongly recommend you ask about details on specifics such as ground-floor rooms, elevators, separate heating and cooling controls, mattress sizes, showers or tubs, age of the establishment, whether your four-footed family members are welcome, and availability of cable TV or Wi-Fi when you make your reservation. You might also inquire about proximity to highways or CSX railroad noise. Other considerations are the distance to your local touring destination and directions from I-64 or whichever route you plan to travel.

When making a reservation, inquire about special discounted rates for AAA members, children, senior citizens, members of the military, and government travelers. You may also want to ask about changes in pricing between in-season and out-of-season times. These periods are defined by the individual lodging, but generally in-season or peak season is from March to November and again during the winter holiday season. Christmas is not the off-season here, as Colonial Williamsburg and Busch Gardens put on their finery and offer many events to commemorate the holiday. Make your reservations well in advance.

Off-season months are generally January, February, and early March, though this can change, depending on when Easter falls. Reservations made well in advance are almost a necessity in peak season.

Unless specifically noted, the lodgings listed below allow children, and the facility is wheelchair accessible. It is now more likely to find a pet-friendly hotel than one that allows smoking. With the advent of online reservations, 800 numbers are going the way of the rotary dial, but Wi-Fi is nearly ubiquitous.

Hotels and Motels Price Code

Based on information available at the time of publication, we offer the following price code as a general guide, with the warning that fluctuations in price and availability, and even chain allegiance, of lodgings often occur. The figures indicate an average charge for double occupancy during peak season.

$	Less than $100
$$	$101 to $200
$$$	$201 to $300
$$$$	More than $301

COLONIAL WILLIAMSBURG LODGINGS

Lodging in one of Colonial Williamsburg's properties offers lots of advantages, but with the exception of CW's budget offering, the Governors Inn, you'll pay substantially more for a night's stay here than elsewhere around town.

These hotels and motels are closest to the Historic Area, so you can park upon arrival and either walk or ride the CW bus for free to get around. Perhaps the three best perks are priority for tee times and dining reservations, and the convenience that anything you purchase from CW shops during your stay will be delivered free to your room.

Guests of the Williamsburg Inn, Providence Hall, any of the Colonial Houses, and Williamsburg Lodge have free use of the Spa of CW's fitness center and pool, and tennis courts at the Williamsburg Inn, and they will receive 2 hours of bike rental as well as exclusive invitations to events, like the nightly root beer sampling at Chowning's Tavern. Check out a full list of benefits at colonialwilliamsburg.com/stay/guest-benefits.

COLONIAL HOUSES, various locations throughout Colonial Williamsburg; (800) HISTORY (447-8679); colonialwilliamsburg.com; $$–$$$$. If you've ever dreamt of waking up in the 18th century, staying in one of these houses is probably the closest you'll come to wish fulfillment. The Colonial Houses offer 75 guest accommodations in 26 separate buildings, some as small as one room, and others as large as 16 rooms. Multiple rooms can be combined within a house to accommodate parties of up to 32. Scattered throughout the Historic Area, many houses overlook brick courtyards, gardens, or Duke of Gloucester Street. Furnished with authentic period reproductions and antiques, many of the houses have canopy beds, sitting rooms, or fireplaces. Guests of the Colonial Houses have recreation privileges at the Williamsburg Inn. ***Note:*** Inquire as early as possible about availability and about the accommodations unique to each. Many book as much as a year in advance for Christmas and Thanksgiving, or in conjunction with events at the College of William & Mary.

PROVIDENCE HALL GUESTHOUSES, 305 S. England St., Williamsburg, VA 23185; (800) HISTORY (447-8679); colonialwilliamsburg.com; $$$–$$$$. Located a short walk from the main Williamsburg Inn building, these rooms offer a tranquil view of a wooded area with a pond from private patios and balconies. The interior decor is contemporary with Asian accents, for those who like a change from colonial architecture for at least part of the day. King- and queen-size beds are available.

THE WILLIAMSBURG INN, 136 E. Francis St., Williamsburg, VA 23185; (757) 220-7978, (800) HISTORY (447-8679); colonialwilliamsburg.com; $$$$. This is arguably the premier accommodation in Hampton Roads, justly proud of its pedigree as a luxury hotel. *Forbes Travel Guide* has awarded it a five-star rating for 2018, 2019, and 2020. It is situated in a dignified, beautifully landscaped setting with the Historic Area and the **Golden Horseshoe Golf Club** on its periphery. Opened in 1937 and built to the exacting standards of John D. Rockefeller and his wife, Abby Aldrich, the inn underwent extensive renovations in 2001. A businessman like Rockefeller would no doubt approve of the changes that brought the inn into the 21st century—the addition of desks in each room, Wi-Fi, larger televisions, minibars, and in-room safes. The main dining room, the Regency Room, is a four-star restaurant in its own right. Afternoon tea is served in the Terrace Room. Cocktails can be had in the Restoration Bar or outdoors on the terrace, with a beautiful view of the golf course. The lobby resembles a sprawling living room with multiple sitting areas. Don't leave without having your picture taken on the sweeping, spiral Queen's Staircase, so named because Queen Elizabeth II was photographed while descending it on her way to dinner during her 1957 visit.

THE WILLIAMSBURG LODGE, 310 S. England St., Williamsburg, VA 23185; (757) 220-7976, (800) HISTORY (447-8679); colonialwilliamsburg.com; $$–$$$$. The Williamsburg Lodge specializes in accommodating groups (of up to 1,000), with 45,000 square feet of conference meeting space, 2 ballrooms, and 323 rooms in 8 separate buildings, connected by covered brick walkways. In addition to refurbished guest rooms in the main building, built in 1939, Tazewell Hall offers rooms with rocking chairs on the patio or balcony and 3 suites with fireplaces. Four brand-new guesthouses—the Ashby and Custis houses with 30 new rooms each, and the Nicholas and Tyler houses with 38 new rooms each—have also been added to the complex. Rooms in the guesthouses feature modern amenities such as Wi-Fi and are decorated in historical colors, with furnishings inspired by folk art from the **Abby Aldrich Rockefeller Museum,** located across the street. Guests have access to the fitness center at the Spa, 2 outdoor pools, and an indoor lap pool. A business center provides a fax, computer, and printer. The Lodge restaurant, Traditions, serves southern—inspired and locally acquired cuisine. In 2017, the Lodge became part of Marriott International Hotels Autograph Collection. Guests who are members of the Marriott Rewards program should book reservations through Marriott if they want to use points or receive their member discount.

WILLIAMSBURG WOODLANDS HOTEL AND SUITES, 102 Visitor Center Dr., Williamsburg, VA 23185; (757) 220-7960, (800) HISTORY (447-8679); colonialwilliamsburg.com; $$. This contemporary three-story facility, with brick and glass exterior, is set amid a pine forest adjacent to the visitor center. The spacious lobby, bathed in natural light from cathedral-ceiling skylights, includes a separate space for a continental breakfast buffet. For full-service dining, a family friendly, 125-seat restaurant is located across from the lobby along the pedestrian promenade to the visitor center. All 204 guest rooms are accessed from interior hallways. Each has 2 full-size beds, a sitting area with a desk, 2 chairs, and a comfortable lounge chair (that converts to a single bed). The 96 suites have king-size beds, a sitting area with a queen-size sofa bed and upholstered chairs, a desk, TV, and a kitchen area with a small refrigerator, microwave, and sink. There is an on-site fitness center. In the summer months, guests can enjoy an outdoor swimming pool, a new Splash Park, and a Kid's "Fun Zone," which includes free miniature golf, horseshoes, volleyball, badminton, table tennis, and shuffleboard.

Other Lodging

Note: Many of the chain hotels offer a popular continental breakfast which has been suspended due to the pandemic. In its place, most hotels who offer breakfast have substituted a brown bag of snacks to go.

BASSETT MOTEL, 800 York St., Williamsburg, VA 23185; (757) 229-5175; bassettmotel.com; $. This no-frills motel is conveniently located within a short walk or drive from most of Williamsburg's attractions, including the Historic Area, Busch Gardens, and Water County USA. Eighteen ground-floor rooms offer individual heating and air conditioning controls, Wi-Fi, and full baths. Open year-round.

BEST WESTERN HISTORIC AREA INN, 201 Bypass Rd., Williamsburg, VA 23185; (757) 220-0880; bestwestern.com; $–$$. Conveniently located between the Historic Area and the outlet shopping district, this budget hotel is popular with both tourists and business travelers. Continental breakfast and Wi-Fi are included in the room rate. An indoor heated pool and Jacuzzi will please the kids or offer relief at the end of a day of traveling or touring. Cracker Barrel and Golden Corral are nearby, as is Pirate's Cove, a popular miniature golf attraction. All rooms are nonsmoking; pets are prohibited. Discounts are offered to senior citizens, military, government employees, and AAA members.

BEST WESTERN WILLIAMSBURG HISTORIC DISTRICT, 351 York St., Williamsburg, VA 23185; (757) 229-4100; bestwestern.com; $–$$. One of the best features of this hotel is its location, just steps from the eastern end of the Historic Area, and a short drive from Busch Gardens and Water Country USA. All guest rooms have been renovated and have two queen beds or one king with coffeemakers, desks, hair dryers, TVs, refrigerators, and microwaves. Select rooms have sofa sleepers and kitchen facilities with microwaves and refrigerators. Wheelchair-accessible rooms are available but limited. Complimentary coffee and Wi-Fi are included in the room rate. There is an on-site business center with a public computer and printer. (Fax and copying services are also available for a minimal charge.) For recreation there is an indoor heated pool and fitness center. A terrific locally owned Mexican restaurant, Taqueria Maria Bonita, is located on the property. The hotel is 100 percent smoke-free and pets can stay for an additional fee. The hotel offers banquet and conference services.

CLARION HOTEL, 3032 Richmond Rd., Williamsburg, VA 23185; (757) 565-2600; choicehotels.com; $$. Located on the western border of Williamsburg, this hotel and conference center is prime lodging for shoppers headed to the outlets. There are 160 rooms, all of which include Wi-Fi, microwave, refrigerator, coffeemaker, iron and ironing board, and hair dryers. A kidney-shaped outdoor pool and an indoor pool will offer balm to tired feet after a grueling day searching for bargains. Jolene's Bar and Grill serves scrumptious food on-site. A complimentary breakfast is available as is a guest laundry and business center. Smoking and wheelchair-accessible rooms are available. This hotel is pet friendly but there is a fee.

COMFORT INN WILLIAMSBURG GATEWAY, 331 Bypass Rd., Williamsburg, VA 23185; (757) 253-1166; choicehotels.com; $$. This 116-room motel changed affiliation and was renovated in 2014. Its central location puts the Historic Area, Richmond Road shopping, Busch Gardens, and Water Country USA just short drives away. Amenities include a heated outdoor pool and fitness business center. All rooms are nonsmoking and include cable TV and Wi-Fi. Wheelchair-accessible rooms are available. The entire fourth floor is a penthouse with a king-size brass bed in the master bedroom. A complimentary continental breakfast is included with your stay, and several restaurants are within walking distance of the hotel, including Denny's. There is a coin-operated guest laundry on-site. Pets, except service animals, are not permitted.

COMFORT SUITES WILLIAMSBURG HISTORIC AREA, 220-A Bypass Rd., Williamsburg, VA 23185; (757) 645-4646; choicehotels.com; $$. This all-suite hotel opened in 2010 in a location convenient to all of Williamsburg's attractions. Every room has either 2 queen-size beds or a king, plus a queen-size pullout sleeper sofa. The kitchen area offers a refrigerator and microwave. The entire building has Wi-Fi, and the whole place is smoke-free. There is an indoor pool with Jacuzzi tub and a fitness center. Daily newspapers and continental breakfast are included in your room charge. The Cracker Barrel and Golden Corral restaurants are just across the parking lot and Rocco's Smokehouse and Jose Tequila restaurants are directly across the street. Pets are not permitted. There are computer terminals for guest use and coin-operated machines for laundry. A market located next to the front desk sells detergent plus snacks, drinks, and sundries.

COUNTRY INN & SUITES BY RADISSON—WILLIAMSBURG HISTORIC AREA, 400 Bypass Rd., Williamsburg, VA 23185; (757) 259-7990; radissonhotels.com/countryinn; $–$$. This modern, 66-room hotel is a favorite for families who need a little extra space. In addition to standard guest rooms, the hotel offers a variety of suites. Indoor pool, Jacuzzi, fitness room, continental breakfast, and Wi-Fi are all included in the room rate. A second Country Inn location at 7135 Pocahontas Trail (US 60), (757) 229-6900, offers the same amenities a bit closer to Busch Gardens.

COURTYARD BY MARRIOTT, 470 McLaws Circle (Busch Corporate Center), Williamsburg, VA 23185; (757) 221-0700, (800) 393-2506; marriott.com; $$. The 151 rooms here underwent an upgrade in 2013 to add luxury bed linens, mini-refrigerators, cable TVs with premium channels, and Wi-Fi. Located 1 mile from Busch Gardens, the hotel is convenient to the Kingsmill championship golf course and just a short drive from the Historic Area. Guests can relax in an indoor or outdoor heated pool, work out in the fitness center, or take care of laundry. An on-site restaurant and the business center are closed until the pandemic threat is over but there are excellent dining options—**Maurizio's Ristorante Italiano**, **Emerald Thai**, **The Whaling Company**—within easy walking distance. Wheelchair-accessible rooms and meeting rooms are available. The property is 100 percent smoke-free. No pets, except service animals, are permitted.

DOUBLETREE BY HILTON, 50 Kingsmill Rd., Williamsburg, VA 23185; (757) 220-2500, (800) 222-8733; hilton.com; $$. If Busch Gardens is your destination, you couldn't get closer than this full-service hotel and conference center. The hotel's 295 guest rooms, some of which are suites, have plush linens, large desks, and Wi-Fi; wheelchair-accessible rooms are also offered. The on-site amenities include a tennis court, indoor and outdoor swimming, fitness center, business center, guest laundry and two restaurants: one which serves full meals and cocktails throughout the day and the Williamsburg Café, open all day offering sandwiches and lighter fare. The hotel is 100 percent smoke-free. At check-in you will be issued one of their warm-from-the-oven chocolate chip cookies. Service animals only. The Anheuser-Busch brewery is within walking distance as are several excellent restaurants and for those in need of a strong cup o' joe, a Starbucks.

EMBASSY SUITES BY HILTON WILLIAMSBURG, 3006 Mooretown Rd., Williamsburg, VA 23185; (757) 229-6800, (800) 284-3930; embassy suites.com; $$. This suites-only hotel tucked behind a former Kmart shopping center offers more quiet than other locations but quick access to attractions and shopping. A major renovation was completed in June 2015, which updated all 168 suites. Like other properties in this chain, each 2-room suite features separate living and sleeping areas, with either a king-size bed or 2 doubles in the bedroom and a sleeper sofa, refrigerator, and microwave in the living room. Each room has its own flat-screen TV. There is also an on-site restaurant, indoor heated pool, whirlpool, fitness room, business center, and meeting space for up to 75 people.

FAIRFIELD BY MARRIOTT INN AND SUITES, 1402 Richmond Rd., Williamsburg, VA 23185; (757) 645-3600, (800) 228-2800; fairfieldinn .com; $$. This chain hotel got a makeover in 2014, adding to its appeal as its central location puts visitors almost equidistant from Colonial Williamsburg and the shopping hot spots to the west on Richmond Road. Every room has the standard amenities: coffeemakers, irons and ironing boards, cable TV, and Wi-Fi. There's an indoor pool, fitness room, and business center. Wheelchair-accessible rooms are available. No pets are allowed. The hotel is 100 percent smoke-free. There is a market near the front desk selling snacks and sundries but this location puts you within walking distance of excellent restaurants in every price range—Five Guys, Chipotle, the Tipsy Beans Café, and Le Yaca, a French restaurant which ranks among Williamsburg's best places to dine.

FORT MAGRUDER HOTEL AND CONFERENCE CENTER BY WYNDHAM, 6945 Pocahontas Trail (US 60), Williamsburg, VA 23185; (757) 220-2250; wyndham.com; $. The most unique feature of this hotel is that it sits on the site of the Civil War's 1862 Battle of Williamsburg. With 303 guest rooms, this is one of the larger hotels in the area, with 26,000 square feet of conference space and meeting rooms named Lee's Redoubt, Grant's Redoubt, and one that always stops first-time visitors in their tracks: Hooker's Redoubt—named for the Union general. Visitors can gaze at an actual redoubt from the earthworks of Fort Magruder on the hotel's grounds and examine Civil War artifacts on display in the hotel lobby. Wyndham Hotels took over management in 2016; all guest rooms now have cable TV and Wi-Fi. You'll also find a seasonal outdoor pool, indoor pool, fitness center. There are two on-site restaurants, under renovation in 2020. All rooms are nonsmoking. The hotel has 12 wheelchair-accessible rooms, including 4 with roll-in showers. Pets under 40 pounds are welcome, with a one-time cleaning charge of $25 per day for up to two pets per day. Except for the passing trains, this is a quiet section of town but a terrific restaurant, **Old City Barbeque,** is a 5-minute walk away.

GREAT WOLF LODGE, 549 East Rochambeau Dr., Williamsburg, VA 23188; (757) 229-9700, (800) 551-WOLF (9653); greatwolf.com/williams burg; $$$–$$$$. This is less a hotel than an indoor water park with a place to sleep attached. The main attraction here is liquid and loud: The 55,000-square-foot play area features a 4-story, 12-level tree fort that dumps 1,000 gallons of water every few minutes. There's a serpentine wave pool, 8 slides, two 7,000-gallon hot tubs, a lazy river, and more. It's completely irresistible if you like to be wet, but get ready to pay for the fun. This is one of the priciest places to lay your head in the area. With all that this theme complex offers, you may never make it outside where there is another pool (open only in summer) with water "geysers" to splash through. Lifeguards abound.

The hotel itself is a four-story faux-log structure, with a stone fireplace in the lobby, wood beam ceilings, and wild animal decoys. The outdoorsy motif carries over to the guest rooms, all with modern amenities set amid a rustic decor. Some rooms have their own fireplaces, whirlpools, and vaulted ceilings. Some have log forts or tent areas—complete with televisions—for the kids. There are also several restaurants on the premises, ranging from fast food to snack bar. Reservations include a deposit of the first night's charge, plus tax, and be sure to check on the penalties for cancellation, which can be steep.

HAMPTON INN & SUITES WILLIAMSBURG HISTORIC DISTRICT, 911 Capitol Landing Rd., Williamsburg, VA 23185; (757) 941-1777, (855) 271-3622; hamptoninn.com; $$. There are three Hampton Inns in Williamsburg. This one is located in a quiet area, a mile off the interstate, a mile north of the historic district, and 2 miles west of Busch Gardens and Water Country USA. The hotel has 109 well-equipped rooms, including five designed for wheelchair accessibility. This is a 100 percent smoke-free property. Wi-Fi is included in the room rate. All rooms have cable TV, microwaves, refrigerators, and hair dryers; some have separate living rooms. There is a business center, guest laundry, indoor pool, and Jacuzzi. The other Hampton Inn locations are at 718 Bypass Rd. (757-229-7330) and 1880 Richmond Rd. (757-229-4900).

HILTON GARDEN INN, 1624 Richmond Rd., Williamsburg, VA 23185; (757) 253-9400, (877) 609-9400; Hilton.com; $$. If you're visiting Williamsburg to shop, this hotel is located closer to Premium Outlets than many equivalent choices. Standard amenities include satellite TV, refrigerator, Keurig coffeemaker, microwave, hair dryer, and Wi-Fi. Business travelers will appreciate the desk in each room, ergonomic chair, and remote printing service. Business center, indoor pool, whirlpool, and fitness center are open 24 hours.

The Seafare of Williamsburg, a neighboring restaurant, provides room service. Rte. 60, featuring barbecue, is steps away, and the lobby boasts a well-stocked grab-and-go-style pantry. The entire hotel is smoke free. Pets are prohibited, except for service animals. Planning a reunion? The inn offers meeting space for up to 100 people.

HOLIDAY INN—GATEWAY, 515 Bypass Rd., Williamsburg, VA 23185; (757) 229-9990, (800) HOLIDAY (465-4329); holidayinn.com; $$. This five-story inn opened in 2006 in a location convenient to all of Williamsburg's attractions. The rooms are well-equipped with all the standard amenities, plus Wi-Fi, microwave, and refrigerator. Kids 12 and under eat free at the on-site restaurant, Bistro 515, and they'll enjoy the heated indoor pool and whirlpool. There's also a fitness center, business center, guest laundry and meeting rooms. Pets, except service animals, are not permitted.

HOLIDAY INN EXPRESS—WILLIAMSBURG NORTH, 720 Lightfoot Rd., Williamsburg, VA 23188; (757) 220-0062, (877) 859-5095; ihg.com/holidayinnexpress; $–$$. This former Days Inn underwent a reincarnation in 2013, making it one of the spiffiest "new" hotels in Williamsburg. Located just off I-64 (exit 234) on the northwest end of town (adjacent to **Williamsburg Pottery**), this property has 118 rooms, an indoor pool, fitness center, coin-operated laundry, and all the standard in-room amenities. The business center is open 24 hours and offers fax, copy, and printing services. Wi-Fi and breakfast are included in the room rate. The property is 100 percent smoke-free. A second Holiday Inn Express at 1452 Richmond Rd. (757) 941-1057; (877) 859-5095 offers the same amenities and services at a more central location.

HOMEWOOD SUITES BY HILTON, 601 Bypass Rd., Williamsburg, VA 23185; (757) 259-1199, (855) 277-4942; hilton.com; $–$$$. This property offers one- and two-bedroom suites with queen- and king-size beds, a fully equipped kitchen, and TVs in the living area and bedroom. A well-equipped fitness center features an indoor swimming pool. Wi-Fi, breakfast, and the "Manager's Reception," with a light meal, Mon through Thurs, from 5 to 7 p.m., are included in the room rate. A full laundry facility is provided, and a sundry store in the lobby stocks necessities and snacks. This property is located about a mile from the city's Historic Area, Merchants Square shopping, and the College of William & Mary. It is a 100 percent smoke-free hotel. Service animals only. A limited number of wheelchair accessible rooms are available.

KINGSMILL RESORT, 1010 Kingsmill Rd., Williamsburg, VA 23185; (757) 253-1703, (800) 832-5665; kingsmill.com; $$$–$$$$. Designated a four-diamond property by AAA, Kingsmill offers luxury-resort amenities in a gorgeous setting: The 2,900-acre property, formerly a plantation, overlooks the

James River on one side and is surrounded by three world-class golf courses. (The River Course has played host to PGA and LPGA tournaments for three decades. The Woods Course is for full golf members only.) Guests can also play tennis, kayak, fish, use Jet Skis or paddleboards, or relax at the spa. In 2012, Kingsmill added a third swimming option, the River Pool, which might make a trip to Water Country USA superfluous for some families. The River Pool complex features a waterslide, a winding lazy river with tubes, a zero-depth entry pool with fountains, a sandy beach, a fire pit, and a beautiful view of the James. Open seasonally.

Area attractions are a short drive away—you can almost get to Busch Gardens without hitting a traffic light. A free shuttle takes guests there or to Water Country USA or to Colonial Williamsburg. During spring break weeks and summer, a Kids Camp for children ages 5 to 12 is available for an additional fee, as well as Kids Night Out on weekend evenings, so parents can enjoy dinner by themselves at one of the resort's three restaurants.

There are 425 fully appointed, villa-style rooms, including one-, two-, and three-bedroom suites, some providing working fireplaces with complimentary wood during the winter. In 2015, the resort opened Cottages on the James, four impeccably appointed homes, with three or four bedrooms, each with its own en suite. (A fifth cottage is being used as a model, in case you want them to build you your own within the community.)

A marina with 15 itinerant boat slips allows guests to cruise to Williamsburg and dock riverside. Various packages are also available. If this doesn't break the budget, Kingsmill is one of the most pleasant accommodations in the Williamsburg area.

LA QUINTA INN, 600 Bypass Rd., Williamsburg, VA 23185; (757) 220-2800, (800) SLEEPLQ (753-3757); lq.com; $. This former Days Inn changed hands and underwent a makeover in 2015. Located one mile from Colonial Williamsburg and within easy driving distance of Busch Gardens and Water Country USA, it offers standard budget hotel amenities, including Wi-Fi and the outdoor pool. It is 100 percent smoke-free, but pets are welcome, without a charge.

MARRIOTT'S MANOR CLUB AT FORD'S COLONY, 240 Ford's Colony Dr., Williamsburg, VA 23188; (757) 258-1120; marriott.com; $$–$$$. This resort, set within a planned community, is off the beaten track. But if you are willing to brave a slightly longer trek into Williamsburg's attractions, you'll find a quiet, beautiful retreat with lots of amenities and well-appointed rooms. Choose from guest rooms or one- and two-bedroom private villas with full kitchens, separate living and dining areas, Wi-Fi, washer/dryers, enclosed balconies or patios, and fireplaces. There's also a spa, fitness center, indoor and outdoor pools, and tennis courts. Play golf at the adjacent **Ford's Colony Country**

Club, which has the only restaurant on the property. Jogging and hiking trails wind throughout the development.

PARK INN BY RADISSON, 2007 Richmond Rd., Williamsburg, VA 23185; (757) 220-3888, (888) 288-8889; radissonhotels.com; $–$$. Located along Richmond Road's commercial district, this older budget hotel has an indoor heated swimming pool with exterior sundeck, and 127 rooms, all with Wi-Fi, cable TV, coffeemakers, hair dryers, irons, and ironing boards. Continental breakfast, weekday newspaper, and local phone calls are included in the room rate. Pets are prohibited. Pretty much whatever you feel like eating is available within walking distance—Red Lobster, Carrabba's, and the Fireside Chop House are steps away. Fax and copy services are available as are wheelchair-accessible rooms and whirlpool suites. Discounts offered to military and government employees, senior citizens, and AAA members. There is a guest laundry on-site.

RESIDENCE INN BY MARRIOTT, 1648 Richmond Rd., Williamsburg, VA 23185; (757) 941-2000, (800) 331-3131; marriott.com/phfrw; $–$$. This hotel is popular with William & Mary parents and alumni for its location just west of campus. All 108 suites have kitchens; select from studio suites with king-size beds or one- or two-bedroom suites. Other amenities include Wi-Fi, outdoor pool, and fitness room. Several national chain restaurants and local favorites, **Food for Thought,** Kephi Greek Kitchen, and **Seafare,** are within easy walking distance. Two pets per room (under 75 pounds each) are allowed with a $100 nonrefundable fee. This facility is 100 percent smoke-free. Wheelchair accessible rooms are available. There is guest laundry that accepts debit or credit cards, a business center, and a market near the front desk for snacks and sundries. Complimentary coffee and hot tea are available throughout the day.

RODEWAY INN & SUITES, 7224 Merrimac Trail, Williamsburg, VA 23185; (757) 229-0400, (800) 228-2000; choicehotels.com/rodeway-inn; $. This 32-room motel is a favorite of budget-minded families for its large, no-frills suites and its location near Busch Gardens and Water Country USA. Rooms are equipped with a refrigerator, microwave, and Wi-Fi. Continental breakfast is included in the room charge, and there is a large outdoor pool to splash around in during the warm months. There are some rooms in which smoking is permitted. Wheelchair access is very limited. A second Rodeway Inn, at 309 Page St. (757-229-1855, 800-228-2000) is a short walk away from the east end of the Historic area and **La Tolteca,** an inexpensive but terrific Mexican restaurant, is right around the corner.

SLEEP INN HISTORIC, 220 Bypass Rd., Williamsburg, VA 23185; (757) 259-1700; choicehotels.com; $–$$. This attractive motel offers fine accommodations in a range of prices. In addition to 65 rooms, this property offers two Jacuzzi rooms, each with a king-size bed and a Jacuzzi for two. All rooms have cable TV, Wi-Fi, and walk-in showers. Continental breakfast is included in the room rate. The heated indoor swimming pool and exercise room are open year-round. Wheelchair-accessible rooms are available. This is a 100 percent smoke-free facility. There is a Cracker Barrel next-door and Denny's, Jose Tequila, and **Rocco's Smokehouse Grill** are just across the street. Pets are welcome for an additional $25 fee. There is a business center, coin-operated and guest laundry on-site. Coffee, tea, and hot cocoa are available in the lobby 24 hours a day.

SPRING HILL SUITES BY MARRIOTT, 1644 Richmond Rd., Williamsburg VA 23185; (757) 941-3000, (800) 676-3069; marriott.com; $–$$. This moderately priced, all-suites property is located in the heart of Richmond Road's commercial corridor. Each suite has a trundle bed and either two queen-size beds or one king. The rooms have separate eating areas and a pantry with a refrigerator. Other amenities include indoor pool, business center, guest laundry, and exercise room. The entire hotel offers Wi-Fi, and the property is 100 percent smoke-free and pet-free. Several restaurants—Chili's, Rocco's Smokehouse Grill, and local favorite Food for Thought—are located within easy walking distance. The Ripley's Believe It or Not attraction is directly across the street. Wheelchair-accessible rooms are available upon request.

BED AND BREAKFASTS

Newcomers to Virginia soon learn that there is a history to everything here, and if you choose to lodge with Williamsburg residents, you'll be continuing a tradition dating back more than 200 years, when, during "publick times" twice each year, the legal and governmental business of the colony took place, and the city was as crowded with visitors as it can get during high season today.

In the early days of the Historic Area restoration, there were no hotels in town. The response was to do what folks in the 'Burg have always done: open their doors to visitors and offer them hospitality. And while a contemporary hotel/motel room may meet your lodging needs, staying in a tastefully appointed bed and breakfast sets a certain tone for your visit. The people who run Williamsburg's small inns and B&Bs are also some of the most knowledgeable residents when it comes to directing you for making best use of your time.

Today, Williamsburg has a well-established roster of exquisite bed and breakfasts, some of them world-class, national-award winners. Each offers modern amenities and has a unique decor and personality all its own. Some are close to the Historic Area, while others are as far afield as Charles City County, where you can stay in a true southern plantation house dating from colonial times, if you're willing to drive a bit.

Keep in mind, too, that the bed and breakfast establishments offer some of the finest food served in the area. Breakfasts take on grand proportions in some of the lodgings, and, no, you don't have to sit at a large table with a bunch of strangers in all cases. "That's one thing we learned over the years," said Sandy Hirz, who along with her husband, Brad, runs the **Liberty Rose Bed and Breakfast.** "We discovered that some people simply prefer to enjoy a quiet, private breakfast at a table for two."

Today's hosts will not require you to sleep three or more to a bed and to bring your own linen—and food—as was customary in colonial times. Most houses date from the Colonial Revival of the 1920s onward. The City of Williamsburg's Architectural Review Board in 1993 designated several of the houses as "historically significant" in helping define the city's character and representing architectural styles and cultural periods from the city's past: Applewood, Colonial Capital, Liberty Rose, and Williamsburg Manor. The West Williamsburg Heights Architecture Preservation District includes some of the listings, and you may wish to discuss the architectural importance of the area with your hosts.

Most of the homes take their own reservations. But many of the bed and breakfast owners also belong to the Williamsburg Hotel-Motel Association (888-882-4156; visitwilliamsburg.com), which handles reservations on their behalf. AirBnB also operates in Williamsburg.

Most establishments accept Visa and MasterCard. If you plan to use another credit card, a personal check, or traveler's checks, confirm this with the inn when you make your reservation. Wheelchair accessibility can be tricky at bed and breakfasts. Discuss any special needs with your host ahead of time.

Many bed and breakfasts also offer special seasonal packages, particularly romance packages, where guests can stay two or more nights and receive extras such as gift certificates to dinner or flowers and champagne in their room for a special price. Often, this information is listed on their website, but be sure to mention any special occasion you're celebrating when you make your reservation. Some of the larger residences also host weddings and other events as well.

Some of the bed and breakfasts sell tickets to local attractions. Be sure to ask your hosts when you make your reservation if they provide this added-value service.

Note: There are three bed and breakfasts—the **Hornsby House Inn,** the **Marl Inn,** and the **York River Inn**—located in Yorktown, 15 miles northeast of Williamsburg, and close to the Yorktown historical attractions and the Riverwalk shopping and dining district. See our complete description in the Jamestown and Yorktown chapter later in this book.

The dollar signs in each entry indicate a range of rates for double occupancy (two persons) per night. During peak season (generally anytime other than January, February, and March), rates are higher. Also, some establishments offer lower rates for single occupancy, and some may require a minimum two-night reservation on select weekends. Please confirm your rate with your hosts at the time you book your visit.

ALDRICH HOUSE, 505 Capitol Ct., Williamsburg, VA 23185; (757) 229-5422; aldrichhouse.com; $$. Innkeepers Tom and Sue Patton opened this bed and breakfast in 1997. The house, 2 blocks east of the Historic Area, was built in 1986 in the style of a colonial saltbox home and decorated in 18th-century fashion. Each room is a mix of current-day luxuries (TV, Wi-Fi) and historic charm. A full breakfast, served family-style, consists of fruit, eggs, pancakes, waffles, or oven-baked French toast, a breakfast meat, and sometimes country sausage gravy and biscuits. They offer several packages aimed at lovers of wine, history, or love itself.

ALICE PERSON HOUSE, 616 Richmond Rd., Williamsburg, VA 23185; (757) 220-9263; alicepersonhouse.com; $$. Innkeepers Jean and Harry Matthews operate this Colonial Revival home, located 1 block from the College of William & Mary campus and the Historic Area. Built in 1929, the house is reminiscent of early 20th-century Williamsburg accommodations, replete with high ceilings and spacious rooms furnished with antiques and Oriental rugs. The house features a formal parlor with a fireplace on the first floor, available for guest use, and three guest rooms, each with private bath, cable TV, and VCR. The house has secure Wi-Fi. European linens and plush towels and robes make for luxurious lounging.

Breakfasts are served family-style and include biscuits, quiche, crepes, and waffles served with Virginia sausage or bacon, seasonal fresh fruits, yogurts, fresh-ground coffees, and teas.

There is a two-night minimum stay during high season, and a three-night minimum stay on holiday weekends. Off-street parking is available, but no pets and no smoking. Children ages 10 and older are welcome.

APPLEWOOD COLONIAL BED AND BREAKFAST, 605 Richmond Rd., Williamsburg, VA 23185, (757) 903-4306; williamsburgbandb.com; $$. This elegantly appointed home is located four short blocks from the city's Historic Area, near the College of William & Mary. Built by a Colonial Williamsburg craftsman, the house dates from 1928 and features Flemish bond brickwork, colonial decor, fireplaces, and antiques throughout. Each room is appointed with a queen-size bed, cable TV, Wi-Fi, a small refrigerator stocked with refreshments, a coffeemaker, iron and ironing board, and a private bath.

Guests enjoy a full breakfast with treats such as peach French toast, hash-brown quiche, baked oatmeal, eggs, meats, rolls, and muffins. Mention any dietary restrictions when reserving your room.

Innkeepers Monty and Denise Fleck are happy to make special occasions more memorable by having any particular items in the room before arrival.

Children 10 and older are welcome. This is a nonsmoking, air-conditioned house. A private patio in back is available for relaxing, and bicycles are available for guest use.

THE CEDARS OF WILLIAMSBURG, 616 Jamestown Rd., Williamsburg, VA 23185; (757) 229-3591, (800) 296-3591; cedarsofwilliamsburg.com; $$. A front garden welcomes guests to The Cedars, located across from the William & Mary campus and a short walk from Merchants Square. Owner Alexander Vlk offers a variety of accommodations: a freestanding cottage, two-room suites in the main house, and other sleeping rooms, all with private baths. Antiques and 18th-century reproductions throughout the house convey an elegant, historic ambience, fitting to the place known as "Williamsburg's oldest and largest guesthouse."

Brace yourself for a day of touring with a full gourmet breakfast ranging from a personal loaf of banana bread, sharp cheddar quiche with shrimp. and much more. Conversation is key as the breakfast room is the ideal location to talk history and your vacation. The Cedars is a nonsmoking house. You'll find off-street parking in the rear.

COLONIAL CAPITAL BED AND BREAKFAST, 501 Richmond Rd., Williamsburg, VA 23185; (757) 645-4525; ccbb.com; $$. Three blocks from the Historic Area and within walking distance of William & Mary's football stadium, this 3-story Colonial Revival has been welcoming visitors since 1926. Antique furnishing and Oriental rugs throughout the house suggest luxury; a plantation parlor on the main floor is kept cozy by a wood-burning fireplace.

Five large guest rooms, each with private bath, offer a variety of accommodations. The Potomac Room has a private porch with rocking chairs. The York is a favorite for honeymoons and anniversaries, with its queen-size, turned-post canopied high-rope bed and en suite bath with original claw-foot tub. All rooms have remote-controlled ceiling fans, TVs, and VCRs. Beds are turned

ACCOMMODATIONS

down nightly—look for a pillow mint. There is zoned central air-conditioning and Wi-Fi.

Breakfast is a decadent affair with French toast, western omelets, soufflés, and a variety of casseroles.

Children older than 8 years old with well-behaved parents are welcome. Single occupancy rates are available year-round. This is a nonsmoking inn.

COLONIAL GARDENS BED & BREAKFAST, 1109 Jamestown Rd., Williamsburg, VA 23185; (757) 220-8087; colonial-gardens.com; $$. This split-level brick home, located a mile west of the William & Mary campus, sits on a landscaped acre that lends a country air to its central location. Romantic getaways are the specialty—the entire inn can be rented out for weddings, and owner Karen Watkins has 6 marriage commissioners in her Rolodex for those who want to say "I do" on the lush grounds.

The house has 4 guest rooms, each with private bath, telephone, and flat screen TV with DVD and cable. All beds have luxury mattresses and fine linens. Plush bathrobes are provided to all guests.

Breakfasts are "elaborate. We might have bananas Foster crepes with baked eggs or poached pears with honey. I'm a good cook," Watkins says. Complimentary refreshments are served in the sunroom, overlooking the gardens. A designated refrigerator holds wine, sodas, and water for whenever guests need to slake their thirst. Hot tea, coffee, chips, and biscotti are offered to nosh on throughout the day.

Colonial Gardens hosts an average of 40 weddings a year, and prospective brides and grooms can view photographs of previous ceremonies on the home's excellent website listed above.

Children older than 12 are welcome, but pets are not. This is a nonsmoking inn.

EDGEWOOD PLANTATION, 4800 John Tyler Hwy. (VA 5), Charles City, VA 23030; (804) 829-2962; edgewoodplantation.com; $$. This historic plantation is located 30 minutes west of Williamsburg but provides a unique lodging experience. The mansion, with its double spiral staircase and 10 fireplaces, is a National Historic Landmark. A gristmill on the property dates from 1725. There is a ghost: Legend has it, Elizabeth "Lizzie" Rowland died of a broken heart waiting in vain for her lover to return from the Civil War. Don't let her intimidate you. There's a good night's sleep in any one of the seven bedrooms or in the separate cabin behind the main house. *Gone with the Wind* fans will enjoy the third floor, with its sitting and common area rooms, called Scarlett's Room and Melanie's Room. All rooms have king- or queen-size canopy beds.

On the grounds, you will find formal gardens and a swimming pool. Breakfast is candlelit, and it may include fresh fruit, orange juice, crepes, quiche, croissants filled with fruit and cheese, or sometimes a country breakfast of Smithfield ham biscuits and fried apples. Special features available upon request include Victorian teas and tours, including a haunted tour. If Christmas is your favorite season, you will enjoy Edgewood's 18 decorated Christmas trees.

No smoking is permitted; pets are accepted in Dolly's Room only.

FIFE AND DRUM INN, 411 Prince George St., Williamsburg, VA 23185; (757) 345-1776; fifeanddruminn.com; $$–$$$. The building that houses the Fife and Drum—1 block off Merchants Square—has been in the same family since A. W. Hitchens built it to replace the general store and pasture he sold to the Colonial Williamsburg Foundation in 1933. Granddaughter Sharon Scruggs and her husband, Billy, talked for years about turning it into a small inn—and in 1999, they got their chance. It's the only inn in "downtown" Williamsburg.

The inn's seven rooms and two suites are tucked into one of the best locations in Williamsburg—100 yards from the Merchants Square entrance to the colonial area. The inn is packed with historical bric-a-brac, collected into a theme for each room.

The George Washington Room features a collection of antique postcards celebrating the Father of Our Nation's birthday. The Richneck Room, named for the home of Thomas Ludwell, a 17th-century secretary of the Virginia Colony, includes archaeological artifacts from that historic site.

Fife and Drum also comes with "two innkeepers who grew up here," as Sharon says. Guests get more than just insider recommendations of shops and restaurants—they get local color and stories.

For all the history, the inn has every modern amenity: luxury linens, plush towels, delicious breakfast, afternoon refreshments, Wi-Fi, and cable TV in each room. The inn welcomes children over age 8; children under 14 must stay in a room with an adult (two of the rooms sleep three). The inn is nonsmoking, and pets are not permitted.

GOVERNOR'S TRACE, 303 Capitol Landing Rd., Williamsburg, VA 23185; (757) 229-7552; governorstrace.com; $$. Conveniently located just a minute away from George Washington's favorite tavern in the Historic Area, this Georgian brick house was built during the restoration of Colonial Williamsburg and occupies a half-acre of a former peanut plantation that extended the length of what is now Capitol Landing Road. Nearby, thirteen of Blackbeard's pirates were hanged. Today's visitors receive a much more cordial welcome than the pirates did. Hosts Sue and Dick Lake are happy to help tailor your touring itinerary.

The three guestrooms, each named for an 18th-century governor, are more spacious than most and splendidly decorated in period fashion. Each has a porch and private bath.

Governor's Trace serves a candlelight breakfast in each room and provides cozy robes so guests need not "dress" for breakfast. This is a nonsmoking accommodation. It offers off-street parking. No pets are allowed.

NEWPORT HOUSE, 710 S. Henry St., Williamsburg, VA 23185; (757) 229-1775; newporthousebb.com; $$–$$$. A 5-minute walk from the Historic Area, the Newport House is a reproduction from a 1756 design by colonial architect Peter Harrison, whose buildings spanned the British Empire from America to India and who was the architect of the Williamsburg Statehouse rebuilding in 1749. The building is furnished with period antiques and reproductions—even guests' blankets are historically authentic. In recognition of how sultry the Virginia summers can be, however, there is air-conditioning, and each bedroom has two four-poster canopy beds (an extra-long queen-size and a single) and a private bath.

Breakfast is based on 18th-century recipes and includes Rhode Island johnnycakes, scuppernong jelly, and baked goodies. Pancakes and waffles are served with honey from the owners' own beehive, and fresh berries and apples—when in season—come straight from the property's garden. The morning meal is also usually accompanied by a historical lecture from host John Fitzhugh Millar. He is a former museum director and captain of a full-rigged ship, as well as author and publisher of many books of history.

On Tuesday evening, you may participate in colonial country dancing in the ballroom. Beginners are welcome to join in or watch. A harpsichord is available, and with a few days' advance notice, guests may rent colonial clothing either for their entire stay or for dinner at one of the colonial taverns. Newport House does not allow pets and or smoking in the house.

NORTH BEND PLANTATION, 12200 Weyanoke Rd., Charles City County, VA 23030; (804) 829-5176; northbendplantation.com; $$. One of the oldest bed and breakfast structures in the area (built ca. 1801 and enlarged in 1853), North Bend Plantation is on the National Register of Historic Places and also is designated a Virginia Historic Landmark. The National Park Service features it on its Civil War and birding trails. Your hosts here are George and

ACCOMMODATIONS

Ridgley Copland, fifth-generation owners. The home was originally built for Sarah Harrison, George's great-great-aunt and sister of William Henry Harrison, the ninth US president.

The main house's Greek Revival design is situated on 500 acres just east of Charles City Court House and 1 mile off VA 5, about a 25-minute drive west of Williamsburg.

Possessions treasured and displayed by the family include old and rare books, colonial antiques from related plantation families, and an antique doll collection. Modern fun is to be had, as well: a fine swimming pool, billiards room, croquet, horseshoes, volleyball, and a full country breakfast including fresh fruit, juices, waffles, omelets, bacon, sausage, and biscuits.

Accommodations include varying combinations of bed sizes and styles, and all rooms feature private baths. The Magnolia Room features a canopied queen-size rice bed and a shower. The Sheridan Room features a high queen-size tester bed (ca. 1810–40) that belonged to Edmund Ruffin, George Copland's great-great-grandfather. The headboard was shot at in the Civil War. General Sheridan's desk and a sitting area are in the room. The Federal Room features an iron and brass queen-size bed. The Rose Room has a queen-size canopy bed, a fireplace, and a sitting area. The Maids Quarters connects to the Magnolia Room and has a double bed. An upstairs sunporch (one of three) is available for guests' enjoyment.

Guests are treated with refreshments on arrival: cookies and lemonade or hot cider, depending on the season. Children 6 and older are welcome, but pets are not.

PINEY GROVE AT SOUTHALL'S PLANTATION, 16920 Southall Plantation Ln., Williamsburg, VA 23187; (804) 829-2480; pineygrove.com; $$. Three generations of the Gordineer family have welcomed travelers to this Virginia Historic Landmark, which is listed on the National Register of Historic Places. Built ca. 1790 on 300 acres first occupied by the Chickahominy Indians, Piney Grove is the oldest existing example of log architecture in Tidewater Virginia. Another home on the property, the Ladysmith, is a modest Greek Revival plantation house built in 1857. Both houses have been restored to their original appearance yet include modern conveniences.

Six spacious guest rooms—each with a private bath, working fireplace, small refrigerator, and coffeemaker—are tastefully appointed with family heirlooms as well as antiques and artifacts that chronicle four centuries of Virginia home life. Suites are available for parties of up to four guests.

A nature trail, garden walk, and pool invite outdoor activity. Mint juleps, hot toddies, cider, and nightcaps of brandy are offered in every season. A candlelight plantation breakfast is served in the 1790 Log Room.

No pets or smoking are permitted. Children are welcome, and young guests will particularly enjoy the barnyard animals. Credit cards are not accepted. The inn takes checks, cash, or traveler's checks.

WAR HILL INN, 4560 Longhill Rd., Williamsburg, VA 23188; (757) 565-0248, (800) 743-0248; warhillinn.com; $$. Set on a 32-acre estate 4 miles from downtown Williamsburg, this house was built in 1968 for hosts Shirley and Bill Lee under the guidance of a Colonial Williamsburg architect. Crickets, frogs, owls, and Angus cattle are the closest neighbors, and it is easy, upon awakening, to imagine yourself having traveled 200 years back to a peaceful setting in the colonial period.

Among War Hill's attractions is a reproduction colonial cottage, the Washington Cottage. It offers a canopy bed for a comfortable rest, a private bath, and a whirlpool tub for your relaxation and enjoyment. The Jefferson Cottage also features a fireplace, whirlpool bath, and kitchenette. Four other rooms in the main house all have private baths, antique furnishings, and TVs. Children are welcome here; smoking is not. The hosts are not serving continental breakfast for the foreseeable future and to maintain a safe environment, they require a three-night minimum stay in the cottages and a seven-night minimum stay in the Manor House.

WEDMORE PLACE, at the Williamsburg Winery, 5310 Wessex Hundred, Williamsburg, VA 23185; (757) 941-0310; wedmoreplace.com; $$–$$$. The luxury accommodations offered on the manicured grounds of the **Williamsburg Winery** are styled as a "European country hotel." All 28 rooms have king-size beds and wood-burning fireplaces. Two conference rooms are suitable for private functions or executive retreats. An outdoor pool with sundeck, a well-stocked library, and dining at the vineyard (**Gabriel Archer Tavern**) make this a full-service retreat for those who want an upscale escape. The winery, located just steps away, offers tours (by reservation only). There are four room styles, ranging from traditional to suites. Special offers are outlined on the website, which also offers photographs of the well-appointed rooms and gorgeous grounds.

WILLIAMSBURG MANOR BED AND BREAKFAST, 600 Richmond Rd., Williamsburg, VA 23185; (757) 220-8011, (800) 422-8011; williamsburg manor.com; $$. This 1929 Georgian brick Colonial Revival house is just a 5-minute walk from Merchants Square and steps away from the College of William & Mary. Innkeepers Laura and Craig Reeves opened it to guests in 1992 and offer a wealth of expertise about the area. Interior spaces and gardens have been updated with modern amenities. All rooms feature queen-size beds with private full baths, flat panel TVs, iPod docking stations, and Wi-Fi.

The innkeepers are also professional caterers and prepare a delicious array of southern breakfast favorites. They can accommodate special diets and allergies. The Manor is available for weddings, family reunions, private parties, and other special occasions. More information about the Reeves' catering business, The Catering Company, can be found at williamsburgoccasions.com.

Well-behaved children and pets are welcome. Smoking is restricted to the back patio. Off-street parking is available to guests.

WILLIAMSBURG SAMPLER BED AND BREAKFAST, 922 Jamestown Rd., Williamsburg, VA 23185; (757) 220-8011, (800) 422-8011; williams burgsampler.com; $$. Across the street from the College of William & Mary and within a 10-minute walk of Merchants Square, this stately brick home in the style of an 18th-century plantation manor house is decorated throughout with antiques, books, a magnificent pewter collection, other Americana, and—how did you guess?—a host of hand-stitched samplers that innkeeper Ike Sisane has collected.

Excellence is a hallmark here. The Sampler has won accolades for its hearty and delectable "Skip Lunch" Breakfast, which has been featured on CBS TV. When actor Ray Romano comes to Williamsburg, this is where he stays.

Four of the guest accommodations offer fireplaces. King-size, rice-carved four-poster beds are available, and Thomasville furnishings, a private bath, and a comfortable sitting area with wing chairs or daybed are features of every guest room. Two two-room suites open to a rooftop garden overlooking the grounds and woods below. Air-conditioning, Wi-Fi, and TVs in every room are welcome non-colonial features.

Beautiful grounds at the rear invite a stroll just downhill from a replica of Colonial Williamsburg's 18th-century Coke-Garrett Carriage House. Or you can work off that breakfast at the fitness center in the carriage house. Off-street parking is provided. Children over 13 and pets are welcome. Smoking outside only.

A WILLIAMSBURG WHITE HOUSE, 718 Jamestown Rd., Williamsburg, VA 23185; (757) 229-8580; awilliamsburgwhitehouse.com; $$. This unique bed and breakfast, located 4 blocks from the Historic Area, does everything but play "Hail to the Chief" for visitors. Innkeepers Deborah and John Keane have remodeled a three-story, 105-year-old colonial in presidential style. There are five suites, one of which has two bedrooms, all with private baths and Wi-Fi. Each is named for a former president and decorated in a style befitting his taste. The Roosevelt Suite, for instance, celebrates Teddy's love of train travel with a queen-size railroad-like berth. Teddy might also appreciate the Wi-Fi.

Guests awake to made-to-order breakfasts, served on fine china in the Reagan Dining Room or at a table for two in the JFK Library, where they can peruse the extensive collection of historical and political books. Afternoon sweets, wines, ports, and sherry are served in the Diplomatic Reception Room. Party politics extends even to the parking lot where spaces bear "Democrats only" and "Republicans only" designations.

The inn offers its 1.5-acre lawn for weddings. Special elopement and vow renewal packages are available.

YORKTOWN

BATTLEFIELD COTTAGE, 121 Lafayette Rd., Yorktown, VA 23690; (757) 879-0438; vrbo.com/1123028; $$$. Formerly the studio of renowned folk artist Nancy Thomas, this renovated cottage is located on a bluff just above the York River, less than a mile across the battlefield to historic Yorktown. One of 40 homes laid out in the 1920s as summer retreats for those who wanted to swim, fish, and crab in the York River, it is the only neighborhood completely within the confines of the Colonial National Historic Park, and it sits directly on the Revolutionary War battlefield.

The cottage has a full kitchen (coffee, tea, and bottled water included), toiletries, linens, golf clubs, and fishing gear. (The Yorktown fishing pier does not require a license.) Sleeps two. No pets. A two-night minimum stay is required.

HORNSBY HOUSE INN, 702 Main St., Yorktown, VA 23690; (757) 369-0200; hornsbyhouseinn.com; $$–$$$. Built in 1933 by J. W. Hornsby, a prosperous local businessman, this Georgian-style home and property is situated on the bluff overlooking the York River and across a quiet street from the Yorktown Victory Monument. Designed by the same architects John D. Rockefeller hired to restore Colonial Williamsburg, the stylish house is a local treasure, decorated with American and English antiques. In 2012, brothers David and Phil Bowditch, grandsons of the original owner, converted the spacious home into a bed and breakfast. A top-notch breakfast is served at 8:45 a.m., wine and cheese or high tea are served at 5 p.m. Spa services are available in the on-site carriage house. The battlefield is steps away in one direction, the beach and Riverwalk's shops and restaurants in the other. The tastefully appointed rooms include high-end linens and Wi-Fi; the Monument Grand Suite, which can sleep four, has its own fireplace. The house is not wheelchair accessible nor set up to serve children. (They will make exceptions on a case-by-case basis.) Pets and smoking are not allowed.

MARL INN, 220 Church St., Yorktown, VA 23690; (757) 898-3859; marl innbandb.com; $$. This charming bed and breakfast, 2 blocks from Yorktown's Riverwalk district and just 20 minutes from Colonial Williamsburg, adds another layer of experience to your tour of the Historic Triangle—owner Tom Nelson is a descendant of Thomas Nelson, signer of the Declaration of Independence. Nelson operates this B&B with his wife, Poppet. There are four guest rooms, and a full breakfast is provided—unless you don't want one. The Nelsons will take $20 off the room rate if you'd prefer the continental breakfast they lay out in the dining room. (Poppet Nelson reports 80 percent of the guests take the continental breakfast option!)

The Marl Inn has Wi-Fi and is child and pet friendly (the Nelsons have two dogs of their own). There is no smoking.

ACCOMMODATIONS

YORK RIVER INN BED & BREAKFAST, 209 Ambler St., Yorktown, VA 23690; (757) 887-8800, (800) 884-7003; yorkriverinn.com; $$. Innkeeper William Cole thinks of his inn as "a home with frequent guests," and he carries out that philosophy in every detail, from the warm greeting you receive to the elaborate breakfasts. The inn provides cable TV in each room, fresh flowers, Wi-Fi, plush bathrobes, fax services, and other amenities. Cole's local knowledge—19 years with Colonial Williamsburg and four as director of the Watermen's Museum—will help you spend your time here wisely.

The first-floor public area has a deck with a panoramic view of the York River and Coleman Bridge. Guest rooms are upstairs. (Some overlook the river.) The largest room, on the third floor, has a Jacuzzi.

A hearty breakfast might include a clam casserole, three-cheese quiche, or fresh honeydew-pineapple-kiwi salad.

This is a nonsmoking inn, and neither pets nor children can be accommodated. It is not wheelchair accessible.

Dining

Williamsburg has been feeding visitors for several hundred years. The original public establishments here were the taverns you now will find in the city's Historic Area.

Since then, the variety of cuisines offered locally has expanded quite a bit so that you can now get fine Vietnamese food, down-home southern cooking, and everything in between. You can order grits at a pancake house, but you'll also see them at the most expensive restaurants in town—often served with shrimp.

Arguably the best thing to happen on the Williamsburg restaurant scene has nothing to do with the food. In 2009, a new state law went into effect prohibiting smoking in restaurants that did not have a separate ventilation system for their smoking areas. As a result, nearly every restaurant in Virginia, a state that relied on tobacco as its primary cash crop and economic bulwark for hundreds of years, is now nonsmoking.

Two beverage notes: Iced tea is the drink of choice to accompany all southern meals, but it is served sweetened. Those folks in Boston may have thrown their tea into the harbor, but southern colonials and their progeny maintain that sugar, not saltwater, is the best companion. Make sure to ask for your tea unsweetened if you think otherwise.

If you are looking for places that serve or sell adult beverages, the designation is "ABC," short for the commonwealth's Alcoholic Beverage Control, the agency that regulates the sale of beer, wine, and spirits. Beer and wine are sold in supermarkets, but liquor is sold by the state in ABC stores only.

Fido Ate Here

Any town where Main Street is commonly referred to as "Dog Street,"—short for Duke of Gloucester—is sure to have its share of fido-friendly restaurants and Williamsburg does, beginning on DoG Street itself with the DoG Street Pub. If you are traveling with your pup, we have noted which local restaurants have outdoor seating which welcomes canines with the initials DF. Be advised that state law requires dogs to enter directly onto the outdoor seating space. Don't bring your pup into the restaurant itself. If dogs are not a good companion for you, be sure to ask to be seated away from the dog-friendly area.

Price Code

Area restaurants almost universally accept Visa and MasterCard, so we only note exceptions. Both the state and local government add taxes to prepared meal charges.

The following code indicates the average price of two entrees only—without appetizer, dessert, beverages, tax, or gratuity.

$	Less than $30
$$	$31 to $50
$$$	$51 to $75
$$$$	More than $75

18TH-CENTURY EATING FOR 21ST-CENTURY TASTES

Many people feel their visit to Williamsburg would be incomplete without the experience of being served by a waitress in a mobcap, serenaded by a strolling balladeer, or having the origins of their Sally Lunn bread explained. These are the special features of the meals served at Colonial Williamsburg's restored taverns, which serve 18th-century favorites adapted for 21st-century tastes. (Somehow children survived 250 years ago without chicken nuggets; no such dire circumstances exist now—each of the taverns has something for the kids.)

All of the taverns are located in the Historic Area and are open to the public. (You do not need a Colonial Williamsburg ticket to eat at the taverns.) Free parking is available for tavern patrons.

A centralized number, (757) 229-2141 or (800) TAVERNS (828-3767), handles reservations for the taverns, as well as Colonial Williamsburg's other restaurants—the **Williamsburg Inn's Regency Room** and **Golden Horseshoe,** and the **Williamsburg Lodge** (see our listings for those restaurants in this chapter). Dinner reservations, in season, are a must. You can also peruse all the restaurants' menus at colonialwilliamsburg.com.

CHRISTIANA CAMPBELL'S TAVERN, 101 S. Waller St., Williamsburg, VA 23185; $$$. George Washington favored meals at this establishment, opposite the eastern end of the Capitol building, and one of unique pleasures here is listening to servers recount his favorable critiques of the place, taken from his diary. The cuisine these days focuses on traditional seafood dishes—chowder, oyster salad, crab ragout, crab cakes, and the like. The entrees are complemented by longtime tavern favorites of cabbage slaw, spoon bread, and sweet potato muffins. During the holiday season, the tavern hosts tea with Mrs. Campbell, who entertains guests with accounts of her 18th-century contemporaries and the quaint customs of the period. Dinner is served Tues through Sat from 5 p.m. Reservations are required, and parking is available behind the tavern.

DINING

JOSIAH CHOWNING'S TAVERN, 109 E. Duke of Gloucester St., Williamsburg, VA 23185; $$. Capitalizing on the craft beer craze, Chowning's Tavern reopened in 2015 as a colonial-era alehouse, with a brighter decor, new menu, and brews created by small batch breweries including **Williamsburg Alewerks,** using authentic 18th-century beer recipes. They'll be served alongside other beers, Virginia wines, cocktails, and nonalcoholic beverages. Menu changes include shepherd's pie and light fare such as pork sliders, flatbreads, corn chowder, and salads. Weather permitting, the arbor garden behind the tavern will offer a full-service bar and dining tables overlooking Market Square. On select dates, Chowning's hosts "Beers in the 'Burg" from 4 to 7 p.m., a ticketed ($25) event that allows guests to sample 10 different beers. Tickets are available at CW ticket locations, by calling (855) 296-6627, or online at colonialwilliamsburg.com. The tavern is open from 11:30 a.m. to 11 p.m. daily, with no reservations required. Live music and plenty of other types of revelry is offered every evening.

KING'S ARMS TAVERN, 416 E. Duke of Gloucester St., Williamsburg, VA 23185; $$ (lunch), $$$ (dinner). In its decor and its menu, this restaurant reflects the refined tastes of the colonial gentry who dined here. The house specialties include fried chicken, peanut soup, prime rib, and Sally Lunn bread. The bar offers specialty drinks such as "rummer" and punch royal. After your meal, try the 18th-century favorite, syllabub, a concoction of cream, white wine, sherry, sugar, and lemon that separates into a meringue-like topping with the wine and sherry at the bottom of the glass. Open Thurs through Mon for lunch from 11:30 a.m. to 2:30 p.m. and for dinner from 5 p.m. until closing. Closed Tues and Wed.

SHIELDS TAVERN, 422 E. Duke of Gloucester St., Williamsburg, VA 23185; $$$. Operated by James Shields in the 1740s, this tavern has been carefully appointed to serve visitors the foods of colonial Virginia in a setting that predates the other taverns by 25 years. Menu selections are inspired by the food served to the period's "middle class"—lesser gentry and traveling merchants—so dinner choices include Seafood Pye, Barnyard Chicken, and Forest Mushroom Fricassee.

Shields also features a full bar menu, with specialty drinks such as apple cider, rum punch, champagne cocktails, and spiced wine; beers and ales; and favorites such as Chowning's root beer and King's Arms Tavern ginger ale. Strolling balladeers and character interpreters welcome guests. Open for lunch and dinner Tues through Sat. Dinner reservations are required.

MORE WILLIAMSBURG FAVORITES

ABERDEEN BARN, 1601 Richmond Rd., Williamsburg, VA 23185; (757) 229-6661; aberdeen-barn.com; $$$. Best known for its aged steaks, this restaurant opens at 4:30 p.m. for dinner only. The decor is rustic, subdued, and candlelit—think old-fashioned steak house. This is not the place to begin a diet—a popular starter is a basket of sesame sticks accompanied by a crock of cheese spread. Guests rave about the prime rib. A kids' menu adds appeal for families, as does The Mother Lode, a dessert for two consisting of a chocolate-chip brownie topped with ice cream and hot fudge. Reservations are recommended.

AMBER OX PUBLIC HOUSE, 525 Prince George St., Williamsburg, VA 23185; (757) 790-2299; amberox.com; $$$; DF. Not too long ago the only reason to wander this stretch of Prince George Street, a block off Merchants Square proper, was if you were lucky enough to have scored a reservation at A Chef's Kitchen. Now this area has blossomed into a bustling little offshoot with The Hound's Tale and the Corner Barkery, both owned and managed by the Aromas' group, a popular ramen house, Oishii, and this new upscale restaurant. Amber Ox features an expansive bar area, locally sourced cuisine, specialty cocktails and microbrews from the Precarious Beer Project, whose distillery was originally located next door. The menu has a wide variety of "boards and bar snacks," including the Southern favorite, whipped pimento cheese, lots of salads and a rotating list of entrees with an emphasis on Virginia and North Carolina produce and meats. The sidewalk patio area is a convivial meeting spot. Open 3 to 10 p.m. Mon, Wed, and Thurs; 10 a.m. to 10 p.m. Sat; 10 a.m. to 9 p.m. Sun. Closed Tues.

AMIRAJ MODERN INDIAN KITCHEN, 204 Monticello Ave., Williamsburg, VA 23185; (757) 565-3200; amiraj.com; $$. The coronavirus ended what had been one of the most popular offerings at this fine restaurant located in a nondescript shopping center: the lunchtime all-you-can-eat buffet. In its place, Amiraj (formerly Nawab) is offering lunch specials starting at $11 that include soup or salad, naan, rice, and an entrée. There's also a three-course, $19 brunch on Sat and Sun that offers beer, wine, or a mango lassi, appetizer, entrée, dessert, and coffee or tea. The attractive interior—crisp white linens, soft lighting, tinkling water feature—make for a relaxing meal. The extensive menu offers lots of excellent Northern Indian cuisine: tandoori specialties, curries, kebabs, and Indian staples such as raita, mango chutney, basmati rice, and specialty breads including garlic naan, roti, and paratha. There are ample options for vegetarians. Open daily for lunch and dinner.

AROMAS, 431 Prince George St., Williamsburg, VA 23185; (757) 221-6676; aromasworld.com; $; DF. Some days it seems everybody in Williamsburg is at Aromas, the coffee spot of choice, 1 block off Merchants Square. Whether you want caffeine, a snack, or a full meal, it's hard to go wrong. Decor and service are casual (order at the counter, pick it up yourself). The menu features egg dishes, sandwiches, wraps, baked goods, soups, and salads. Breakfast is served daily beginning at 7:30 a.m.; dinner specials are available after 5 p.m. The kids' menu was obviously designed for picky eaters—actual description: "The nachos are fixed how kids like 'em, PLAIN." Decadent desserts and a full range of specialty coffees and loose-leaf teas are available. There's a whole calendar full of programming: game night, open mic, live music. Evenings, the drink of choice shifts from coffee to wine or beer. Because of its popularity, grabbing a table can be tricky at peak times. Most days, even in the winter, the outside tables are a great option. Free Wi-Fi is available, too.

BAKER'S CRUST, 5234 Monticello Ave. (Settler's Market shopping center), Williamsburg, VA 23188; (757) 253-2787; bakerscrust.com; $–$$. This Virginia-only chain has locations in Ashburn, Richmond, Norfolk, Chesapeake, Virginia Beach, and this one in the New Town mixed-use development off Monticello Avenue. High-backed leather booths ring the dining room; a separate bar area is a popular spot for a glass of wine during happy hour. The real draw here is, however, the fresh-baked breads, salads (full and half portions), burgers, soups, and crepes—prepared both as entrees (shrimp and jumbo lump crab or steak and mushroom) and desserts (the Wimbledon crepes contain fresh strawberries and whipped cream). Several varieties of Mediterranean flatbread pizzas work as appetizers for the table; the roasted tomato and house-made mozzarella panini is warm, gooey, and full of iron-rich baby spinach leaves. Don't limit yourself to trying just one thing—the most popular items on the menu are the soup/salad/sandwich combos. Steam rises from the liquid center of the chocolate lava mini-bundt cake—cool it off with the scoop of vanilla bean ice cream served alongside. There are plenty of gluten-free options, and children are welcomed with seven smaller plate options.

Takeout and catering menus are available. Open at 11 a.m. for lunch and dinner Mon through Fri; open at 8 a.m. for breakfast on Sat and Sun. Dinner is served until 9 p.m. Sun through Thurs; until 10 p.m. on Fri and Sat.

BERRET'S SEAFOOD RESTAURANT AND TAPHOUSE GRILL, 199 S. Boundary St. (Merchants Square), Williamsburg, VA 23185; (757) 253-1847; berrets.com; $$–$$$; DF. This is actually two restaurants in one, located directly behind the shops on Duke of Gloucester Street. Locals consistently rate Berret's seafood (especially the crab cakes) the best in town. Specials are chosen based on what local fishermen have brought in that day: shad roe, soft-shell crabs, sea trout, and striped bass in the spring; flounder, cobia, tuna, wahoo, and bluefish in the summer; and rockfish, red fish, and sea bass each fall. Thanks to aquaculture, local natural oysters and clams can be offered year-round.

The open-air Taphouse serves food, but the attraction is the full bar that includes wine and beer menus featuring unique selections from across the state and local microbrews. There's live music almost every night April through October. Thursday nights you can "Steal the Pint" by sampling a new brew. Try the beers; keep the glass. Open 4 p.m. daily, weather permitting about 9 months of the year.

BLUE TALON BISTRO, 420 Prince George St., Williamsburg, VA 23185; (757) 476-2583; bluetalonbistro.com; $ (breakfast), $$ (lunch), $$$ (dinner). Any short list of Williamsburg's best restaurants would include this charming, French-inflected bistro, which is open for breakfast, lunch, dinner, and Sunday brunch at an unbeatable location 1 block off Merchants Square. Cafe tables on the sidewalk and the fare—"Champagne, sausages, fromages"—stenciled on large-pane storefront windows lend a Parisian air. Inside, the space evokes early 20th-century elegance—hammered tin ceiling, tile floor with inlaid mosaics, light wood, and rattan furniture. It's a nice change from the pervasive colonial motif.

Owner-chef David Everett's focus is "serious comfort food," but his menu is European and traditional. Onion soup gratinée, sautéed calf's liver, foie gras, pâté, escargot, sweetbreads, braised goat, lamb steak, cassoulet, potpies, and all manner of crepes are standards. The wine list is extensive. The chocolate mousse, a cloud of intense flavor scooped tableside from a porcelain lion's head bowl into a bowl of sliced strawberries, dusted with powdered sugar, and drizzled with chocolate sauce, could feed a small nation. Cappuccino, made with Italian Illy coffee, is prepared with the precise amount of microbubbles in the milk so as to leave a heart-shaped inset of foam—the so-called Illy apple—on the surface.

An excellent website allows guests to take a behind-the-scenes tour, book a reservation, check current menus, and learn about the bistro's many specials and event dinners.

Traveling alone? An especially nice place to dine is at the Zinc Bar, within easy reach of a selection of newspapers hanging from hooks on a half wall that separates the bar area from the front dining room. Bar seating is always first-come, first-served, and don't ask them to change the channel to ESPN. The bar TV runs a perpetual spool of Julia Child reruns.

Vegetarian entree options are pretty limited. Open 8 a.m. 'til close except Wed.

i The Indians taught the Jamestown colonists the secret behind the famous Virginia cured ham. Their methods of salting, smoking, and aging venison were adapted by the Europeans. Today, the distinctive taste of salt-cured ham is achieved by following essentially the same process used by the early settlers.

Close-up

Take Off for Charly's

If you want to find Williamsburg's most popular off-the-beaten-path restaurant, look up. In the skies above Rte. 199 you'll often see little two- and four-seaters headed to the Williamsburg-Jamestown Airport, a private landing strip dug out of vacant acreage 50 years ago, a family affair that's grown into an established hub for private plane owners.

Indisputably, part of the draw of this facility is **Charly's Airport Café**, a restaurant located in the nondescript terminal with just 32 seats, some picnic tables for eating outside when the weather permits, and a playground so mom and dad can linger while the kids play. Whatever image "airport food" conjures up for you, think the opposite. Everything at Charly's is fresh, a lot of it is homemade, and the prices are low. It's not nouvelle cuisine. It's hot and cold sandwiches served on fresh-baked bread (try the Bavarian!), seafood bisque, a hot dog they call the Pablo. Dinner is served only one night a week—Friday—but they make it special with crab cakes and a two-man band playing rock 'n' roll covers.

Save room for dessert because the pies are famous. Flavors vary but there is almost always chocolate cream, coconut cream, bumbleberry, and pecan. The pies are a legacy. When Larry and Jean Waltrip built this airport from scratch in the 1970s, Jean's pies became famous. New owners Dan and Audra Hausman took over four years ago but you don't mess with success. The pies remain.

The restaurant and its patio have a clear view of the runway so you can watch takeoffs and landings while dining. Of course, there are no scheduled flights in or out of this facility, so if you're coming for the view, pick a clear day on which a private pilot might decide to take a spin. (There are over 60 airplanes based here, plus a flight school, the Williamsburg Air Center.) The restaurant is so popular with hobby flyers that people are known to touch down on a nice day just for lunch. Pilots call it the "$100 hamburger," because the menu prices are reasonable, but jet fuel is not cheap.

Charly's doesn't advertise and you're not going to stumble across it. Follow the signs to the Williamsburg Winery from Rte. 199 and before you get to the grapes, make a left on Marclay Road. You'll pass a landfill and some warehouses before reaching the airport. Open at 11 a.m. Tuesday through Sunday for lunch, and for dinner at 5 p.m. on Friday nights only.

Charly's Airport Café, Williamsburg Jamestown Airport, 100 Marclay Rd., Williamsburg, VA 23185; (757) 258-0034; williamsburgairport.com/restaurant/; $; DF.

DINING

CARROT TREE KITCHENS, 1303 Jamestown Rd., Williamsburg, VA 23185; (757) 229-0957; carrottreekitchens.com; $. The Carrot Tree began (30 years ago) as a home business with owner Debi Helseth selling cakes she baked out of her garage. Now there is a restaurant with a full menu which relocated from Jamestown to the edge of Williamsburg (Colony Square Shopping Center) and a second location in Yorktown's Riverwalk. (See our chapter on Jamestown and Yorktown for details.) The delectable array of baked goods continues to evolve, too. In addition to the ever-popular selection of pies, the cafe now offers something called Hybrid cake, a three-layered cake of chocolate cake sandwiched between layers of carrot cake and slathered in cream cheese icing. The breakfast and lunch menus have made this more than just a place to pick up dessert. The house specialties are Brunswick stew, ham biscuits, and crab cakes. There is always a freshly made quiche of the day and a wide variety of sandwiches and wraps. In the summer months, the gazpacho made from fresh tomatoes is a must. (It and many other menu items are sold for takeout by the pint and quart.) Open Tues through Fri from 10 a.m. to 6 p.m., Sat 8 a.m. to 4 p.m., Sun 10 a.m. to 3 p.m., Mon closed.

THE CHEESE SHOP, 410 Duke of Gloucester St. (Merchants Square), Williamsburg, VA 23185; (757) 220-0298; cheeseshopwilliamsburg.com; $; DF. If you ask where to get a quick lunch in the Historic Area, chances are good you will be directed to The Cheese Shop. Its well-deserved reputation for terrific sandwiches was built on their roast beef special, served on fresh-baked French bread with "top secret" house dressing. These days their reputation extends to an almost endless number of delicious offerings—Virginia ham on rye, smoked turkey on sourdough, provolone and prosciutto on ciabatta. Everything you need to make a meal—side salads, beverages, chips, and desserts—is of top-notch quality and available near the rear of the store, where orders are placed. The front of the store offers a wide assortment of gourmet food products and, of course, a cheese counter where you can sample fresh cheese, semisoft cheese, semihard cheese, blue cheese or even wash-rind cheese before purchase.

Recently, the store arranged to have its famous house dressing bottled for resale. Any alum of the College will want this, with a $1 bag of "bread ends," long considered a staple of the William & Mary student's diet. Downstairs is the newly renovated wine cellar, with a standout collection of reasonably priced reds, whites, roses, and sparkling wines. There is (limited) seating in the storefront and on outdoor patios, but The Cheese Shop would need another building to seat the crowds that want lunch during high season. Open daily 10 a.m. to 6 p.m.

Insider tip: Call in your order (or order online) for pickup at the outdoor window, which opens onto the breezeway between The Cheese Shop and **Wythe Candy and Gourmet Shop.** The window is open for the lunch crush— 11 a.m. to 3 p.m. daily. The entire sandwich menu can be viewed online at cheeseshopwilliamsburg.com.

Where the College Kids Eat

You don't need a calendar to tell when school's in session at the College of William & Mary: You can tell by how crowded the eating and drinking establishments are along the stretch of Richmond Road between Scotland Street and Merchants Square. You might want to steer clear of certain college hangouts at peak times—it's dangerous to get between a hungry undergrad and his $1 bag of bread ends from The Cheese Shop.

The Delis' Triangle

When they can break away from studying at Swem Library (which houses a branch of Aromas Café, open to the public), members of the Tribe make their presence known at the pubs across from Zable Stadium, an angular intersection where Scotland Street ends at Richmond Road. This triangular corner is home to **Paul's Deli,** the **College Delly,** and the **Green Leafe Cafe.** Unlike that famous triangle off the coast of Bermuda, nobody actually disappears here, at least not for more than a few hours. All three restaurants are now under the control of the same owner, but each has carved out a unique identity. Check their websites if you want to know who's hosting trivia night, open mic night, live music, karaoke, or offering happy hour specials.

Merchants Square

Retro's, the hamburger and milkshake joint on Prince George Street near Merchants Square, is popular for its low-priced, tasty grub. The **LoKal Café** (loKated right next to Retro's) offers vegan and vegetarian fare, and the cafe tables at **Aromas,** also on Prince George Street, are usually full of students wielding MacBooks, taking advantage of the Wi-Fi and bracing themselves for their next class with a jolt of joe.

But perhaps the most enduring Tribe food favorite is also one of the best bargains in the 'burg. The $1 bag of "bread ends" at **The Cheese Shop** on Duke of Gloucester Street. Many alumni will admit that during their college days they feasted on these heels of baguettes cut off during sandwich production, which are bagged for sale while fresh—sometimes barely cooled from the oven—and paired with the shop's famous house dressing (various sizes beginning at 50 cents). The Cheese Shop's owner, Mary Ellen Power Rogers, doesn't remember why or when they started bagging baguette heels for sale but knows there isn't any possibility they can stop. "I think there would be a mutiny if we did," she said.

COCHON ON 2ND, 311 Second St., Ste. 106, Williamsburg, VA 23185; (757) 229-1199; cochonon2nd.com; $$$. Tucked behind a consignment shop on a corridor of mostly car dealerships and small businesses is this elegant, white-tablecloth gem, that will delight true foodies. Chef Neil Griggs, a graduate of the Culinary Institute of America, grew up in Williamsburg and his menu showcases his affinity for local ingredients: fried oysters, sticky ribs, pan-seared crab cakes, pork chops in a fig wine reduction. Try not to fill up on the farmhouse bread and house-made butter. One specialty is potatoes au gratin made with 30 razor-thin layers of tuber, heavy cream, and Maytag bleu cheese. Save room for the crème brulee. Despite a concrete floor and exposed pipes, the dining room has a gracious feel and features an 8-seat chef's table overlooking the kitchen, where wood-grilled entrees are cooked on the area's largest Big Green Egg. The bar area boasts an extensive wine list and offers handcrafted cocktails, making it a good spot to enjoy a glass and a tasty bite before a show at the nearby Williamsburg Playhouse. Open 5 to 9 p.m. Tues through Sun.

More interested in a picnic or take-out? The same crew runs **Moody's Kitchen's,** opened in 2020 a mile south at 7129 Merrimac Trail, which specializes in high quality catering and made-from-scratch gourmet to-go meals. Soups by the quart, salads, sandwiches, paninis, thin-crust pizza (smoked duck and fig is one offering), baked goods, and hand-cut steaks that can be cooked at home. "Fare to share" includes wings, chicken tenders, spiced peel-and-eat shrimp and the to-die-for Moody's Ribs. Order in person or by phone: (757) 229-1195. Open Tues through Sun 11 a.m. to 8 p.m.

COGAN'S, 4324 C-2 New Town Ave., Williamsburg, VA 23188; (757) 645-3351; cogansdeli.com. Sports, live music, and daily drink specials make this one of the liveliest spots in New Town. Cogan's brags it has the best Reuben in Williamsburg; and there is a daily homemade soup special. All their sandwiches are made with Boar's Head meats. But the big draw here is the full slate of entertainment. Every Mon it's a jazz jam session, Wed is acoustic, and Fri and Sat feature a rotating assortment of local bands. Open 10 a.m. to 11 p.m. Mon through Thurs, 10 a.m. to midnight Fri and Sat, and 11 a.m. to "whatever" Sun.

COLLEGE DELLY, 336 Richmond Rd., Williamsburg, Va 23185; (757) 229-3915; collegedelly.com; $$; DF. This sandwich shop is a longtime favorite with students ($8 pitchers!), locals, and tourists looking for a quick, tasty meal or a friendly place to watch a sporting event. Reading the sandwich ingredients—all made with Boar's Head brand meats—will certainly fire up your appetite. There's also the freshly made Italian and Greek dishes (especially the souvlaki and shish kebab), homemade soups, and stews to consider. There's a friendly competition between this establishment and **Paul's Deli** as to who makes the best Hot Holly, a sub sandwich of roast beef, cheese, turkey, bacon, lettuce, tomato, and pickle on a toasted roll. You'll have to try both on successive days and decide for yourself. Hungry night owls will appreciate that the restaurant is open until 2 a.m. daily.

THE CORNER POCKET, 4805 Courthouse St., Williamsburg, VA 23188; (757) 220-0808; thecornerpocket.us; $$; DF. This upscale pool hall features creative takes on pub food in a smoke-free environment. Meals are graced with little touches that show a well-trained chef working with fresh ingredients. The roasted fish tacos, Reuben, and jambalaya get raves (the latter is so popular it's known to run out).

When the weather cooperates, which is most of the year, food and drinks are served outdoors on a covered patio that wraps around two sides of the building.

And the billiards? Thirteen tables including three 9-foot professional tables with great lighting and plenty of room. In addition to billiards tournaments, the Corner Pocket also has a thing for the blues and for jazz; every Thurs, weather permitting, they offer live music on the patio, followed by karaoke.

Opens at 11:30 a.m. Mon through Fri, 4 p.m. on Sat and Sun. Dinner is served till midnight, making this one of the latest places to get a full tasty meal. Closing time is 1 a.m. Sun through Tues; 2 a.m. Wed through Sat.

CRAFT 31, 3701 Strawberry Plains Rd., Williamsburg, VA 23188; (757) 378-3268; craft-31.com, $$–$$$.; DF. Another gem a tourist won't naturally come across, this newish restaurant is located between William & Mary and New Town on a quiet two-lane road. The menu here leans to pub fare: gourmet burgers, wings, extensive raw bar options, and a loaded "bottoms up" pizza—a nice match with the many TVs tuned to sporting events. There is an open-air patio with a roof and outdoor fireplaces and a full bar. As the restaurant's name suggests, the craft beer choices are nearly endless. Open daily at 11 a.m. except Sun, open at 10 a.m.

DoG STREET PUB, 401 W. Duke of Gloucester St., Williamsburg, VA 23185; (757) 293-6478; dogstreetpub.com; $ (lunch), $$ (dinner); DF. The folks behind the **Blue Talon Bistro** identified a vacuum on Merchants Square's main strip, Duke of Gloucester Street: no pub. The DoG opened in 2012 in a renovated bank building, offering microbrews to slake any thirst (and steel bowls of water on its street-facing patio, in case you are an actual dog). The beer selection is vast—17 varieties on draft and more than 100 bottled brews—but the knowledgeable bar staff can guide you to the right match with their pub fare, which includes fish and chips, sliders, fried green tomatoes, and even tikka masala. The DoG is doing its best to become not just a downtown pub but a community builder. Every Mon night they sponsor a family- (and dog-)

DINING

friendly 5K, starting at the pub. Registration is at 5, race at 6, and a pint when you finish. Open 11:30 a.m. to 9 p.m. Sun through Thurs; 11 a.m. to 10 p.m. Fri and Sat.

EMERALD THAI, 264G McLaws Circle (Marketplace Shops Shopping Center), Williamsburg, VA 23185; (757) 645-2511; $$. Thai standards are done exceptionally well here. Small touches make the difference—chunks of pineapple in the cashew chicken; a hint of heat in the peanut salad dressing. The acid test for Thai fare, of course, is pad thai noodles—and Emerald's pass, nicely. This is not San Francisco or New York Thai cuisine, however. The dishes are kept on the mild side. If you want heat, you have to ask for it.

The location, near the Kingsmill Resort and Busch Gardens, makes this spot more convenient to those attractions' visitors than to guests staying near the Historic Area. Open at 11:30 a.m. for lunch and dinner Mon through Sat, dinner only on Sun, beginning at 4:30 p.m.

FAT CANARY, 410 W. Duke of Gloucester St., Williamsburg, VA 23185; (757) 229-3333; fatcanarywilliamsburg.com; $$$. Recipient of a four-diamond designation from AAA every year during its first decade of existence, this upscale restaurant has a lot of things going for it, beginning with its fine pedigree—the owners, the Powers family, have a long history in Williamsburg, having operated the adjacent Cheese Shop for decades. The restaurant also occupies prime real estate in Merchants Square. To top it off, the food is exceptional.

The fare offered is a mix of carefully crafted seafood and meat dishes with special attention paid to local resources—crispy Rappahannock oysters or a caprese salad variation that adds Edwards' ham. Steaks are tender, the fish is fresh. The graces that accompany each entree are always creative.

There is no children's menu, and given the price of the entrees, this is the night you'll want to spring for a babysitter.

The wine list is drawn from a wine cellar, open to the public, beneath the restaurant. Dinner served 5 p.m. to 10 p.m. daily. Reservations are encouraged, especially in season. Dinner is also served at the bar, but seating is on a first-come, first-served basis.

FOOD FOR THOUGHT, 1647 Richmond Rd., Williamsburg, VA 23185; (757) 645-4665; foodforthoughtrestaurant.com; $$. Located on "restaurant row" and about equidistant from Premium Outlets and Colonial Williamsburg, this popular spot offers eclectic fare: American comfort food and select dishes from a variety of ethnic cuisines—Jamaican jerk chicken, Thai One On, baked eggplant marinara. Vegetarians (and those on gluten-free diets) will find plenty of choices, and so will kids—here's a rare children's menu that offers more than grilled cheese and chicken tenders. There's pot roast, meat loaf, ribs, and a veggie option. The soups are house-made (try the roasted veggie bisque), and the complimentary bread is freshly baked.

Open at 11 a.m. daily for lunch and dinner, 8 a.m. Sat and Sun; reservations are taken for parties of three or more. A line can form: Save yourself some time by calling ahead to have your name put on their priority seating waitlist.

GABRIEL ARCHER TAVERN, 5800 Wessex Hundred (Williamsburg Winery), Williamsburg, VA 23185; (757) 564-8869; williamsburgwinery.com; $–$$. If you're looking for a pleasant lunch in a beautiful setting, this cafe's on the grounds of the winery fits the bill. Located off-the-beaten-path, west of Rte. 199, you won't stumble across this hidden gem. An expanded menu offers salads, sandwiches, tacos, crab cakes and more. Oysters are very popular here and there is often programming designed around their availability. There is a different menu for dinner, served Thurs through Sat, beginning at 5 p.m. Wine flights are available and if the weather is nice, lunch on the patio with a view of the grapes is a world-away experience. Open daily. 11 a.m. to 4 p.m. Sun through Wed; 11 a.m. to 8 p.m. Thurs through Sat.

GIUSEPPE'S, 5525 Olde Towne Rd., Williamsburg, VA 23188; (757) 565-1977; giuseppes.com; $$. Owner Joe Scordo offers a pleasing blend of carefully prepared fine food, a comfortable, upbeat dining room, and friendly service in his trattoria, with alfresco dining in season. An unusual and varied menu with a wide variety of prices offers pizza, pasta, risottos, seafood, steaks, several vegetarian entrees, an outstanding lentil and sausage soup (featured in *Bon Appétit* magazine), and contemporary versions of old Italian standby desserts such as tiramisu and cannoli. Everything is made to order, yet the small kitchen churns out meals quickly, so there's no waiting between courses. Because of the fine quality of the food, this is an extremely popular restaurant for both lunch and dinner. Reservations for weekend nights are highly recommended. Open 11:30 a.m. to 2 p.m., Mon through Sat. Open from 5 to 9 p.m. for dinner Mon through Thurs, until 9:30 p.m. Fri and Sat. Closed Sun.

GREEN LEAFE CAFE, 765 Scotland St., Williamsburg, VA 23185; (757) 220-3405; greenleafe.com.; $$. Open since 1974, this is the most enduring nightspot in town. (It even says so in the *New York Times* review that is framed and hanging on the wall.) This venerable institution (if, by venerable, one means "smells like decades-old spilt beer") underwent a major renovation and can no longer be classified as everybody's favorite dive bar. The bar was lengthened and replaced with marble. There's a whole wall of boutique whiskeys and 35 beers on tap (They offer another 40 or 50 in bottles or cans). The tile floor looks new and freshly mopped. These developments will no doubt disappoint those who remember the Leafe's scruffier days. Luckily, there's still a winning combination of cold beverages and tasty grub, including loaded fries, fried pickles, and the old standbys: shepherd's pie, bangers and mash, and half-price burgers on Mon nights. It's reportedly the closest bar in the US to a college football stadium (William & Mary's Tribe football team plays directly across the street) so come early on game days if you want a seat. Check their Instagram account (@green-leafe_cafe) for a schedule of themed beer nights, specials on "shakers and 'tinis," live music, open mic events, and trivia contests. Food served from 11 a.m. until 1:30 a.m.; the bar is open until 2 a.m.

JAMESTOWN PIE COMPANY, 1804 Jamestown Rd., Williamsburg, VA 23185; (757) 229-7775; buyapie.com; $; DF. The slogan of this small, takeout-only establishment is "Round food is good food," and they're underselling it. The gourmet pizza, open-top potpies, and 28 varieties of dessert pies—nut, fruit, and specialties like coconut custard—are sinfully delicious. (They have salads and sandwiches, too. They are not round.) This is the last chance for picnic fare before you reach Jamestown Island; if you time it right (call ahead to place your order if you want pizza or potpies—each takes 15 to 30 minutes to prepare), you can pack a wonderful lunch (or dessert) and have your picnic before touring the settlement or the national park, or you can pick up something delicious here before you begin a leisurely drive along the scenic Colonial Parkway, which has its western terminus in Jamestown.

The house specialty is pecan pie, but a unique alternative is the Virginia peanut pie (also available in chocolate) and the bumbleberry. The Pie Company makes 18 different types of fruit pies, but some are only available in season. Prices range from $14.99 to $19.99. Open daily 9 a.m. to 9 p.m., but occasionally they open a little late on Sun mornings.

Special note: The Pie Company does not have indoor seating. There are a few picnic tables on the grounds, but if it's raining, plan to take your food to go.

KYOTO JAPANESE STEAK HOUSE & SUSHI BAR, 1621 Richmond Rd., Williamsburg, VA 23185; (757) 220-8888; kyotoofwilliamsburg.com; $$–$$$. In a town where family dining is a major draw, this restaurant has a formula sure to entertain youngsters and delight their parents as well. Select from the hibachi menu and your showman chef prepares it tableside. Things get downright fun if you're willing to applaud your chef, who is spurred on by appreciative guests. All meals come with soup, salad, hibachi shrimp appetizer, vegetables, rice, and hot tea. Entrees include teriyaki chicken, hibachi shrimp or steak, bonsai scallops, sukiyaki steak, or teppanyaki filet mignon. For those who prefer fish, there is a sushi menu with lots of variety. Vegetarian and children's meals are also offered. Reservations are recommended. Open 4 to 11 p.m. daily.

LA CASONA, 1784 Jamestown Rd., Williamsburg, VA 23185; (757) 808-5595. This dog-friendly Mexican restaurant specializes in all the traditional menu favorites plus barbecue and grilled items. Located at the last intersection before the Jamestown history attractions and the Scotland Ferry, this is a good place to stop for lunch or dinner in what is a bit of a food desert. (La Casona is directly across the street from the Jamestown Pie Company and adjacent to Toby's Dog House, a converted motel and former home of the Carrot Tree). They serve a margarita that is actually big enough for a bird to bathe in. Birthday guests are serenaded (adorably) by the guitar-playing staff. Open 11 a.m. to 10 p.m. Mon through Thurs, 11 a.m. to 11 p.m. Fri and Sat (bar open until 1 a.m.), 10:30 a.m. to 3 p.m. Sun.

LA PIAZZA, 403 W. Duke of Gloucester St. (Merchants Square), Williamsburg, VA 23185; (757) 229-8610; DF. This Italian-themed restaurant has big shoes to fill, replacing The Trellis, founded by Chef Marcel Desaulniers, who earned fame and a national reputation with his "Death by Chocolate" desserts. In its heyday, The Trellis came as close to a landmark as anything in Williamsburg. So like Harry Truman following FDR or Jay Leno following Johnny Carson, the bar had been set high for this spot and so far La Piazza is not quite meeting it. The glaring problem in its opening months—a rocky start in the middle of a pandemic—has been, the desultory service. But the Italian quotient of the food here lacks authenticity and the quality is inconsistent. That said, this is some of the best restaurant real estate in town and the people running it are pros. Moving tables to the center of DoG Street has added a European air to all of Merchants Square. The menu needs tweaks and the staff needs to be professionalized. Odds are good that both those things will happen. Open 11:30 a.m. to 9 p.m. Tues through Fri; 10 a.m. to 9 p.m. Sat and Sun. Closed Mon.

LA TIENDA TAPAS BAR AND MARKET, 1325 Jamestown Rd., Williamsburg, VA 23185; (757) 808-5344; latienda.com. If you are looking for a taste of Spain—small plates of olives, ham croquettes, Iberico bacon-wrapped dates—this is a must stop. The spacious restaurant spans several rooms, keeping the noise level low for conversation. The menu features creative takes on traditional Spanish foods: paella for the table with calasparra rice, chicken, chorizo and smoked paprika; gazpacho, a selection of Spanish cheeses and cured meats. Ask about the daily specials. The sangria rojo is fruity and delicious. A retail area sells specialty foods, including all the ingredients you need to make your own paella, olive oils and, of course, Spanish wines. Open noon to 8 p.m. Tues through Sat.

LA TOLTECA, 3048 Richmond Rd., Williamsburg, VA 23185; (757) 253-2939; 135 2nd St., Williamsburg, VA 23185; (757) 259-0958; latolteca2

.com; $–$$. These popular, locally run Mexican restaurants offer standard fare with fresh ingredients. The menu includes a lengthy list of vegetarian selections; if you like shrimp, the slightly spicy camarones al mojo de ajo is excellent, served with a delicious avocado salad and seasoned rice. The Richmond Road location offers a lunch and Sunday brunch buffet. Frequent specials include buy one fajita, get the second fajita half off. The bar offers happy hour and an impressive variety of Mexican beers, 12 types of tequila, and margaritas in every possible variation, including mango and peach. Kids have their own menu of Mexican specialties. Both restaurants are small, so don't be surprised to find a line at the Richmond Road location, a problem that is less common at the harder-to-find 2nd Street restaurant (latoltecawilliamsburg.com/location.aspx).

LE YACA FRENCH RESTAURANT, 1430 High St. (The Shops at High Street), Williamsburg, VA 23185; (757) 220-3616; leyacawilliamsburg.com; $$$. Long one of the area's finest restaurants, Le Yaca moved from its location near Kingsmill to this more central spot in 2014. The cuisine specializes in using fresh, high-quality ingredients in season. The setting is elegant (not easy to pull off in a shopping center, but they do). This is as good a choice for a five-course dinner as it is for the popular Mon through Thurs happy hour featuring $5 premium wines and $6 appetizers from 5 to 7 p.m. (The crab crepes are superb.) One not-to-be-missed menu item is the onion soup—a puree of onions in a rich stock, nicely spiced, and served with grated cheese and house-made croutons. At least once you must order La Marquise au Chocolat for dessert.

Open for lunch and dinner, seven days a week. A $29 four-course table-service brunch is about the most decadent way you can possibly start a week—or end a weekend. Reservations are highly recommended.

MANHATTAN BAGEL, 1437 Richmond Rd., Williamsburg, VA 23185; (757) 259-9221; manhattanbagel.com; $. Perhaps driving around town has convinced you that everybody here eats pancakes and waffles for breakfast. Not so! (But see our Close-up on The Pancake Tour, later in this chapter.) If you instead crave an authentic New York bagel, this is the place. Choose from 24 different flavors, including the hard-to-find-in-the-South salt bagel, baked continuously throughout the day, and offered with myriad accompaniments. Open daily 6:30 a.m. to 3 p.m.

MAURIZIO'S ITALIAN RESTAURANT, 264 McLaws Circle (Festival Marketplace), Williamsburg, VA 23185; (757) 229-0337, (866) 604-9616; mauriziositalianrestaurant.com; $$. This authentically Italian restaurant (owner Maurizio Fiorello hails from Palermo, Sicily) offers deliciously prepared food in a setting that makes the most of its shopping center location, a stone's throw from Busch Gardens. The service here is friendly and attentive. All dishes are made to order from scratch, using fresh ingredients. The variety is a notch above typical Italian restaurant fare—there are not too many other places in town one can get Carciofi Adriana—marinated artichokes and fresh mozzarella wrapped in prosciutto de Parma and drizzled with herb-infused olive oil. Tender osso buco is served over saffron rice. For dessert, try the Tronchetto Limone, a cheesecake-filled pastry dusted with cinnamon and sugar, served in a pool of lemon-flavored crème brûlée, and drizzled with milk chocolate. Crunchy garlic knots dripping with butter are so good you must force yourself not to fill up. A children's menu offers kid-friendly options like ravioli and chicken tenders. Pizza and subs are available for those with less-adventurous taste buds. The tomato sauce is so popular that it's bottled for takeout, with three generations of Fiorellos—Maurizio, his father, and son—smiling on the label.

Outdoor seating is available when the weather permits. Open daily from 11 a.m. to 10 p.m., until 11 p.m. on Fri and Sat.

MELLOW MUSHROOM, 110 S. Henry St. (Merchants Square), Williamsburg, VA 23185; (757) 903-4762; mellowmushroom.com; $$; DF. A southern chain with a menu as lengthy as the Manhattan phone book (what's a phone book?), there is something here to please everyone: soups, salads, wings, sandwiches, pizzas, all made to order. The interior is rather dark—cool on a hot day—but the back patio is a lovely spot when the weather is nice. Open 11 a.m. to 9 p.m. Mon through Thurs and Sun; 11 a.m. to 10 p.m. Fri and Sat.

NEW YORK DELI, 6546 Richmond Rd. (Gallery Shops at Lightfoot), Williamsburg, VA 23188; (757) 564-9258; newyorkdelipizza.com; $. Subs, pizza, and Greek specialties draw hungry visitors to this casual restaurant on the western edge of town. If you're in the mood for New York deli fare—say, corned beef and swiss on rye, piled-high roast beef, grilled pastrami, kosher dills—the fare here will hit the spot. Open Tues through Sun 11 a.m. to 10 p.m.

OLD CHICKAHOMINY HOUSE RESTAURANT & ANTIQUES, 1211 Jamestown Rd., Williamsburg, VA 23185; (757) 229-4689; oldchickahominy.com; $–$$. First established in 1955 on the banks of the Chickahominy River, this popular restaurant moved to its current location a few miles from the Historic Area in 1962. The recipient of the *Virginia Gazette*'s 2007 "Best Kept Secret" award, locals keep the Chickahominy hopping during the off-season. The rest of the year, the place is packed with visitors who remember a good

DINING

thing and return. Luckily, there are rocking chairs on the porch, and three floors of antiques, jewelry, handbags, Virginiana, and seasonal decorative items to browse through in the gift shop.

The restaurant is decorated in the style of a colonial tavern, but the real attraction is the reasonably priced breakfasts and lunches. The menu includes fresh chicken and dumplings, a delicious traditional Virginia ham biscuit, and hearty Brunswick stew. Miss Melinda's Special is a sampler plate perfect for first-time guests. (Miss Melinda is the cat. Be careful not to let her slip out as you enter through the colonial-style louvered doors.) Save room for a slice of homemade pie. Try the buttermilk—it is excellent. Open for breakfast and lunch only, but everything on the menu can be packaged for takeout. Hours 8:30 a.m. to 2:30 p.m. Tues through Thurs; 7:30 a.m. to 2:30 p.m. Fri through Sun. Closed Mon. Fully cooked hams are available for shipping.

OPUS 9, 5143 Main St. (New Town), Williamsburg, VA 23188; (757) 645-4779; opus9steakhouse.com; $$$–$$$$. Opus 9 is arguably Williamsburg's premier steak house, winning the title of "Best Steakhouse" in the *Virginia Gazette*'s competition in just its second year of operation, among a crowded field. Prime, aged steaks highlight the entree selections, including Steak Oscar 9, New York strip au poivre, and a unique bone-in filet mignon, but there are delicious seafood options including Maine lobster, crab cakes, and nightly fresh fish specials. House-made desserts are a standout—tiramisu, crème brûlée, and bananas Foster cheesecake.

This is one of the pricier (and more popular) places to dine out, so consider taking advantage of specials: a lunch menu featuring "12 under $20" entrees and half-price bottles of wine with Sunday dinner. Open every day for lunch and dinner. Reservations are recommended.

PAUL'S DELI & RESTAURANT, 761 Scotland St., Williamsburg, VA 23185; (757) 229-8976; paulsdelirestaurant.com; 4345 New Town Ave. (New Town), Williamsburg, VA 23188; (757) 565-2380; paulsdelineighbor hoodrestaurant.com; $. The original Paul's, across Richmond Road from Zable Stadium and the William & Mary campus, is a college hangout alumni love to revisit. The place is packed for sporting events that are shown on numerous wall-mounted televisions. Huge sandwiches, pizzas, Greek and Italian dishes, and daily entree specials (see the daily chalkboard on their Facebook page: facebook.com/paulsdeli) provide something for almost every palate. Happy hour from 5 to 9 p.m. features beer specials.

PETER CHANG, 1203 Richmond Rd., Williamsburg, VA 23185; (757) 345-5829; peterchangrestaurant.com; $–$$. In a 2010 profile in the *New Yorker* titled "Where's Chang?," the writer Calvin Trillin chronicled the obsessive search some foodies had undertaken to follow the "mysteriously peripatetic"

Peter Chang, a Chinese chef whose delectable food might have had an even larger following if he would simply stop changing jobs. A year later, Chang opened his own restaurant in Charlottesville, but instead of sinking roots there, he began a campaign to colonize Virginia, opening new restaurants in Virginia Beach, Richmond, Arlington, and this outpost, just northwest of the William & Mary campus.

That makes the new game not "Where's Chang?" but "Where's Chang cooking today?"

The Williamsburg location does not seem to be his home base. You can get a really delicious meal here at a bargain price—lunch with soup, shrimp roll, entree with rice for $10—but Chang's specialty is Szechuan, and the heat that normally accompanies authentic Szechuan cooking is often missing in the dishes served here. That said, the cilantro-stuffed spring rolls and ginger-seasoned flounder are delicious and fresh. The orange beef, bamboo fish, and tea-smoked duck with fried onions are menu standouts. Normally, we say no to crispy noodles, but the house-made noodles served here are irresistible.

Located in a nondescript building, the interiors decorated in pistachio and baby-aspirin orange, the room could use a makeover. But if Chinese is what you're craving, it's worth asking who's in the kitchen tonight.

Open daily 11 a.m. to 9:30 p.m. Mon through Thurs; until 10 p.m. Fri and Sat; until 9 p.m. Sun.

PIERCE'S PITT BAR-B-QUE, 447 E. Rochambeau Dr., Williamsburg, VA 23188; (757) 565-2955; pierces.com; $–$$. See our full description of this Williamsburg institution, one of the most popular places to eat in town since 1971, in the Barbecue section at the end of this chapter.

PRECARIOUS BEER HALL, 110 S. Henry St. (Merchants Square), Williamsburg, VA 23185; (757) 808-5104; precariousbeer.com; $–$$. Definitely not your father's corner bar, although it is on a corner. This decidedly non-Colonial addition to Merchants Square has quickly become a popular hotspot, with its pleasing mix of craft beer on tap (16–18 ever-shifting varieties), street tacos, wings, live music, outdoor seating, and "retro" arcade games. (In Williamsburg, "retro" usually means centuries ago but these games only go back as far as the '80s. The 1980s.) Families are welcome during the day but when the lights go down, the picnic table-style seating fills up with the college crowd and young professionals. The cavernous beer hall itself is flanked on two sides by outdoor patio seating and one highly in-demand fire pit. (Construction is underway to make it three sides with the addition of a back patio facing the parking lot.) Tuesdays' special is special: three tacos and a full pour of your choice for $11. Open at noon Tues through Fri, at 11 a.m. Sat and Sun. Closing time varies depending on the crowd but closed all day Mon.

RETRO'S, 435 Prince George St., Williamsburg, VA 23185; (757) 253-8816; retrosgoodeats.com; $. Retro's combination of yummy dogs, burgers, and frozen custard can make this place busier than the mall on Black Friday if you happen to hit it when a school field trip descends. Timing is everything, because for cheap eats, you can't do better in Merchants Square. Retro's serves its Black Angus beef dogs anyway you want 'em—cheese, relish, slaw, sauerkraut, three kinds of mustard, jalapeños, onions, Carolina barbecue. The burgers are similarly tasty. The frozen custard is a dense, creamy concoction served in a cone with sprinkles, or made into a shake, float, or sundae. Just reading the dessert menu has been known to add calories. Wine and beer are available but the best thing on draft might be the root beer and the most refreshing beverages could be the lime- and lemonades, made fresh daily.

Takeout is available; phoned-in orders are welcomed. Open every day from 11 a.m. to 7 p.m. in the winter, later in the warmer months, Apr through Nov.

SAL'S BY VICTOR, 1242 Richmond Rd. (Midtown Row), Williamsburg, VA 23185; (757) 220-2641; salsbyvictor.com; $–$$. Sal's has a lot going for it: good location, delicious pizza, huge menu, and a long-standing fan base. The veal dishes here are particularly good, as is the fresh pasta. The espresso creations pair well with the homemade cannoli. Be sure to check the chalkboard or ask your server about daily dinner specials, because they often are too good to pass up. This is truly a family restaurant, and children are not only welcome but there's a section of the menu devoted especially to them. FYI: Sal's delivers after 5 p.m., for free. After a busy day of touring or playing, the pizza here cannot be beat—especially when it is delivered freshly made and hot. Open 11 a.m. to 11 p.m., with a midnight close on Fri and Sat.

SAL'S RISTORANTE ITALIANO, 835 Capitol Landing Rd., Williamsburg, VA 23185; (757) 221-0443; salsristoranteitaliano.com; $. Hot and cold appetizers, specialty pizzas, and "the largest sandwiches in town" complement a wide selection at this casual dining restaurant that's a bit off the beaten path. Pastas and breads are fired in the brick hearth, which imports a special, smoky flavor that is unmistakable. Located across from the International Housing Village, it is often busy with European students who come to Williamsburg in season to work at Busch Gardens and Water Country USA. Children are welcome.

THE SEAFARE OF WILLIAMSBURG, 1632 Richmond Rd., Williamsburg, VA 23185; (757) 229-0099; seafareofwilliamsburg.com; $$$. If it swims, it's likely they serve it here. Lobster is a specialty, but all the fish and seafood is very well prepared, as you would expect at this price point. For dry-land diners, options include milk-fed veal, prime beef dishes, and tableside gourmet preparations. A wine steward will help you select a vintage to enjoy with your meal, and cocktails also are available. You might select one of the flambé desserts to top off a pleasant dinner. The restaurant is open for dinner Mon through Sat from 4 to 10 p.m., Sun from noon to 10 p.m.

SECOND STREET, 140 2nd St., Williamsburg, VA 23185; (757) 220-2286; secondst.com; $$$. The large menu here has something to please everyone: local seafood, chicken, steak, burgers, pasta, overstuffed sandwiches, kid-friendly foods, munchies, fresh soups and salads, plus an extensive wine list. Open daily at 11:30 for lunch and dinner; Sun through Thurs, they close at 10 p.m., Fri and Sat at 11 p.m.

TAQUERIA MARIA BONITA, 6618 Mooretown Rd., Ste. D (Victory Village Shopping Center), Williamsburg 23188; (757) 378-2352; taqueria mariabonita.com; $. After a stint in hospitality at Colonial Williamsburg, Guadalupe Arreola returned to her roots, opening this storefront restaurant featuring authentic Mexican cuisine. The menu offers 11 different types of tacos including the usual beef and chicken but also the harder-to-find tripitas (beef intestines) and lengua (beef tongue). The variety here is matched by the freshness—all the sauces and sides are made on-site and Arreola's mother makes the tamales and tortillas by hand each day. The burritos are big enough for two and elegantly presented with a generous dollop of guacamole and a squiggle of cheese.

Daily specials include discount nachos on Mondays and, of course, $2 taco Tuesday (beef or chicken only). Try the pamazo bread dipped in a red guajillo pepper and filled with mashed potatoes, chorizo, lettuce, sour cream and queso fresco. Open daily at 11 a.m. until 8 p.m., Mon through Thurs, until 9 p.m. Fri and Sat, and until 7:30 p.m. Sun. A second location inside the Best Western Inn at 351 York St. (near Colonial Williamsburg) opened in June 2020. The CW location has the same hours except it is closed Mon.

WAYPOINT SEAFOOD AND GRILL, 1480 Quarterpath Rd., Williamsburg, VA 23185; (757) 220-2228; waypointgrill.com; $$$. Hidden in a Harris Teeter shopping center off VA 199 (across from the entrance to the Kingsmill community), this restaurant features "Chesapeake ingredients" and locally sourced produce, fish, and meats. Locals rave about not only the freshness of the ingredients but also the attentive staff and lovely decor, especially the wine room that can accommodate private parties, rehearsal dinners, and the like. Open for lunch 11 a.m. to 2 p.m. and for dinner from 5 to 9 p.m. Tues through Sun. Closed Mon.

WILLIAMSBURG INN REGENCY ROOM, 136 E. Francis St., Williamsburg, VA 23185; (757) 220-7754, (800) TAVERNS; colonialwilliamsburg .com; $$$$. Long considered one of the finest restaurants in the Tidewater area, the Regency Room is consistently recognized with fine-dining awards: a

Mobil four-star, AAA four-diamond facility, featured in the *Guide to Distinguished Restaurants of North America*, and recipient of *Wine Spectator's* Award of Excellence. That said, the vibe here can feel like you've wandered into a ballroom that time forgot, with a small orchestra playing and impeccably dressed couples swaying on the dance floor. A requirement that men wear jackets and ties has been relaxed, but the elegant room hasn't been able to shake its reputation that this is very much "your father's Oldsmobile." And perhaps it doesn't want to. This is a super-expensive place to dine, with classic continental dishes (chateaubriand, quail, caviar, roast duck) and the kind of staff attention that can be impressive to one diner and a tad intrusive to the next: Empty dishes are whisked away with brisk efficiency; water glasses refilled after almost every sip, it seems. Some of this rigor is less evident at breakfast and lunch. If you want to see what all the fuss is about, a late lunch, overlooking the famed golf course, may be the way to go. Dinner reservations are recommended but not required.

YORKTOWN

CARROT TREE KITCHENS, 323 Water St. (Riverwalk Landing), Yorktown, VA 23690; (757) 988-1999; carrottreekitchens.com; $. This is where the locals eat in Yorktown. After years of operation inside the historic Cole Digges House (Yorktown's oldest home, built in 1720), this popular restaurant squabbled with its landlord (the federal government) when it defied orders and stayed open during the 2013 government shutdown. The two parted ways shortly after, and the Carrot Tree reopened in the heart of Riverwalk Landing in 2014. Like the original restaurant in Jamestown, this one serves fresh, homey foods with an emphasis on regional favorites—Brunswick stew, crab cakes, chowders—and wraps, salads, and sandwiches, with modern updates like their signature sauce, carrot chipotle aioli. Save room for dessert. The carrot cake might not even be the yummiest among the offerings, although it is exceptional. Open daily 10 a.m. to 4 p.m.

UMI SUSHI, 327 Water St., Yorktown, VA 23690; (757) 989-6464; $$. The riverfront's newest restaurant offers authentic Asian cuisine including sushi and the signature Korean dish, bibimbap. Slake your thirst with premium sake, beer, wine, and a variety of teas. Open daily 11:30 a.m. to 8 p.m.

WATER STREET GRILL, 323 Water St., Yorktown, VA 23690; (757) 875-1522; riverwalkrestaurant.net. $$–$$$. This waterfront restaurant is the centerpiece tenant of Riverwalk Landing and occupies perhaps the best real estate in town, with gorgeous patio views of the York River. The adjacent restaurant, Riverwalk, was closed for renovation in 2020 but look for its reinvention as the more upscale choice of the two, coming in 2021.

The big attraction at the Water Street Grill is liquid: more than 20 craft microbrews on tap, listed on an electronic menu on one wall that lets quaffers know when individual kegs are running low. The fare at the grill suits the pub atmosphere: burgers, brick oven pizza, seafood. Lunch and dinner are served Sun through Thurs daily 11 a.m. to 9 p.m. On Fri and Sat, they're open until 10 p.m.

YORKTOWN PUB, 540 Water St., Yorktown, VA 23690; (757) 886-9964; yorktownpub.com. $. If you want good, basic pub food in a rollicking, even raucous, atmosphere, the Yorktown Pub is the place. The menu features the usual array of burgers, sandwiches, and local seafood.

As a watering hole, the pub draws an eclectic mix of locals, tourists, and the many military people stationed nearby. As you'd expect of a beach pub, it's very casual, with plenty of jeans in evidence, knotty pine walls, and worn wooden booths. The pub is open daily 11 a.m. to 11 p.m. (kitchen closes at 10 p.m.).

NEWPORT NEWS

CIRCA 1918, 10367 Warwick Blvd., Newport News, VA 23601; (757) 599-1918; circa1918.com; $$–$$$. Arguably the best restaurant in Newport News, this way-too-small storefront in Hilton Village never disappoints. The staff is friendly and attentive, but the food is the star. House-made soups are inventive and delicious (carrot-ginger with lump crab . . . so yummy), as are the sautéed crab cakes, crispy salmon, and homey favorites like meat loaf. Even humble sides like French fries are given an upgrade, sprinkled with garlic and parsley and served upright in a metal cone. Desserts are executed with similar flair. There is an extensive collection of superior wines and craft brews. Because of its size, you must have a reservation. In 2020, the restaurant closed for remodeling but was serving from its food truck, parked out front, and open from noon to 7 p.m. There is also an option to purchase family meals. Check the restaurant's Facebook page for news about reopening and current menus for the food truck and pickup options.

CRAB SHACK ON THE JAMES, 7601 River Rd. (inside Huntington Park, at the east end of the fishing pier), Newport News; (757) 245-2722; crab shackonthejames.com; $$. As popular with locals as it is with tourists, the Crab Shack serves up some of the best hard-shell crabs, crab cakes, oysters, shrimp, and even calamari, on the peninsula. It would be a shame to miss this place even if seafood is not your thing because the setting—a long closed-in porch jutting out over the James—makes the trip from Williamsburg worth-while. Time your visit to see the sun set over the James—it can look like a painting. Open 11 a.m. to 10 p.m. daily for lunch and dinner.

DINING

INDULGE BAKERY AND BISTRO, 10359 Warwick Blvd., Newport News, VA 23601; (757) 594-1399, indulgebakeryandbistro.com; $–$$. This establishment, opened in 2015, offers exquisite baked goods and savory fare in an elegantly remodeled storefront. Breakfast and lunch entrees include quiche, croissant sandwiches, biscuits and gravy, and the "Kickstarter," a buttermilk biscuit filled with spinach sautéed in garlic, egg, cheese, and sriracha sauce. Top it off with a house-made Napoleon, hazelnut tart, or owner Michelle Smith's Nutella swirl pound cake. Save room for the affogato—espresso served over vanilla gelato. Open 8 a.m. to 4 p.m., Tues through Sat, 8 a.m. to 3 p.m. for Sunday brunch.

NAWAB INDIAN CUISINE, 11712 Jefferson Ave., Newport News, VA 23606; (757) 591-9200; nawabonline.com; $$. If you were transported into this cool, elegant dining room without entering from the parking lot, you'd never guess you're in a Food Lion shopping center. Beginning with the tinkling water feature at the entranceway, the vibe here is calm and relaxed, a little less so, perhaps, during lunch when they serve up a very popular all-you-can-eat buffet. Dinners begin with complementary *papadan* with a delicious green tamarind sauce. Standouts from the menu include the garlic naan, crab masala, *dal makhni* (spicy lentils), *palak paneer* (creamed spinach), curries, and tikka dishes. The attentive staff inquires about the heat level you want if you order something labeled as spicy. A sister restaurant on Monticello Avenue in Williamsburg is equally as good. There are also Nawab locations in Norfolk and Virginia Beach. Open 11:30 a.m. Mon through Fri for lunch; at noon on Sun and for dinner daily at 5 p.m.

SMOKE BBQ RESTAURANT & BAR, 10900 Warwick Blvd., Newport News, VA 23601; (757) 595-4320; smokenn.com; $–$$. Roll down your windows as you pass this newly remodeled restaurant on US 60 and, if the wind is blowing the right way, the scent from the outdoor smoker might make your mouth water. Smoke cures its meats on-site, and the hardwood-smoked ribs, pulled pork, and brisket are tops in town (or so said voters in *Coastal Virginia Magazine*'s "Best of the 757" poll). It's probably not the best choice for a vegetarian, but there are salads and fish on the menu. Everything is tasty; portions are huge. A new (covered) porch opened in 2015, either to accommodate the ever-growing popularity of the food here or to let people inhale the aroma wafting from the smoker outside. Open 11 a.m. to 10 p.m. daily.

HAMPTON

ANTHONY'S SEAFOOD, 2600 W. Mercury Blvd., Hampton, VA 23666; (757) 827-7000; facebook.com/AnthonysSeafood; $. Don't be dissuaded by the nondescript storefront that houses this family-owned Vietnamese sub shop. Curb appeal is lacking but the menu may contain the tastiest bargain sandwich you'll ever encounter—the $5 Banh Mi sub, made with your choice of grilled pork, sausage or ham, and topped with pickled carrots, daikon, cucumber spears, and cilantro. It's about the length of your arm and every bite is savory. Anthony's also serves bread and fried wings, a variety of po boys, including catfish, tilapia and oyster, and soft-shell crab as a sandwich or on a platter. Bring your appetite but plan to take your food to go. Seating is limited and the dining room closed until further notice because of the pandemic. Open 9 a.m. to 7 p.m. Mon through Thurs; 9 a.m. to 7:30 p.m. Fri and Sat. Closed Sun.

BARKING DOG, 4330 Kecoughtan, Hampton, VA 23669; (757) 325-8352; $. If you didn't drive through a scruffy Hampton neighborhood to get to this wooden shack on Sunset Creek, you might think you're in Key West or the Outer Banks. It's decidedly low-key, off the beaten path, and a relaxed place to have a tasty meal. As the name suggests, the house specialties are hot dogs— the El Diablo comes with onions and crumbled bacon—and cased sausages, including alligator. The burgers are good; the crab cake sandwich and tuna tacos are standouts. The place is small: 4 picnic tables, 5 tables with bench seating, and a couple of counter stools that face the creek. With two dozen types of beer, there's sure to be something to slake your thirst, but don't overdo it: You'll need room in your tummy for the house-made banana pudding. Open daily 11 a.m. to 8 p.m. When the weather gets cold, this all-outside-on-the-covered-patio institution reduces its hours, closing at 3 p.m. on weekdays and 5 p.m. on Sat and Sun.

> **i** America's first seven astronauts trained at NASA Langley Air Force Base in Hampton.

DEADRISE, 100 McNair Dr. (Fort Monroe), Hampton, VA 23651; (757) 788-7190, $–$$. The exterior of this restaurant is not much to look at and the name is going to have some people scratching their heads. (It has nothing to do with zombies. The "deadrise" is the traditional fishing boat used by Chesapeake Bay watermen.) But put those concerns aside and enjoy this second-floor restaurant's two exceptional features: the waterfront view (there is outdoor and indoor seating) and the delectable seafood being served here. Seared scallops, crab cakes, seafood pasta, grouper tacos—you can't go wrong if you love the fruits of the sea. Located inside historic Fort Monroe at the Old Point Comfort Marina, you can pull up dockside if you're in your own deadrise. Open daily 11 a.m. to 10 p.m. except Sun and Mon when they close at 9 p.m.

DINING

The Pancake Tour

A Williamsburg fact that is just a little less well-known than its historic origins is that it has the world's highest per capita ratio of pancake and waffle houses. So prevalent are these establishments that a new entry is actually named "Not Another Pancake House." (We highly recommend it!) There are fewer than 8,000 year-round residents in the 'Burg. Driving along Richmond Road and Pocahontas Trail, you begin to wonder if the pancake houses might outnumber the people. Could tourists really need this many flapjacks? Is it the William & Mary undergrads who are scarfing down all these waffles?

Sadly, now that this claim to fame has been brought to light, a rather sinister trend must also be mentioned. The tremendous influx of chain hotels offering "free" continental breakfasts may eventually spell the demise of Williamsburg's pancake and waffle industry. Already, several have closed. So please, help Williamsburg keep its carbo-loading tradition alive by ladling some syrup onto a stack of silver dollars before you leave town. These are our favorites.

The Astronomical Pancake House, 5437 Richmond Rd., Williamsburg, VA 23185; (757) 253–6565; facebook.com/pages/Astronomical-Pancake-House/174910482560931; $. If what you're looking for in your pancakes is size, this is the place for you. The pancakes almost exceed the diameter of the plates on which they are served. How do they flip them, one wonders?

GOOD FORTUNE, 225 Fox Hill Rd., Hampton, VA 23669; (757) 851-6888; goodfortunehamptonva.com; $. Readers of the *Daily Press* have repeatedly voted this storefront restaurant in Willow Oaks Shopping Center as the "Best Chinese Food." The menu is what you would expect, but the ingredients are fresh, and everything is made without MSG. The shredded pork with string beans is a favorite, as are the wonton soup and the Vietnamese spring rolls. Large portions mean you usually have food to take home. Ample parking in a quiet setting. Open 11 a.m. to 10 p.m. Mon through Thurs; 11 a.m. to 10:30 p.m. Fri; noon to 10:30 p.m. Sat; and 11:30 a.m. to 10 p.m. Sun.

DINING

They come in a wide variety of flavors or reliable buttermilk. The breakfast potatoes, too, are very well done. Open 7 a.m. to 2 p.m. daily.

The Capitol Pancake House, 802 Capitol Landing Rd., Williamsburg, VA 23185; (757) 564-1238; capitolpancakehouse.com; $. Every variety of pancake, including a gluten-free option, is available here, but if you want to branch out, there are Belgian waffles, French toast, and every imaginable combination of eggs, bacon, and sausage. Open daily 7 a.m. to 2 p.m.

The Colonial Pancake House, 100 Page St., Williamsburg, VA 23185; (757) 253-5852; $. Established in 1955, local businesspeople and college faculty have made this family-owned restaurant an informal clubhouse. Pancakes will fill up those headed to Water Country USA or Busch Gardens, which are nearby, and there are gluten-free options. Open daily 7 a.m. to 2 p.m.

Not Another Pancake House, 1803 Richmond Rd., Williamsburg, VA 23185; (757) 585-7195; $$. The latest entrant (opened in 2019) in the 'Burg's pancake pantheon may have the most decadent offerings. Consider one weekly special: the Cannoli-stuffed French toast which features three drenched slices, stuffed with cannoli cream and chocolate chips and topped with cannoli shell crumbles and chocolate syrup. If that triggers fear of diabetes onset, there's also cinnamon twirl waffles or pancakes drizzled with lemon cream cheese glaze and topped with fresh blueberries, powdered sugar, and a scoop of homemade whip cream. They don't have a website but check their Facebook page for specials. Students with an ID receive a 20 percent discount. Open daily 7 a.m. to 2 p.m.

MUSASI JAPANESE RESTAURANT, 49 W. Queens Way, Hampton, VA 23669; (757) 728-0298; musasihampton.com; $–$$. Japanese and Korean cuisine are served in a cozy cafe within walking distance of all the downtown attractions. The sushi here is fresh, expertly made, and delicious; standouts are spicy tuna and Philadelphia rolls. The Korean fare is perhaps an even bigger draw because it's harder to find in this area: bibimbap in a stone pot, bulgogi, and *katsu donburi* are rarely seen on Hampton Roads menus. Udon noodles, shrimp dumplings, and humble miso soup also receive rave reviews. Open 4 to 9:30 p.m. Mon; 11 a.m. to 2:30 p.m. and 5 to 9:30 p.m. Tues through Thurs; 11 a.m. to 2:30 p.m. and 5 to 10:30 p.m. Fri; 3:30 to 10:30 p.m. Sat; noon to 9:30 p.m. Sun.

HOW SWEET IT IS

Like elsewhere in the country, Williamsburg's sweet tooth has benefited from a wave of new cupcake-only and frozen yogurt shops. There are also two can't-miss donut shops in town.

CELLI'S CHOCOLATE CHIPS, 5223 Monticello Ave., Ste. B, Williamsburg, VA 23188; (866) 923-5547; cellischocolatechips.com. Cookies are all they make here but, boy, are the cookies terrific. Organic, small-batch, and concocted without any preservatives, these are treats for the most discriminating sweet tooth. Though the Cellis offer a dozen different flavors including dark chocolate coconut, lemon glazed, milk chocolate caramel sea salt, the signature offering is the chocolate chip, a rich, not overly sweet disc the size of a saucer. Open 10 a.m. to 4 p.m. Tues, Wed, and Sat; until 5 p.m. Thurs and Fri. In-store availability is limited and cookies are only available for purchase on a daily basis until they run out—and they do. Preorder is required for orders of a dozen or more. Celli's will ship their sweets just about anywhere.

DUCK DONUTS, 4655 Monticello Ave. (Monticello Marketplace-Shoppes), Williamsburg, VA 23188; (757) 258-DUCK (258-3825); duckdonuts.com; $. It's hard to imagine how a donut could be improved upon after sampling the slightly crunchy vanilla cake donuts made here in front of your eyes and to order. Have yours bare or choose from 10 coatings, including powdered sugar, cinnamon sugar or glaze, or a flavored icing (lemon, strawberry, chocolate, orange, vanilla, maple bacon, peanut butter). Then add a topping: shredded coconut, sprinkles, chopped peanuts, bacon bits, or Oreos.) Finally, drizzle hot fudge,

Duck Donuts offers unique and fun flavors.
Bobby Talley

salted caramel or marshmallow. At $1.75 a donut (or $15.50 a dozen), this treat is a terrific bargain, too. Open Mon through Wed daily 6 a.m. to 6 p.m.

EMILY'S DONUTS, 7123 Merrimac Trail, Williamsburg, VA 23185; (757) 345-3602; emilysdonutcafe.com; $. They serve donuts here, but you want the warm-from-the-oven apple fritter. Really. You do. This massive, gooey confection is what has drawn people to this off-the-beaten track, reincarnated sub shop north of the Historic Area and west of Busch Gardens. The coffee is excellent, and the tasty donuts come in interesting flavors: blueberry, caramel sea salt, peanut butter stripes. A word of warning: Made fresh every morning on the premises, the most popular donut flavors have been known to run out early. Open Wed through Sun 7 a.m. to noon.

EXTRAORDINARY CUPCAKES, 1220 Richmond Rd., Williamsburg, VA 23185, (757) 645-2122; extraordinarycupcakes.com; $. The heavenly smell from inside this adorable shop just west of the William & Mary campus beckons you (by your nose) to the artfully created cupcakes, almost too pretty to eat. But eat you must. (Maybe take a photo first.) Seven flavors are offered daily (including a gluten-free option) plus monthly and seasonal specials. The bestsellers include Marvelous Madagascar ($3.50), a vanilla bean pound cake with vanilla buttercream frosting, and the Sinfully Salted Caramel ($4), vanilla cake filled with caramel, topped with caramel frosting and a dash of French sea salt ($4). Enjoy your selection with a gourmet coffee, organic iced tea, or Fanta de Mexico soda in 5 flavors. Open Mon through Fri 11 a.m. to 5 p.m., Sat 10 a.m. to 5 p.m. Closed Sun.

REGIONAL CUISINE

Part of the fun of traveling is learning what's unique about a new place, including the food that's special to a particular region. Who could go to Philly and not get a cheesesteak? Or to New Orleans and leave without licking the powdered sugar from your lips after biting into a beignet?

The regional specialties in Williamsburg evolved from the early bounty of Virginia's fields and, especially, its rivers. No less than Captain John Smith himself recorded in his diary in 1614 that the waters of Hampton Roads were so full of fish he could have walked across Chesapeake Bay on the backs of its inhabitants—rockfish, blue crabs, sturgeon, herring, shad roe, mussels, oysters, and clams.

Sadly, over the centuries, development has taken a toll on Virginia's waterways; some species are highly endangered. Sturgeon is hard to find, and there is a concerted effort among oystermen (and women) to reinvigorate beds depleted by overharvesting. But area fishermen still reel in plenty of blues, croakers, shad, spot, pike, bass, and other varieties of freshwater and saltwater fish.

On local piers you're likely to see weekend anglers patiently baiting their lines for crabs. Virginia's most common crab is the blue crab, or *Callinectes sapidus*, which translates as "savory, beautiful swimmer." This ornery-looking creature lives two or three years and periodically molts, shucking off its exoskeleton. For a short stretch of time after molting, the blue crab is soft and vulnerable, but a new hard shell quickly forms. Commercial crabbers harvest this tender prey to sell as soft-shell crab, considered a delicacy locally but apt to make the novice ask, "You mean I'm supposed to eat it legs and all?" Hard crabs are harvested, too, of course.

While commercial fishermen work from their boats, dropping large baited crab pots made of specially treated steel wire into area waterways, the simple way to catch a crustacean dinner is to tie chicken necks or fish heads to kite string, grab a dip net, and head for the shallows. The trick to this method of crabbing is to gently lure a nibbling crab close enough to net him from underneath. Crabs are smart enough to be frightened by abrupt movements or a sudden play of shadows on the water, such as a body blocking the sun. But they're not smart enough to stop coming back for more, so don't give up. You also can buy small crab pots to use from piers in local sporting goods stores. Crabbing is a time-honored way to spend a leisurely morning in eastern Virginia.

Naturally this quirky crustacean, so important to the culture and economy of the Hampton Roads area, long ago captured the imagination of cooks and consumers, spawning an endless variety of recipes from the humble crab cake to crab imperial. Backfin crabmeat is considered the tastiest and is often served simply—sautéed with butter or chilled with mayonnaise. You'll also see crabmeat served as a stuffing for avocados, tomatoes, or mushrooms. Heated, it combines with shrimp, lobster, and other seafood for a variety of baked dishes and casseroles.

Local cooks spar to create the best crab cakes, with feuds developing over whether cornmeal, cracker crumbs, or bread and eggs provide the most suitable base. Fresh soft-shell crab season runs roughly from May to early fall. If you see the dish offered at other times of the year, you're probably getting a frozen product, which is not recommended.

Crab bisques, soups, and gumbos (both hot and chilled) are perennial favorites around here as well. Hampton crab bisque is made with cream, Tabasco, and sherry. Crab soups are sometimes based on fish stock, sometimes tomato broth. She-crab soup, which combines sauterne or sherry with whipping cream, butter, and lots of crab—including the roe—is just too good to miss.

Here are some other local specialties you may want to sample while you're in town:

Brunswick Stew

Local restaurants serve this hearty mixture by the gallon. While the original version of this savory dish called for a couple of freshly shot squirrels and rabbits, the meat you find in today's dishes typically is chicken, with a little beef or ham tossed in for good measure. Onions, celery, corn, okra (if it's available), lots of tomatoes, potatoes, butter beans, and generally whatever else is ripe in the garden are added, as are vinegar, sugar, salt, pepper, and even ketchup. To get it just right, this thick concoction must be simmered all day in a big iron pot. By the way, you may have heard some apocryphal tales about the true origins of Brunswick stew. Brunswick County, North Carolina, claims it, along with several other East Coast Brunswicks. We believe Virginia lore, which says intrepid hunters back in the early 1700s created the dish in the Old Dominion's Brunswick County, relying on resourcefulness and whatever happened to cross their paths out in the wilds. In other words, squirrels and rabbits were all the game they bagged that day.

Frequently, you can find Brunswick stew on sale at any number of outdoor festivals or church bazaars. To assure yourself of getting a stew of the highest quality, check out the **Old Chickahominy House** (see listing earlier in this chapter).

Ham

Pigs do not stand a chance around here. Can a state have a "most famous meat"? If it can, then Virginia's candidate is certainly ham. Its popularity dates from colonial times, when hog and hominy were an essential part of the early settlers' diets. Ham was easy to preserve—an important quality in a time before refrigeration. After slaughter, pig meat was smoked, dried, sugar-cured, even pickled. Virginia ham became so well-known that it was soon being exported to the North and even abroad.

Before we go any further, let's clear up the great ham confusion. On local menus you may see entrees prepared with Virginia ham, Smithfield ham, Williamsburg ham, Edwards ham, or sometimes simply "country ham." While all of these pork products are similar in that they are salt-cured, there are some important differences among them. The one basic difference between Virginia hams and other cured hams is that Virginia hams are dry salt-cured before smoking. Technically, only hams cured in Smithfield, a small town across the James River from Williamsburg, can be called Smithfield hams. These hams, left in the skin and aged for up to a year, have a stronger, smokier taste than younger Virginia hams, sometimes known as Williamsburg or country hams. Smithfield hams are coated with pepper during the curing process, which enhances the hams' flavor. You may see these hams hanging in burlap sacks in local stores. They require overnight soaking before cooking.

Once your Smithfield ham is prepared correctly (those knowledgeable recommend soaking it for at least 24 hours, simmering it for about 20 minutes per pound, then baking it in a 350 degrees Farhenheit oven for 20 to 25 minutes, basting frequently), it should be consumed sparingly, thinly sliced. Typically, it is nestled in a buttermilk biscuit, but, like its Italian sibling prosciutto, Smithfield ham works well as an appetizer, for example, wrapped around melon.

Barbecue

Those who are not native to the American South may not know or care about the finer distinctions between varieties of this pit-cooked, chopped-pork delight, but barbecue aficionados will tell you Virginia barbecue tends to have a delicate, smoky flavor. The sauce adds a tang, not a kick. Down in the Carolinas, they make their barbecue with a stronger vinegar base, and you'll sometimes see references to pulled barbecue, which is more strip-like than chopped.

Here in the Tidewater area of Virginia, there's plenty of debate over who makes the best barbecue. We've listed a few of our favorite purveyors so you can try them all and cast your vote.

COUNTY GRILL & SMOKEHOUSE, 1215A George Washington Memorial Hwy., Yorktown, VA 23693; (757) 591-0600; countygrill.com; $$. Traditional Carolina-style barbecue, beef or pork, served in sandwiches or on a platter. Tables are decked out in butcher paper and equipped with half a dozen different barbecue sauces—Eastern North Carolina, Memphis, Southwest Texas, Kansas City, Savannah, and Lexington, so you can doctor the fare exactly how you like it. Wash it down with one of the microbrews on tap. Daily specials are available. This spot has been a favorite of *Daily Press* readers for several years running. Open 11 a.m. daily for lunch and dinner.

OLD CITY BARBEQUE, 700 York St., Williamsburg, VA 23185 (757) 378-5125; oldcitybbq.com; $–$$. This convivial restaurant offers pulled pork, brisket, and ribs, all smoked out back over hardwood coals. It boasts of its "nose to tail" love of the pig but you can also get a delicious organic fried chicken sandwich here. An expansive rectangle of a bar area is a good place to meet for televised sports (especially if like whiskey—they have dozens of varieties) while the outdoor patio is dog friendly, although the view of Highway 60 and the railroad tracks is not inspiring. Side dishes are standouts: the excellent cole slaw is savory and the waffle fries are to die for. Ask about their daily specials. A full children's menu offers five entrees, each with one side, for $6.50. Open at 11:30 a.m. for lunch and dinner every day except Mon.

PIERCE'S PITT BAR-B-QUE, 447 E. Rochambeau Dr., Williamsburg, VA 23188; (757) 565-2955; pierces.com; $–$$. Decades ago, when highway construction on I-64 restricted access to Pierce's, barbecue fans parked their cars and trucks on the new highway's shoulder and walked through the woods to get their 'cue. The highway department put up a fence. No problem. What's a little ol' fence to a determined barbecue connoisseur? It was knocked down and scrambled over until finally the DOT gave up.

These days, it's much easier to get to Pierce's but no matter when you arrive, you are almost certain to have at least a short wait in line, because people are still clamoring to get at Pierce's pulled pork barbecue, made on the premises (you can follow your nose to Pierce's on a clear day). Beachgoers en route to the Outer Banks stop in Virginia to stock up on this Carolina-style favorite, because Pierce's sells just about everything on its menu by the pint and quart, packed to go if you need to be on your way. In addition to pork, Pierce's now serves barbecue chicken. They also have slaw, beans, collard greens, onion rings, and homebaked cookies and cakes.

In 2021, Pierce's celebrated its 50th anniversary. The restaurant, which first made a name for itself by selling 85-cent barbecue sandwiches, marked the occasion with 50th anniversary mugs and a special edition hot sauce. What began in a 25-foot by 14-foot building that only offered walk-up service has grown into an institution. The current restaurant seats 100 and smokes more than 3,000 pounds of pork a week. In 2019 *Southern Living* magazine named Pierce's the best BBQ in Virginia.

When the trees are bare, you can see Pierce's through the woods along the eastbound lanes of I-64—it's between exits 234 and 238. From exit 238, turn left at the stop sign at the top of the ramp, then right at the first traffic light. That's Rochambeau Drive. Pierce's is 3 miles west. From exit 234, make a right at the top of the ramp onto VA 199. Travel 1 mile to the E. Mooretown Road exit, then turn left at Lowe's onto Rochambeau Drive. Pierce's is 2 miles east. Open 10 a.m. to 8 p.m. daily except Thanksgiving, Christmas, and New Year's Day.

ROCKY MOUNT BAR-B-Q, 10113 Jefferson Ave., Newport News, VA 23605; (757) 596-0243; rockymountbbq.com; $. In the restaurant business longevity pretty much says it all. Rocky Mount has been cooking North Carolina–style barbecue for more than 40 years. The shredded or sliced pork here has a vinegar tang, a perfect contrast to the warm, sweet hush puppies that accompany your meal. Platters and sandwiches are served with a wide variety of sides—coleslaw, baked beans (made with ground beef), lima beans, collards, sweet potato casserole, onion rings, and more. (They offer the side dishes as a meal itself: the four veggie platter.) Check their website for daily specials and save room for the delicious banana pudding. Takeout and catering are available. The restaurant also stocks many of the products its kitchen uses—Atkinson's corn bread and hush puppy mix, their own special vinegar sauce, and Hub's Peanuts. Open Mon through Sat 11 a.m. to 8 p.m. Closed Sun.

SMOKE BBQ RESTAURANT & BAR, 10900 Warwick Blvd., Newport News, VA 23601; (757) 595-4320; smokenn.com; $–$$. Roll down your windows as you pass this newly remodeled restaurant on US 60 and, if the wind is blowing the right way, the scent from the outdoor smoker might make your mouth water. Smoke cures its meats on-site, and the hardwood-smoked ribs, pulled pork, and brisket are tops in town (or so said voters in *Coastal Virginia Magazine*'s "Best of the 757" poll). It's probably not the best choice for a vegetarian, but there are salads and fish on the menu. Everything is tasty; portions are huge. A new (covered) porch opened in 2015, either to accommodate the ever-growing popularity of the food here or to let people inhale the aroma wafting from the smoker outside. Open 11 a.m. to 9 p.m. daily.

Peanuts

Southeastern Virginia has lost thousands of acres to development over the past few decades, but the region is still a leading producer of peanuts—32,000 tons in 2013. Suffolk and Isle of Wight Counties, just south of Williamsburg, usually account for about a third of the state's total crop. So, yes, this is still considered Peanut Country. If you need proof, drive through downtown Suffolk, where the most beloved statue is not of some Civil War general but of Mr. Peanut, the advertising icon of the Suffolk-based Planters Peanut company. Don't leave Williamsburg without stocking up.

THE PEANUT SHOP, 414 Prince George St. (Merchants Square), Williamsburg, VA 23185; (757) 229-3908, (800) 637-3268; thepeanutshop .com. Crunchy home-style peanuts prepared in a mind-boggling variety of ways, including our favorite: chocolate covered.

WHITLEY'S VIRGINIA PEANUTS AND PEANUT FACTORY, 1351 Richmond Rd., Williamsburg, VA 23185; (757) 229-4056, (800) 470-2244; whitleyspeanut.com. You'll find delicious "homecooked" Virginia peanuts, Virginia hams, gift baskets, and other goods from the commonwealth, all available for carryout or mail order.

i The weather is typically very mild in Williamsburg in January and February (highs in the 40s to 50s with only occasional snow) but the crowds are gone. Local restaurateurs would like to tempt you to visit with 10 days of special deals during Restaurant Week, typically scheduled for late January or early February. Forty local restaurants offer special menus with discount pricing for breakfast, lunch, and dinner. For more information or specific dates, check WaraRest.com or call (757) 345-1219.

DINING

Shopping

While it may be history that brings visitors to the Historic Triangle, once they get here they want to shop. This is nothing new: Merchants Square dates to 1935 and bills itself as one of the oldest shopping malls in the country. West of town, the granddaddy of outlet shopping, the Williamsburg Pottery Factory, started drawing visitors in 1938 and has spawned many an imitator along Richmond Road, including some upscale competition.

What follows is a list of where to find what, beginning with the Historic Area. In general, you'll find specialty shops offering unique fine-quality items grouped near Merchants Square. If you're looking for manufacturers' outlet stores, head westward out Richmond Road (US 60), where shopping centers give way to outlet malls, consignment shops, craft bazaars, and finally to the Pottery. Though many of these businesses have Williamsburg addresses, the further west you go the more likely you are really in Lightfoot, Norge, or Toano. There are enough interesting shops in this stretch to plan a full day making the Richmond Road circuit, between Rte. 199 and **Charlie's Amazing Stones,** an outdoor wonderland of rock rarities and lawn sculptures. The **New York Deli,** 6546 Richmond Rd., is a good place to stop for sandwiches (get the onion rings!) The Flipping Flea, 6927 Richmond Rd., recently opened its own coffee shop (wait for it)—the **Sipping Flea**—which also sells mini-donuts in an assortment of flavors. Bet you can't eat just one.

For shopping specialists, we've broken out those places where you can browse bookshelves, shop for Christmas decorations, or pick up a unique item of Virginiana. If unique is what you're looking for, browse our listings of the area's second-hand shops, which sell everything from antiques to vintage tchotchkes. With a large population of retirement-age residents, there is a lot of down-sizing going on in Williamsburg. You can find some unique bargains in the consignment shops.

THE HISTORIC AREA

Along Duke of Gloucester Street are many restored shops where you can buy items crafted on the premises by artisans you can observe at work. (You do not need to have a Colonial Williamsburg ticket in order to shop here.) Historic Area shops are open daily in season but their hours vary throughout the year. Call the Colonial Williamsburg information line at (757) 229-1000 for the operating hours during the time of your visit.

The **Golden Ball Shop** offers metalcraft items, including ladies', gentlemen's, and children's fine jewelry in silver and gold, which can be engraved to order.

The **Raleigh Tavern Bakery** has counter service. Pick up some Sally Lunn bread, sweet potato muffins, or ginger cake for a quick snack.

M. Dubois Grocer's Shop offers Smithfield hams, jams, relishes, and other colonial fare.

General merchandise shops include **Prentis Store, Tarpley's Store,** and **Greenhow Store,** carrying pottery, hats, games, toys, baskets, candles, pipes, handwoven linens, leather and wooden crafts, jewelry, and many more items.

These shops are open year-round and are the places to find a memento of your visit or a unique gift.

MERCHANTS SQUARE

Centered on the western end of Duke of Gloucester Street, Merchants Square was established in 1935 expressly to create a shopping center for the redeveloping Williamsburg community. Businesses formerly scattered throughout the Historic Area were relocated here, primarily to cater to residents because the tourist trade at that time was humble. The architecture synthesized colonial and early 19th-century design, a deliberate choice made so that the business district would blend as seamlessly as possible with the Historic Area.

As Williamsburg and the surrounding counties grew, more businesses opened elsewhere, leaving Merchants Square to focus on providing goods and services demanded by tourists. In a way, this also protected Merchants Square from market forces that have afflicted many American downtowns. Business here is very much alive and flourishing. The ambience is charming without

Merchant Square in spring.
2017 Michael Ventura Photography

feeling fake. The buildings are human-scale, the brick walkways dotted with benches, the main block closed to vehicular traffic. When restaurants reopened here following the 2020 pandemic shutdown, many moved tables both to the sidewalk and into the street. Begun as a life-saving measure for these businesses, the al fresco options have become enormously popular. Look for the open-air trend to continue even after pandemic restrictions are lifted.

All in all, a few hours spent strolling Merchants Square is a very pleasant activity. Many others have recognized this—in 2005, Merchants Square was added to the National Register of Historic Places. In 2009, the American Planning Association recognized Duke of Gloucester as one of its "10 Great Streets."

Though there are about 40 stores in a 2-to-3-block area—a combination of specialty shops, fine restaurants, and upscale chain stores, including Chico's, Lululemon, and Talbots. We have listed some local favorites below. Places to eat are detailed in our Dining chapter.

A word about parking: If you can, leave your car wherever you're lodging and take the CW bus, the city trolley, or walk. Parking behind the shops is free for 2 hours but difficult to find. There is a paid lot on Francis Street and one behind the college bookstore which charge $2 an hour. Your best bet (and value) is the city parking garage at 230 N. Henry Street. It has 362 spaces and charging locations for electric vehicles. There are two Universal Charging Stations on the ground level and two Tesla Charging Stations on the second level. Parking is $1 an hour. (The first 30 minutes are free, and the maximum charge is $12 a day.) Credit and debit cards only; payment is fully automated using license plate reader technology. Download the Passport Parking app to pay using your phone. The garage is open daily from 6 a.m. to midnight. Overnight parking is not allowed.

Stores in Merchants Square are open daily, generally beginning at 10 a.m. During summer months, many stay open until 9 p.m.; in the off-season, most close at 6 p.m. For information about hours specific to the time of your visit, check merchantssquare.org.

Clothing

THE CAMPUS SHOP, 425 Prince George St., Williamsburg, VA 23185; (757) 229-4301. Gifts and apparel featuring the logo of the College of William & Mary.

CAROUSEL CHILDREN'S BOUTIQUE, 420 W. Duke of Gloucester St., Williamsburg, VA 23185; (757) 229-1710; carouselchildrens.com. Unique children's clothing and accessories.

R. BRYANT LTD., 429 W. Duke of Gloucester St., Williamsburg, VA 23185; (757) 253-0055. Traditional men's and boys' clothing with a flair for fresh designs in classic items.

> Every summer Merchants Square sponsors a free concert series featuring fun party bands (dancing is encouraged) and the area's finest military bands. Concerts are scheduled from 7 to 9 p.m. Wed. The band sets up in the middle of Duke of Gloucester Street. Bring a lawn chair or blanket— the public benches fill up quickly. To check the lineup of performers, visit the sponsor's website at merchantssquare.org.

SHOE ATTIC, 409B W. Duke of Gloucester St., Williamsburg, VA 23185; (757) 220-0757; shoe-attic.com. This store is located in an alley between DoG and Prince George streets and carries the outrageously funky designs of Irregular Choice, a London shoe designer, plus a wide variety of women's clothing and accessories. Owner Brittany Rolston offers 10 percent off to anybody with a student or a military ID.

THREE CABANAS: A LILY PULITZER SIGNATURE STORE, 411 W. Duke of Gloucester St., Williamsburg, VA 23185; (757) 561-7099. A must stop for the Lily lover with racks of Pulitzer prizewinners. Even in winter, it feels like a day poolside inside this bright shop, located in the alley between DoG and Prince George streets.

Food

BLACKBIRD BAKERY, 407 W. Duke of Gloucester St., Williamsburg, VA 23185; (757) 229-8610; blackbirdbakerywilliamsburgva.com; $. Though the address is DoG Street, this charming bakery actually faces the parking lot behind the shops on the eastern end of Merchant Square. It's worth seeking out because of the fresh breads and delectable sweets offered here (but baked around the corner at The Trellis, also owned by David Everett). Pick up some truffles, giant cookies, scones, or whole loaves of bread. Custom cakes for all occasions, from birthdays to weddings, can be ordered. Open daily 8 a.m. to 8 p.m.

THE CHEESE SHOP, 410 W. Duke of Gloucester St., Williamsburg, VA 23185; (757) 220-0298; cheeseshopwilliamsburg.com; $. In addition to terrific made-to-order sandwiches, The Cheese Shop's shelves groan with gourmet food products and, of course, a wide variety of specialty cheeses (which they will be happy to let you sample). Oenophiles will want to make a special trip downstairs to the cellar, where the knowledgeable staff will help you choose a high-quality wine that is also a good value. The cellar is also where you'll find a selection of 120 craft brews, from local ales to rare European beers.

ILLY CAFFE, 435 W. Duke of Gloucester St., Williamsburg VA 23185; (757)208-0006; facebook.com/illyCaffeWilliamsburg. Coffee shop and cafe by day; cocktail stop at night. This European-style bistro's signature drink may be a caffeinated beverage with a heart-shaped image in the foam but it's also a great place for breakfast, lunch, or a postprandial dessert and a glass of wine. Open 7 a.m. to 7 p.m. daily.

KILWIN'S, 421 Prince George St., Williamsburg, VA 23185 (757) 378-2727; kilwins.com. Are you in the mood for a huge slice of fudge (in a wide variety of flavors?) A caramel apple? Ice cream? The diet busters abound at this locally-owned confectionary.

THE PEANUT SHOP, 414 Prince George St., Williamsburg, VA 23185; (757) 229-3908, (800) 637-3268; thepeanutshop.com. Crunchy homestyle peanuts prepared in a mind-boggling variety of ways, including our favorite: chocolate covered.

SECRET GARDEN, 110 S. Henry St., Williamsburg, VA 23185; (757) 808-5318; secretgarden-café.com. Conveniently located just across the street from the Colonial Williamsburg bus stop and ticket office at the western edge of the Historic Area, this cafe offers breakfast (Liege waffles!) and a wide variety of refreshing drinks, including every kind of bubble tea you can imagine.

> **i** On Saturday mornings, downtown Williamsburg transforms into a bustling farmers' market featuring local produce, seafood, flowers, organic vegetables, herbs, baked goods, pasture-raised meats, fresh breads, and many other items. That may sound like fun to adults, but—weather permitting—there also are kid-friendly activities like face painting, food tasting, and live music. The market has (at least temporarily) moved from DoG Street to the parking lot on West Francis Street since DoG Street has been taken over by al fresco dining. It opens 8 a.m. to noon each Sat, as long as the weather allows. For more information, check the market's website: williamsburgfarmersmarket.com.

WYTHE CANDY AND GOURMET SHOP, 414 Duke of Gloucester St., Williamsburg, VA 23185; (757) 229-4406. A perennial favorite for all visitors with a sweet tooth. The homemade fudge is excellent, but there are too many other choices to just settle on one thing. Can't eat sugar? The shop has a wonderful selection of sugar-free goodies, too.

Gifts and Accessories

BLINK, 413 W. Duke of Gloucester St., Williamsburg 23185; (757) 585-7477. Blink and you'll miss this unique collection of eclectic furniture, gifts, artwork, and fashionable accessories. Located on the alley linking DoG and Prince George streets, this boutique is one flight up but worth the climb.

BRICK & VINE, 435 W. Duke of Gloucester St., Williamsburg, VA 23185. This flagship store selling CW branded products moved into the two-story, 13,000-square-foot, former Binn's Department Store, which closed in 2018. Merchandise previously sold at Williamsburg at Home, the Williamsburg Craft House, and Boxwood and Berry will now be available under one roof. There will be direct entrance from Brick & Vine to the adjacent Illy Café so shoppers can grab a quick coffee or glass of wine without even leaving the building.

DANFORTH PEWTER SHOP, 417 W. Duke of Gloucester St., Williamsburg, VA 23185; (757) 229-3668; danforthpewter.com. Traditional pewter handicrafts and jewelry.

EVERYTHING WILLIAMSBURG, 415 W. Duke of Gloucester St., Williamsburg, VA 23185; (757) 565-8476; williamsburgmarketplace.com. From tees to tavernware, a broad selection of exclusive Colonial Williamsburg logo products.

J. FENTON GALLERY, 110 S. Henry St., Williamsburg, VA 23185; (757) 221-8200. Contemporary American-crafted items, including flax linen clothing, handbags, watches, jewelry and jewelry boxes, pottery, games, metal wall sculptures, and whimsical and humorous gifts in all price ranges. The emphasis is on unusual individual pieces by American artists, many from Virginia. Selected stained-glass, hand-blown glass and glass fountains, kaleidoscopes, puzzle boxes, and a collection of Judaica.

PERFECTLY NATURAL SOAP, 423 Prince George St., Williamsburg, VA 23185; perfectlynaturalsoap.com. It smells really good in this elegant shop, which sells artisan soaps, bath, and body "luxuries." The local owner operates two other storefronts at 4021 Richmond Rd., Williamsburg, and in downtown Smithfield, at 202 Main St.

THE PRECIOUS GEM, 423 W. Duke of Gloucester St., Williamsburg, VA 23185; (757) 220-1115; thepreciousgems.com. Owner and master craftsman Reggie Akdogan, trained in Turkey, is known for his exquisite jewelry designs featuring diamonds, sapphires, and rubies in solid gold and platinum.

R.P. WALLACE AND SONS GENERAL STORE, 424 W. Duke of Gloucester St., Williamsburg, VA 23185; (757) 229-2082. Need a kitschy souvenir? (And who doesn't?) This is your place.

SCOTLAND HOUSE LTD., 430 Duke of Gloucester St., Williamsburg, VA 23185; (757) 229-7800; scotlandhouseltd.com. Imported ladies' and gentlemen's apparel, tartan, heraldry, and gifts from the United Kingdom.

WILLIAMSBURG CELEBRATIONS, 110-A S. Henry St., Williamsburg, VA 23185; (757) 565-8642; williamsburbmarketplace.com. Byers' Choice, Department 56, Jim Shore, and other collectibles. Seasonal floral arrangements, holiday decorations, and garden accessories galore.

ANTIQUES, CONSIGNMENT, AND BAZAARS

CHARLIE'S AMAZING STONES, 7766 Richmond Rd., Toano, VA 23168; (757) 784-7870; charliesantiques-va.com. To give you an idea of the size of Charlie and Susie Crawford's collection of antiques, reproduction furniture, Asian art and decoratives, bric-a-brac, marble and bronze sculpture and statuary, ornamental iron, and outdoor furniture, please note that Charlie's has its own speed limit: 8 miles per hour. Enter the sprawling property, 20 minutes west of Williamsburg, and slow down so you can catch a glimpse of the ferocious bears (sculptures) lining either side of the rutted driveway. Many an hour can be whiled away strolling through the goods here, especially for those looking for unique furnishings and souvenirs. There's also a large collection of natural stones and pavers for landscaping needs—decorative pebbles, garden stones, large boulders, fieldstones for water gardens, pathways, and walls. Sold by the pound or ton. (A sign warns, "No returns on rocks.") A second location, **Charlie's Antiques** at 6500 Richmond Road, carries furniture, mineral specimens, and vintage accessories but no bears. Both locations are open 11 a.m. to 5 p.m., Thurs through Mon. (Sun, they open at noon.) Closed Tues and Wed.

CLASSIC CONSIGNMENTS, 7405 Richmond Rd., Ste. A, Norge, VA 23188; (757) 220-1790; classicconsignments.shop. The specialty here is home decor, with an emphasis on seasonal decorations but there is also a large, rotating selection of gently used furniture and accessories. Open 10 a.m. to 5 p.m. Mon through Sat. Closed Sun.

THE FLIPPING FLEA (1 & 2), 6927 and 7003 Richmond Rd., Lightfoot, VA 23188; (757) 645-5172; theflippingfleamarket.com. Fleas may be small but this collection of specialty shops now spans two storefronts in adjacent shopping centers with a companion coffee shop—the Sipping Flea—located between them. Open 10 a.m. to 4 p.m. Tues through Sat; 11 a.m. to 4 p.m. Sun.

JONI'S CONSIGN & DESIGN, 1303 Jamestown Rd. (Colony Square Shopping Center), Williamsburg, VA 23185; (757) 504-5886; jonisconsignanddesign.com. Lightly used furniture and decor pieces with an emphasis on original artwork. The range is from antique to contemporary but the vibe is quirky. Open 10 a.m. to 5 p.m. Mon through Sat.

LADYBUG CONSIGNMENT AND BOUTIQUE, 5251 John Tyler Hwy., Ste. 44, Williamsburg VA 23185; (757) 345-6633; ladybugconsign.com. Ladies' clothing, accessories, shoes, and jewelry. A children's consignment shop, Two Trolls, is located in the same shopping center. Open 10 a.m. to 5 p.m. Mon through Fri, 10 a.m. to 4 p.m. Sat.

THE MOLE HOLE, 1425 Richmond Rd., Williamsburg, VA 23185; (757) 220-8609. This locally owned shop carries estate jewelry, (previously owned) high-end handbags, silver, artwork, home decor, and ladies and baby clothing and gifts. Open 10 a.m. to 7 p.m. Mon through Sat.

SUGAR & SPICE KIDS CONSIGNMENT, 6536 Richmond Rd., Lightfoot, VA 220-1661; sugarandspiceconsignmentboutique.com. Clean, well-organized shop featuring lightly used kids' clothes from newborn to teens. Open 11 a.m. to 5 p.m. Tues through Fri; 10 a.m. to 3 p.m. Sat.

TK ASIAN ANTIQUES, 1654 Jamestown Rd., Williamsburg, VA 23185; (757) 253-0769; tkasian.com. This unique business collects and sells ancient Chinese artifacts such as bronze and pottery ritual vessels and sculpture. Other inventory includes a selection of 18th- and 19th-century Chinese furniture and rare Chinese art deco furniture (ca. 1930). Prices range from hundreds of dollars to millions per piece. Restoration services are also provided. Open 9 a.m. to 5 p.m. Tues through Fri. (Closed from noon to 1 p.m. for lunch.)

A TOUCH OF EARTH, 6580 Richmond Rd. (The Gallery Shops), Williamsburg, VA 23188; (757) 565-0425; atouchofearthgallery.com. Located 20 minutes west of Williamsburg on US 60, this unique space is the oldest American crafts gallery in the area, offering highly prized American craft work by fine artists in many media. Their "Gloom Chaser" makes a memorable souvenir. Open 9:30 a.m. to 5:30 p.m., Mon through Sat; noon to 5 p.m. Sun.

VELVET SHOESTRING, 311 Second St., Williamsburg, VA 23185; (757) 220-9494; thevelvetshoestringinc.com. This cavernous but well-organized store offers high quality pre-owned furniture, glassware, brass and silver accessories, rugs, bric-a-brac, lamps, and more. Located in the same complex as the excellent restaurant, Cochon on Second—a good place for a repast after shopping. Open 10 a.m. to 5 p.m. Mon through Sat; 11 a.m. to 5 p.m. Sun.

WILLIAMSBURG ANTIQUE MALL, 500 Lightfoot Rd., Williamsburg, VA 23188; (757) 998-8450; antiqueswilliamsburg.com. Just off Richmond Road in Lightfoot is this 45,000-square foot warehouse, home to 300-plus dealers of antiques and collectibles. This place is unique in that you wander freely, picking up goodies you wish to buy (they supply handy baskets to hold your newly found treasures), and then leave via a central checkout area. You'll find just about anything: furniture, jewelry, glass, old photos, baseball cards, coins, clocks, pottery, framed artwork, clothing and decorative textiles, vintage toys, and more. Open daily 10 a.m. to 6 p.m. except Sun, noon to 5 p.m. Closed Christmas, Easter, and Thanksgiving.

WILLIAMSBURG BAZAAR, 5625 Richmond Rd., Ste. F120 (Premium Outlets), Williamsburg, VA 23188; (757) 206-1405; williamsburg-bazaar .business.site. A one-stop shop for home decor, ladies clothing, pet accessories, jewelry, vintage items, and specialty foods. The friendly staff prides itself on running the store with "no employees." Each of the stores 50-plus vendors takes turns on the sales floor. (A second location, **Norge Bazaar,** 7521 Richmond Rd., sells similar items in the same format but—yum—they also sell ice cream.) Open daily 11 a.m. to 7 p.m., Fri and Sat until 8 p.m.

WILLOW GROVE PRIMITIVES, 7445 Richmond Rd., Norge, VA 23188; (757) 740-0228. Located on the very fringe of the Williamsburg area, this unique store specializes in reproduction furniture and decor in the early colonial America style. Most of the merchandise is handmade, including exclusive items produced by local craftspeople. Open 10 a.m. to 5 p.m. Tues–Sat; 1 to 5 p.m. Sun.

BOOKSTORES

BARNES & NOBLE, 5101 Main St. (New Town), Williamsburg, VA 23188; (757) 564-0687; barnesandnoble.com. Located in the New Town development off of Monticello Avenue, this store anchors the central shopping district. The store has regular story hours for kids, frequent book signings, and school book fairs. Open Mon through Sat 10 a.m. to 10 p.m., Sun 10 a.m. to 9 p.m.

BOOK WAREHOUSE, 5625 Richmond Rd., Ste. F130 (Premium Outlets), Williamsburg, VA 23188; (757) 565-9801, book-warehouse.com. This 4,000 square foot store located on the southern end of the sprawling outlet center is a bookbuyer's dream, with hardcover titles selling for half their retail price. Many are overstocks (unsold inventory from full-price bookstores designated by a black dot or slash on the top edges of the pages. All genres are offered plus audiobooks, magazines, book-related gifts and stationery. Teachers get an additional educator discount. Open 10 a.m. to 9 p.m., Mon through Sat; 11 a.m. to 7 p.m. Sun.

COMIC CUBICLE, 4809-2 Courthouse St. (New Town), Williamsburg, VA 23188; (757) 229-5299. A Williamsburg fixture since 1992, this is a must-stop shop for comic aficionados. Welch carries the latest releases in addition to collectible comics, graphic novels for kids and adults, collector cards, and related merchandise. Like elsewhere in the US, the first Sat in May is always free comic book day. Open 11 a.m. to 7 p.m. Mon through Sat, except Wed, when Welch opens at noon to get the latest issues on sale; 1 to 5 p.m. Sun.

WILLIAM & MARY BOOKSTORE AND CAFÉ 345 Duke of Glouces-ter St. (Merchants Square), Williamsburg, VA 23185 (757) 221-1651; wm .bncollege.com. Located at the western entrance to the Historic Area, this store is run by Barnes & Noble College and functions as William & Mary's official bookstore. In addition to textbooks and school supplies, there are a good selec-tion of general interest books, a modest children's department and lots of green and gold T-shirts and hoodies. A cafe on the second floor offers ample seating for studying—or a break from the heat in summer. Open Mon through Sat 9 a.m. to 5 p.m., Sun noon to 5 p.m.

CHRISTMAS ALL YEAR

CHRISTMAS MOUSE, 1991 Richmond Rd., Williamsburg, VA 23185; (757) 221-0357. Through the windows you'll see dozens of trees lighted and decorated with unique items. Inside you'll find more things associated with the holidays than you ever imagined possible. A second store is located several miles west at 7461 Richmond Rd., Norge, VA 23187. Open daily 9 a.m. to 11 p.m. (Norge store open daily 10 a.m. to 6 p.m.)

THE CHRISTMAS SHOP, 415 W. Duke of Gloucester St., Williamsburg, VA 23185; (757) 229-2514. The vast array of decorations offered for the tree and home includes many that are uniquely Williamsburg—pineapples, fifers, drummers, painted images of the Governor's Palace, and the like. Open 10 a.m. to 5 p.m. Sun through Thurs; 10 a.m. to 6 p.m. Fri and Sat.

COOKE'S CHRISTMAS (AT COOKE'S GARDENS), 1826 Jamestown Rd., Williamsburg, VA 23185; (757) 220-0099; cookesgardens.com/christmas/. The Schell family has operated a garden center from this site since 1990, but vacationers who like to pick up a special item for the tree while traveling will be most interested in the Christmas shop adjacent to the nursery, which sells a wide array of seasonal decorating items. "Themed" trees boast special ornaments for the teacher, the bride and groom, musicians, you name it—there's even a whole tree of dog ornaments. A wide variety of Mark Roberts Santas and fairies are available, and there's an entire section of the store devoted to wreath making. Beginning the Sun after Thanksgiving each year, Santa stops by to take requests from those who would like an audience with the big man. Bring your camera. Open 10 a.m. to 3 p.m. Mon through Fri, by appointment only Sat and Sun.

GROCERIES AND SPECIALTY FOODS

THE CORNER BARKERY, 501 Prince George St., Williamsburg, VA 23185; (757) 221-6678; DF. Easily the most unusual establishment in Williamsburg, this combination retail space and bar is completely dog friendly. The front of the shop sells dog treats and doggy-themed gifts. A six-seat bar separates the shop from the back patio where Fido can rest at your feet while you order from a menu provided by the Hound's Tail, a restaurant operated by the same owners located two doors down.

EDWARDS VIRGINIA HAM SHOPPE OF WILLIAMSBURG, 5541C Richmond Rd., Williamsburg, VA 23185; (757) 220-6618; edwardsvaham .com. This shop sells Surry hickory-smoked hams and bacon direct from the family smokehouse, plus a variety of Virginian specialty foods, including jellies, jams, flours, cake and pie mixes, bacon-coated chocolate bars, and more. They'll ship, too. Open 10 a.m. to 6 p.m. Mon through Sat. Closed Sun.

THE FRESH MARKET, 5231 Monticello Ave., Williamsburg, VA 23188; (757) 565-1661. Classical music, ambient lighting, bins of fresh flowers, artfully displayed—wait. This is a grocery store? Indeed it is. This upscale North Carolina–based chain makes grocery shopping seem like something more than a chore. Top-of-the-line meat, seafood, and produce; fresh herbs; hard-to-find spices; and small-label packaged goods are attractively arranged. The deli counter makes terrific sandwiches and side salads, and the baked goods are yummy. Pick a bottle from their impressive wine section and you've got the makings of a deluxe picnic. Open daily 8 a.m. to 9 p.m.

THE PEANUT SHOP, 414 Prince George St. (Merchants Square), Williamsburg, VA 23185; (757) 229-3908, (800) 637-3268; thepeanutshop .com. Crunchy homestyle peanuts prepared in a mind-boggling variety of

Close-up

New Town

Perhaps unique to an American city that's been around as long as Williamsburg, there is no "downtown" here. Merchants Square was organized in the 1930s to bring scattered businesses to a central location. Though many residents shop and dine here in the off-season, from April to October, it's given over to the tourist trade. Moreover, government offices are located elsewhere; the majority of the people who live in what would pass as Williamsburg's downtown are students at William & Mary.

All of that was part of the impetus for New Town, a 365-acre, mixed-use community, on the drawing boards since 1997 and still a work in progress. Designed according to the architectural and planning principles of the New Urbanism school, this area along both sides of Monticello Avenue west of the historic district was jointly developed by the College of William & Mary and the C. C. Casey Company. Though the project, like everything else, took a few hits during the economic downtown at the end of 21st-century's first decade, New Town has mostly fulfilled its promise of creating a second city center for Billsburg.

There are more than 300,000 square feet of shops, restaurants, and business space in New Town, including a **Barnes & Noble,** which anchors the main retail street, and a 12-screen movie theater. A national chain, **Brass Cannon Brewing Company,** now occupies a prominent corner of commercial real estate on Main Street, joining locally owned businesses like the **Corner Pocket,** an upscale billiards hall. There are destinations for kids, too: **Comic Cubicle** brings fans of Ironman and the Green Lantern to New Town for the latest issues. New Town has all the amenities you'd expect in a small town—doctor's office, hair salons, fitness centers, banks, courthouse, and post office.

"The thing I love about New Town is that it's such a good mix," said Mark Welch, who moved his comic bookstore, Comic Cubicle, to New Town in 2006. "There's a really healthy combination of owner-occupied businesses and national chains."

When it's finished, the residential component will include about 1,000 households, a mix of garden apartments, town houses, and traditional homes, many with front porches. There are also live/work loft apartments above some storefronts. Walking and biking trails link the whole community, part of an effort to design a place where it's impossible not to know your neighbors. For a complete list of New Town businesses, visit newtownwilliamsburg.com.

ways, including our favorite: chocolate covered. Open 10 a.m. to 5 p.m. Sun through Thurs; 10 a.m. to 6 p.m. Fri and Sat.

WHITLEY'S VIRGINIA PEANUTS AND PEANUT FACTORY, 1351 Richmond Rd., Williamsburg, VA 23185; (757) 229-4056, (800) 470-2244; whitleyspeanut.com. You'll find delicious homecooked Virginia peanuts, Virginia hams, gift baskets, and other goods from the commonwealth, all available for carryout or mail order. Open daily 9:30 a.m. to 6 p.m.

OUTLET SHOPPING

WILLIAMSBURG POTTERY, 6692 Richmond Rd., Williamsburg, VA 23188; (757) 564-3326; williamsburgpottery.com. A $30 million renovation, which added three new buildings and another half mile of sales floor, has not yet brought this shopping institution—dear to the hearts of longtime Williamsburg residents—out of its slump. From its completely humble start in 1938, when a local potter laid some factory seconds out on a table in front of his home 7 miles west of Williamsburg, the Pottery grew into one of the largest bargain centers on the East Coast. A no-frills retail complex where rock-bottom prices could be offered because nothing was spent on the backdrop, the Pottery developed a following that brought shoppers here by the busload in its heyday.

But as the Pottery grew, so did the retail choices elsewhere. Outlet shopping is now commonplace. What made the Pottery unique is now ho-hum. That said, you can still spend a day wandering the vast offerings here, and if you invest the time, you can find bargains. Open Mon through Sat 9 a.m. to 8 p.m., Sun 10 a.m. to 6 p.m.

WILLIAMSBURG PREMIUM OUTLETS, 5715 Richmond Rd., Williamsburg, VA 23188; (757) 565-0702; premiumoutlets.com/williamsburg. With more than 135 stores, this sprawling complex is more like a small city than a shopping center. There are more than two dozen places just to buy shoes. Premium Outlets advertises savings of 25 to 65 percent off regular retail prices and bills itself as one of the most popular outlet malls in the country, but some days and weeks are better for bargains than others—end of season sales usually offer your best bet to save big.

But without a doubt, Premium Outlets is popular. On weekends and holidays, parking can be a challenge. There's potentially a lot of walking involved in a day spent at the outlets, and that might be just from your car to the stores. Definitely leave your high heels at home. It's worth taking a look at the site map online (premiumoutlets.com/pdfs/williamsburg.pdf) before you head out. The mall's most recent expansion amassed many of its upscale stores in a new wing on the property's southeast side. If discount high fashion is what you're after, you might want to focus on just that one U-shaped collection of stores that includes Lucky Brand, True Religion, Kate Spade, Burberry, Juicy Couture, and Charlotte Russe.

When you arrive, stop by the guest services booth, located in the food court, to pick up a coupon book for $5. It's a good idea to flip through the coupons first and make a list of must-stop stores before you begin to wander. Nearly half of the center's stores offer 10 percent off to seniors (50 and up) who shop on Tuesday; many stores also offer a variety of discounts to military and to students (with ID). Truly organized bargain hunters may want to sign up for Premium Outlets e-mails when planning their Williamsburg trip—the loyalty club sends out regular postings with coupons and information about special offers. Visit premiumoutlets.com to join.

YORKTOWN

AUNTIE M'S AMERICAN COTTAGE, 330 Water St., Yorktown, VA 23690; (757) 369-8150; auntiemsamericancottage.com. Handcrafted American art and crafts. Watch self-taught artist "Auntie M" (Marilyn West) produce original folk art in her studio area or sign up to create artful projects in the workshop area. The emphasis is on using recycled goods in artful ways. Open daily 11 a.m. to 6 p.m. except Sun noon to 6 p.m.

BLACK DOG GALLERY, 114 Ballard St., Yorktown, VA 23690; (757) 989-1700; blackdoggallery.net. The owners of this gallery (with a second location in Virginia Beach) have unique expertise in 18th-century decorative arts and fill a unique niche with the wares they offer: handcrafted picture frames, custom-painted floor cloths, and antique and reproduction prints. You'll see their work in some of the country's best known historic houses and museums, including

Yorktown Trolley
York County Tourism

Close-up

Riverwalk Landing

Yorktown's historical waterfront got a much-needed 21st-century makeover when the county spent millions renovating the shopping and dining district, recasting the area as Riverwalk Landing in 2005. A mile-plus brick riverwalk stretches along the beach side of Water Street from the battlefield, all the way up the hill to the American Revolution Museum (formerly Yorktown Victory Center). The central shopping and dining area gives the town a heart—a place to host a popular farmers' market (every Sat, 9 a.m. to 1 p.m., May through Dec), several concert series (outdoors in the summer, indoors at the old Freight Shed in the winter), and other seasonal events like a Civil War weekend (Memorial Day), an annual wine festival (October), and Christmas celebration with a lighted boat parade.

And, of course, the riverfront also serves as the centerpiece of events on July Fourth, and October 19, the anniversary of Cornwallis's surrender, known locally as Yorktown Day.

Most of the events are hosted on Riverwalk Plaza—an open area with a small bandstand that stretches eastward toward the beach, the most popular being "Shaggin' on the Riverwalk," a free weeknight concert series. (The Colonial Shag Club provides dance lessons in case you don't know how to shag.) Next door is the restored Freight Shed, variously used since the 1930s as a ferry terminal and US post office. It was renovated and moved a few hundred yards as part of the county's revitalization plan; it's now available for receptions and meetings.

A word about parking: While the 270-space parking terrace across from Riverwalk is convenient, it fills quickly on weekends and during special events. (If there's rain in the Saturday morning forecast, the farmers' market moves to the parking structure's ground floor, making things even tighter.) Other surface parking lots are available throughout town; park elsewhere, then take the free Yorktown Trolley, which runs every 20 to 25 minutes.

Mount Vernon and Monticello. Open Tues through Fri 10 a.m. to 5 p.m.; Sat 10 a.m. to 2 p.m.; by appointment only on Sun and Mon.

VICCELLIO GOLDSMITH & FINE JEWELRY, 325 Water St. (Riverwalk Landing), Yorktown, VA 23690; (757) 890-2162; viccelliogoldsmith.com. Hank Viccellio, a master goldsmith and precious metals craftsman, offers a line of beautiful and distinctive fine jewelry from this shop he opened in his hometown. Preview his exquisite offerings on his Facebook page, under Viccellio Goldsmith. Open 11 a.m. to 4 p.m., Tues through Sat or by appointment.

THE WATERMEN'S MUSEUM GIFT SHOP, 309 Water St., Yorktown, VA 23690; (757) 887-2641; watermens.org. This excellent shop on the museum's grounds offers a variety of interesting and unusual items relating to the water that showcase local artists and artisans. A good place to find a souvenir, a personal keepsake, or a gift. Open Apr through Dec, 10 a.m. to 4 p.m., Tues through Sat, 1 to 4 p.m. Sun. (Closed Christmas Eve and Christmas Day.)

YORKTOWN BOOKSHOP, 328 Water St. (Riverwalk Landing), Yorktown VA 23690; (757) 969-6626; yorktownbookshop.com. Quality used books at 50 to 70 percent off the publisher's price are sold by an attentive and knowledgeable staff in an elegant space that invites you to browse and relax. If only they served coffee. Open daily noon to 6 p.m.

SHOPPING ON THE PENINSULA

Both Newport News and Hampton have overhauled their shopping districts in recent years—and in all cases they've opted for the "mixed-use" model of retail blended with apartments, condos, and homes.

Two such centers in Newport News straddle either side of Jefferson Avenue in the center of the city—Port Warwick, a mixed-use development with shops and businesses arranged pleasingly around a village green, and the new City Center development, which has apartments rather than single-family homes, and shops, restaurants, government offices, and a Marriott hotel and conference center. Port Warwick opened first, but its no-national-chains approach may have contributed to its apparent difficulty to pull in crowds. City Center, by luring national brands like Talbots, Chico's, and the Marriott, seems to have had more initial success.

The stores and restaurants are more unique in Port Warwick, but if you're looking for familiar favorites, City Center is a better choice. There's also the Patrick Henry Mall at the intersection of I-64 and Jefferson Avenue, an area that has become the nucleus for lots of big-box retail: Best Buy, Wal-Mart, Target, and the shops in the new Tech Center at Oyster Point development, a $250 million, mixed-use development on the southeast corner of Jefferson Avenue and Oyster Point Road, which opened in 2015.

In Hampton there's Old Hampton (downtown) and the bustling Coliseum Central corridor along Mercury Boulevard. If you're looking for ambience while you browse, stroll along the quaint tree-lined brick streets of Old Hampton. Here you will find dozens of specialty shops selling everything from British imports to elaborate doll collections. The Peninsula Town Center in the Coliseum Area continues to evolve since its 2010 debut.

Newport News

CITY CENTER, 701 Town Center Dr., Newport News, VA 23606; citycenter oysterpoint.com. From I-64, exit at J. Clyde Morris Boulevard (exit 258A) and turn right at Thimble Shoals Boulevard. (You can't miss the incredibly huge, neon-lighted spears above the gold-lettered sign.) Continue for 1 mile. The first structure you'll see is the parking garage. You might want to circle around the area once to figure out where your interest lies and park somewhere else—this is a rather sprawling complex, although the most popular stores are on Mariner Row. The Cinemark 12 shows movies in an upscale setting. During the warmer months, special events in past years have included a weekly farmer's market and a concert series called Fridays at the Fountain featuring live music from 5 to 9 p.m.

HILTON VILLAGE, Warwick Boulevard, between Post and Hopkins streets, Newport News, VA 23601. People who live in Hilton easily understand why the American Planning Association named it one of "America's Top 10 Neighborhoods." The humble but charming 2-block shopping district was "mixed--use" before anybody coined that term. Built in 1918 during the World War I shipbuilding boom, most of the shop fronts on Warwick Boulevard still have apartments on their upper floors. The lovely streetscape, brick-paved walkways, and well-maintained landscaping make this an attractive place to stroll. A community theater group stages regular productions at the Village Theater on one end of the district; a bakery (details below) offers sumptuous treats at the other.

PORT WARWICK, off Jefferson Avenue at Loftis Boulevard, Newport News, VA 23606; portwarwick.com. Located on the west side of Jefferson Avenue; turn at Port Warwick Boulevard (near the Sonic hamburger restaurant) and go straight to reach this home to more than 40 locally owned businesses, including several restaurants, a yoga studio, and a bridal salon. Parking around the square is free. A popular art and sculpture festival is held annually in October; concerts are held near the gazebo on William Styron Square from 6 to 9 p.m. on Wed, May through Aug. Want to see what the area looks like? View the 24/7 live webcam of the square by visiting the web address listed above.

Some Shops to Visit

ACT II, 10253 Warwick Blvd., Newport News, VA 23601; (757) 595-0507. Billed as the "Peninsula's premier consignment shop," this huge store offers quality reruns at discount prices. Well-organized and clean, the atmosphere here is more like a department store than you'll find at most second-time-around places. Bargains are to be had for a good cause: Proceeds support Women's America ORT, a nonprofit that offers skills and job training to the unemployed. Open 10 a.m. to 5 p.m. Mon through Sat.

THE BEAD STORE, 10375 Warwick Blvd., Newport News, VA 23601; (757) 591-0593; beadstore-va.com. Check out the "Wall of Beads" that offers an array in every color, shape, texture, and finish. There's "open beading" around the table on Wednesday, for free help with any project, an ornament of the month tutorial, and "Project Friday," with free instruction on how to make bracelets. Open 11 a.m. to 5 p.m. Tues through Sat.

COUTURE CAKES, 10373 Warwick Blvd., Newport News, VA 23601; (757) 599-6452; couturecakesbynika.com. Master baker Nika Covington offers luxurious baked goods at a price almost anybody can afford, like Choco-late Overload Cupcakes for $2.50, and buy one, get one free on Thursday. Her cakes are so beautifully constructed you may feel bad about eating them. A baby shower cake in the shape of a diaper bag looks like you could walk off with it slung over one arm. Open Tues through Sat 10 a.m. to 7 p.m.

PLANTIQUES, 10377 Warwick Blvd., Newport News, VA 23601; (757) 595-1545. This rambling, multiroom house at the northwestern end of Hil-ton's shopping district is like a mini antique mall under one roof. Individual purveyors offer jewelry, vintage clothing, home accents, decorative items, and collectibles. Owner Pam Phillip will also whip up a cappuccino for you from her coffee bar. Open 10 a.m. to 5 p.m. Mon through Sat.

PRIMROSE, 10345 Warwick Blvd., Newport News, VA 23601; (757) 369-4697. Jennifer Gambill runs this charming gift shop while her husband, Shawn, cuts hair in the back room, and Hannah, their very mellow dog, feigns constant hunger. The shop reflects Jennifer's relaxed vibe and elegant taste— unique jewelry, accessories for the home and garden, doggy accessories, baby gifts, and many hand-painted (some by Jennifer herself) and one-of-a-kind items. Open Tues through Thurs 10 a.m. to 5 p.m.; Fri 10 a.m. to 2 p.m.; Sat 10 a.m. to 5 p.m.

Hampton

Old Hampton

BLUE SKIES GALLERY, 26 King St., Hampton, VA 23669; (757) 727-0028; blueskiesart.com. This cooperative gallery offers 5,000 square feet to showcase the creative work of local artists and artisans. Its selection includes sculpture, paintings, clothing, and crafts in silver, acrylic, wood, fiber, fabric, paper, and glass.

THE VIRGINIA STORE, 555 Settlers Landing Rd., Hampton, VA 23669; (757) 727-0600; thevirginiastore.org. If it's made in Virginia, they sell it here. They'll even make you a beautiful gift basket full of Virginia products: wine, peanuts, sauces, jams, jellies, spices, and more. Open 9:30 a.m. to 5:30 p.m. Mon through Sat; 12:30 to 5:30 p.m. Sun.

Coliseum Central

This is the main business district in Hampton. Located on either side of Mercury Boulevard, the area is named after the nearby Hampton Coliseum, a concert venue that's highly visible from I-64.

PENINSULA TOWN CENTER, West Mercury Boulevard, Hampton, VA 23666; (757) 838-1505; peninsulatowncenter.com. The centerpiece of Coliseum Central is this mixed-use development, built on the site of a bulldozed '70s-era enclosed mall. It's anchored by Target and Barnes & Noble, with a blend of local shops, national chains, and restaurants. The project was completed in 2011, underwent an overhaul again in 2015, and now has a full (but seemingly rotating) array of shops.

Attractions

Years ago, *the* reason people came to Williamsburg was the extraordinary restoration of a pre-Revolution colonial village. These days, there are more magnets: the world's faster roller coaster at Busch Gardens, the cool pull of the Hubba Hubba Highway at Water Country USA, the shopping at Premium Outlets, and a burgeoning array of craft beer breweries. Read through our list as you're planning your trip—you might want to add another day or two to your vacation to experience it all.

AMUSEMENT PARKS

BUSCH GARDENS, 1 Busch Gardens Blvd. (exit 243A off I-64), Williamsburg, VA 23185; (757) 229-4386; buschgardens.com/va. When Busch Gardens opened in 1975, it was a secondary diversion: Tourists would come to Williamsburg for the history, then spend a day at the theme park. Today, it's the opposite—nearly 3 million visitors a year pass through the turnstiles at Busch Gardens and its sister park, Water Country USA, compared with about 650,000 paid admissions to Colonial Williamsburg. For many, the reason to come to Williamsburg is roller coasters. They may, or they may not, take in some of the history while they're here.

Located 3 miles east of Williamsburg on US 60, Busch Gardens celebrated its 45th anniversary in 2020. In that time, it has cemented its reputation as one of the most beautiful—and cleanest—amusement parks in America, set on a hilly, well-manicured 100-acre tract. It's a quiet part of southeastern Virginia, so the screams from the roller coasters can be heard clearly in France. (The park is organized around the idea that visitors are traveling through 17th-century Europe. Even the parking lots are named for European countries.)

Among the more than 50 rides and attractions 7 are major roller coasters (8 if you count a kiddie coaster)—3 of which have opened since 2012, including Tempesto and InvadR, which opened in 2015 and 2017 respectively. In 2009, the park also relaunched its children's ride area built around Sesame Street characters.

Arriving in 2021 is Pantheon, already voted a Top 10 "Most Anticipated Roller Coaster" by *USA Today*. Pantheon will be the World's Fastest Multi-Launch coaster. Located in the Festa Italia village, Pantheon features two inversions, four launches, five air-time hills, a 95-degree drop, a height of 180 feet, and a record-breaking top speed of 73 mph. The all-new coaster incorporates five mighty gods including Pluto, Mercury, Jupiter, Minerva, and Neptune, with an aspect of the track reflecting their respective powers. In this one-of-a-kind

Busch Gardens Roller Coaster
Kathy Kirby

multilaunch experience fit for the gods, Pantheon is sure to delight even the most daring mortal thrill-seekers.

Getting There

The park opens for the season in late March—mostly weekends only, but some daily operation around Easter to catch spring breakers and school vacationers. From Memorial Day through Labor Day, it operates daily. In late September through November 1, it reopens for "Howl-O-Scream," sinister tricks and terrifying fun leading up to Halloween. After Thanksgiving, the park retools for Christmas, featuring one of the largest light displays in North America with over 11 million twinkling lights, holiday shows, festive food including hot chocolate, fresh baked Christmas cookies and, of course, Santa. "Christmas Town" typically runs through the first week of January. Hours can vary; check the website for specific days if you're planning to go. Indeed, opening and closing times vary throughout the season. The park can close as early as 8 p.m. in spring or as late as 11 p.m. on holiday weekends. The website has an updated calendar for each day of the season, which includes schedules for the park's shows and special events.

Getting to Busch Gardens is easy: Take I-64 to the Busch Gardens exit (exit 243A), which leads directly to the park entrance. If you're coming from the Historic Area or the western part of the Williamsburg area, take US 60 East, past Kingsmill and the Anheuser-Busch brewery; the park entrance will be on your right. A parking fee is required for nonmembers. Trams are used to shuttle people from lots to the entrance but, be aware, there is a lot of walking during a day at Busch Gardens.

A Busch Gardens membership is the best value for those who plan on visiting multiple times, and Howl-O-Scream and Christmas Town are included, plus free parking and in-park discounts. Single-day tickets are pricey: $75 per adult, $65 for children ages 3 to 9.

Various discount programs are available: active-duty military discounts, multiday tickets, and combo tickets with Busch Gardens' sister park, Water Country USA. Check the website for details; also search for discounts and coupons online. Admission gets you unlimited rides, access to the park's regular

The Big Thrills

The major rides at Busch Gardens include the following:

Alpengeist—This floorless steel roller coaster hurtles passengers through the air at nearly 70 mph. Make sure your cell phone is tucked deep into a pocket. Located in Germany.

Apollo's Chariot—This is the tall, humpbacked coaster visible from I-64. It has the biggest drop (210 feet) and fastest speeds (73 mph) of Busch Garden's coasters. In Italy.

The Battering Ram—A swooping pendulum ride that is best not experienced directly after lunch. In Italy.

Battle for Eire—a marriage of a motion-based theater simulator with state-of-the-art 360-degree virtual reality headsets, creating an innovative experience unlike any other in the attraction industry.

Da Vinci's Cradle—This ride is flat but somehow still manages to make one's internal organs lurch. In Italy.

Escape from Pompeii—One part boat ride, one part volcanic eruption, you can get cooled off by this ride just by standing nearby to watch it descend. Good on a hot day! In Italy.

Finnegan's Flyer—Riders soar high and swing out over the cliffs of the Celtic coast on this "Screamin' Swing" ride located in the Irish village, adjacent the Loch Ness Monster roller coaster. This breathtaking attraction features two pendulum-like arms, seating 32 riders that fly progressively higher with each swing, reaching a height of more than 80 feet at a speed of 45 mph. Riders can (briefly) take in beautiful views of the park.

Griffon—Imagine falling 200 feet straight down, at 70 mph, with nothing beneath your feet but the sky. That's the start. In France.

InvadR—Hold on to your Viking helmet and feel the wind in your beard on the park's first-ever wooden coaster. Situated in New France, this coaster opened April 2017 and reaches speeds of 48 mph and features a 74-foot drop and nine air-time hills

Le Scoot—A fairly tame log flume for those who prefer their rides to be mild.

Loch Ness Monster—The park's oldest coaster, dating to 1978, features interlocking loops and a long, dark helix tunnel. In Scotland—where else?

Mäch Tower—The tallest attraction in the park lifts riders nearly 240 feet in the air, rotates them for a lovely view, and then drops them into a 60 mph free fall. In Oktoberfest.

Pantheon—scheduled to open in 2021, Pantheon is billed as the world's fastest multilaunch coaster, featuring two inversions, four launches, five air-time hills, a 95-degree drop, and a record-breaking top speed of 73 mph.

Roman Rapids—A gentle, serene raft ride—for at least 10 feet. Then it's neither gentle nor serene. Bring a towel. In Italy.

Tempesto—Located in Festa Italia, this multilaunch coaster with a high-speed station experience and a 154-foot inversion reaches speeds of 63 mph.

Verbolten—Opened in 2012, this ride imagines a drive through the Black Forest on the Autobahn and includes sounds and light effects, high speed turns, and an 88-foot drop into the water. In Oktoberfest.

show lineup, in-park transportation, and other entertainment, but additional fees may be charged for arcade games, and certain special events. The admission price does not include food and drink. If you want front-of-the-line priority access to some of your favorite roller coasters and attractions, check out the Quick Queue® products before your visit.

Getting around Inside

The park sprawls over 100 acres and has a number of significant hills that surround its central waterway, the Rhine River (actually a pond formed by a dam across a branch of Grove Creek). The park's main entrance places you at England—roughly at 5 o'clock if you imagine the park as the face of a clock. Continuing clockwise, you pass through Italy, Germany, France, Ireland, and Scotland.

Various paved walkways and bridges link the different sections of the park, but the hills can be a killer, especially after a long, hot day or if you have a group of kids in tow. The park's internal transportation systems can be a savior at those times. The Aeronaut Skyride's triangular route connects England to France to Germany and back on aerial cars. They offer terrific views of the park and surrounding woods. Three steam locomotives circle the park clockwise, with stops at Scotland, Italy, and France.

Still, plan to do plenty of walking, wear sensible shoes, and grab a park map on your way in. Strollers and wheelchairs (including electric wheelchairs) can be rented near the ticket windows, but the numbers are limited.

The Countries

Busch Gardens groups its attractions into areas named for European countries, each occupying its own portion of the park, plus a wild life area, named in honor of zookeeper Jack Hanna, and Oktoberfest, an extension of Germany with Das Festhaus, a 2,000-seat beer hall (it's not called *Busch* Gardens for nothing) as its centerpiece. They needn't be explored in any particular order. In fact, many park regulars have their own definite—and often contradictory—opinions on the "best" way to maximize fun and avoid crowds. Unfortunately, some days there is no way to avoid crowds. The consistently best option is to be at the park the moment it opens.

Each of the nations has various dining and shopping options, some (but not all) themed to the cuisine and wares of that country. We'll take them clockwise from the main entrance.

England

This area, just inside the park's main entrance, is designed to evoke an English village. It's home to a Big Ben–like clock tower (which makes for a great meeting place if your party plans to split up) and a replica of Shakespeare's Globe Theatre, where specialty acts perform throughout the season.

Close-up

Don't Try This at Home

The fictional Tempesto, for whom Busch Garden's roller coaster is named, is a bicyclist in the mold of a turn-of-the-20th-century daredevil who performed as "Diavolo" and was best known for having mastered the loop-the-loop, a full vertical loop on a bicycle, defying gravity by being upside down at the top of the loop—kind of an X Games move, or something more commonly completed on a Hot Wheels track with a tiny metal car.

The roller coaster built as an homage to this stunt rider lets passengers experience his signature move.

Instead of a traditional steady climb up an incline, Tempesto teases passengers with a small burst of power that sends them only partway up the 154-foot loop. The cars roll backward into the loading station (in full view of those waiting to board) and up a second incline where the ride peters out again. Finally, the cars coast forward to a loading station and receive a full dose of propulsion, revving the train up to 63 mph. That gives them just enough juice to make it all the way up and over the huge loop. A lot of loops turn riders upside down, but this one twists firsts, placing the train on the outside of the arc and keeping riders in an upright position as they scale the coaster's apex. It isn't until passengers are about to exit the loop that they get the inversion, a second twist that will send them barreling upside down. After that, there's just the 90-degree free fall to return to the loading station, which the cars race past for a third time before losing steam and falling backward into the station to end the ride. The whole thing takes about a minute, but you will have aged about 10 years.

To the left of England is "Sesame Street: Forest of Fun," a collection of many of the park's "kid-siderate" child rides. Among them are Grover's Alpine Express (a kid-friendly roller coaster), Bert and Ernie's Loch Adventure (a miniature log flume), and wet and dry play areas.

Italy

This village is dominated by its thrill rides—Escape from Pompeii, Apollo's Chariot, and Tempesto, and coming in 2021, Pantheon, the park's newest roller coaster.

Escape from Pompeii starts as a pleasant, gentle boat ride that quickly becomes a simulated trip through a volcano, complete with bursts of flame, and ends with a long, flume-like drop. (Stand back: Spectators usually end up wetter than the riders and on hot summer days there are definitely people hoping to get drenched.)

Apollo's Chariot is one of the park's signature coasters—a hypercoaster to aficionados, with a height of 170 feet, and a 210-foot drop. (How? Those hills—it takes advantage of one of the park's natural valleys. Not that you'll be able to tell as you top out at 73 mph.) See our Close-up in this chapter of the park's newest coaster, Tempesto.

Also in Italy is Roman Rapids, a raft expedition that sends riders swirling past ruins, through fog, and down the rapids. Obey the warnings on this one: You'll get wet. That doesn't mean you *might* get wet, or *could* get splashed. You'll be doused, then soaked. Leave the phone with someone for safekeeping, or spring for a locker.

Germany and Oktoberfest

Clockwise from Italy, across a long footbridge, is the biggest area of the park which includes Germany and Oktoberfest. It's home to the park's excellent bumper-car arena (Der Autobahn), kid's airplane ride (Der Roto Baron), a lovely restored antique carousel (Kinder Karussel), and the Das Festhaus dining, drinking, and entertainment hall. Board the Rhine River Cruise here for a unique view of the park from its waterways.

The thrill rides here are Alpengeist and Mäch Tower, and the roller coaster, Verbolten, which opened in 2012.

France

At 12 o'clock on the park's imagined clock face, France has the requisite log flume (Le Scoot), the Trappers Smokehouse dining area (more French Canadian then French), and the Royal Palace Theatre, home to special events.

It also has a dive-style roller coaster called Griffon that opened in 2007. It's named for the mythical beast (half eagle, half lion), and the weak-stomached might prefer to be eaten by a griffon rather than ride this one. You're hauled in a floorless car up 205 feet, dangled over a precipice—then dropped, straight down (it takes almost 4 seconds). Before your stomach can catch up, you're yanked up into an inverted Immelmann loop (named after a WWI German

i Busch Gardens is a big park, and its staff doesn't page for lost persons. Your best bet is to prearrange a central meeting place should members of your party get separated. Some suggestions: the Big Ben clock in England, in front of Das Festhaus in Germany, or in front of the Royal Palace Theatre in France.

> ## Where's the Wolf?
> Frequent visitors may wonder about the Big Bad Wolf, an aggressive steel coaster that featured a 99-foot drop toward the surface of the Rhine water-way. Alas, it closed at the end of the 2009 summer season. After 25 years of operation, it had reached the end of its designed service life. Rather than refurbish the ride, park management choose to retire it.

fighter pilot). Not enough? You do it *again* on a smaller (130-foot) drop into a second Immelmann before scrubbing off the speed in a shallow splash pool. Best not to do this one right after a big lunch. Or maybe just get on the Skyride here and have a nice look at the scenery from high above it.

Ireland

This newest village, at roughly 2 o'clock on the clockface, features most of the park's wildlife shows. Jack Hanna's Wild Reserve features Wolf Valley, home to a small pack of gray wolves; the Eagle Ridge preserve for injured bald eagles; the Lorikeet Glen, and other animals in the Conservation Station.

Ireland also is the site of the park's newest motion simulator ride, Battle for Eire—a marriage of a motion-based theater simulator with state-of-the-art 360-degree virtual reality headsets. Cool off inside the Abbey Stone Theatre with a live show, Celtic Fyre, featuring musicians, singers, and really loud step dancing.

Scotland

The faux-Scottish village occupies the rough center of the park. There's nothing faux about the wildlife here, though. The exhibit features a variety of Scottish animals—border collies, blackface sheep, and majestic Clydesdale horses.

Also wild in Scotland: the Loch Ness Monster roller coaster. In some ways, it's tame compared to its cousins elsewhere in the park—it *only* reaches 60 mph and drops 100 feet. But it's a sentimental favorite for many aficionados—it opened in 1978 and was the first coaster in the world with interlocking loops.

WATER COUNTRY USA, 176 Water Country Pkwy., Williamsbug, VA 23185; (757) 229-4386; watercountryusa.com. This wild and wet place to cool off during Virginia's mostly muggy summers sits on 40 acres of wooded land 3 miles northeast of Busch Gardens on VA 199. The largest water theme park in Virginia, Water Country USA offers more than a dozen water rides as well as pools, 1,500 lounge chairs for sunbathing, a variety of restaurants, arcades, and, of course, bathhouse facilities.

Visitors will be able to see one of the coolest slides as they pull up to the gates: Colossal Curl, true to its name, is a mega-slide that starts with a funnel feature, which will swish and swirl guests before whisking them through the ride's enclosed colorful tubes on their way to a wave element that hurtles them high above the park. (Sorry, tots. Riders have to be at least 48 inches tall to experience the Curl.)

Like its sister park, Busch Gardens, this is a beautifully maintained facility, landscaped with palms, ornamental grasses, pines, and bold, bright flowers like hibiscus, hot pink geraniums, and blazing yellow marigolds. Bare feet abound, but swim shoes or waterproof sandals will protect from hot pavement and stubbed toes. If you don't want to wear shoes on some of the rides, there are "sneaker keepers" at the base of many attractions. Strollers are available near the main concession area.

This family-friendly park boasts rides suited to all ages and all levels of swimming ability. Pools and rides are temperature-controlled, a feature especially helpful for early-season splashing. And while thrills are the main business of this attraction, relaxation hasn't been forgotten. Beach bums can catch a wave at Surfers' Bay, then grab a few rays on the four-tiered sundeck. Parents can sit on deck chairs while the kids splash around in the supervised play area. In fact, visitors anxious about water dangers will be pleased to know Water Country USA has been rated among America's safest theme parks by Barclay & Associates, an independent risk-management firm.

Getting Inside

Water Country USA typically opens in mid-May and closes in early September. From Memorial Day through mid-August hours generally are 10 a.m. to 8 p.m., although the park typically closes at 6 p.m. both earlier and later in the season. On hot summer days, it's a good idea to get there when it opens. If you want front-of-the-line priority access to some of your favorite water park attractions, check out the Quick Queue® products before your visit.

To reach the park from I-64, take exit 243A and follow VA 199 for 0.25 mile to the entrance. There is a parking fee, although free parking is included with most memberships. A membership is the best value for those who plan on visiting multiple times, Single-day tickets are available for adults and children ages 3 to 9 and various discounts are offered for multiday ticket packages and combo tickets with Busch Gardens. Check the website for details; also search for discounts and coupons online. Admission gets you unlimited slides and attractions. Additional fees may be charged for arcade games and certain special events. The admission price does not include food and drink. Check the website for detailed information, cabana rentals, and dining options.

Unless a member of your group is staying dry for the whole day, consider renting a locker for your valuables (cash, car keys, identification) and dry clothes for the ride home. A convenient way to pay for expenses throughout the day is with a Cashless Wristband, a waterproof payment method that allows you to swim and slide without worrying about where your wallet is. Visit Guest

Relations or any ticket booth window to receive a complimentary wristband and link it to a credit card, debit card, or cash. If you're like us and can't get by without sunglasses, they, too, should be worn on some type of head-hugging cord. One last word of advice: Take towels with you, and park them on lawn chairs at Surfers' Bay or one of the children's play areas. That way you'll have a home base to return to when you just want to sit a while or test the waters in the wave pool.

The park has a large supply of free life vests for nonswimmers and small children. Because you can find them on racks throughout the park, many people pick them up and drop them off as needed. We have found that after 2 p.m.

The Rides

Now that you've stashed your valuables and suited up, it's time for the main event. What follows are individual descriptions of each of the water rides and play areas.

Cutback Water Coaster—This is Water County's newest ride. It's the only "RocketBlast" coaster on the eastern seaboard and Virginia's first hybrid water coaster. This water propulsion ride merges two unique technologies—a water jet propulsion system and an exhilarating saucer feature. With the RocketBlast technology, Cutback will drive bigger boats, at higher speeds, and move riders up longer, steeper inclines. Thrill-seekers board a four-person raft, speed along an 856-foot slide, jet through tunnels, and slide onto the wide-open space of massive saucer-shaped features. The steep angles of the saucers provide a drop-and-dive sensation as riders race along the edges. Cutback Water Coaster features the latest in turbine technology and takes water propulsion coasters to a whole new level with heart-stopping turns, lightning-fast drops and thrilling speeds.

Aquazoid—Named for a 1950s' mutant movie monster, parties of four travel on rafts through big black tubes into a pitch-dark tunnel, passing through curtains of water while their senses are assaulted by beams of light and howling sound effects. Escape the 864-foot ride by plunging 78 feet into a splash pool.

Big Daddy Falls—This 670-foot water ride splashes through twists and turns, slips into a dark tunnel, then plunges into a slow-moving river alive with waterfalls before racing around the bend to a final splashdown.

Colossal Curl—Mentioned above, this newest ride is a 622-foot long slide, which swirls riders into a funnel-style opening on cloverleaf-shaped inner tubes before rocketing them through tunnels high above the park where they hit a wave wall and experience a weightlessness akin to riding a huge ocean wave.

Cow-A-Bunga—This children's play area features a 4,500-square-foot heated pool, an interactive speedboat with a water skiing cow ("udder" silliness), a curving water flume, a short but slick triple slide, and several fountains. Ample deck seating allows parents to watch the action from the sidelines.

H2O UFO—The largest interactive children's play area has a sci-fi theme and features a fun combination of slides and spray jets. There's even a fairly long, scaled-down waterslide for kids (and their parents) who aren't quite ready to take a walk on the wilder side. Park your gear on one of the many lawn chairs.

Hubba Hubba Highway—A lazy river attraction that covers 3.5 acres, featuring a jet stream that gently pushes you along. Enter through a shallow 2,000-square-foot lagoon. Watch out for the coconuts and the geysers!

Jet Scream—Water Country USA's flume ride is one of the longest in the nation at 415 feet. Start 50 feet off the ground and streak down one of four twisting waterslides at 25 mph into a splashdown pool.

Kritter Koral—Splash fun for the tiniest of tots, complete with scaled-down waterslides, play equipment, and fountains. A word to tweens and teens—the lifeguards will shoo you out immediately to keep the pool safe for the little ones.

Malibu Pipeline—A twisting, two-person tube ride through enclosed double flumes, complete with strobe lighting, waterfalls, and a splash pool at the bottom.

Nitro Racer—If you like competition, this super-fast, slippery drag race is for you. Six contestants race down a 320-foot-long slide to see who can reach the finish line first.

Rock 'n' Roll Island's Jammin' Jukebox—Three body slides, The Twist, The Hully Gully, and The Funky Chicken, shoot from the top of a 33-foot-tall slide tower. In addition, there are nearly 600 feet of twisting and turning tubes, and a 700-foot "lazy river" surrounds the 9,000-square-foot pool.

Surfers' Bay—Virginia's largest wave pool seems more like an ocean with its 650,000 gallons of water. Periods of mechanically produced 4-foot waves alternate with times of smooth surf for relaxation. Sit back on one of the 1,000-plus lounge chairs on the wood sundeck surrounding the bay or head for one of the bright canopied cabanas. Grab seats early as they go fast.

Vanish Point—Inspired by the point on a wave where water and gravity form a perfect partnership, this summit supplies two wicked-wet ways to drop out of sight.

Wild Thang—A 500-foot-long double-inner-tube ride passes jungle scenes, goes under waterfalls, and winds through tunnels.

it's hard to locate one of the smaller children's vests—it might be a good idea to hold on to one for your entire visit. Plastic swim diapers, required throughout the park, can also be purchased.

Dining

Whether you're looking for a full meal, quick bite, refreshing drink, or tasty dessert, the park has something for everyone. For those with allergen concerns, Boardwalk Southwest Grill is our designated allergy-friendly dining location.

There are nine eateries offering burrito bowls, sandwiches, wraps, hot dogs, pizza, pretzels, subs, fries, funnel cakes, ice cream, lemonade, sports drinks, beer, and slushy adult beverages. Snack bars are situated around the park and open for business. Guests can eat at shaded outdoor tables, and a catering facility may be reserved in advance for groups of 20 or more. Food is pricey, lines can be long on the busiest days, and service can make kids—who just want to get back in line for another ride—fidgety. If you can, pack a picnic in a cooler and eat at the tables on grassy areas in the parking lot (no food or beverages may be brought into the park). The tables are on grassy median strips and most are shaded by umbrellas, so it's both a cheap and pleasant alternative. There's also a shaded pavilion for picnicking off to the right of the park entrance. Make sure to have your hand stamped at the gate so you can get back inside the park.

Safety Features

Water Country USA has an excellent reputation as a safe, fun place to enjoy water without hitting the beach. The park employs more than 80 certified lifeguards and stations supervisors at each ride and attraction. Lifeguards are trained in CPR, first aid, and accident prevention, and they participate in ongoing training programs and drills. Life vests and inner tubes are provided free for anyone who would like one. Each year American Red Cross–certified volunteers offer swim lessons to area residents.

A first-aid station is open during all operating hours, paths are treated with salt to prevent falls, pool depths are clearly marked, and individual safety rules are posted at each ride. Children younger than 8 must always be in the company of a parent or other adult. Bad weather? One component of safety

i When lightning strikes—hang on to your ticket! Water Country USA prides itself on its safety record, one element of which is closing all water rides if lightning is seen in the area. The park may reopen within as little as 30 minutes if the clouds pass quickly, but if the park closes, you can use your ticket to gain entry another day.

policy is to close the park immediately if there is lightning. This combination of rules and features at Water Country USA set the standards for safety among the nation's water parks. Precisely because the park is so safety-conscious, visitors can truly relax and enjoy a wet and wild adventure.

HISTORY ATTRACTIONS

COLONIAL WILLIAMSBURG, various locations within the Historic Area, roughly defined by Henry Street on the west, Lafayette Street on the north and east, and Francis Street on the south; Williamsburg, VA 23185; (844) 585-1168; colonialwilliamsburg.com. The massively ambitious restoration project that began here in the early 20th century was a hymn to democracy, a way of honoring and ensuring the memory of the birth of a nation. Over the decades it has morphed into something else. It's one thing to restore buildings, quite another to hobnob with Thomas Jefferson or share tea with Martha Washington. Colonial Williamsburg (CW) realized that no matter what the original mission, if they wanted the story of America's beginnings to continue to be told, it had to be about more than buildings; it had to be about people.

That's why, strolling down Duke of Gloucester Street, you are meant to eavesdrop. Listen to the talk of taxes, politics, and religious freedom. A visit to CW is much more than leafing through the pages of a history book—it's a chance to put yourself, at least momentarily, in the shoes of British citizens who had the temerity, the guts even, to think about overthrowing the king. Imagine! After all, when all this discourse about independence was brewing, do you think most Virginians believed they could win?

The historical interpreters here emphasize the political and social history of the day. Because of the restoration, you get to experience that in a way that allows you to employ all your senses. There is probably nowhere else in the US where the sights, sounds, tastes, and even smells of the past come alive in the present as they do in Williamsburg, including the occasional waft of horse manure.

The latest iteration of the CW experience is an effort to be more inclusive, to correct what was perhaps the unintentional whitewashing of that history. The contributions—and circumstances—of America's first African population have taken center stage. It's a slice of American history that hasn't gotten the attention it deserved until now. That's true not just at CW but at all of the area's historic attractions: adding the stories of the first African American—and the continent's original inhabitants—is of paramount importance.

The other big development at CW involves the Art Museums—the **DeWitt Wallace Decorative Arts Museum** and the **Abby Aldrich Rockefeller Folk Art Museum**—which reopened in 2020 after a $42 million renovation which added 65,000 square feet of exhibit space among many other improvements.

In total, CW offers 301 acres of 18th-century history along with a full slate of lectures, concerts, theatrical performances, and militia exhibits year-round. The city is portrayed on the brink of revolution, when the air is tense with rumors of rebellion, espionage, and possible war. Throughout the Historic Area, costumed interpreters toil at their trades without modern conveniences like, say, electricity. In colonial taverns, balladeers serenade their audiences with the bawdy tales that were popular with previous generations, while learned gentlemen of the time discuss the political issues that were at the forefront of everyone's mind.

With 88 original structures, 300 major reconstructions, 40 exhibition buildings, and 90 acres of gardens and greens, Williamsburg isn't a city you can see in a day—or even two. Allow enough time to listen to a morning reveille, dance in the candlelit House of Burgesses, and participate in a military drill. The memories you'll come away with are unlikely to be duplicated anywhere else. To start you on your trip to another era, we begin with a comprehensive look back at how it all began.

One program, for instance, explores the paradoxical issue of freedom in a society that fought to win its independence from the British Crown while practicing and condoning slavery. CW also has used grant monies to improve and more fully assimilate interpretation of the 18th-century African American experience into its presentations. The role religion played in the daily lives of colonists is being more fully explored and interpreted for the benefit of visitors through lectures, tours, and concerts. Each year, Black history, women's history, music, and religion are observed with special programming. Reenactments and re-creations of historical events—from a day of fasting, humiliation, and prayer in response to the Boston Tea Party to a mock trial and burning of Britain's chief minister, Lord North—occur on a regular basis throughout the Historic Area.

Costumed tradespeople at nearly 20 sites around the Historic Area also invite visitors to roll up their sleeves and assist them with their 18th-century trades, whether shoemaking, basket weaving, or silversmithing. In addition, Thomas Jefferson, Patrick Henry, and other Founding Fathers now engage

i Children get a different perspective on history when they wear colonial costumes. Girls can don an elegant white 18th-century lawn dress with a colored sash and boys can sport a hunting shirt, haversack, and imitation rifle. For more information on costume rental see colonialwilliamsburg.org/explore/shop/costume-rentals. (Costumes are available for children between the ages of 5 and 10.)

visitors with compelling discourse on such topics as democracy, slavery, marriage, and the "Mother Country" of England.

The best way to find out what's on tap when you're in town is to consult the online calendar at colonialwilliamsburg.org/events-calendar. Walking through the Historic Area is free, but some scheduled events require tickets.

Getting Started

Buying Tickets

The visitor center building is closed. Guests are encouraged to purchase tickets online. The visitor center parking lot is open. Guests may park there and take the complementary shuttle to the Historic Area. There is also free parking at the Art Museums. Shuttle buses provide transport to all key spots in the Historic Area though new safety procedures will limit the number of passengers per bus to accommodate physical distancing. In accordance with state law, face coverings are required to ride the shuttle.

Touchless tickets are available for purchase online. Additionally, a map of the Historic Area and weekly program guides are available digitally on the Colonial Williamsburg website. Guests are strongly encouraged to purchase tickets online but there are ticket windows at the Art Museums, 301 S. Nassau St., and the Lumber House (at the intersection of South Henry and Duke of Gloucester streets). Beginning April 1, both locations are generally open from 9 a.m. to 5 p.m. daily.

Tickets

You can feel transported back to the 18th century just by roaming the historic streets of Colonial Williamsburg free of charge, but visitors need a ticket to enter exhibition buildings and historic trade shops, ride the buses provided by CW, or take part in guided walking tours.

Tickets can be purchased online, which allows you to see the range of choices and take advantage of specials and discounts that are offered, especially in the off-season. The CW website is colonialwilliamsburg.org.

Prices, which can vary seasonally, range from $14.99 for a youth ticket (ages 6 to 12) to $74.99 for an adult annual pass. Children 5 and under are admitted free. There are also multiday passes, and a special rate for students and for Williamsburg residents. Guests staying at Colonial Williamsburg lodgings receive substantial discounts.

Every CW ticket includes admission to the historic area, where costumed interpreters offer guided tours of the Governor's Palace, Capitol, and Courthouse; admission to trade sites to see and speak with expert masters, journeymen, and apprentices practicing 18th-century trades; and daily performances on the Charlton Stage and in the Hennage Auditorium. Ticketed guests may also enter the Art Museums of Colonial Williamsburg, 301 S. Nassau St.

Special-ticket programs include ghost walks for all ages and musical, interpretive, and craft programs.

Hours of Operation

Colonial Williamsburg is open 365 days a year, but its hours and the availability of certain buildings and attractions vary. During the summer months, most buildings in the Historic Area are open from 9 a.m. to 5 p.m. with some variations. In the winter, open hours are generally shortened to 9:30 a.m. to 4:30 p.m. Double-check online before you make specific plans.

Transportation

A fleet of Colonial Williamsburg buses circulates throughout the Historic Area, stopping at major points of interest. They carry visitors continuously from morning until about 10 p.m. (earlier in the off-season), and ticket holders may board at any stop. Special assistance and shuttle bus service are available to visitors with disabilities. If you need these services, call the toll-free number (844-585-1168). As we mentioned in our Getting Here, Getting Around chapter, parking in the Historic Area is extremely limited, and many streets are typically closed to vehicles from 8 a.m. to 10 p.m.

Guests of the **Williamsburg Inn** or **Williamsburg Lodge** are entitled to 2 hours of free bike rental during their stay; bikes can also be rented for $15 (per bike) for 2 hours, or $40 for 8 hours. Call the Fitness Center at (757) 220-7690 or (800) 688-6479 for more information.

Historic Area Attractions

While it's impossible to absorb everything Colonial Williamsburg has to offer in a day or two, some visitors can't stay longer. Even a short visit will be memorable if you take the time to plan your tour in advance. Before you visit, it's worth spending some time surfing colonialwilliamsburg.org to get a general idea of what is happening during the time you'll be in the area.

Below we highlight the major buildings and exhibits you won't want to miss, no matter how brief your stay. While we mention which buildings and exhibits require special reservations, it's always best to check the day you plan to tour a specific site, as hours of operation vary, and buildings are occasionally closed to the public.

The Buildings

Bruton Parish Church

On Duke of Gloucester Street, west of the Palace Green, Bruton Parish Church is one of America's oldest Episcopal churches, in use since 1715. While Bruton Parish is not owned by Colonial Williamsburg, the public is welcome to tour the church from 10 a.m. to 4 p.m. Mon through Sat and from 12:30 to 4:30

Bruton Parish Church, Williamsburg, Virginia
Lee Snider/GettyImages

p.m. Sun. The church was fully restored in 1940. Walls and windows are original. The stone baptismal font, according to legend, was brought from an earlier Jamestown church. The churchyard holds many 18th-century graves. Buried inside the church is Francis Fauquier, one of Virginia's royal governors. Evening organ recitals, chamber music performances, and choral concerts frequently are presented at the church.

Due to the coronavirus pandemic, the church has canceled tours. You can watch a live-stream service through their YouTube channel (youtube.com/user/BrutonParish), and they are conducting limited outdoor services in the churchyard.

CAPITOL

Prior to the Revolutionary War, the House of Burgesses and a 12-member council met in this ornate structure at the east end of Duke of Gloucester Street. Many important political events that involved Virginia in the Revolutionary War took place here. The most significant was on May 15, 1776, when Virginia's legislators adopted a resolution declaring independence from England, two months before the Continental Congress adopted the Declaration of Independence in Philadelphia. Once war began, and until 1780 when the capital was moved to Richmond, it housed the state government. Foundations were laid in 1701 for the H-shaped building, designed with two wings to hold the bicameral legislative bodies that made up colonial government. Like the Governor's Palace, the original Capitol building suffered fire damage, burning in 1747. Its replacement, neglected after the capital moved to Richmond in 1780, eventually burned also. What you see today is a reconstruction of the first Capitol, about which more architectural evidence was found. Here, you can tour the House of Burgesses, Council Chambers, and General Courtroom, and join in a number of special evening programs.

> i During your stroll through colonial times, get involved in what is happening around you. The teaching of history is a primary goal in Colonial Williamsburg, and the historical interpreters here embrace their mission with the passion of a great classroom teacher. To engage visitors, there are a many hands-on learning presentations. But don't just watch! Walking along Duke of Gloucester Street, you might run into Patrick Henry or George Washington—ask them a question! When are you going to get another chance?

George Wythe House

This spacious original Georgian-style home affords an understanding of gracious living in 18th-century Williamsburg. The house, featuring two great chimneys and large central halls, was used as George Washington's headquarters before the Battle of Yorktown. Owner George Wythe was the nation's first law professor and an influential teacher of Thomas Jefferson. A $750,000 redecorating project involved replacing marble fireplace mantels with more authentic ones of red sandstone and installing custom hand-printed wallpaper after a painstaking analysis revealed that the Wythe House most likely was wallpapered during Wythe's lifetime (1726–1806).

Behind the house you'll find symmetrical gardens, tree box topiaries, and an arbor of shady hornbeam. Be sure to stop by the poultry pens and observe some of the rare breeds.

Governor's Palace

Set on 10 acres of restored gardens, this elegant mansion housed seven royal governors and the Commonwealth of Virginia's first two elected governors, Patrick Henry and Thomas Jefferson. The original construction began in 1706 and took 17 years to complete; alterations and redecoration continued until the December 22, 1781, fire that left only the foundation. At the north end of the Palace Green, the reconstructed mansion, with its entrance hall, parlor, ballroom, dining rooms, bedchambers, waiting areas, and even a wine cellar, is opulently furnished from an inventory of more than 12,000 items dating to the period of Lord Dunmore, Virginia's last royal governor. Lord Dunmore and his family lived in the Governor's Palace in the early 1770s. Check out the incredible crown moldings and wall coverings (that's leather on the walls in the upstairs meeting room), and don't miss all the interesting details throughout the palace. The chairs in Lady Dunmore's upstairs bedchamber are made to simulate bamboo, there really were Venetian blinds on the windows, and the small statues lining the dining room mantel are the actual figurines representing the costumed characters from the masquerade ball commemorating King George III's 21st birthday.

In the 18th century the Governor's Palace was the scene of many get-togethers of early America's well-to-do. Dances, for example, were held about every three months in the palace ballroom, each typically lasting up to 18 hours, because many visitors had journeyed three or more days on horseback to reach Williamsburg and it would have been exceedingly impolite to send them home too soon. Evening dances still occur here at 7 p.m. Sat (ticket required).

On the palace grounds you will find a stable and carriage house, laundry, and hexagonal bagnio, or bathhouse, a real frill in colonial times. The kitchen and scullery are often active; let your nose lead you to the preparation of hearty onion soup, candied pineapple, or even beer. Take the time to stroll through the formal gardens, similar to early 18th-century English gardens, which lead to

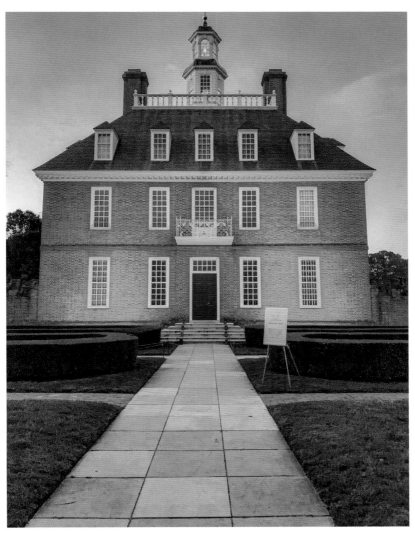

Governor's Palace at dusk
Kathy Kirby

informal terraces and a fishpond. Children love running and playing hide-and-seek in the boxwood maze. The palace, which opened to the public in 1934, is one of Colonial Williamsburg's most popular attractions.

MAGAZINE AND GUARDHOUSE
Across Duke of Gloucester from Chowning's Tavern is the octagonal Powder Magazine, which was built in 1715, by order of Lieutenant Governor Alexander

Spotswood, to store arms for the protection of the colony and for trade with the Indians, and a Guardhouse, reconstructed in 1949. The Magazine played an important role during the French and Indian War (1754–1763), when it became evident that the wooden stockade surrounding it served as woefully inadequate protection from enemies.

Perhaps the biggest conflict surrounding the Powder Magazine occurred before dawn on April 21, 1775, when British soldiers removed 15 half barrels of gunpowder from the storehouse, stirring a protest from Williamsburg's angry citizenry and fanning the fires that led to the Revolution. After the Revolution, the Magazine housed a market, meetinghouse, dance school, and livery stable. Humble as they seem, these interim uses probably saved the original building from abandonment and destruction.

PEYTON RANDOLPH HOUSE

The Peyton Randolph House at Nicholson and North England Streets is among Williamsburg's oldest and finest 18th-century homes. The west wing of the house has stood at its current location since about 1715, sheltering the likes of General Rochambeau, the Marquis de Lafayette, and its namesake, the first president of the Continental Congress. Sir John Randolph purchased the west wing in 1721. A few years later he bought the adjacent one-and-a-half-story house that later became the structure's east wing. Sir John's son, Peyton, speaker of the Virginia House of Burgesses in the years leading to the Revolution, built a spacious and well-appointed two-story central section that connected the two houses via a hall and magnificent stairway. Today this well-preserved center section contains some of the best surviving paneling in Williamsburg as well as much of the original edge-cut pine flooring. The parlor doors have unusually fine brass hinges and locks.

---

i Guests of Colonial Williamsburg can leave their car keys in their hotel room and tour Duke of Gloucester Street the 18th-century way in one of CW's horse-drawn coaches. The coach and livestock program has been operating these unique tours continuously since 1947. Today, more than 50,000 guests embark on the 15- or 30-minute journey through Colonial Williamsburg annually. Tickets can be purchased at any ticket sales location but make a reservation if this is on your bucket list. Space is limited. All carriage rides begin at the Lumber House Ticket Office on Duke of Gloucester Street.

Colonial Williamsburg began restoring the Peyton Randolph House in late 1939 and finished a few months later. Further restoration was completed in the late '60s. The center and west portions of the house opened for visitors in 1968. In recent years the house once again has been painstakingly restored. All of the work that was done was based on two decades of research and a remarkable room-by-room inventory of the house taken at the time of Peyton Randolph's death in 1775. Many of the outbuildings—including a smokehouse, dairy, storehouse, and 2,000-square-foot kitchen—were reconstructed.

Public Gaol

Behind the Capitol on Nicholson Street is the Public Gaol (pronounced "jail"), with partially original walls and wholly authentic grimness. Shackles that were excavated while the gaol was under restoration are on display. Take a look in the small, dank cells hung with leg irons, and consider spending a winter night in such a place with only a thin blanket for cover. Among the 18th-century inhabitants of these cells were Blackbeard's pirate crew, runaway slaves, Indians, insolvent debtors, and, occasionally, the mentally ill. During the Revolution, British captives, accused spies, and Tory sympathizers were cordially allowed to use the gaol facilities. Part of the gaol has been refurbished to reflect its other function—home to the gaol keeper and his family. Furnishings are representative of those owned by a typical family of the period.

Raleigh Tavern

Revolutionary heroes like Patrick Henry and Thomas Jefferson gathered to discuss politics and reach important conclusions in this famous Duke of Gloucester Street tavern, the first of Colonial Williamsburg's reconstructed buildings to open for public viewing. Built around 1717, the tavern was the axis around which 18th-century Virginia society, business, and politics revolved. George Washington dined here often and mentions the tavern in his diary. The Phi Beta Kappa Society was founded here in 1776. Slaves were sold on its steps. The tavern burned in 1859, but original foundations and drawings aided architects in the 1930s reconstruction. Behind the tavern is the Bake Shop, where visitors line up for Sally Lunn bread, sweet potato muffins, and ginger cake.

The Gardens

The Historic Area's 100 or so gardens have been re-created with meticulous attention paid to the style of Dutch, English, and southern traditions of the 17th and 18th centuries. Archaeological digs conducted on many sites often revealed the remains of walkways, brick walls, and fence lines, which served as blueprints for the gardens and outbuildings eventually erected on each lot.

Most of Colonial Williamsburg's gardens were planted from the 1930s through the 1950s and reflect the Colonial Revival style, which tends to be rather refined and elegant. Ongoing research suggests that this interpretation of ℹ Some people think no visit to Williamsburg is complete without sampling the fare in one of the popular restored taverns. See our Dining chapter for details about the fare at Chowning's, the King's Arms, Christiana Campbell's (where Washington dined), and Shields Tavern.

our nation's colonial gardens may not be accurate; thus Colonial Williamsburg gradually is reworking its gardens in simpler form.

As you stroll through these gardens, you will enjoy a profusion of greens, including English boxwood, hollyhock, and yaupon holly. Seasonal flowers—everything from the wandering phlox to the purple crocus—provide a wash of color that changes with the passing months. Kitchen and vegetable gardens are yet another part of the landscape. While corn, tobacco, wheat, cotton, and flax were grown in the fields, it was the much smaller kitchen gardens that provided the fruits and vegetables used at the table and for preserving.

As part of its regular programming, Colonial Williamsburg offers a guided Garden History Walk through its restored grounds. Check colonialwilliamsburg.org for specific dates.

TRADE SHOPS AND DEMONSTRATIONS

Scattered throughout the Historic Area are costumed craftspeople, journeymen, and apprentices practicing the various old trades that were part of life in the 18th century. At the **Printing Office** on Duke of Gloucester Street, visitors can see newspapers printed on an 18th-century press, learn about bookbinding, and watch periodic demonstrations of typesetting, papermaking, and decorating. At the **James Anderson Blacksmith Shop,** seven reconstructed forges operate, demonstrating smithing techniques. Silversmiths craft mote spoons—decoratively perforated and good for straining tea—at **The Golden Ball,** where you can also buy gold and silver jewelry. The **Margaret Hunter Millinery Shop** re-creates the atmosphere and activity of an 18th-century milliner's shop, with hats, gloves, purses, shoes, and embroidery pieces.

Next door to the **King's Arms Tavern,** a wigmaker uses goat, horse, yak, and human hair to conjure up a few curls. Nearby, coopers shape and assemble staves to form casks, piggins, and other wooden containers. In addition, harness- and saddle-makers, shoemakers, cabinetmakers, brass founders, gunsmiths, wheelwrights, carpenters, cooks, and basketmakers go about their business.

MERCANTILE SHOPS

While some of the historic trade shops sell crafted items, several operating mercantile shops accurately re-create 18th-century business premises, offering wares and services representative of colonial times. Finest among these is

Prentis Store, an original building dating from 1740 that features reproductions of 18th-century wares. **Tarpley, Thompson & Co.** sells pottery, educational toys, and soaps, while the **Greenhow Store's** inventory includes candy, three-cornered hats, and fifes. At the **M. Dubois Grocer's Shop,** you can pick up a bottle of tavern sparkling cider.

Other Buildings and Exhibits

If you have time to explore more restored or reconstructed sites in the Historic Area, here are a few we particularly recommend.

Courthouse

With its cupola, weather vane, and round-headed windows, the Courthouse is visible up and down Duke of Gloucester Street. A series of special programs allows visitors to experience the day-to-day functioning of early American jurisprudence. Costumed interpreters and guides lead visitors through participatory scenes, such as trials and impromptu dialogues. Interesting furnishings include the chief magistrate's throne-like chair and clothbound docket books used by colonial clerks and sheriffs.

Great Hopes Plantation

The original Great Hopes was in York County, Virginia. This re-creation, on the edge of the Historic Area (near the visitor center) is a representation of the "middling" plantations that existed around the colonial capital. Those plantations were the homes of most of the rural middle class, the ones who weren't shop and tavern keepers or tradespeople in town. Only 5 percent of the colonial population was what Patrick Henry would have called "well-born." About a third or more were lower class, or "lesser sort," depending on where you lived. The rest of the people were "middling;" that is, hardworking, honest people

> **i** One of the true pleasures of living near Colonial Williamsburg—or visiting in spring—is meeting each year's new litter of lambs. CW's animals graze within fenced pastures on local streets. When there are newborn lambs (the progeny of Leicester Longwool Sheep) they meet the public in public, and watching them leap and gambol as they learn to move in the world is just pure joy. In spring 2020, CW's ewes gave birth to nearly two dozen lambs, including two sets of triplets and four sets of twins. The historic area also has a herd of working horses, oxen, plenty of goats, chickens, and pigs.

who owned 100 acres or more, and ten or so slaves. Learn here about enslaved African Virginians and their masters, and how they lived and worked on a typical middle-size Virginia farm. The barns are home to many of CW's rare-breed animals, including American Milking Devon cattle, Ossabaw Island pigs, and a variety of chickens and English fowl.

Close-up

Christmas in Colonial Williamsburg

In colonial times feasts and celebrations were the highlights of the Christmas season. Families and neighbors gathered together to celebrate with the best their tables could offer. In the 18th century, the holiday season began on December 24 and culminated with a large celebration on the Twelfth Night, January 6.

These days, the holiday season is still one of the most popular times to visit Colonial Williamsburg. The first Christmas celebration organized for visitors took place in 1936, and the celebrations have gotten even grander in recent decades, adding modern touches to time-honored colonial traditions. It's a perfect time to see the village decked out in colonial holiday decor, take in a holiday concert, and taste some traditional Yuletide dishes.

The Christmas season is officially ushered in on the first Sunday in December with the **Grand Illumination.** Candles and cressets are lit around the Historic Area, and musical and theatrical performances are held in several areas. Finally, three impressive fireworks displays take place over the Governor's Palace, the Powder Magazine, and the Capitol.

And look for concerts of music played on 18th-century or reproduction instruments at the candlelit House of Burgesses or the Governor's Palace. In addition, the Fifes & Drums offer an annual concert of international military music and Christmas tunes.

Be sure to make reservations early, as many hotels and restaurants book up well in advance. For more information, visit colonialwilliamsburg.org, or call (844) 585-1168.

James Geddy House

The James Geddy House, on Duke of Gloucester Street just across the Palace Green from Bruton Parish Church, was home to a family of artisans who worked in bronze, brass, pewter, and silver. Visitors to the house can learn about the life of an 18th-century tradesman and his children by helping out at the foundry or assisting Grandma Geddy (mother of eight) with the laundry.

Thomas Everard House

One of the oldest houses in Williamsburg, the Thomas Everard House on the Palace Green is known for its carved woodwork. The yard is paved with original bricks found during excavation, and the smokehouse and kitchen are original restored structures. One of three buildings included in a $2.5 million renovation project that added air-conditioning and heating, fire detectors, security systems, and computerized humidity and temperature controls, historians had a rare opportunity to explore the structure's innards while the work was going on and readjust their thinking about its history. The Colonial Williamsburg tour focuses on the life of Everard, who arrived from London as an orphaned apprentice and became a wealthy planter and Williamsburg's mayor.

Wetherburn's Tavern

Wetherburn's Tavern, an original building, was carefully refurnished using information gleaned from a detailed inventory left of Henry Wetherburn's estate and from artifacts uncovered during excavation at the site. Tours spotlight the lives of Wetherburn's family and slaves. The house is on Duke of Gloucester Street next to Tarpley, Thompson & Co.

BASSETT HALL, East Francis Street (near Lafayette Street), Williamsburg, VA 23185; (888) 965-7254. A tour of Bassett Hall, the two-story, 18th-century

> **i** If you need bricks to repair an 18th-century structure you can't just dash over to the Home Depot. You have to make your own. So every November, CW's brickmasons make thousands of bricks the old-fashioned way, firing them in a kiln constructed at the intersection of Nicholson and Queen Streets. The bricks were formed from tons of wet clay shaped and dried in the sun during the summer (often with help from CW visitors who "volunteer" to help). The bricks are cooked the week before Thanksgiving, at temperatures reaching up to about 2,000 degrees Fahrenheit.

More Art Than Ever

For decades, the way a visitor entered Colonial Williamsburg's world-class museums—the **Abby Aldrich Rockefeller Folk Art Museum** and the **DeWitt Wallace Decorative Arts Museum**—was by walking through the **Public Hospital** and descending to the basement. As entrances go, this one was the opposite of grand.

Now that's changed with a $42 million renovation of the entire space that has added an elegant new above-ground entrance, 65,000 square feet of new exhibition space, large windows that bathe the lobby in natural light, bigger work spaces for the staff, dressing rooms for the Henmage Auditorium, a new cafe, and retail space.

Private donors picked up the bill for the improvements.

Horse-drawn carriages and women in mob caps might be the most familiar images of CW but the real impact of the investment made by CW is its educational programs and in the vast collections preserved, exhibited, and interpreted by the people who work at these museums. The archaeological holdings alone number 60 million pieces. Even with the additional new space, there isn't room to have permanent displays of all of the more than 67,000 period antiques and 7,000 pieces of folk art the museums own.

The Abby Aldrich is the oldest institution in the US dedicated solely to the preservation of American folk art, housing the nation's premier collection from the 18th, 19th, and 20th centuries. Exhibits feature paintings, drawings, furniture, ceramics, whirligigs, weather vanes, carvings, toys, quilts, musical instruments, and other folk works representing many diverse cultural

frame house that was the Williamsburg home of John D. Rockefeller, Jr. and his wife, Abby Aldrich Rockefeller, tops most people's lists of the best thing to see while in Colonial Williamsburg. Visitors learn about the Rockefellers themselves and about their contribution to the restoration of Colonial Williamsburg. Bequeathed to the foundation in 1979, the house is set on a 585-acre tract of woodlands, and the property includes a teahouse, called the Orangerie, and three original outbuildings: a smokehouse, kitchen, and dairy. Bassett Hall reopened in 2002 after undergoing renovations that include a new exhibition of the history of the Rockefellers at Bassett Hall and a return of the extensive gardens to their 1940s appearance. The house is open to tours only three days a week (usually Wed, Thurs, and Sat).

traditions and geographic regions. John D. Rockefeller, Jr. established the museum in 1957 in honor of his wife, Abby, who began collecting folk art early in the 20th century. In 1939, she gave her core collection of 425 objects to the Colonial Williamsburg Foundation. Today the collection of more than 7,000 objects includes items dating from the 1720s including "Portrait of an Enslaved Child," an 1830 watercolor with pencil and ink by Mary Anna Randolph Custis, "Music and Dance in Beaufort County," an 18th-century watercolor of an al fresco scene showing two groups of African American interacting in South Carolina, and a 19th-century Noah's Ark toy set, part of the exhibition of "German Toys in America."

The **DeWitt Wallace** is devoted to British and American decorative arts from 1670 through 1840. It is home to the world's largest collection of Southern furniture and one of the largest collections of British ceramics outside England. Charles Willson Peale's iconic "Washington at Princeton," is on display as are portraits of Thomas Jefferson and James Madison, whose painting by Gilbert Stuart was rescued by Dolley Madison before British forces set fire to the White House during the War of 1812. Among the finest pieces are a full-length portrait of King George III, painted by English artist Allan Ramsay and a burled-walnut and gilt Tompion clock, which is among a handful of the most important pieces of English furniture in the US.

It would be easy to spend the better part of a day (or days) here (but children might not be so engaged), browsing through each museum's vast collections. Fortunately, the new cafe has a full kitchen serving lunch, tea, and light refreshments. A gift shop selling reproductions and decorative arts journals is also on the premises. Both museums are located at 301 S. Nassau St., Williamsburg, VA 23185; (757) 220-7724, (844) 585-1168. Admission is included with your Colonial Williamsburg ticket. Entering the cafe and museum store does not require a ticket. Open daily 10 a.m. to 7 p.m.

PUBLIC HOSPITAL OF 1773, 326 W. Francis St., Williamsburg, VA 23185; (844) 585-1168. It's only slightly macabre to suggest that, while on vacation, you visit this reconstruction of the first public institution for the mentally ill to be built in colonial America. Originally opened in 1773 and known as the Hospital for Lunaticks, this facility treated its inmates more like prisoners than patients, as the early, small cells indicate. Nineteenth-century scientific and medical advances improved treatment, which the hospital's interpretive exhibits chronicle, but on display are a number of devices used on patients, some of which resemble implements of torture. Open daily from 10 a.m. to 7 p.m.

Family Programs

Most family programs are offered beginning in mid-June and continue through Labor Day. Because activities vary not only from day to day but also from hour to hour, check colonialwilliamsburg.org for specific times and locations.

In general, programs allow kids to help craftsmen (or craftswomen) make bricks, cook, fashion a wheel, or watch as pewter or iron is forged or a horseshoe is applied to a hoof.

Many homes include a demonstration of 18th-century games; you'll often see kids trying to roll the hoop on the Palace Green. The historic area is also home to an incredible variety of animals: cattle, sheep, horses, hogs, pigs, and chickens. A particular joy comes each spring when you can hang on a fence post and watch the baby lambs make their first wobbly frolic through the grass.

Children can sign up to serve in the Continental Army and learn about life in a military encampment.

But perhaps the best experience for school-age children is the street theater, which brings the past they've been reading about in their textbooks to vivid, sometimes wrenching, life. Few will forget the experience of horror of watching a husband and wife sold to separate masters at a slave auction, or not feel a tingle along their spine hearing Patrick Henry insist he be given liberty or death.

Evening Events

Evening performances require a separate ticket (prices range from $15 to $20 for adults; about half that for children, and less for annual pass holders). Check the calendar at colonialwilliamsburg.org for specific dates, times, and locations during the week you are visiting. As we noted earlier, programming changes frequently, so selections may be different during the time you are in town. The programs include music, dancing, ghost tours, and theater. One of the most popular programs is **"Cry Witch,"** a re-creation of an early 18th-century witch trial (not suitable for young children). Audience members may question the witnesses, weigh the evidence, and determine the guilt or innocence of the "Virginia witch," Grace Sherwood, who was tried for witchcraft in 1706. Also popular is the long-running **"Grand Medley of Entertainments,"** an 18th-century "variety show," perhaps the forerunner of modern circuses and vaudeville, that includes music, magic, feats of strength, and other amusements. You can bring the kids to this one.

Other Programs and Events

The Colonial Williamsburg Fifes & Drums

Beating drums or trilling fifes, this colorful group makes regular marches down Duke of Gloucester Street throughout much of the year. On various dates, visitors can enjoy the 18th-century ceremony of reveille in the morning at Market Square Green. In the early evening the corps does its retreat, a time when pickets are posted, flags lowered, and the soldiers relieved of their daily duties.

Colonial Williamsburg Fife & Drums
David M. Doody/The Colonial Williamsburg Foundation

All told, the corps performs in and around Colonial Williamsburg nearly 500 times during the year, in daily programs from Apr through Oct and during special programs on major holidays. In the spring and summer, the corps usually marches at 5 p.m. on Wed and 1 p.m. on Sat, weather permitting.

Founded in 1958, the corps traditionally has been made up of boys ages 10 through 18. Girls were admitted for the first time in 1999. Typically, applicants to the program are placed on a waiting list around age 5 and must participate in the required training before they can become active members. Nearly 100 youths perform as members of the corps' two units: a junior corps and a senior corps. Over the years the corps has served as Colonial Williamsburg's musical ambassadors across the nation, performing at Macy's Thanksgiving Day Parade in New York, the Pentagon in Washington, D.C., Independence Hall in Philadelphia, and the Art Institute of Chicago.

For specific Colonial Williamsburg Fifes & Drums performance times during your visit, consult the online calendar at colonialwilliamsburg.org.

Other History Attractions

Churches

THE FIRST BAPTIST CHURCH, 727 W. Scotland St., Williamsburg, VA 23185; (757) 229-1952; firstbaptistchurch1776.org. One of the earliest Baptist congregations in the country (slogan: "Saving Souls in Williamsburg since 1776"), it is also one of the first African American churches in America. Blacks had been allowed to worship in Bruton Parish Church, where they were seated in the North Gallery. Because they were not included in the worship service, they left the parish and worshipped at a site near **Greensprings Plantation** west of town, sometimes in secret. This site was remote from the city, so they moved again, closer to Williamsburg. Finally, a sympathetic resident made his carriage house available to Blacks in the city. The group that met there organized in 1776 as the First Baptist Church.

For more than a century, the congregation worshipped in a brick church building built on South Nassau Street, believed to be long gone. During the four-year renovation of the nearby art museums, ground-penetrating radar indicated the remains of that early church might be found deep beneath an existing parking lot. Archaeologists from Colonial Williamsburg and the Jamestown Rediscovery Foundation, under the guidance of the church, began a full-scale excavation of the site, with help from students at the College of William & Mary. There is evidence of a late 18th- or early 19th-century structure buried beneath later buildings erected on the site. There may also be burial sites which both the church and CW want to protect.

In 1956, the congregation moved into its present home. In the lower level of this church is a fascinating display tracing the history of this important congregation; furnishings of the earlier church are used in various parts of the current edifice. Closed until further notice due to COVID-19 restrictions; they are streaming the Sunday morning service.

HICKORY NECK EPISCOPAL CHURCH, 8300 Richmond Rd., Toano, VA 23168; (757) 566-0276; hickoryneck.org. The Virginia landscape is dotted with small brick churches dating from the colonial period, many associated with plantations, others with small communities that vanished in the ensuing years. One worship site of historic interest is Hickory Neck Church on the west side of Toano. The edifice was built about 1740 and is still in use by an active Episcopal parish. On April 21, 1781, it housed militia opposing the British army. Later that year the militiamen fought in the siege of Yorktown. Standing with your back to busy US 60, it is still possible here to glimpse a vista without 21st-century encroachments. If you're interested in attending worship services, they are held at 8, 9, and 11:15 a.m. on Sun (8 a.m. and 10 a.m. during the summer months). The church is temporarily closed due to COVID-19 restrictions, but they are streaming Sunday services.

i On Easter Sunday a consortium of religious leaders representing various faiths leads a "sunrise service," usually beginning at 7 a.m., at the historic cross on Jamestown Island. Check the religion pages of the *Virginia Gazette* to get specifics each Easter.

HISTORIC JAMESTOWNE, 1368 Colonial Pkwy., Williamsburg, VA 23185; (757) 229-4997; nps.gov/jame/index.htm. In the beginning, all America was Virginia, wrote William Byrd in 1732, and this scruffy island on the banks of the James is where Virginia, named for Queen Elizabeth I, the so-called Virgin Queen, began.

Programs offered here are coadministered by the National Park Service, which bought 1,500 acres of the island in 1934, and Preservation Virginia, whose leaders first saw the need to ensure this spot be maintained. They bought, and continue to hold, 22.5 acres of the island in 1893. A new visitor center opened in 2007, a little farther inland than the old one, which offers an interpretive introduction to the island. There is an extensive collection of 17th-century Jamestown artifacts on display and an 18-minute orientation film. Here is where you pay your admission fee, hook up with one of the rangers leading a tour, or pick up a self-guiding leaflet if you prefer to go at your own pace.

Once outside, be sure to check out the interactive "virtual viewer," a panoramic camera that superimposes images onto the existing, vacant land to show visitors where buildings stood, where objects were recovered, and what the fort looked like 400 years ago. With the press of a button, monitors then show short films re-creating pivotal events from Jamestown history that occurred at these sites, like the burning of Swann's Tavern during the Bacon Rebellion, or the 1635 meeting of the Virginia Assembly at which Governor John Harvey was arrested for treason. Way cool.

Begin your tour of the grounds at the Tercentenary Monument, a 103-foot shaft of New Hampshire granite that was erected in 1907 to mark the 300th anniversary of Jamestown's founding. River tides have washed away part of the early town site, but you can explore the 1639 Church Tower, the sole 17th-century structure still standing, and view ruins of the original settlement made visible by archaeological exploration. These include foundations of some of the early statehouses and ruins of the original glass furnaces built in 1608. Near the Church Tower along the James River waterfront is the Jamestown Rediscovery archaeological excavation site, where you can watch researchers sift through the remains of the James Fort, once believed lost forever, and talk to interpreters about the latest dig finds. Excavation on the site began in 1994 after archaeologist William Kelso led the team that discovered that the fort was not lost under the James River, as was formerly believed. It is estimated that about 85 percent of the fort still exists on land. Of that, about 20 percent has been uncovered so far.

You'll also see statues of John Smith and Pocahontas as well as the Dale House, which sits near the seawall, just beyond the Confederate earthwork. The Dale House serves as a snack bar, now that its former tenants—the archaeologists—have moved into a beautiful building of their own, called the

ATTRACTIONS

Archearium. Sit on the patio if the weather's nice: The Dale House offers a gorgeous view of the James River for miles in either direction.

Next, pause at the Memorial Cross, which marks some 300 shallow graves that were dug by the settlers during the so-called starving time, the dismal winter of 1609–1610. Walk to the other side of the visitor center and you will find the New Towne Site, which contains reproductions of ruins built over original foundations, including those of the Ambler Mansion, a two-story home built in the mid-1700s. Also in New Towne is the Manufacturing Site, where a number of commercial endeavors—including brickmaking, pottery making, and brewing—occurred in the mid-1600s.

New in 2015 is the Ed Shed, which houses fun family activities and is where to get the newest version of the Jamestown Adventure game booklet for kids. Previous versions have explored the world of Pocahontas and sent kids on a hunt for a Spanish spy. Youngsters will also be able to act like an archaeologist by sifting through millions of potential finds at a Sorting N' Picking station.

After you've toured the town site, take one of the loop drives around **Jamestown Island.** These 3- and 5-mile self-guided automobile tours through a wilderness of pine and swamp will bring you close to the vision early colonists must have beheld when they set foot in America—a natural environment at once beautiful and frightening. Herds of deer still roam the forested ridges of the island, sometimes coming close to the ruins under cover of dusk. Muskrats hide in the Jamestown marshes; you might glimpse one paddling leisurely through the swamp. A profusion of waterfowl, including ospreys, herons, and mallards, make seasonal stops. Roll down your windows, listen to the music of songbirds, feel the stillness all around you. If time permits, pull over to read the markers inscribed with interesting historical and botanical data.

Save time to visit the reconstructed **Glasshouse,** which is actually located on the mainland, across the bridge that brings you to the island, but included in your park admission fee. Costumed craftspeople demonstrate 400-year-old techniques, making glassware much like that created and used by settlers. While hardwoods such as hickory and oak fueled the kilns in 1608, today natural gas heats the fiery furnace. The products, which register a red-hot 2,000 degrees Fahrenheit when first pulled from the heat, are lovely. Clear and green goblets, bell jars, flasks, wineglasses, pitchers, and the like can be purchased here. A display case also shows off some of the glassblowers' after-hours work—the vases and such they make to perfect their skills after the tourists have gone home.

You may want to return to the visitor center for souvenirs before leaving. Reproductions of colonial stoneware, glassware made at the Glasshouse, and a vast selection of books, videotapes, toys, games, and other keepsakes are for sale.

Admission to Jamestown Island is $20 per adult, age 16 or older, and covers reentry for up to a week, as well as entry to the Yorktown Battlefield. Children 15 and younger are admitted free. Interagency Annual, Senior, and

> ### Did You Remember to Send a Card?
> On a spring day more than 400 years ago, one of history's most unlikely couples were wed in a small chapel on the banks of the James River at what is now called Historic Jamestowne. Despite the Romeo and Juliet nature of their families' histories, the bride's father ultimately gave his blessing; the groom's big request was that his wife be baptized before she took her vows. The interior of the church was lit by opening the building's broad windows; local flowers served as decoration. The bride's brothers sat on cedar pews alongside then-governor Thomas Dale who hoped (futilely) that the marriage would be "another knot to bind this peace stronger." This was the wedding of Pocahontas and John Rolfe, in April 1614. The state's longtime advertising slogan—Virginia is for lovers—has been true for centuries, it seems.
>
> Though the church where the Rolfes married no longer exists, archaeologists recently unearthed its deeply buried foundational posts, allowing them to pinpoint its precise location inside James Fort and even state its modest dimensions: 64 feet long by 24 feet wide.

Access passes are accepted. Educational groups are admitted free of charge with advance notice and a written fee waiver. Open daily at 8:30 a.m. and closes at 4:30 p.m. except Thanksgiving and Christmas. Parking is free.

Interpretive Programs

To truly get a feel for the place and the era, children may participate in a number of special programs. These include the Pinch Pot program during the summer months, in which children can make their own pot out of clay, and the Colonial Junior Ranger programs, in which children 12 and younger can learn about Jamestown while enjoying a series of activities with a chance to earn a patch. Most programs are either free with admission or have a small materials cost per child.

JAMESTOWN SETTLEMENT, 2110 Jamestown Rd., Williamsburg, VA 23185; (757) 253-4838; jyfmuseums.org. Opened in 1957, 350 years after the founding of America's first permanent English colony, Jamestown Settlement, a museum of 17th-century Virginia history and culture, underwent major renovations in 2006, in time for its 400th anniversary—the quadricentennial. New museum galleries doubled the size of the exhibition space, added classrooms, and expanded the cafe, with indoor and outdoor seating for 300. Combined with the outdoor living-history exhibits, the programs offered here re-create both the early colonists and the Virginia Indians habitats and customs in a lively manner without sacrificing historical authenticity. Museum-goers can board replicas of the ships that brought the English settlers to the New World in 1607, which are docked along the James River; grind corn; play quoits; and watch as tools are made and muskets are fired. If you are traveling with kids, especially young children, and have time to visit just one of the two Jamestown sites, the settlement is likelier to offer a richer experience for all.

Tickets are available in the high-ceiled lobby. Start your visit by watching an introductory film, *1607: A Nation Takes Root*, shown every 30 minutes, which presents a dramatic overview of the first decades of the British colonial experience in the Virginia colony. After the film, make your way through the expansive galleries, where exhibits use artifacts, maps, and full-scale dioramas to illustrate a chronological journey of life in Virginia from 1600 to 1699, with a special emphasis on the native Powhatans and the Africans who first began arriving here when tobacco cultivation became the dominant economic enterprise.

A short walk from the galleries, the outdoor exhibits offer a hands-on way of learning about American history. Costumed interpreters reenact the quotidian details of life in colonial Virginia. Here is a museum where visitors are actually *encouraged* to touch and use the items on display—climb into a dugout canoe, play ninepins, lie down in a bunk aboard the *Susan Constant*.

At the Powhatan Village, visit the Virginia Indian houses made of sapling frames covered with reed mats. These dwellings are re-creations based on archaeological findings and eyewitness drawings made by a New World explorer. Walk around the ceremonial circle made up of seven carved wooden poles. Historical interpreters dressed as Powhatans make tools from bone or smoke fish over a fire and cook it on a baking stone. Children can play cob darts, a game of pitching dried corn ears through a hanging vine hoop.

Three Ships

Follow the path down from the village to the pier, where full-size replica ships of the *Susan Constant*, *Godspeed*, and *Discovery* are docked. The *Susan Constant* replica, built at the settlement from 1989 to 1991, is brightly painted and fully rigged. Go on board the 116-foot-long ship and imagine calling it home for nearly five months with 70 other men and boys. You can climb down to the 'tween deck, where passengers were quartered, for an idea of just how cramped conditions were. (And remember during the voyage from England, the 'tween deck probably was loaded with cargo waist high.)

Take note that the *Susan Constant*, *Godspeed*, and *Discovery* are functional ships, which occasionally sail from Jamestown Settlement to participate in a maritime event or take part in an educational demonstration. (Visitors always have access to at least one of the ships.) Costumed crew members describe life at sea, unfurling sails, dropping anchor, posting colors, and letting eager visitors try their hand at steering or nautical knot tying. Children learn the role of 17th-century ship's boys and may be asked to ring the ship's bell or read directions on the compass. Other demonstrations may include raising sails or operating a pulley (to show how simple machines work). A 20-by-50-foot pier shelter near the three ships is designed to resemble a waterfront building and is used for demonstrations, such as piloting and navigation.

James Fort

When you're ready to stand on solid ground again, debark and head up to re-created James Fort. Enter these stockade walls, and you'll experience the rough-and-ready life of the settlers from 1610 to 1614—thatched roof, wattle-and-daub houses with rudimentary furnishings, the smell of wood smoke, the ceaseless worry and toil of survival. Inspect a cannon, try on armor, help a colonist tend the garden. Children might be interested in learning to fetch water the old-fashioned way—with a pole draped over their shoulders and heavy buckets attached to either end. Historical interpreters may be engaged in early Virginia industries, manufacturing lumber, blacksmithing, or doing chores such as daubing a house or preparing food.

In addition to regular exhibits and activities, Jamestown Settlement sponsors a number of special programs throughout the year. These include Jamestown Day in May, a November Foods & Feasts presentation that demonstrates how the early colonists prepared and preserved food, and "A Colonial Christmas" in December.

Cafe and Gift Shop

The cafe is open from 9 a.m. to 5 p.m. and serves a variety of sandwiches, salads, and snacks. The gift shop carries everything from reproductions of 17th-century glassware and pottery to a variety of souvenirs, books, toys, and jewelry.

Jamestown Settlement is open from 9 a.m. to 5 p.m. daily. It is closed Christmas and New Year's Day. Ask about the guided tours that are offered throughout the day. It's best to visit when skies are clear, but even on a rainy day, the film and the museum's expansive exhibits are worth seeing. In the summer, river breezes help make all but the hottest of days tolerable. Allow at least 3 hours for a thorough exploration.

Admission to Jamestown Settlement is $18 for adults; $9 for children ages 6 to 12, and free to children under 6. A combination ticket for both the settlement and the American Revolution Museum (formerly Yorktown Victory Center) costs $28.90 for adults and $14.45 for children ages 6 to 12. Residents of York and James City Counties and Williamsburg are admitted free.

PLANTATIONS

While Virginia's Historic Triangle offers visitors plenty to see and do, it also provides easy access to myriad attractions just a short drive outside the immediate Williamsburg area. Of particular interest to history and architecture buffs are the historic **James River Plantations** in James City and Charles City Counties.

How many neighborhoods in America can claim to be the homeplace of not one but two US presidents? Both William Henry Harrison (9th) and John Tyler (10th) grew up in this riverfront community. Descendants of both men remain in the area. In fact, though Tyler died in 1862, one of his grandsons, Lyon Gardiner Tyler, only passed away in 2020 at age 95. (John Tyler's own father, also named John Tyler, was college roommates at William & Mary with Thomas Jefferson! Lyon Tyler's father, also named Lyon Tyler was president of the school. If this fascinates you, do read the entry below on Sherwood Forest Plantation.)

For those whose idea of Southern architecture has been shaped by *Gone with the Wind*, the estates these men called home may surprise you. Predating the era of Greek Revival columns and other such adornments, the refined Georgian architecture of the buildings, executed in rich redbrick or in white wood, is understated and takes its elegance from simplicity and tasteful detail. These were among the first mansions in the country, and their history is, in a sense, ours. These magnificent estates are located along the James River because that was the area's main artery when they were built. Luckily, many are open to the public. In cases where the houses are not open, visitors usually are welcome to tour the grounds. The trip on VA 5 from Williamsburg to Richmond to visit the plantations is gorgeous, passing through thick, overarching forests, wide open farmlands, and over at least one very narrow bridge. It was colonial Virginia's premier land route and remains a favorite route west, especially in autumn, and especially these days by cyclists using the Virginia Capital Trail, a bike path that links Virginia's colonial capitals—Jamestown and Williamsburg—with its current seat of government, Richmond.

BERKELEY PLANTATION, 12602 Harrison Landing Rd., Charles City, VA 23030; (804) 829-6018, (888) 466-6018; berkeleyplantation.com. This was the site of the first official Thanksgiving in North America, celebrated by English settlers on December 4, 1619. Located just off VA 5, halfway between Williamsburg and Richmond, Berkeley was the birthplace of Benjamin Harrison, a signer of the Declaration of Independence, and his third son, William

---

i Jamestown is not only a drawing card for history buffs. Best-selling mystery writer Patricia Cornwell visited in the summer of 1999 to gather material for a novel. *The Last Precinct* was published in October 2000 and picked up where the heroine, Dr. Kay Scarpetta, left off in *Black Notice*. Cornwell also has donated $50,000 from the proceeds of the novel *Black Notice* to the Jamestown Rediscovery project.

See It Like a Native

Want to see Jamestown the way the first settlers did? Jamestown Discovery, a 90-minute boat tour, churns the same watery path that three ships of Virginia Company of London did when British colonists first sailed into the area, dubbing both the river and their 1607 landing spot in honor of their king. "I take them up the James River and all around Jamestown Island so they can see it just the way Captain John Smith did," said Corey Fenton, the Williamsburg native and waterman who operates the cruises. "Most people ride around here on little carts so they get to see everything, but it's a whole different feel to see the area from a boat. It's really neat." Boats launch out of Eco Discovery Park, which is located just off the Colonial Parkway, between Jamestown Settlement and the national park site. Call Jamestown Discovery for hours of operation: (757) 253-TOUR (8687).

Henry Harrison, the ninth president of the US. The plantation was established in 1618, and the stately Georgian mansion, overlooking the James River, was built in 1726 of brick fired on the site. It is said to be the oldest three-story brick house in Virginia and the first with a pediment roof. The handsome Adam woodwork and double arches in the Great Rooms were installed by Benjamin Harrison VI in 1790 at the direction of Thomas Jefferson. The rooms in the house are furnished with period antiques. As you approach the site, watch for the sharp curve onto a side road that leads to the plantation drive.

Two tidbits of Berkeley history deserve particular attention. "Taps" was composed here by US General Daniel Butterfield in 1862 during the Civil War while Union troops were encamped on the site. And the first bourbon whiskey in America was distilled here in 1621.

Allow about 90 minutes for your visit. The plantation is open daily from 9:30 a.m. to 4:30 p.m. (Last tour begins at 4 p.m.) Hours are shortened in winter, and the house is closed Thanksgiving and Christmas Day. Tickets cost $15 for adults, $7 for children. Discounted tickets are offered for senior citizens, military, and AAA members.

EDGEWOOD PLANTATION, 4800 John Tyler Hwy. (VA 5), Charles City County, VA 23030; (804) 829-2962; edgewoodplantation.com. This Gothic Revival house (ca. 1849), reputed to have a ghost in residence, operates as an opulent bed and breakfast inn (see our listing in Accommodations). Advance reservations are needed for tours, which are scheduled based on demand. Luncheon and candlelight tours are the most popular. Check the website for details.

NORTH BEND PLANTATION, 12200 Weyanoke Rd., Charles City County, VA 23030; (804) 829-5176; northbendplantation.com. The original plantation house was built in 1819 for Sarah Harrison, the wife of wealthy landowner John Minge and a sister to US president William Henry Harrison. In 1853, the house was doubled in size, and a total renovation was completed in 1982 by the Copland family, descendants of noted agriculturist Edmund Ruffin and current owners of the house. Even after all the changes, North Bend's main house survives as the best-preserved example of the academic Greek Revival style of architecture in Charles City County. Of special historic note is the plantation's 1864 occupancy by General Phillip Sheridan and his 30,000 Union troops.

Today, the plantation operates as a bed and breakfast (see our listing in Accommodations). Day and evening tours for groups of 10 or more are offered by appointment. If you just happen to be in the neighborhood, the 500-acre grounds are open daily from 9 a.m. to 5 p.m. for a self-guided tour. To begin your tour, pick up a brochure at the kiosk on the grounds. Points of interest include the smokehouse and dairy house, both built around 1819, slave quarters, and the site of the 1853 cookhouse. The tour ends just outside the house, where tables and chairs have been set up to give visitors an opportunity to sit a while and take in the view.

PINEY GROVE AT SOUTHALL'S PLANTATION, 16920 Southall Plantation Ln., Charles City County, VA 23030; (804) 829-2480; pineygrove .com. Piney Grove was built ca. 1790 on the 300-acre Southall's Plantation, a property first occupied by the Chickahominy Indians, and the oldest and best-preserved example of log architecture in southeastern Virginia. In recent years, the house has operated as a beautifully appointed bed and breakfast inn. (See our listing in Accommodations.) The grounds are open for a self-guided tour, which takes visitors along a splendid nature trail that begins beneath a century-old cedar, meanders around a swimming hole and past a gazebo, and then winds along the edge of a ravine where the trail is canopied by beech, hickory, and white oak trees. A short path leads down into the ravine to Piney Springs, where constantly flowing water eventually funnels into the Chickahominy River. Past the ravine, the trail skirts a horse corral and pasture, offering a scenic view of Piney Grove, as well as a view of Moss Side Barn, once part of Southall's Plantation. Grounds are open daily, 9 a.m. to 5 p.m. Admission is $3. Guided tours are offered for groups only, with advance reservation.

SHERWOOD FOREST PLANTATION, 14501 John Tyler Hwy. (VA 5), Charles City County, VA 23030; (804) 829-5377; sherwoodforest.org. One of the loveliest homesteads in this part of Virginia belonged to US president John Tyler. Built about 1730, the original structure was altered and renovated by President Tyler in 1844. The house today looks very much like it did when

Tyler retired here from the White House in 1845. He brought with him his new bride, Julia Gardiner of Gardiner's Island, New York. Since then, the plantation has been continuously occupied by members of the Tyler family and has been a working plantation for more than 240 years. John Tyler's last living grandson, Harrison Ruffin Tyler, is the current owner.

The house features a private ballroom 68 feet in length and is furnished with an extensive collection of 18th- and 19th-century family heirlooms. President Tyler's china, porcelain, silver, mirrors, tables, chairs, and other furnishings are still in use here. In the library are the books of Governor Tyler (President Tyler's father), John Tyler, and his son, Dr. Lyon Gardiner Tyler, who served as president of the College of William & Mary.

A self-guided grounds tour costs $10; guests under age 15 are admitted free. The grounds are open daily, except Thanksgiving and Christmas Day, from 9 a.m. to 5 p.m. House tours, which cost $35 for adults and $25 for those under age 18, are by reservation only and should be made at least a week in advance by calling the number listed above or by emailing info@sherwood forest.org, and leaving your name, the date and time of the call, phone number, date of tour request, and number in the party. Reservations are contingent on the availability of the house. Parties of 10 or more may request a guided plantation tour or house tour using the same number or email address.

SHIRLEY PLANTATION, 501 Shirley Plantation Rd., Charles City County, VA 23030; (804) 829-5121; shirleyplantation.com. Perhaps the most famous of Virginia's plantations, this estate on the banks of the James is a National Historic Landmark. Shirley was founded in 1613 and granted to Edward Hill in 1660. Construction of the present mansion house began in 1723 by the third

---

The Progressive Plantation Tour

One way to try to get a good feel for all of Charles City County's historic estates is to sign up for the James River Plantation Progressive Tour, offered through Piney Grove at Southall's Plantation. This two-hour experience is offered on select Saturdays. (Groups of ten or more can make arrangements for the tour on weekdays.)

The tour includes interior visits to Piney Grove, Ashland, and Ladysmith, as well as grounds visits to Duck Church, Dower Quarter, the Lanexa Farm Stand, and the Harwood Family Cemetery. Visitors will learn about the history and architecture of each building as well as the history of James River Plantation country. On October weekends the tour switches gears to focus the ghostly legends of the area. Register for either tour at pineygrove.com. Expect to pay $20 per person.

Close-up

Country Fun

Though Williamsburg prides itself on a sophistication you wouldn't normally find in a city of approximately 8,000 year-round residents, one need not travel very far to feel completely removed from city life. Two popular examples are **Fox Wire Farm,** which opens its barns for the public to meet its adorable herd of alpacas. The alpaca tours leave from the farm's retail store at 8105 Richmond Rd. in Toano, a rural area about 20 minutes west of Williamsburg. The store sells yarn, clothing, and even alpacas, if you are in the market for one. Book online at foxwirefarmalpacas.com. School groups are welcome. One very popular annual event is the annual shearing, which takes place in April.

A little closer to town is **Sweethaven Lavender,** 2301 Jolly Pond Rd., a 134-acre farm on the outskirts of Williamsburg. This farm has animals, too, but the main attraction is seven acres of pick-your-own lavender. Farm owner Kerry Messer and her coworkers mix their crop into lip balms, soaps, skincare, and artisan gifts sold at their on-site farm shop and online. The best time to visit is spring and early summer when the lavender is in full bloom. Lavender Festival Days are held at the harvest's peak season, usually over successive weekends in May and June. Reservations can be made online at sweethaven lavender.com. You can also order a box lunch if you want to spend the whole day in an exceptionally fragrant countryside setting.

Edward Hill, a member of the colonial House of Burgesses, for his daughter Elizabeth. It was finished in 1738 and is largely in its original state.

The house is a recognized architectural treasure. Its famous walnut-railed staircase rises three stories without a visible means of support and is the only one of its kind in America. The mansion is filled with portraits, crested silver, and other family heirlooms. George Washington, Thomas Jefferson, John Tyler, Teddy Roosevelt, and John Rockefeller have all been guests at Shirley. Robert E. Lee's mother, Anne Hill Carter, was married to "Light Horse" Harry Lee in the parlor.

The grounds open at 10 a.m. Tues through Sat and the last self-guided tour begins at 4 p.m. (Closed Sun and Mon, Thanksgiving, and Christmas.) The grounds remain open until 5 p.m. Admission is $11 for adults, $7.50 for ages 6 to 18. Seniors, military, and AAA members are offered discounts. Children younger than 6 are admitted free. Guided house tours are available in a modified form to comply with safety concerns related to the pandemic. Check the website for details.

YORKTOWN

As at Jamestown, the history of Yorktown is neatly captured in the complementary approaches of the federal government's National Park Service battlefield site and the American Revolution Museum, operated by the state-chartered Jamestown-Yorktown Foundation.

The Park Service facilities focus on preservation; the foundation focuses on interpretation through historic re-creations.

ALLIANCE TALL SHIP SAILING, Riverwalk Landing Dock, Yorktown, VA 23690; (888) 316-6422; sailyorktown.com. These schooners offer 2-hour cruises on the York River that let you see the area as Cornwallis did as he fled the battlefield for Gloucester. Passengers are encouraged to help raise the sails, meander the decks, or just relax and enjoy snacks and beverages. "Capt. Mayhem's School of Piracy" is geared toward kids ($27 for children 12 and under). Morning, afternoon, and sunset cruises for adults ($39) focus on sightseeing. The ships operate daily Apr through Nov. Purchase tickets online or by calling the number listed above.

THE AMERICAN REVOLUTION MUSEUM AT YORKTOWN (formerly Yorktown Victory Center), 200 Water St., Yorktown, VA 23690; (757) 253-4838, jyfmuseums.org. If the national park is a place to imagine the horrors of war through the stillness of the battlefield, the rechristened American Revolution Museum is the place to experience what life was like for colonists and members of George Washington's army through film, artfully curated exhibitions, and a re-creation of Yorktown during the Revolutionary War period.

It's also the newest thing in a town whose claim to fame is its very old stuff. An 80,000-square-foot museum building opened in 2015, part of a $50 million overhaul that began in 2012 and was completed in 2017.

Visitors are welcomed in an expansive two-story entrance lobby, with access to a museum gift shop, a cafe, and an introductory video about the new center. In 2016, a new film about Yorktown premiered in the 170-seat museum theater.

Next to the theater is a 5,000-square-foot space for future special exhibitions. A timeline corridor leading to the museum's outdoor living-history areas includes 22,000 square feet of permanent exhibit space. The corridor provides a visual journey tracing the evolution of America from the 13 British colonies in the 1750s to westward expansion of the new country in the 1790s. A short video at the end of the corridor introduces visitors to the museum's outdoor re-creation of a Continental Army encampment and Revolution-era farm.

Yorktown reenactor
Courtesy of Visit Williamsburg

The Revolutionary War encampment offers a glimpse into life in Washington's army. You'll learn how many soldiers shared a tent (too many), peek into a field hospital for a look at colonial-era medicine (and learn why if wounds didn't kill you, disease or the "medicine" might). You'll see colonial-era laptops (yep, they called 'em that) to understand why the quartermaster had the hardest job. Less frightening—but no less revealing—is the colonial-era farm.

Costumed historical interpreters will proudly show off the farmhouse, home of a rising middle-class family; you can tell so because of its sheer size (one room, almost 200 square feet, plus an upstairs sleeping loft for the children), and because it has a separate kitchen/smokehouse to keep the open cooking fire away from the living quarters. (Only the poor would think to cook and sleep in the same place!) On any given day, an interpreter may be making pork loin with potatoes and carrots from the garden, carrot pudding ("When the carrots are ripe, we think of every possible thing you can make with them," said one cook), or gingerbread, all in dutch ovens placed over a fire.

At other outbuildings, you'll learn how to break flax to make linen, and how tobacco—the king of the postrevolutionary economy—wasn't just a cash crop; it was *cash*. Watch out for the chickens. Just as in the colonial era, they walk around freely.

A section of the new museum building serves student groups, with a separate entrance for group check-in and classrooms to support the curriculum-based educational programming that is offered.

In addition, the new building houses a library, historical clothing workshop, and special-event space on the second floor that offers a panoramic view of the York River.

Open daily 9 a.m. to 5 p.m. Admission is $16 for adults, $8 for children ages 6 to 12. A combination ticket with Jamestown Settlement is $28.90 for adults, $14.45 for children 6 to 12.

i For a small town, the various attractions at Yorktown actually sprawl across a large, hilly area. It's about 1.5 miles from the National Park Service visitor center to the American Revolution Museum (formerly the Yorktown Victory Center) at the other end of Water Street, for example. On holidays and weekends, parking can be at a premium, too. Once you've found a spot, use the free Yorktown Trolley to shuttle to the various places. From mid-March through mid-November, the trolley runs a daily continuous loop every 20 to 25 minutes, from 11 a.m. to 5 p.m., stopping at nine locations, including the park service center, the Yorktown Victory Monument, the beach, Riverwalk, the Watermen's Museum, the American Revolution Museum, and the county government center. From mid-November through Christmas, it runs on Fri, Sat, and Sun only. For more information, call the Tourism Development office at (757) 890-5900

Yorktown National Cemetery

Not far from Surrender Field lay the gravestones of more than 2,200 fallen American soldiers—but not from the Revolutionary battle fought at Yorktown. These dead gave their lives during the **Civil War** battle here.

Some 80 years after the siege that led to independence, Yorktown was the site of a second, smaller battle, triggered by the same strategic location alongside a deepwater river port.

In 1862, the North successfully blockaded Hampton Roads harbor and Norfolk, and held control of Fort Monroe at the harbor's mouth. Union general Richard McClellan used the ability to bring in troops and supplies to Fort Monroe to launch an offensive up the Virginia Peninsula. His aim: end the war quickly by seizing the Confederate capital of Richmond.

The Confederates countered by building a defensive line along the natural obstacle of the Warwick River, supplementing it with earthen works and dams that strategically blocked other routes to Richmond with floodwaters. The Confederates choose Yorktown as the northern terminus because it still had leftover fortifications from the Revolutionary War.

McClellan's troops heavily outnumbered the Confederates—but instead of attacking, he chose to besiege and bombard Yorktown. McClellan may have been looking for a crushing blow, like Washington and Rochambeau before him. Instead, the delay caused by his fastidious preparations gave the Confederates time to slip away.

A few weeks later, as McClellan pushed to the outskirts of Richmond, the Confederate Army of Northern Virginia was turned over to a new commander—General Robert E. Lee. He routed McClellan in the bloody Seven Days Battles of June and July, and sent the Union troops retreating back to the safety of Fort Monroe.

In the Civil War's Battle of Yorktown, the remains of 632 Union dead were buried in the heart of the **Revolutionary War battlefield**—not far, in fact, from **Moore House,** the Yorktown home where Cornwallis's surrender was negotiated.

Later, the Yorktown cemetery was chosen to serve as a national cemetery for those killed in the Civil War throughout the region. More than 1,500 others were disinterred from their hastily made wartime graves and reburied with military honors at Yorktown.

VICTORY MONUMENT, Main Street, Yorktown, VA 23690; (757) 898-2410; nps.gov/york. On October 29, 1781, a resolution of the Continental Congress called for the creation of a Yorktown monument. It took a century, however, before the cornerstone was laid on October 18, 1881. The monument is the record of the centennial celebration that took place in the town that year. The stirring inscriptions around its base are worth reading. (There is parking across the street.) The monument is maintained by the National Park Service.

THE WATERMEN'S MUSEUM, 309 Water St., Yorktown, VA 23690; (757) 887-2641; watermens.org. Located directly on the York River, this local gem operates more like a community center than a museum. Though the stated mission is to preserve and interpret Tidewater Virginia's relationship with the water and its bounties, the programming is inventive and expansive. Yes, there are artifacts, exhibits, ship models, and photographs of crabbers and clammers at work, but there are also summer educational programs for kids that teach crabbing, seining, boatbuilding, and—why not?—how to be a pirate. On any Friday night, there might be a fish fry on the grounds (nearly 4.5 riverfront acres) with live music. On the second Wednesday of every month, they host a folk music jam in the Carriage House. Yorktown is a magnet for historic tall ships; when the replica of the Marquis de Lafayette's *Hermione* stopped in Yorktown on its 2015 transatlantic tour, it was the Watermen's Museum that threw a party for the crew, public invited.

The main building is a 1935 Colonial Revival house, a masterpiece of engineering that was floated 3 miles across the York River from its original site in Gloucester County in 1987. The renovated Carriage House, which also was brought from Gloucester to Yorktown, features a riverside dock that can be rented for wedding receptions, private parties, and meetings. The well-stocked gift shop is worth a visit by itself. Careful not to step on the chilled-out cocker spaniel splayed across the entrance.

Admission is $5 for adults and $4 for senior citizens and students. Active military are admitted free. Groups of 15 or more may make arrangements to visit anytime—even during the off-season—by calling in advance. Discounted rates are offered for group tours. The museum is open 10 a.m. to 5 p.m. Tues through Sat; 1 to 5 p.m. Sun; closed Christmas Eve and Christmas Day.

YORKTOWN BATTLEFIELD VISITOR CENTER, 1000 Colonial National Pkwy., Yorktown, VA 23690; (757) 898-2410; nps.gov/york. The National Park Service's visitor center is a small brick building nearly hidden by the 10-foot-high earthworks. The center has an interesting set of indoor exhibits (including the actual tents George Washington used as his field headquarters), and a 16-minute film using re-creations to give some sense of the siege.

In other words, the visitor center is intentionally understated and serves to keep the attention where it's due—the acres of open fields and earthen fortifications. To truly appreciate the scale of the battle, you need only walk the fields or drive the 7-mile self-guided tour of the sprawling battlegrounds.

You can view samples of the types of cannon and mortar the siege forces used, tucked behind earthworks 0.5 mile south of the visitor center. You can stare across the fields—just as Washington, Rochambeau, and Cornwallis did—to gauge the distances and effect of the artillery.

Most evocative, however, is Redoubt 9—one of two earthen fortifications that were linchpins of the British defensive line. (Nearby Redoubt 10 is fenced off—the meandering banks of the York River have washed out chunks of the river bluffs over the past 200-plus years, leaving the redoubt teetering at the edge of a cliff.)

In a few bloody minutes one moonless night, a few hundred British, French, Americans, and German mercenaries fought hand to hand. The Franco-American allies prevailed. Within a few hours, their artillery was firing into town at almost point-blank range; within three days, British general Charles Lord Cornwallis surrendered.

There is no single preferred way to view the battlefield. The 15-minute film *The Siege at Yorktown* provides excellent context (the actor portraying Cornwallis lays on arrogance to the verge of campiness), and a re-creation of a Revolutionary-era warship gives a glimpse of life aboard (hint: duck).

Outside, park service rangers lead 30-minute guided walking tours that describe the historical context and the allies' siege tactics. To get a broader view (including some insight into the difficulties of marching massive troop numbers through a marshy, heavily forested region), pick up a free map at the visitor center and take the self-guided driving tour through the fortifications or the slightly longer 9-mile tour that includes the troop encampments.

Many visitors, however, simply choose to walk the grounds, taking in the sweep and imagining the epic events that occurred on these quiet, wide fields.

Admission to the park is $15, good over a seven-day period for both Yorktown Battlefield and Historic Jamestowne. An annual pass is available for $45. Visitors 15 and younger are admitted free.

Historic Buildings

Structures dating from the colonial period attest to the wealth citizens gained from Yorktown's prominence. Some of the most notable are listed here.

ARCHER COTTAGE, Water Street, Yorktown, VA 23690. This former waterfront tavern, originally built "under the cliff" in the early 1700s, was reconstructed atop its stone foundation after an 1814 fire. The earliest homes in Yorktown were built on the bluff and away from the beach. The location of this cottage under the cliff suggests it served as a spot to quench one's thirst in the bustling, hard-drinking port. The building belongs to the National Park Service and is used as an office. It is not open to the public.

THE AUGUSTINE MOORE HOUSE, Moore House Road, Yorktown, VA 23690. This is the historic home where the terms of surrender were drawn in 1781. It has been restored and furnished to its 18th-century appearance. A living-history program tells the interesting story of the arguments that took place during the negotiations. The house is open spring through fall. For specific dates and times, contact the National Park Service at (757) 898-2410.

GRACE EPISCOPAL CHURCH, 111 Church St., Yorktown, VA 23690; (757) 898-3261; gracechurchyorktown.org. In colonial times this church, which dates to at least 1642, was known as the York-Hampton Church. The church has been damaged several times by war and by fire, but the original walls have been standing since 1697 and have been incorporated into a number of reconstructions. It remains the place of worship for an active Episcopal parish. A bookshop offers theological and devotional literature, gifts, and cards. The church is open for viewing from 9 a.m. to 3 p.m. Mon through Fri, noon to 3 p.m. Sat, except during services, weddings, and funerals.

THE NELSON HOUSE, 501 Main St., Yorktown, VA 23690; (757) 898-2410. With its Georgian design, glazed Flemish bond brickwork, and lovely formal gardens, the Nelson House was once home to one of Yorktown's wealthiest men, Thomas Nelson Jr., a governor of Virginia, commander of the Virginia militia, and signer of the Declaration of Independence. Cornwallis used the home as headquarters during the siege, and colonial cannonballs still are lodged in the wall facing the American siege line. Legend has it that Thomas Nelson, Jr. himself gave the order to fire those cannons, even though it might have meant the destruction of his home and possibly his fortune, an act putting literal force behind his pledge in the Declaration of Independence. The Nelson House is open spring through fall. Admission is included in the $14 fee to the Yorktown Battlefield. Call park headquarters at the number listed above for specific hours and times.

OLD CUSTOM HOUSE, 410 Main St., Yorktown, VA 23690. Reputed to have been built by Richard Ambler in 1720 as his "large brick storehouse" and used by him while he served as customs collector, this sturdy monument to Yorktown commerce is administered by the Comte de Grasse Chapter of the Daughters of the American Revolution. Believed to be the oldest custom house in the US, the Yorktown structure was named to the Virginia Landmarks Register in 1999. Over the years, the custom house has been a dwelling, a store, the headquarters of Confederate general John B. Magruder during the Civil War, and the medical offices of African American physician D. M. Norton. Its restoration—sponsored by the Daughters of the American Revolution, who staged tea parties, cake sales, and masked balls to raise needed funds—is considered a milestone in the historic preservation movement. Open by appointment only. Message them via facebook.com/Yorktown-Custom-House.

POOR POTTER SITE, 221 Read St., Yorktown, VA 23690; (757) 898-2410. The site of the largest-known pottery factory in colonial America tells the story of how this industry flourished in Yorktown during the early 1700s. Operated by the National Park Service, hours are seasonal; call ahead before you visit.

NEWPORT NEWS

ENDVIEW PLANTATION, 362 Yorktown Rd. (exit 247 off I-64), Newport News, VA 23603; (757) 887-1862; endview.org. One of the few remaining colonial-era homes on the Lower Peninsula sits on 500 acres that belonged to the politically influential Harwood family for 350 years—originally part of the holdings of Captain Thomas Harwood, an early émigré to the colonies who served as speaker of the House of Burgesses (the equivalent of a parliament for the colony). His descendant, William Harwood, built a simple white clapboard house in 1769, a solid but hardly opulent home that was representative of the middle tiers of the landed gentry at the time.

Historians and curators have been at work restoring the house since the city purchased the property in 1995. The plantation was an important element of the Confederacy's defenses during the Peninsula Campaign early in the Civil War, when Harwood's great-grandson, a doctor, commanded a company of volunteers, the Warwick Beauregards, ran a field hospital on the site, and quartered two generals.

Today, Endview is a living-history museum with both Confederate and Union camps represented. A variety of programs and events are scheduled throughout the year, including a Civil War reenactment early each spring; summer camps devoted to the study of the Civil War; and holiday season events in December. Admission is $8 for adults, $7 for seniors (62+), and $6 for children ages 7 to 18. Some programs may cost extra. Open 10 a.m. to 4 p.m. Thurs through Sat; closed Sun through Wed and New Year's Day, Easter, Thanksgiving, Christmas Eve, and Christmas.

FORT EUSTIS/US ARMY TRANSPORTATION MUSEUM, 300 Washington Blvd. (Fort Eustis, exit 250A off I-64), Newport News, VA 23604, (757) 878-1115; transportation.army.mil/museum. Military leaders have a maxim: Amateurs study tactics; professionals study logistics. Nowhere is this truer than Fort Eustis, 11 miles southeast of Williamsburg, home to the army's command and training center for air, sea, rail, and land transportation.

Most of the base is restricted to the public, but the excellent US Army Transportation Museum, just inside the base gates, is open for tours. As prosaic as the topic may sound, the museum brings the nitty gritty of military campaigns to life—the movement of food, munitions, and fuel to frontline troops. Visitors can explore more than 200 years of Army transportation history through miniatures, dioramas, experimental models, and exhibits focusing on the personal stories of Army personnel during Operations Desert Storm and Desert Shield. Kids will enjoy seeing a truck and a jeep that flies. There also are four outdoor parks where aircraft, trains, ships, land craft, and jeeps are on display.

Open Tues through Sat from 9 a.m. to 4:30 p.m. Closed Sun, Mon, and federal holidays. Fort Eustis is a limited-access military installation. US citizens must stop at the guardhouse and receive a visitor's pass to tour the museum. Noncitizens must apply for entry; see the website for details. Admission is free; donations are accepted.

LEE HALL MANSION, 163 Yorktown Rd. (exit 247 off I-64), Newport News, VA 23603; (757) 888-3371; leehall.org. If nearby Endview Plantation is a fine example of colonial-era architecture for the middle class, Lee Hall is a glimpse of the lifestyle of wealthy landowners just before the Civil War shattered the "Old South." Restored by the city and opened as a museum in September 1998, Lee Hall affords historical interpretations of the antebellum era and of the 1862 Peninsula Campaign.

The Italianate mansion was built in the 1850s by wealthy planter Richard Decauter Lee. Typical of the time, the home was built for entertainment: Curators have restored a ladies' parlor, music room, and two of the home's bedrooms. Lee didn't get to enjoy his lovely home for long. By 1862, Union troops were pushing northwest from their stronghold at Hampton's Fort Monroe. The Lees fled, and Confederate general John B. Magruder used the home as his field headquarters. He built earthworks as part of a network from the James to the York, and he even launched tethered hot-air balloons from the mansion's front yard to provide reconnaissance of the advancing Yankees.

Today, the home features artifacts and historical interpretations of that campaign (which very nearly ended the war three years early). Among the artifacts are a tablecloth from the USS *Monitor* and items recovered from a nearby battle site.

Admission is $8 for adults, $7 for seniors (62+), and $6 for children ages 7 to 18. Some programs may cost extra. Open 10 a.m. to 4 p.m. Thurs through Sat; closed Sun.

MARINERS' MUSEUM AND PARK, 100 Museum Dr. (exit 258A off I-64), Newport News, VA 23606; (757) 596-2222; marinersmuseum.org. This world-renowned museum, founded in 1930, boasts the nation's most extensive collection of maritime treasures, including ship models, scrimshaw, maritime paintings, decorative arts, carved figureheads, navigational instruments, and working steam engines. The centerpiece is its collection from the USS *Monitor*, the Union's first ironclad and the key Union combatant in the Battle of Hampton Roads. During the Civil War, the *Monitor* sank in a storm off the coast of Cape Hatteras, but divers located the wreck in the 1990s and brought up artifacts, including the ship's massive rotating gun turret. Museum curators spent years painstakingly restoring the finds, now on exhibit in a 2004 addition the museum built specifically to tell the *Monitor* story.

The museum is also a boon for scholars. Its research library and archives house more maritime-related documents than any other American institution: photographs and negatives, nautical charts and maps, ships' logs, and thousands of other archival items, including Mark Twain's pilot license.

Scholarly lectures and popular guest speakers appear throughout the year. While the museum was closed in 2020 because of the coronavirus pandemic, an abundance of digital content and a full calendar of free virtual lectures moved online. The Virtual Programming page on the website now links to recorded lectures on YouTube.

In summer, the museum hosts various days for kids, and a free live music event—Thursdays on the Lake—from June through early Sept. A gift shop offers maritime books, prints, and sea-related gifts. An on-site cafe opens midday for lunch and snacks. A 550-acre park surrounds the site featuring a 5-mile trail with 14 pedestrian bridges that span Lake Maury and its shady creeks. Paddleboats are available for rental. In late 2020, the park and the Noland Trail, a five-mile path that circles through the woods that surround the museum, reopened to the public. There is no admission charge.

It is open daily 6 a.m. to 7 p.m. except Thanksgiving and Christmas. When the museum itself reopens, hours are generally 9 a.m. to 5 p.m. Mon through Sat, 11 a.m. to 5 p.m. Sun except Thanksgiving and Christmas. Thanks to a $10 million grant from The Batten Foundation of Norfolk admission was permanently reduced to $1 per person in 2016.

NEWSOME HOUSE MUSEUM AND CULTURAL CENTER, 2803 Oak Ave. (exit 3 off I-664), Newport News, VA 23607; (757) 247-2360; new somehouse.org. Built in 1899, the Newsome House is a modified Queen Anne structure that was home to Joseph Thomas Newsome, one of the first Black attorneys to argue before the Virginia Supreme Court. Newsome also was the editor of a Black newspaper, cofounded a Newport News church, and formed the Colored Voters League of Warwick County. His home, in the city's East End, houses an exhibit on the Newsome family and extensive archives on the African American community in Newport News. Monthly programming on the African American experience in Virginia is offered. Open 10 a.m. to 5 p.m. Thurs through Sat. A $2 donation is suggested to offset operating costs.

> **i** If kids need a break from museum hopping, **Fort Fun** in Huntington Park is just the ticket. A 14,000-square-foot playground, on a bluff overlooking the James River, has a pirate theme, with 2 play apparatuses that resemble ships, slides, swings, climbing walls, and more. Located in southern Newport News off Warwick Boulevard, just north of US 17. See Huntington Park listing under Parks.

VIRGINIA LIVING MUSEUM, 524 J. Clyde Morris Blvd., Newport News, VA 23601; (757) 595-1900; thevlm.org. The Living Museum is an intriguing hybrid: part zoo, part botanical gardens, part observatory and planetarium, with native bird and aquatic life exhibits thrown in for good measure. It's hard for a kid to have a bad time at the Living Museum, so the place is usually crawling with that young human life, too.

Opened in 1987, the museum underwent a $22 million expansion in 2004, which added a 62,000-square-foot exhibits building, allowing visitors to seemingly walk through a Chesapeake Bay deepwater aquarium, explore a Shenandoah Valley cave, and study the environments of an Appalachian cove and cypress swamp. You'll find fossil exhibits, a touch tank for hands-on learning about marine life, and a two-story glass aviary with native songbirds. Younger visitors get a special thrill from putting their hands in the authentic footprints of a 210-million-year-old dinosaur or from petting a docile horseshoe crab.

Outside, a boardwalk winds through a nature preserve where animals—everything from regal bald eagles to coyotes to endangered red wolves—can be viewed in their natural habitats. In the Coastal Plain Aviary, a net canopy encloses a marshy ecosystem for herons, egrets, ducks, pelicans, cormorants, and other birds, as well as turtles and a variety of plants indigenous to wetland areas. In a separate building (part of the original facility), the planetarium features multi-image shows and telescope observation.

Admission is $20 for adults, $15 for children ages 3 to 12. Planetarium shows carry an additional charge. Open 9 a.m. to 5 p.m. daily except Thanksgiving, Christmas Eve, Christmas, and New Year's Day.

VIRGINIA WAR MUSEUM, 9285 Warwick Blvd. (inside Huntington Park), Newport News, VA 23607; (757) 247-8523; warmuseum.org. This museum offers a detailed look at US military history from 1775 to the present. Kids will particularly like the array of artillery on the lawn allowing for close-up looks. More than 60,000 artifacts, including an 1883 brass Gatling gun, a

World War I Howitzer tank, and a Civil War blockade-runner's uniform, are on display. In the summer, the museum runs a popular day camp.

Admission is $8 for adults, $7 for seniors, and $6 for children ages 7 to 18. The Duffle Bag gift shop offers books, posters, and shirts. Open 9 a.m. to 4 p.m. Thurs through Sat. Closed on Thanksgiving, Christmas, and New Year's Day.

HAMPTON

THE AMERICAN THEATRE, 125 E. Mellen St., Phoebus, VA 23663; (757) 722-2787; hamptonarts.net/the-american-theatre. Built in 1908 as a vaudeville and movie house, this was the first integrated theater in Virginia. It fell into decline and closed in the 1990s but reopened in 2000 after a $3 million makeover. The theater offers plays, concerts featuring international artists, classic movies, and children's programs.

BLUEBIRD GAP FARM, 60 Pine Chapel Rd., Hampton, VA 23666; (757) 825-4750; hampton.gov/139/Bluebird-Gap-Farm. This 60-acre farm is home to numerous animals, including pigs, deer, goats, sheep, cows, chickens, ducks, and an occasional horse. A playground area is perfect for picnicking, and public restrooms and vending machines are available. Open daily 9 a.m. to 5 p.m. Closed Thanksgiving, Christmas, and New Year's Day. Admission is free, but bring a couple of quarters for the food machines if you want to feed the animals. Do not bring your own food to feed the animals; it upsets their diets.

CHARLES H. TAYLOR VISUAL ARTS CENTER, 4205 Victoria Blvd., Hampton, VA 23669; (757) 727-1490; Hamptonarts.net. Housed in Hampton's 1926 library, the center displays the work of local artists and photographers as well as traveling exhibitions. The center also is home to the Hampton Arts Commission, which stages the Great Performers Series at the American Theatre. The center is open 11 a.m. to 4 p.m. Wed, Thurs, and Sat or by appointment. Admission is free.

FORT MONROE / CASEMATE MUSEUM, 20 Bernard Rd. (on the grounds of Fort Monroe), Hampton, VA 23651; (757) 788-3391; fortmonroe.org. Fort Monroe, formerly the headquarters for the US Army Training and Doctrine Command, holds the title of the largest stone fort ever built in America. It's located at one of the most historic—and strategically important—places in Virginia, where the James River and Hampton Roadstead meet the Chesapeake Bay. The Jamestown settlers stopped here briefly on their way upstream, and Old Point Comfort has been the site of a military base since 1609, when the Virginia Company established Fort Algernourne to protect Jamestown from waterborne assault from other European nations.

Within its walls, you'll find the Casemate Museum, which chronicles the history of the fort and the Coast Artillery Corps. During your tour, you will see the cell in which captured Confederate president Jefferson Davis was imprisoned, as well as weapons, uniforms, Frederick Remington drawings, and other military artifacts. You also will learn how "Freedom's Fortress" helped shelter thousands of slave refugees. Other nearby points of interest include Robert E. Lee's quarters, now a private residence, seacoast batteries, and the Old Point Comfort Lighthouse. Open 10 a.m. to 3 p.m. daily. Admission is free.

The Deadrise, a restaurant serving tasty lunches and dinner, is located inside the fort, as well. See the full listing for this eatery below.

HAMPTON CAROUSEL PARK, 602 Settlers Landing Rd., Hampton, VA 23669; (757) 727-1610 (Hampton History Museum); hampton.gov/Facilities/Facility/Details/1. Pony up a dollar and take a ride on Hampton's beautifully restored 1920s merry-go-round, one of fewer than 100 antique wooden carousels still existing in the US. Built in 1920 by the Philadelphia Toboggan Company, this beautiful example of American folk art is housed in its own weather-protected pavilion. Its stately chariots and prancing steeds are hand carved and intricately painted. The carousel was delivered to Buckroe Beach Amusement Park in 1921, where it delighted thousands of visitors until the park closed in the 1980s. The city bought the historic gem and had it painstakingly restored. After two years of work, the ponies—painted in shades of cream, yellow, and brown—were ready to be ridden once again. Open Apr through Dec, 11 a.m. to 8 p.m. Tues through Sun.

HAMPTON HISTORY MUSEUM, 120 Old Hampton Ln., Hampton, VA 23669; (757) 727-1610; hamptonhistorymuseum.org. A showcase for the history of the nation's oldest continuous English-speaking settlement, this museum opened in 2003 with 9 permanent galleries: Native American, 17th Century, Port Hampton, 18th Century, Antebellum, Civil War, Reconstruction, Late 19th Century, and Modern Hampton. Open 9 a.m. to 4 p.m. Tues, Thurs, and Fri; 1 to 3 p.m. Wed; 9 a.m. to 3 p.m. Sat and Sun. Admission is $5 for adults and $4 for children ages 4 to 12.

HAMPTON UNIVERSITY MUSEUM, Huntington Building, 14 Frissell Ave., Hampton, VA 23668; (757) 727-5308; museum.hamptonu.edu. Founded in 1868, the Hampton University Museum is the second-oldest museum in Virginia and the oldest devoted to African American art in the US. Its remarkable collection contains more than 9,000 objects and works of art from cultures and nations worldwide. Among the works housed at the museum are nine paintings by the renowned African American artist Henry O. Tanner. The museum also holds an American Indian collection of more than 1,600 art and artifact objects from 93 tribes, gathered beginning in 1868 by faculty, friends of the school, and American Indian students sent by the federal government to receive an education at Hampton University. Most artifacts are from Plains Indians, but some pieces of contemporary Pamunkey pottery are also part of the collection.

The museum is housed in a beautiful expanded facility—a former Beaux Arts–style library, which includes a Fine Arts Gallery; the African Gallery, with objects from nearly 100 ethnic groups and cultures; the Hampton History Gallery, which traces the university's own historical contributions; plus galleries devoted to changing exhibits by contemporary artists, the Harlem Renaissance, and a studio gallery that showcases the works of Hampton's students.

All campus buildings closed to the general public during the pandemic but museum hours when open are 8 a.m. to 5 p.m. Mon through Fri; noon to 4 p.m. Sat; closed most holidays. Admission is free. In addition to the museum, the university is also the site of six National Historic Landmarks, including the **Emancipation Oak,** where President Abraham Lincoln's Emancipation Proclamation was first read to the slaves of Hampton in 1863 (see the sidebar in this chapter).

Emancipation Oak

Its low branches stretch impossibly wide, creating a cool canopy over a grassy patch of land a stone's throw from what is now I-64. The tree's been here a lot longer than the traffic. It was here, under the sturdy limbs of what is now called the Emancipation Oak that residents of Hampton first learned that slavery had been outlawed in the US. In 1863, Lincoln's Emancipation Proclamation was read aloud for the first time in the South, according to historians at Hampton University.

The peaceful shade of the Emancipation Oak, located at the entrance to Hampton University, also served as the first classroom for newly freed men and women eager for an education. It had already been a classroom for slaves: Before the Civil War, Mary Peake, a prominent educator who was the daughter of a free colored woman and a Frenchman, broke the law to teach classes to slaves and free Blacks under this tree. The Emancipation Oak, 98 feet in diameter, is designated as one of the 10 great trees of the world by the National Geographic Society. A live oak, the tree's foliage remains green year-round.

ST. JOHN'S EPISCOPAL CHURCH, 100 W. Queens Way, Hampton, VA 23669; (757) 722-2567; stjohnshampton.org. The oldest continuous English-speaking parish in the US was founded here in 1610. The current church was built in 1728. The tree-lined churchyard holds graves dating from 1701, including a memorial to Virginia Laydon, one of the first persons to survive an arduous birth in the New World. Communion silver made in London in 1618 and a stained-glass window depicting the baptism of Pocahontas are among the church's most prized possessions. When the church reopens for tours, appointments can be made by calling between 9 a.m. to 3 p.m. Mon through Thurs. Otherwise, visitors can sign up to attend service at 9:15 a.m. Sunday by filling out a form on the church's website, noted above.

VIRGINIA AIR AND SPACE SCIENCE CENTER, 600 Settlers Landing Rd., Hampton, VA 23669; (757) 727-0900, (800) 296-0800; vasc.org. This $30 million museum, which opened to sellout crowds in April 1992, is designated the official NASA Langley Visitors Center and is considered the pièce de résistance of Hampton's revitalization. A $1.5 million renovation in 2020 made improvements to the IMAX Theater and the Space Explorer Gallery.

The museum features changing exhibits relating to the city's "First from the sea, first to the stars" theme. The Apollo 12 command module is on display here, and vintage aircraft are suspended from the 94-foot ceiling, but the emphasis here is on hands-on (and minds-on) investigation. (The museum added the word "Science" to its official name in 2020 to reflect its commitment to STEM education.) Visitors can get a sense of the evolution of flight with more than 30 aircraft on display, but they can get a real sense of what it feels like to fly when they take the controls at a number of flight simulators. The five-story-high IMAX theater offers a cool and often dramatic escape from summer heat. There's an on-site cafe and gift shop. The center also offers summer and school holiday camps for children.

Open 10:30 a.m. to 4 p.m. Mon through Sat, noon to 4 p.m. Sun. Tickets are $20 for adults, $18 for seniors, and $16.50 for children 3 to 18, which includes IMAX admission. Tickets just for IMAX films are also sold separately from museum admission.

Entertainment

Grammy Award–winner Bruce Hornsby is, without a doubt, one of Williamsburg's favorite sons. But if your timing isn't right to catch Hornsby on a Williamsburg stage, don't despair. Although this isn't a rowdy, rocking kind of town, it's usually possible to find something fun to do once the sun goes down.

The local bar scene is decidedly low-key: The live music is mostly jazz, blues, or oldies. There are sports bars, and other unusual diversions—from candlelit ghost tours (on land or by sea!) to 18th-century-style concerts. The Precarious Beer Project, on the southeasternmost corner of Merchants Square, is drawing families during the day and young adults at night with its pleasing mix of craft beers, street tacos, live music, outdoor seating with an inviting fire pit, and arcade games.

If you're in the mood for Broadway or opera and have the whole night to spare, you might plan a trip to Norfolk, about an hour's drive east on I-64, or Richmond, 45 minutes west. If you're looking for big name musical acts, check out the schedules at the coliseums in Hampton, Norfolk, and Richmond or the amphitheater in Virginia Beach. We give you the information you need to map out your itinerary in our Out-of-Town Nightspots section near the end of this chapter. For ticket information and availability, call the numbers listed or contact Ticketmaster at (800) 653-8000 or visit ticketmaster.com.

The best way to find out what's happening in and around Williamsburg is to check the *Virginia Gazette* (published Wed and Sat) or the *Daily Press* (particularly "Ticket Weekend," published Fri, featuring entertainment news, and the "Sunday Ticket" section, which offers a guide to arts and leisure activities). You can visit the *Daily Press*'s entertainment website at hrticket.com.

Other sources for entertainment news include *Williamsburg Magazine* (a free monthly publication you can pick up just about anywhere) and *Colonial Guide* (a seasonal publication available free at numerous locations around the greater Williamsburg area).

LIVE MUSIC

AROMAS, 431 Prince George St., Williamsburg, VA 23185; (757) 561-1516; aromasworld.com. This popular coffee shop offers live music from 8 to 10 p.m. Fri and Sat and open mic night for singers, comedians, and poets from 7:30 to 9 p.m. every Thurs. (Arrive early to get on the list.)

BERRET'S SEAFOOD RESTAURANT AND TAPHOUSE GRILL, 199 S. Boundary St. (Merchants Square), Williamsburg, VA 23185; (757)

253-1847; berrets.com. A Merchants Square institution, this popular restaurant has live music almost every night of the week.

COGAN'S, 4324 C-2 New Town Ave., Williamsburg, VA 23188; (757) 645-3351; cogansdeli.com. Sports, live music and daily drink specials make this one of the liveliest spots in New Town. Cogan's brags it has the best Reuben in Williamsburg; and there is a daily homemade soup special. But the big draw here is the full slate of entertainment. Every Mon it's a jazz jam session, Wed is acoustic and Fri and Sat feature a rotating assortment of local bands. Open 10 a.m. to 11 p.m. Mon through Thurs; 10 a.m. to midnight Fri and Sat; 11 a.m. to "whatever" Sun.

THE CORNER POCKET, 4805 Courthouse St. (New Town), Williamsburg, VA 23188; (757) 220-0808; thecornerpocket.us. This upscale billiards parlor has terrific food (see our description in the Dining chapter) and a great atmosphere. Thirteen tables, including three 9-foot professional tables with great lighting, and plenty of room offer the best facility around for billiards, making the Corner Pocket a frequent host to area tournaments. Occasionally, however, they cover the tables and install a stage, bringing in blues, jazz, and zydeco acts for live performances. They also offer live music on the patio that surrounds the restaurant, weather permitting. Check the website for upcoming shows.

Dinner is served here till midnight, making this one of the latest places around to get a full tasty meal. Closing time is 1 a.m. Sun through Tues, 2 a.m. Wed through Sat.

GREEN LEAFE CAFE, 765 Scotland St., Williamsburg, VA 23185; (757) 220-3405; greenleafe.com. Open since 1974, this is the most enduring nightspot in town. (It even says so in the *New York Times* review that is framed and hanging on the wall.) See our full description of this college watering hole in the Dining chapter. On weekend nights, there's usually a DJ, but there's always a party or, at the very least, trivia night or karaoke. It's no surprise *USA Today* named the Green Leafe to its "Top 10 Bar" list. Themed beer nights, specials on "shakers and 'tinis," live music, and sports viewing occur weekly. Tasty food served from 11 a.m. until 1:30 a.m.; the bar is open until 2 a.m.

PRECARIOUS BEER PROJECT, 110 S. Henry St. (Merchants Square), Williamsburg, VA 23185; (757) 808-5105; precariousbeer.com. Williamsburg doesn't typically produce hotspots but this is one: a cavernous beer hall on a prominent corner in Merchants Square that serves on small batch beers, street tacos, live music, outdoor seating with an inviting fire pit, and arcade games. See our full description in the Dining chapter.

RIVERWALK LANDING, Riverwalk Plaza, Water Street, Yorktown, VA 23690. Possibly the most fun you can have for free is at Yorktown's free concert series: "Shagging on the Riverwalk," featuring beach music and Motown hits, held Thurs during the summer from 6:30 to 9:30 p.m., or "Rhythms on the Riverwalk," a jazz and swing series on Wed nights. All concerts are held at the outdoor bandstand on Water Street. Bring a blanket, a picnic dinner, a bottle of wine, and your dancing shoes.

SUMMER BREEZE CONCERT SERIES, Merchants Square, Duke of Gloucester Street, Williamsburg, VA 23185; (757) 220-7751; merchantssquare.org. Free concerts featuring not-to-be-missed party bands rock DoG Street from 7 to 9 p.m. Wed throughout the summer. Bring folding chairs and blankets for these outdoor performances, held on W. Duke of Gloucester Street near the Dog Street Pub.

THE WATERMEN'S MUSEUM, 309 Water St., Yorktown, VA 23690; (757) 887-2641; watermens.org. On any Friday night, there's live music, organized around a theme. There might also be a fish fry on the grounds (nearly 4.5 riverfront acres), which means you don't have to eat somewhere else first. On the second Wed of every month they host a folk music jam in the Carriage House. This museum rocks.

WILLIAMSBURG REGIONAL LIBRARY, 515 Scotland St., Williamsburg, VA 23185; (757) 259-4070; wrl.org. The Dewey Decibel Concert Series brings folk, bluegrass, country, classical, and jazz musicians to the library's 268-seat auditorium at bargain prices. Past performances have included Robin and Linda Williams, Tommy Emmanuel, and Stephen Bennett, as well as free concerts by the Langley Winds (a woodwind quintet from the US Air Force's Heritage of America Band). Concert dates vary—check the monthly calendar at the website listed above—but most shows start at 8 p.m. Some concerts are free, but for the most part ticket prices are $16 or less and usually half price for those younger than 16. Call ahead to have tickets held at the door. Tickets can

> **i** If you like chamber, organ, or choral music, visit Bruton Parish Church on Duke of Gloucester Street at 8 p.m. Tues and Sat, Mar through Dec or at the same time on Thurs from June through Dec. The church also presents some special evening concerts throughout the year. A free-will offering is collected at each performance. There are no admission charges. For more information call (757) 229-2891 or go to brutonparish.org.

A Ghostly Evening

Let's just say the Historic Triangle—scene of some of the bloodiest battles in American history—has more than its share of ghosts. Clever capitalists have responded by producing spirited tours featuring the area's favorite haunts, one for every appetite. Read on.

Since Colonial Williamsburg runs the place, their ghost tour—Haunted Williamsburg—is the only one op with exclusive access to historic outdoor and indoor spaces—you know, where the ghosts are. The specialty here is costumed storytellers sharing authentic 18th-century tales. The one-hour candlelit tours take brave visitors through town, into gardens and beyond the barriers to "our most haunted sites." Tours begin at the Play House Stage on Palace Green and are considered suitable for children aged 8 and older. (All children must be accompanied by an adult.) The tours operate rain or shine, except in cases of severe inclement weather. Tickets are $19 for adults, $12 for children aged 12 or younger.

The **Original Ghosts of Williamsburg Candlelight Tour** bills itself as family friendly and the "second oldest ghost tour in the country." Based on the book by L. B. Taylor, Jr., the 90-minute, one-mile walking tour gathers in front of the Barnes & Noble, 345 Duke of Gloucester St., at 8 p.m. nightly Mar through Oct, rain or shine. Tickets are $14 per person (children 6 and under are free).

The "extreme" version of this tour, which includes "ghost-hunting equipment," begins at 9:15 p.m. in front of Bruton Parish Church, 201 W. Duke of Gloucester St and takes about two hours. Tickets are $17 (not recommended for young children).

Need a stiff drink to conquer your fear? Then there's the **Extreme Murder Pub Crawl,** which sets out to prove that the scariest thing in Williamsburg are not ghosts but real people. This tour hops to local pubs where guests can enjoy "murder-themed" cocktails. Held on select Fridays and Saturdays from 8 to 11 p.m., the tour starts from 199 S. Boundary St. This one costs $25 and is also not for children.

If you already know all about Williamsburg's ghosts, you can sashay east to Yorktown to meet their ghouls. Tours are offered nightly at 8p.m. beginning at 209 Church St. Tickets are $13 per person.

A word of caution: The streets here are dark, unpaved, or occasionally made with oddly shaped cobblestones; sensible walking shoes are a must. Especially on the pub crawl.

Not big on walking? Have the wrong shoes? Try the **Haunted River Cruise of Jamestown Island** which also operates on "select nights" at 9:15 p.m. and 10:30 p.m., departing from the James City County Marina, 2054 Jamestown Rd., at the southern end of the Colonial National Parkway. Tickets are $27 per person.

Tickets for all tours must be purchased in advance, online, at theghost tour.com. Questions? Check the website for this entire ghostly enterprise at theghosttour.com or call (757) 342-6599.

be reserved as far as two months in advance with payment either by telephone with a credit card or in person with cash, check, or credit card.

MOVIES

Williamsburg has three very different choices for filmgoers: an art house, a cinema that offers full meals, and a multiplex in the New Town area.

KIMBALL THEATRE, 428 Duke of Gloucester St. (Merchants Square), Williamsburg, VA 23185; (757) 565-8588, (844) 585-1168; kimballtheatre .com. This restored 583-seat theater, owned by the Colonial Williamsburg Foundation, has a full schedule—lectures, concerts, art films, and documentaries. Current offerings can be heard by calling the local number listed above or visiting the website; advance tickets can be purchased by calling the toll-free Colonial Williamsburg reservation line. A second, 35-seat theater inside the building—dubbed the "screening room"—shows films, too.

MOVIE TAVERN, 1430 Richmond Rd. (High Street Shops), Williamsburg, VA 23185; (757) 941-5362 (box office); movietavern.com. Sure you can get popcorn here, but you can also have a burger, a beer, or a sandwich wrap and a glass of wine brought to your table as you watch first-run films. At 9 a.m. Sat and Sun, "Breakfast and a Flick" offers morning meals and a kid-friendly film. Some of the screens are reserved for art-house films and documentaries. Call the box office for current movies and showtimes, or visit the website.

NEW TOWN CINEMAS 12, 4911 Courthouse St. (New Town), Williamsburg, VA 23188; (844) 462-7342, ext. 4018 (recorded movie listings); reg movies.com. The 12 screens at this Regal Cinema offer first-run movies in a shopping and entertainment district.

> **i** On summer Sunday evenings through Labor Day, watch a family-friendly movie outdoors on Prince George Street near the Historic Area. The movies are free and begin at dusk. Bring a lawn chair or blanket. The audience gathers in the street outside the Blue Talon Restaurant, a major sponsor of the event. See the schedule of flicks at merchantssquare.org.

OUT-OF-TOWN NIGHTSPOTS

Hampton

HAMPTON COLISEUM, 1000 Coliseum Dr., Hampton, VA 23666; (757) 838-5650 (event information); hamptoncoliseum.org. When big acts come to the peninsula, this is where they play, in a spaceship-looking arena about 40 minutes east of Williamsburg on I-64 (exit 263). To find out what's happening for the dates you plan to be in town, call the box office or visit the website listed above.

Norfolk

HARRISON OPERA HOUSE, 160 E. Virginia Beach Blvd., Norfolk, VA 23510; (757) 877-2550 (box office), (866) OPERA-VA (673-7282); vaopera.org. The Harrison is home to the Norfolk-based Virginia Opera, which was formed in 1975 and performs regularly in Norfolk, Richmond, and Northern Virginia. Recent Norfolk operas have included *Sweeney Todd, La Boheme,* and *Romeo and Juliet.* Check the website for current offerings and ticket information.

NORFOLK SCOPE AND CHRYSLER HALL, 415 St. Pauls Blvd., Norfolk, VA 23510; (757) 664-6464; sevenvenues.com. When big acts come to Southside Hampton Roads, these two venues are where you'll find them. Just a few blocks from the waterfront, the 13,800-seat dome-shaped Scope (it sort of looks like an alien spaceship, too) houses sporting events and big name musicians. The more majestic Chrysler Hall is home to the Virginia Symphony (virginiasymphony.org) and Broadway touring productions, usually beginning in October. Norfolk has aggregated schedule and ticket information for all its cultural attractions at one website, called Seven Venues. To see the full listing, visit the website listed above.

> **i** Southeastern Virginia can lay claim to some landmark places and occasions in rock 'n' roll history. Fort Monroe was the birthplace of country-rock renegade Steve Earle. Rockabilly giant Gene Vincent (think "Be-Bop-A-Lula") hails from Norfolk. Hip-hop princess Missy "Misdemeanor" Elliott was born in Portsmouth. When he played in the marching band at Princess Anne High School in Virginia Beach, friends called Pharrell Williams by the nickname "Skateboard P."

THE NORVA, 317 Monticello Ave., Norfolk, VA 23510; (757) 627-4547; thenorva.com. Housed in a restored vaudeville theater that's nearly 100 years old, the Norva has a well-earned reputation for bringing cutting-edge and up-and-coming musicians to southeastern Virginia. Prince has played here; so did James Brown. Long locally owned, the building was sold in 2014 to AEG Live, a sports and entertainment company based in Los Angeles. Local music fans hope this small-scale venue will continue to host big name acts.

Almost all shows are general admission; the main floor is generally left open, without seats, for standing and dancing. At those shows, there's limited table seating—first come, first served—on the wraparound second-floor balcony. Parking is available at a number of nearby garages, including directly across the street at the MacArthur Center mall. Tickets are available at the Norva's website or through ticketmaster.com.

Virginia Beach

VIRGINIA BEACH AMPHITHEATER, 3550 Cellar Door Way, Virginia Beach, VA 23456; (757) 368-3000; thefarmbureaulive.com. It's at least a 90-minute drive from Williamsburg to Virginia Beach when traffic cooperates—which it usually doesn't, given all the tunnels and bridges between the two towns—but this amphitheater is a regular stop on the outdoor summer tour schedule of many popular acts. There's seating under the pavilion or on the lawn—but go early if you're sitting on the grass and be prepared to brave whatever elements are in play at the time. The amphitheater has 7,500 reserved seats, with room for about 12,500 on the lawn. Two giant screens on either side of the stage provide a view for those in the back. Refreshments are available at every show. To purchase tickets visit the website listed above.

Close-up

Williamsburg's Tasting Trail

For decades, beer lovers in Williamsburg had to be content with calling Budweiser their hometown beer, in recognition of the huge Anheuser-Busch brewery at the south end of town. Then in 2006, **Williamsburg Alewerks** opened, producing small volumes of colonial-style ales, porters, and stouts to the growing appreciation of craft beer lovers.

Now the craft brewery craze is in full swing with almost a dozen new spots for slaking one's thirst. Appoint a designated driver and make this sudsy jaunt around town:

Unless you count the colonial brewmasters who served George Washington and his pals in the taverns, Alewerks is the OG of Williamsburg's micro-breweries, having started life in 2006 in an industrial park off Mooretown Road. Production is modest compared to national brands, but the quality and variety is high—typically 16 drafts rotating daily, available by the glass, flight or growler. They regularly schedule entertainment including music and live comedy—check alewerks.com for the schedule or call them at (757) 220-3670. Tours of the brewery itself are suspended for now but the taproom, at 197-B Ewell Rd., is open 3 p.m. to 9 p.m. daily. The outdoor biergarten is dog friendly; the indoor seating is not.

Alewerks also now operates a **LAB** (for "little auxiliary brewery") at Williamsburg Premium Outlets, 5711-36 Richmond Rd., next to Columbia Sportswear. The LAB site, nicknamed the "Boyfriend Babysitting Club," mirrors mall hours which change a bit seasonally but are generally noon to 7 p.m. The LAB, appropriately, is completely dog friendly. There is no kitchen.

Also along this stretch is **Brass Cannon Brewing Company,** 5476 Mooretown Rd., Williamsburg, (757) 566-0001, which offers kegs, growlers, tasting flights, half pours, and full pint draft selections. In addition to five year-round brews, the brewery offers seasonal selections to enjoy in its tasting room or on the outdoor patio. This microbrewery does not distribute its beer so the only way to try it is in their taproom. The Cannon, as they call themselves, also has an event and entertainment calendar online at brasscannon brewing.com. Open 1:30 p.m to close Mon through Fri; noon to close Sat and Sun.

Billsburg Brewery has set up shop at 2054 Jamestown Rd., near the western terminus of the Colonial Parkway in what had been a beer desert—Jamestown. Long a draw for its history attractions, this area has become a bustling hub for cyclists heading out on the Capital Trail, and commuters headed to the Scotland Ferry. Billsburg is brewing and selling its small batch lagers, pilsners, and ales from the grounds of the municipally-owned James City County Marina. The taproom is small but there is deck with views of the back river. Food trucks roll in to serve the overflow crowd which gathers on the grounds where there is a roofed pavilion and a lot of picnic tables. Dog and family friendly. Check out their selections at billsburg.com or call (757) 926-0981.

Tasting Trail—Beer with Friends
2017 Michael Ventura Photography

If you're looking for craft beer in the Historic Area, **Chowning's Tavern,** 109 E. Duke of Gloucester St., is the spot. Styled as an 18th-century alehouse, the beverage menu includes Dear Old Mom and Old Stitch, two ales from Alewerks. They're served alongside beers from other Virginia breweries. Chowning's is also the home of "Beers in the 'Burg," an occasional (ticketed) festival. Check dates and buy tickets online at colonialwilliamsburg.org. Chowning's is open at 11:30 a.m. daily to close.

In Merchants Square, the **Precarious Beer Project** is the new kid in town and proving to be very popular. Having started life as the beer-making arm of the Amber Ox Public House, on Prince George St., they outgrew that space and opened their own beer hall on Henry Street in 2019. (They are already expanding the patio by adding a whole new seating area that faces the parking lot.) Just off the square is Amber Ox itself, billed as Williamsburg's only brew pub, serving small batch artisan ales brewed on-site. See full descriptions of both restaurants in our dining chapter.

Last but not least is the **Virginia Beer Company,** opened in 2016 showcasing locally made brews as well as international beers. The VBC has staked out a large spot at 401 Second St., for its home base. Sixteen rotating small batch veers are complemented by food trucks and regularly scheduled events. There's a tap room with seating plus a big outdoor biergarten where your pooch is welcome. Check their schedule at virginiabeerco.com or call (757) 378-2903.

But I Don't Like Beer

For those whose tastes run to other spirits, there is the **Copper Fox Distillery,** 901 Capitol Landing Rd., Williamsburg, which specializes in craft whiskies and gin made with hand-malted locally grown barley, smoked and aged with American fruitwoods. See their offerings at cooperfox.biz.

There's also the **Eight Shires Coloniale Distillery**, 7218 Merrimac Trail, Williamsburg, known for its rum and gin made with Virginia grains and molasses using 18th-century techniques. Their stated mission is to research, preserve, teach, and present the "history of distillation from the Colonial American period, 1600–1775." Check online for tours and tasting times at 8shires.com.

The granddaddy of these adult beverage tours is, of course, the **Williamsburg Winery,** 5800 Wessex Hundred, Williamburg. The first Chardonnay vines were planted on this 320-acre farm in 1985. Three years later, the 1988 Chardonnay won the Virginia Governor's Cup, the top prize in a prestigious competition.

Since then the winery has expanded both its varietals and its footprint, adding a tavern and an upscale hotel on-site. Guided tours begin in the 1619 Pavilion, where wine is sold by the glass, bottle, and flight. Capacity was severely restricted by pandemic guidelines so it's imperative to make a reservation in advance. No more than six can tour at one time. The winery is open daily except Thanksgiving, Christmas Day, and New Year's Day. From Mar to Dec hours are noon to 5 p.m.

There is also a **Williamsburg Winery Tasting Room** in Merchants Square, open noon to 5 p.m. Thurs through Sun.

Finally, the **Silver Hand Meadery,** 224 Monticello Ave., Williamsburg, produces an ancient drink known as mead or honey wine. The storefront hosts free tastings and something called the Honey Tasting Experience. Call (757) 378-2225 or check silverhandmeadery.com for specific times.

Where to Grind Your Axe

They've been holding axe-throwing demonstrations at Colonial Williamsburg for decades and now finally the public has gotten their chance. **Axe Republic** has become a popular nightspot for visitors seeking an uncomplicated and therapeutic exercise. Located in New Town, the space is arranged much like a bowling alley, with twelve individual lanes, each flanked by a seating area for two to six players and a small table to hold snacks and drinks. Instructors give each customer a brief tutorial, showing players how to (safely) lift the axe over their head, let the blade hang between their shoulder blades and then lift and let go, pitching the axe into a spin and (hopefully) right into the bull's eye. The bell clangs if you hit the spot. This is not a place for quiet conversations.

Owner Nikki Montero (handily, a school nurse by day) sampled axe throwing at a venue in Virginia Beach and was instantly hooked. "I'm a very competitive person," she admits. She went back twice with her college age kids before she and her husband decided to open their own center in Williamsburg. "When we decided to go for it, I said we have to act on it fast." Axe Republic opened in March 2019.

The kitchen serves up a limited menu of pub fare (wings, sliders, loaded tater tots) as well as beer and soft drinks.

Like other centers in the burgeoning competitive axe-throwing universe, Axes Republic runs weeknight leagues. Teenagers 14 and up are welcome to play if they are accompanied by an adult. All players must wear closed-toe shoes. "In the event of an axe bounce-back," Montero says. "It happens."

Axe Republic, 4919 Courthouse St. (New Town), Williamsburg, VA 23188; (757) 808-5397; axerepublic.com. Open at 5 p.m. Wed through Fri; 11 a.m. to 10 p.m. Sat; noon to 6 p.m. Sun. Reservations are recommended.

Kidstuff

With Busch Gardens and Water Country USA in your backyard, it's hard to imagine that there isn't enough for kids to do in Williamsburg, but some like less overwhelming diversions. (Even some kids do.) It's also tough to justify the entrance fee at some attractions if you have less than a whole day to spend there. Here are some alternatives when you have just a few hours to spare, or if you want a more unusual experience out of your time in Williamsburg.

ATTRACTIONS

THE ADVENTURE ZONE, inside the Williamsburg Indoor Sports Complex, 5700 Warhill Trail, Williamsburg, VA 23188; (757) 253-1947; thewisc .com. Active kids and rainy day? This indoor sports complex has a solution: the Adventure Zone which features a climbing wall, a "ninja warrior gym," laser maze, arcade games, and a 1,400-square-foot playground for little ones. Pricing for the different areas varies, but there's a bundle for $20 that includes 90 minutes of laser tag, climbing, and playground use. The facility is open Mon through Fri 6 a.m. to 8 p.m.; Sat and Sun 9 a.m. to 4 p.m. but call ahead for availability as it fluctuates based on the school year.

GO APE!, located inside Freedom Park, 5537 Centerville Rd., Williamsburg, VA 23185; (800) 971-8271; goape.com. Afraid of heights? This is not for you! But the adventurous will enjoy the multiple challenges of this treetop adventure course which allows participants to explore the park from a very unusual perspective: above the tree line, a la Tarzan, using zip lines and swings. There's also a Treetop Junior Course for those not ready to challenge the steep climb up to the zip lines, and "Monkey Drop," a freefall with a soft, safe landing. The park is run by James City County, but is just a few miles northwest of Williamsburg. Admission to the park itself is free but admission prices and reservations for GO APE! can be made either online or by calling the 800 number. Credit cards only. The park is open daily 7 a.m. to sunset.

GO-KARTS PLUS, 6910 Richmond Rd., Williamsburg, VA 23188; (757) 564-7600; gokartsplus.com. Just west of the Williamsburg Pottery Factory on US 60, this family owned and run amusement park features four go-kart tracks, bumper cars, minigolf, blaster boats, a thrill ride from Italy called the "Disk'O," and a newly remodeled video game arcade. Most rides in Kiddieland are geared for children ages 3 to 8; there is also a free playground area called Toddler Town. (There are height requirements for some of the rides, but there are also double-seater karts for a child and adult to ride together.) Admission and parking are free. Rides are paid for with tickets or an "all-you-can-ride" wristband. Discount ticket books, good for the season or as long as you're in town, can help reduce the cost of the rides. There are special offers for military, first responders, and AAA members. Park hours vary depending on the weather and the time of year so call for the current operating hours before you go.

FOX WIRE FARM, 8105 Richmond Rd., Toano, VA 23168; (757) 707-5052; foxwirefarmalpacas.com. This 200-acre farm 20 minutes west of Williamsburg is home to an adorable herd of alpacas and is open to tours by individuals or groups, including school field trips. A working farm, they also offer tractor-pulled hay rides and a summer camp that teaches children about animal husbandry, organic farming, and environmental issues related to farming. A very popular event is the annual shearing demonstration which takes place every April. Tours leave from the boutique on Richmond Road which sells yarn, clothing, and even alpacas, if you are in the market for your own.

PIRATE'S COVE ADVENTURE GOLF, 2001 Mooretown Rd., Williamsburg, VA 23185; (757) 259-4600; piratescove.com. Pirate's Cove minigolf is organized around a pirate theme, with nautical accents—wooden walkways, rope fences, and ship's bow sticking out of the ground, as if Blackbeard himself had sunk it. A waterfall flows down one side of a mountain, and 2 courses run through caves. Pirate's Cove has 36 holes on 2 courses. Adult admission is $9.50 for adults, $8.95 for children. Open 10 a.m. to 11 p.m. daily during the summer, and on weekends Mar through Nov, weather permitting. (Call ahead for operating hours before Father's Day and after Labor Day.)

RIPLEY'S BELIEVE IT OR NOT, 1735 Richmond Rd., Williamsburg, VA 23185; (757) 220-9220; WilliamsburgRipleys.com. The advertising slogan for this gallery of oddities—Visit the Strangest Place in Williamsburg—lures visitors to tour its collection of weird esoterica, like a comic book printed with the ashes of its author (Ew!). There are eleven galleries with more than 350 exhibits, including a 4D theater and "laser race." Admission is $21.99 for kids ages 5 to 12 and $26.99, but check online or in the local tourist magazines in your hotel lobby for discount coupons. Open daily except Christmas, 10 a.m. to 6 p.m. Sun through Thurs; 10 a.m. to 9 p.m. Fri and Sat.

PARKS AND RECREATION

JAMES CITY COUNTY RECREATION CENTER, 5301 Longhill Rd., Williamsburg, VA 23188; (757) 259-4200; jamescitycountyva.gov. This full-service county recreation center offers an expansive list of programming for preschool kids through adults. Youth classes are offered in art, dance, piano, and sports, including swimming. The playground is wheelchair accessible and has adaptive equipment for all children. There are also softball, baseball, and soccer fields. The **Rec Connect Program** offers year-round fitness activities, creative crafts, drama, music, environmental education, and field trips. Programs are available both before and after school, and during school vacation periods.

Open 6 a.m. to 9 p.m. Mon through Thurs; until 8 p.m. Fri; Sat 9 a.m. to 6 p.m.; and Sun 1 p.m. to 6 p.m. Although the center is primarily for area residents, visitors can use the facility for a $10 charge a day for adults, $4 for children ages 5 to 17. There are also nonresident annual and semiannual membership fees.

KIDSBURG, Veterans Park, 3793 Ironbound Rd., Williamsburg, VA 23188; jamescitycountyva.gov/recreation/parks/mid-county-park. This 19-acre park is home to Kidsburg, a 30,000-square-foot playground initially built by more than 1,000 volunteers and now maintained by James City County. Most days you'll find kids swarming the replica of the ship *Susan Constant*, the James Fort Tot Lot, the George P. Coleman Memorial Bridge, and two theaters. Admission is free. Hours are from sunrise to dusk.

SKATE PARK, 5301 Longhill Rd., Williamsburg, VA 23188; (757) 259-5360; jamescitycountyva.gov/recreation/parks/skate-park.html. Located directly across the street from the James City County (JCC) Recreation Center, this bowl-style skate park offers 10,000 square feet of concrete jumps and ramps. There are 2 movable ramps, a handrail, and multiple grinding edges. Skateboards, in-line skates, and scooters are permitted to use the facility at the same time, but spectators are not permitted inside the fenced area. Helmets are required. User-fee passes are required. They are free for county and City of Williamsburg residents. Nonresidents may purchase a single day pass for $5 or a season pass for $35. Passes are sold at the JCC Recreation Center. The skate park is open 9 a.m. to 8 p.m. Mon through Sat; 1 to 6 p.m. Sun during the summer months, until 6 p.m. in the spring and fall, and closes at 5 p.m. every day during the winter months.

YORKTOWN WATERFRONT, 423 Water St. (dockmaster's office), Yorktown, VA 23690; (757) 890-3800; yorkcounty.gov/CountyGovernment/GeneralServices/YorktownWaterfront.aspx. A 2-acre beach along the York River provides opportunities for boating, swimming, and fishing. A large picnic area is located east of the beach. Several restaurants within walking distance also are open during the day should hunger strike. Public restrooms, with shower facilities, are available at the west end of the beach and are open Apr through Oct from dawn to dusk. Several trees can offer escape from the midday sun, and the Riverwalk provides a scenic stroll from one end of the town to the other. Be aware: There are no lifeguards on duty.

AMF WILLIAMSBURG LANES, 5544 Olde Towne Rd., Williamsburg, VA 23188; (757) 565-3311; amf.com/williamsburglanes. No bowler is too young to play here. Novices pull up bumpers in the gutters so everyone has a good time—and a decent score at the end of a game. While the place is wildly popular and often crowded with league play, kids are welcome anytime. If you should experience a wait, visit the game room and snack bar. Visit the website to check on daily specials on both play and food. The bowling begins every weekday at 5 p.m. and goes till 11 p.m.; Sat noon to midnight; Sun 2 p.m. to 10 p.m.

RIPLEY'S BELIEVE IT OR NOT, 1735 Richmond Rd., Williamsburg, VA 23185; (757) 220-9220; WilliamsburgRipleys.com. The advertising slogan for this gallery of oddities—Visit the Strangest Place in Williamsburg—lures visitors to tour its collection of weird esoterica, like a comic book printed with the ashes of its author. There are eleven galleries with more than 350 exhibits, including a 4D theater and "laser race." Admission is $21.99 for kids ages 5 to 12 and $26.99 but check online or in the local tourist magazines in your hotel lobby for discount coupons. Open daily except Christmas, 10 a.m. to 6 p.m. Sun through Thurs; 10 a.m. to 9 p.m. Fri and Sat.

WILLIAMSBURG REGIONAL LIBRARY, 515 Scotland St., Williamsburg, VA 23185; (757) 259-4040; 7770 Croaker Rd., Williamsburg, VA 23188; (757) 259-7770; wrl.org. Both locations of this excellent library system provide services for children from birth through high school, including story time for preschoolers and early elementary schoolchildren, "Family Fort Night," an evening event with flashlights and books, author visits, children's theater groups, professional storytellers, puppet theaters, and assorted workshops. Most programs are offered free of charge. For more information call the numbers listed above or check the website.

KIDSTUFF

The Arts

The first performing arts theater in the Americas was located in Williamsburg on the edge of Palace Green. Long gone, that early theater has not been reconstructed, but when it comes to the arts, the Historic Triangle offers plenty to see, hear, and do. There are museums and galleries devoted to the visual arts; theater, music, and dance performances occur here every week.

Travel east to Newport News, Hampton, and points south and you'll find even more: world-class museums of history and art, others with state-of-the-art IMAX movies and interactive exhibits. The state's premier opera company is based in Norfolk, which is also home to multiple theater companies, including the Virginia Stage Company, which performs at the restored Wells Theatre. Almost every municipality in Hampton Roads supports the arts with its own community theater, staging shows throughout the year. The American Theater in Hampton hosts a fantastic lineup of music, theater, and dance year in and year out.

VENUES

In the past, the majority of the performances produced in Williamsburg had been staged at William & Mary's Phi Beta Kappa Memorial Hall, but that facility is closed for a multiyear renovation. In its place, the smaller Kimball Theatre in Merchants Square and the auditorium at the Williamsburg Regional Library are hosting various performances throughout the year.

KIMBALL THEATRE, 428 W. Duke of Gloucester St. (Merchants Square), Williamsburg, VA 23185; (800) 249-0179; Kimball.wm.edu. Extensively remodeled in 2001, this 583-seat chandelier-lit theater now looks essentially as it did when it opened in 1933 as the Williamsburg Theater. Owned by the College of William & Mary, it offered a full schedule—lectures, concerts, limited-run films, and documentaries—prior to the coronavirus pandemic. Check their website for plans on reopening and future events.

PHI BETA KAPPA MEMORIAL HALL, 601 Jamestown Rd. (on the William & Mary campus), Williamsburg, VA 23185; (757) 221-2674 (box office); wm.edu/as/tsd/performances/pbk. Currently closed and undergoing a massive renovation, this 750-seat hall hosts Shakespeare in the summer, lectures, and forums of the highest quality, with the College of William & Mary the most frequent sponsor. William & Mary's theater department—whose graduates include Glenn Close and Linda Lavin—offers a high-quality season of performances here during the academic year, and the music and dance departments provide concerts of equally fine caliber. The William & Mary Concert Series held in the hall is a subscription series of performances by nationally and internationally acclaimed performers and groups presenting symphonies, ballet, chamber music, theater, and solo performances. Ticket sales are publicized in the fall. Think ahead—tickets go very quickly. The hall is wheelchair accessible and has an electronic system for the hearing impaired. Renovations ongoing until at least 2022.

WILLIAMSBURG REGIONAL LIBRARY, 515 Scotland St., Williamsburg, VA 23185; (757) 259-4070; wrl.org. The library has done an extraordinary job of becoming, in effect, the community's cultural arts center. In the center's lobby there are small ongoing exhibits by visual artists working in a variety of media. The auditorium, which seats 268, provides a venue for lectures, debates, forums, and performances of all kinds, from symphonies, chamber concerts, and choral presentations to high school–band rock 'n' roll. Events held here are typically free, but occasionally an event organized by an outside group will charge a minimal fee. The library also hosts a number of national acts with admission ranging from free to $20.

PERFORMING ARTS

Music

Symphonic, operatic, and recital performances by touring professionals and virtuoso students from the College of William & Mary's music department are presented throughout the year. Williamsburg also is home to several professional and skilled amateur musical groups, each presenting a varied program throughout the season. The venues differ depending upon the performance. The best way to get timely information is to monitor the *Virginia Gazette*'s arts and performance sections.

CHAMBER MUSIC GUILD OF WILLIAMSBURG, chambermusic williamsburg.org. Local lovers of chamber music formed this organization more than 3 decades ago to organize an annual series of concerts for classical music aficionados on the peninsula. What was once a small corps of hard-core

> **i** Community members can get on the William & Mary Cultural Events Calendar mailing list. For information about college-sponsored arts happenings, call (757) 221-4000, the college's general information number, between 8 a.m. and 5 p.m., Mon through Fri.

THE ARTS

enthusiasts grew to a base of subscribers large enough to sell out the season every year. Concerts are generally held at the Williamsburg Regional Library's auditorium at 515 Scotland St., Williamsburg. Check the website for its slate of premiere musicians coming in 2021–2022.

SUMMER BREEZE CONCERT SERIES, Merchants Square, West Duke of Gloucester Street, Williamsburg, VA 23185; (757) 220-7751; merchants square.org. Free concerts featuring not-to-be-missed party bands rock DoG Street from 7 to 9 p.m. Wed night throughout the summer. Bring folding chairs and blankets for these outdoor performances, held on Duke of Gloucester Street, just west of Henry Street.

WILLIAMSBURG CHORAL GUILD, PO Box 1864, Williamsburg, VA 23187; williamsburgchoralguild.org. The Williamsburg Choral Guild is an established and esteemed mixed choral group made up of about 100 area volunteer singers. Guild members rehearse from late August through early May, presenting four subscription concerts during that time. The website keeps a current list of upcoming performances. For more information, or to contact the guild to audition, visit their Facebook page.

WILLIAMSBURG SYMPHONY ORCHESTRA, 212 N. Henry St., Williamsburg, VA 23187 (757) 229-9857; williamsburgsymphony.org. Each year, the Williamsburg Symphony Orchestra offers a subscription series in addition to special holiday and family concerts. The WSO is noted throughout the region for the excellence of its programs, typically staging five classical Masterworks concerts, four holiday pops concerts, a cabaret, a family concert, and performing educational outreach to school and youth orchestras. All Masterworks and Family concerts are performed at the Kimball Theatre in Merchants Square. Pops concerts take place in various Williamsburg locations. Check the website for specific information about the symphony's annual programming.

WILLIAMSBURG WOMEN'S CHORUS, PO Box 685, Williamsburg, VA 23187; (757) 220-3035; williamsburgwomenschorus.org. The Williamsburg Women's Chorus is an all-volunteer group who sing in a variety of musical

> **i** Musician and Grammy Award-winning pop artist Bruce Hornsby, who was born and raised in Williamsburg, still lives in town with his wife and two sons. He often can be seen at local sports events, restaurants, and simply walking about town with his family, taking in the sights like everyone else.

THE ARTS

styles from Baroque to Broadway. The chorus performs 2 major concerts a year, inviting middle school choirs to sing with them. At the spring concerts, the recipients of the chorus's vocal scholarship perform onstage. Auditions are required of aspiring new members. Check their website for upcoming concerts and more information. Check the website for specific times and dates.

WILLIAM & MARY THEATRE, 428 W. Duke of Gloucester St., Williamsburg, VA 23185; (757) 221-2674 (Kimball Theatre box office); events.wm .edu/calendar/upcoming/tsd. The college's theater, speech, and dance students stage 4 full-scale productions (and many smaller shows) during the academic year. Ticket prices vary; some performances are free. If you get the opportunity to catch WM's improv troupe, IT, don't miss it. They don't do full-blown shows, but they are an entertaining group and make appearances at local events.

THE WILLIAMSBURG PLAYERS, 200 Hubbard Ln., Williamsburg, VA 23185; (757) 229-0431 (box office); williamsburgplayers.org. For nearly 60 years, this community group has been staging high-quality plays using an all-volunteer cast and crew. In recent years, they've been able to expand their repertoire by greatly expanding their space, doubling the number of seats in their off-the-beaten-path theater. The season usually consists of two musicals and three plays, mixing little-known and more-famous works, with an emphasis on the modern and contemporary. Concessions are served before the show in the well-lit, comfortable lobby. General admission is $20 for adults, $12 for children and students. A $75 season subscription gets you admitted to all five shows.

VISUAL ARTS

Museums

ABBY ALDRICH ROCKEFELLER FOLK ARTS MUSEUM, 301 S. Nassau St., Williamsburg, VA 23185; (757) 220-7724, (844) 585-1168; colonial williamsburg.org. The oldest institution in the US dedicated solely to the preservation of American folk art, this museum houses the nation's premier collection from the 18th, 19th, and 20th centuries. Exhibits feature paintings, drawings, furniture, ceramics, whirligigs, weather vanes, carvings, toys, quilts, musical instruments, and other folk works representing many diverse cultural traditions and geographic regions. John D. Rockefeller, Jr. established the museum in 1957 in honor of his wife, Abby, who began collecting folk art early in the 20th century. In 1939, she gave her core collection of 425 objects to the Colonial Williamsburg Foundation. Today the collection of more than 7,000 objects includes items dating from the 1720s including "Portrait of an Enslaved Child," an 1830 watercolor with pencil and ink by Mary Anna Randolph Custis, "Music and Dance in Beaufort County," an 18th-century watercolor of an al fresco scene showing two groups of African American interacting in South

Carolina, and a 19th-century Noah's Ark toy set, part of the exhibition of "German Toys in America."

DEWITT WALLACE DECORATIVE ARTS MUSEUM, 301 S. Nassau St., Williamsburg, VA 23185; (757) 220-7724, (844) 585-1168; colonial williamsburg.org. This fascinating museum, originally designed by world-renowned architect I. M. Pei, displays prized pieces of Colonial Williamsburg's permanent collection—furniture, textiles, maps, prints, paintings, metals, and ceramics dating from the 1600s to the 1830s—in exhibits designed to instruct viewers in the aesthetics and tastes of the colonial period. Thorough research precedes each exhibition, and the results are presented in understandable and memorable ways. The overall effect on gallery visitors is an understanding of each object in the context of its function, design, and use.

Admission is free with any Colonial Williamsburg ticket, or you can purchase single-day museums ticket ($14.99 for adults, $8.99 for children). The museum is generally open 10 a.m. to 7 p.m. daily, but hours vary seasonally. A cafe serves lunch, tea, and light refreshments. A gift shop selling reproductions and decorative arts journals is also on the premises. The entire museum is wheelchair accessible.

MUSCARELLE MUSEUM OF ART, 603 Jamestown Rd. (on the William & Mary campus), Williamsburg, VA 23185; (757) 221-2700; muscarelle.wm .edu. In the evening this museum, just west of (the under-construction) Phi Beta Kappa Memorial Hall on the William & Mary campus, is easy to spot. Multiple columns of color light one exterior wall; the effect is quite startling when viewed from Jamestown Road for the first time. The museum, designed by famed local

---

Internationally Known Artist Georgia O'Keeffe

The famous artist received her first honorary degree from William & Mary. Although her two brothers attended college here, women were not allowed to enroll when the family moved to Williamsburg in the early 1900s. To mark the award of her honorary degree in 1938, the college put on an exhibition of her work, including eight paintings selected by O'Keeffe's husband, Alfred Stieglitz. Another, *White Flower,* was donated to the event by Abby Rockefeller. It was O'Keeffe's first show in the South, and it remained on view for six days. In 2001 the Muscarelle Museum of Art re-created her exhibit with eight of the original nine paintings. (One was too fragile to travel.) The new O'Keeffe show was on display for five months and also included letters, documents, and a 6.5-minute home movie of her visit to William & Mary to accept her honorary degree.

THE ARTS

architect Carlton Abbott, offers lectures, films, and tours, but the holdings are the major draw. The permanent collection includes works by European Old Masters as well as modern works, and a special holding is the collection of colonial-period portraits of Virginians. The museum also hosts several changing exhibits throughout the year. At the time of publication the museum was only open to W&M students and faculty; check their website for updates on the status of public events. Parking spaces are at a premium on campus, but if you can find an empty space in the lot in front of the building, obtain a permit from the museum in order to park for free. Admission is $10, free to children under 12.

Galleries

ANDREWS GALLERY, Andrews Hall, accessible via Jamestown Road (behind Phi Beta Kappa Theatre and across from Swem Library on the William & Mary campus), Williamsburg, VA 23185; (757) 221-1452; wm.edu/as/andrewsgallery/. This exhibition gallery showcases work in various media, including ceramics, painting, drawing, printmaking, sculpture, and photography, by students and faculty of William & Mary's Department of Art and Art History. Periodic exhibits of traveling shows and invited artists, gallery talks, lectures, and workshops make this a valuable asset to the local art scene. At the time of publication the gallery was only open to W&M students and faculty; check their website for updates on the status of public events.

A TOUCH OF EARTH, 6580 Richmond Rd. (The Gallery Shops), Williamsburg, VA 23188; (757) 565-0425; atouchofearthgallery.com. This gallery features fine decorative and functional crafts by more than 200 contemporary American artists and craftspeople. The selections include pottery, wind chimes in clay and metal, glassworks, jewelry, lamps, musical instruments, kaleidoscopes, candleholders, and textiles—many of them signed, one-of-a-kind pieces. The collection includes hand-built and wheel-thrown stoneware and fine porcelain and unique "Gloom Chasers," intricately decorated and pierced stoneware lanterns. Open from 9:30 a.m. to 5:30 p.m. Mon through Sat; noon to 5 p.m. Sun.

WILLIAMSBURG CONTEMPORARY ART CENTER, 110 Westover Ave., Williamsburg, VA 23185; (757) 229-4949; visitwcac.org. The focus of this gallery, established more than 40 years ago, is work by local, regional, and national contemporary artists who work in various media. Shows change on a regular basis, with an occasional Christmas crafts show in November and December and a spring crafts exhibition. Affiliated with Richmond's Virginia Museum of Fine Arts, traveling exhibits are often featured here, too. Admission is free. Open 11 a.m. to 3 p.m. Tues through Sat; noon to 4 p.m. Sun. At the time of publication the center had canceled their public events due to the coronavirus pandemic, but they offer virtual shows through their website.

Parks and Recreation

Williamsburg and the surrounding communities offer residents myriad recreational opportunities. Anyone interested in sports and recreation information should consult the *Virginia Gazette*'s sports section, which gives extensive coverage to local sports. Another good source of information is the James City County Parks and Recreation's comprehensive seasonal publication, which is available at the JCC-Williamsburg Community Center, listed later in this chapter, or online at jamescitycountyva.gov.

PARKS DEPARTMENTS

JAMES CITY COUNTY PARKS AND RECREATION, 5300 Palmer Lane Rd., Williamsburg, VA 23188; (757) 259-3200; jamescitycountyva.gov/635/Parks-Recreation. This department oversees a wide range of recreation programs throughout the county, including those at the James City County Recreation Center, the Abram Frink Jr. Community Center, Little Creek Reservoir, Veterans Park, and Upper County Park. Office hours are 8 a.m. to 5 p.m. Mon through Fri.

WILLIAMSBURG PARKS AND RECREATION DEPARTMENT, 202 Quarterpath Rd., Williamsburg, VA 23185; (757) 259-3764; williamsburgva.gov/government/department-i-z/parks-recreation. Numerous recreation programs are available through this department, which also oversees Quarterpath Park, Waller Mill Park, and Kiwanis Park. The department's regular office hours are 8 a.m. to 5 p.m. Mon through Fri, although someone is on duty whenever the recreation center is open.

YORK PARKS, RECREATION & TOURISM, 100 County Dr., Grafton, VA 23690; (757) 890-3500; yorkcounty.gov/Parks-and-Recreation. Located at the York County Operations Center off Goodwin Neck Road, the office of York Parks, Recreation & Tourism oversees the operation of six parks, the Yorktown Beach waterfront, and county public boat landings at various sites. The offices are open 8:15 a.m. to 5 p.m. Mon through Fri, except on holidays.

Park Locations and Activities

BACK CREEK PARK, Goodwin Neck Road, Dandy, VA 23697; (757) 890-3850. A free public boat launch keeps this 27-acre park busy year-round. Kayaks are available for rent. Landlubber? There are also 6, well-maintained, lighted tennis courts. Court reservations are recommended and can be made one week in advance. To reserve a court or to rent the ball machine, call the number listed above. There are court fees ranging from $4 to $8 per hour. If staff is not on duty, courts are available for free by calling the York County parks department at (757) 890-3500 or the park to obtain lock combinations. The park has a picnic area with grills and restrooms.

CHARLES BROWN PARK, VA 238, Lackey, VA 23690; (757) 890-3500. Named in memory of a Lackey resident and York County educator who demonstrated a keen interest in youth, this 10-acre park includes a baseball field, 2 basketball courts, 2 tennis courts, picnic shelter, playground area, and restrooms. A 3,000-square-foot community center on-site includes 2 small meeting rooms, 1 large meeting room, restrooms, and a small kitchen.

CHISMAN CREEK PARK, Wolf Trap Road, Grafton, VA 23692; (757) 890-3500. This 13-acre park was reclaimed from a fly-ash site in 1991. It has 2 lighted softball fields, with skinned infields and irrigated outfields. It is used primarily for York County's adult softball program in the spring and summer, and for youth soccer in the fall.

COLLEGE LANDING PARK, 1070 S. Henry St., Williamsburg, VA 23185; (757) 259-3760. This small park on the southern edge of town off South Henry Street is always open. It is built alongside a marsh and has picnic areas, a boat ramp, and a quiet boardwalk. It is wheelchair accessible.

DIASCUND RESERVOIR PARK, 9545 Diascund Reservoir Rd., Lenexa, VA 23089; (757) 259-5360. This James City County reservoir, operated jointly with Newport News and the Division of Game and Inland Fisheries, is open to the public for boating and fishing. To preserve water quality, only electric trolling motors are allowed on the reservoir. Open daily sunrise to sunset.

FREEDOM PARK, 5535 Centerville Rd., Williamsburg, VA 23185; (757) 259-4022; jamescitycountyva.gov. There is a lot to love and a lot to do at this park in James City County, just a few miles northwest of Williamsburg. Nestled within the 600-acre forest here are trails for hiking, including a 1-mile ADA-accessible paved trail. There are also 20 miles of bike paths, designed, built, and maintained by the Eastern Virginia Mountain Bike Association, which also regularly organizes rides through the park.

Perhaps the most fascinating attraction here, though, is the glimpse into what life was like on this land in the centuries ago. This park is the site of an 18th-century cemetery, the Revolutionary War battle of Spencer's Ordinary (1781), and one of the nation's earliest Free Black Settlements, founded in 1803 when William Ludlow Lee released his slaves from servitude upon his death. Historians have re-created three cabins, furnished with items authentic

Close-up

For the Bird(er)s

Five of Charles City County's plantations (Berkeley, North Bend, Piney Grove at Southall's, Sherwood Forest, and Westover) are designated stops on the **Virginia Birding & Wildlife Trail.** Avid naturalists will find the area along this part of the trail, known as The Plantation Loop, offers many diverse habitats that draw a great variety of wildlife and migratory birds. The Audubon Society has been conducting a **Christmas Bird Count** in the Williamsburg area for more than 100 years. In 2019, 73 field observers reported sighting 84 bald eagles, 111 different species and a total of 31,604 birds. For more information on the trail, go to dgif.virginia.gov/vbwt/ and click on the link for the "Coastal Trail," and then on the link for "Plantation."

Elsewhere in the area, there is frequent programming centered on our winged friends. **The Williamsburg Bird Club** meets at New Quarter Park, 1000 Lakeshead Dr., Williamsburg, at 8 a.m. on the fourth Saturday of each month for a bird walk. Bring binoculars if you have them but the park office has extras that may be borrowed. The group meets in the parking lot near the park office.

Wild Birds Unlimited, 4625 Casey Blvd. (New Town), holds regularly scheduled classes on birding basics, with tips of where to see birds, and how to lure them to your own backyard with the right kind of birdhouse and seed.

to the period, which offer a peek into the workaday routines of African Americans in Virginia before the Emancipation Proclamation.

But wait, there's more! The park is also home to the **Williamsburg Botanical Garden,** which displays more than 800 species of native vegetation. The

> **i** Bald eagles are back in record numbers along the James River, just a few decades after they were almost killed off by pesticide pollution. Aerial surveys conducted in 2020 found approximately 310 nesting pairs of eagles had produced young during the spring mating season—that's believed to be the highest number along the James since the colonial era.

WBG also offers monthly educational programs and special events throughout the year.

Finally, there's **Go Ape!,** a treetop adventure course which allows participants to explore the park from a very unusual perspective: above the tree line, a la Tarzan using zip lines and swings. (There's also a Treetop Junior Course for those not ready to challenge the steep climb up to the zip lines.) For specific information on **Go Ape!**, including ticket prices, visit goape.com or call (800) 971-8271.

Admission to the park itself is free and leashed dogs are welcome. The park's interpretive center is open 9 a.m. to 5 p.m. Sat and Sun. The rest of the park is open daily 7 a.m. to sunset.

GREENSPRINGS INTERPRETIVE TRAIL, 375 John Tyler Hwy. (behind Jamestown High School), Williamsburg, VA 23185; (757) 259-5360. This 3.5-mile nature trail loops through a landscape of wetlands, and forest. Signs along the boardwalk offer information about the environment, historic events of the early colonists and Native Americans, and area wildlife. Over 200 species of birds have been documented on this site, which is part of the Virginia Birding Trail. The trail is dog friendly, but dogs must be leashed at all times. Deer are plentiful. Open daily from sunrise to sunset. Park at the tennis courts behind the school and follow the dirt road to the trailhead.

HIGHLAND PARK COMMUNITY PARK, 703 N. Henry St., Williamsburg, VA 23185. This 2-acre mini-park is located on North Henry Street in the Highland Park Community. This facility has playground equipment, half-court basketball, and a picnic shelter with grills.

JAMES CITY COUNTY SPORTS COMPLEX, 5301 Longhill Rd., Williamsburg, VA 23188; (757) 259-5360. Adjacent to the recreation center, this park includes 2 lighted softball fields, 2 lighted natural grass fields, a wheelchair-accessible playground, and a paved 2-mile walking trail. A skate park is located across the street. Open daily sunrise to sunset. Lighted fields may be in use until 10 p.m.

KILN CREEK PARK, Kiln Creek Subdivision, Yorktown, VA 23693; (757) 890-3500. Located in the Kiln Creek community, this 21-acre York County park opened in 1999. The park features a lighted soccer field, lighted baseball field, youth softball/baseball field, 2 outdoor basketball courts, a playground, a picnic shelter, parking, and restrooms. The park is used primarily for the Little League baseball program and the youth soccer program.

KIWANIS MUNICIPAL PARK, 125 Longhill Rd., Williamsburg, VA 23185; (757) 259-3760. In 2019 the city completely overhauled the playgrounds in this 27-acre park, which also provides Little League baseball fields, basketball courts, a picnic shelter, a playground, and lighted tennis courts. The renovation addressed accessibility issues for special needs kids and created separate play areas for kids ages 2 to 5 and those aged 6 to 12. There's a new swing bay, which includes an inclusive freedom swing, an Orbiron, REV8 spinner and a zip line. Nine outdoor exercise equipment stations were located around the perimeter of the playgrounds so parents and guardians can work out while still monitor their kids in the play area. The surface of the new play area is also kid friendly, made of a poured-in-place rubber material. The changes make this park a destination playground for parents looking for a safe, fun, free place to let the kids have some fresh air and fun.

LITTLE CREEK RESERVOIR PARK, 180 Lakeview Dr., Toano, VA 23168; (757) 259-5360. Located off Forge Road, this park is a fisherman's paradise featuring year-round fishing and boating on a 996-acre reservoir, stocked with largemouth bass, bluegill, crappie, stripers, walleye, perch, pickerel, and a variety of sunfish and catfish. There is also a free fishing pier. Use of the boat ramps costs a nominal amount. In summer 2015, the park store was closed and boat rentals suspended due to a lack of a vendor to operate those services; call the county for information about when these services will be reinstated. All fishermen must have a Virginia fishing license. Open daily 7 a.m. Mon through Fri and 6 a.m. Sat and Sun, the park closes daily at sunset.

VETERANS PARK, 3793 Ironbound Rd., Williamsburg, VA 23188 (757) 592-1565; DF. This 19-acre park (formerly called Mid County Park) has courts for every sport: volleyball, pétanque/bocce, basketball, pickleball, and tennis. There's also lots of open space, a wheelchair-accessible trail, picnic shelters, and a memorial to local residents who died in Vietnam. It's also the home of Kidsburg, a 30,000-square-foot lighted playground. (See more about Kidsburg in our Kidstuff chapter.) The park is dog friendly, but canines must be leashed at all times. Open daily sunrise to 10 p.m.

NEW QUARTER PARK, 1000 Lakeshead Dr., Williamsburg, VA 23185; (757) 890-5840. Near the Queens Lake area of Williamsburg, this 545-acre York County park is especially good for group activities. The park has 10 picnic shelters, 9 hiking trails (some with scenic overlooks), a mountain bike trail, an 18-hole disc-golf course, and basketball and sand volleyball courts. There are also horseshoe pits, a large playground, and access to waterways for canoes, kayaks, and fishing. Dogs are welcome but must be leashed at all times. The Williamsburg Bird Club leads a guided bird-spotting walk at 8 a.m. on the fourth Sat of each month. Open daily 8 a.m. to dusk, May through Oct, and from 10 a.m. to dusk, Nov through Apr (8 a.m. on Sat and Sun).

POWHATAN CREEK PARK, 1831 Jamestown Rd., Williamsburg, VA 23185; (757) 259-5390 (parks dept.); (757) 592-1665 (park ranger). Boat launches in this park, which is part of the Chesapeake Gateways Network, provide access to the James River at Jamestown Island, with scenic views of Historic Jamestown. Powhatan Creek is listed on the Natural Resources Inventory as the most biodiverse creek on the peninsula. Scenic views of tidal marshes and an abundance of wildlife highlight trips on this beautiful waterway. The facility consists of a small nonmotorized boat/canoe/kayak launch with gravel parking for up to 20 vehicles, as well as 5 observation/fishing piers. Fishing and boat launch access are available 24 hours a day. Open sunrise to sunset.

POWHATAN CREEK TRAIL, 3131 Ironbound Rd. (behind Clara Byrd Baker Elementary School), Williamsburg, VA 23185; (757) 259-5360. This paved 2-mile long, 8-foot wide multiuse trail connects to the Greensprings Interpretive Trail, the historic site known as Church on the Main, Mainland Farm (considered to be the oldest continuously cultivated farm in America's first English settlement), and the Virginia Capital Trail. Parking is available behind Clara Byrd Baker Elementary School. The trail is open from sunrise to sunset.

QUARTERPATH PARK AND RECREATION CENTER, 202 Quarterpath Rd., Williamsburg, VA 23185; (757) 259-3760. This 23-acre facility includes 3 lighted softball fields; 3 all-weather tennis courts; 2 sand volleyball courts; playground equipment, a picnic shelter, and a 35,000-square-foot recreation center that offers basketball, dance, aerobics, and more. Various instructional classes, athletic programs for youth and adults, sports camps, and special events are held throughout the year at this facility. The rec center is open 8 a.m. to 9 p.m. Mon through Fri, 9 a.m. to 6 p.m. Sat, and 1 to 8 p.m. Sun.

REDOUBT PARK, Quarterpath Road (VA 637, off US 60), Williamsburg, VA 23185. This wooded 22-acre park is the site of the Battle of Williamsburg, waged on May 5, 1862, which resulted in nearly 4,000 Union and Confederate casualties. Benjamin Stoddard Ewell, a West Point graduate and president of the College of William & Mary, conceived the idea of a Williamsburg defensive line to prevent Union troops from reaching Richmond. During the summer of 1861, 14 redoubts were built between College and Queens Creeks. The two preserved in this park were constructed by soldiers and slaves to guard the right flank of the Williamsburg line.

UPPER COUNTY PARK, 180 Leisure Rd., Toano, VA 23168; (757) 566-1451; (757) 259-5360 (parks dept.). An outdoor pool, toddler pool, playgrounds, and sand volleyball and basketball courts make this a popular James City County park from Memorial Day to Labor Day. Entrance to the park is

Many of the region's state parks are dog friendly.
Bobby Talley

free; admission to the pool is $5 for nonresident adults; $4 for nonresidents between the ages of 6 and 12. Children under 6 are admitted free. Residents receive a discount. Seasonal passes are also available. The park is open daily 8 a.m. to sunset.

WALLER MILL PARK, Airport Road (VA 645), Williamsburg, VA 23188; (757) 259-3778. This park features a 300-acre lake for fishing, boating, canoeing, and kayaking with a tunnel connecting the upper and lower sections of the lake. (Boats and fishing gear are available for rent.) Numerous picnic tables, 4 shelters, play fields, and playground equipment are nestled among the trees, providing a scenic picnic area. An 18-hole disc-golf course opened in 2015. (The park has discs to rent for $1, and visitors can buy a day pass for $2.) Hiking trails provide a picturesque walk. A 2-mile asphalt bike trail offers a scenic connection between Mooretown and Rochambeau Roads. A short hike from the park along the asphalt bike trail will bring you to the Lookout Tower, which offers a panoramic view of the water and woodlands. There are separate dog parks for small and large canine pals, but you must pay a small fee and provide proof of required vaccinations. Park admission is $2 per car. Open sunrise to sunset.

WOLF TRAP PARK, 1009 Wolf Trap Rd., Yorktown, VA 23692; (757) 890-3500. Home of the Yorktown United Soccer Club, this 28-acre park has 4 soccer fields, 2 ponds, restrooms, and the York County Memorial Tree Grove, which provides an opportunity for friends, relatives, and organizations to commemorate lost loved ones.

YORK RIVER STATE PARK, 9801 York River Park Rd., Williamsburg, VA 23188; (757) 566-3036; dcr.virginia.gov/state-parks/york-river. This beautiful park lies alongside the York River, which is formed by the joining of the Pamunkey and Mattaponi Rivers at West Point, about 10 miles upriver. Within the park is Croaker Landing, an archaeological site listed on the National Register of Historic Places. Known as Taskinas Plantation in the 17th and 18th centuries, it was the site of a public warehouse, where tobacco planters stored crops destined for shipment to England. Remnants of wooden "corduroy" roads (which are made of logs laid perpendicular to the direction of travel) dating from the period can still be seen at low tide.

Opened as a state park in 1980, more than 2,500 acres provide 30 miles of hiking, mountain biking, and equestrian trails, allowing visitors to explore the marsh, river shoreline, and forests. Stop by Fossil Beach on the Mattaponi Trail to hunt for shark's teeth. A boat ramp, fresh- and salt-water fishing spots, a fishing pier, playgrounds, picnic shelters, and seasonal boat rentals are available. (See more information about the fishing opportunities later in this chapter.) Rangers provide many interpretive programs: fossil and nature hikes, campfire programs, moonlight canoe tours, and after-dark ghost-trail hayrides. Some programs require a fee or reservations. Call the park for details.

The park is open 8 a.m. to dusk and there is a $5 per car admission fee. From I-64, take the Croaker exit (exit 231B). Go north on VA 607 (Croaker Road) for 1 mile, then right on VA 606 (Riverview Road) about 1.5 miles to the park entrance.

YORKTOWN WATERFRONT, 423 Water St. (dockmaster's office), Yorktown, VA 23690; (757) 890-3800. A 2-acre beach along the York River provides opportunities for boating, swimming, and fishing. A large picnic area is located east of the beach. Several restaurants within walking distance also are open during the day should hunger strike. Public restrooms, with shower facilities, are available at the west end of the beach and are open Apr through Oct from dawn to dusk. Trees can offer escape from the midday sun, and the

> **i** A favorite biking trip is the 23-mile Colonial Parkway, which passes through various landscapes and provides wonderful views without the heavy traffic of local streets and highways. Observe Virginia biking laws, which require bikers to ride in the same direction as the flow of traffic at all times.

Riverwalk provides a scenic stroll from one end of the town to the other. Be aware: There are no lifeguards on duty.

Newport News

HUNTINGTON PARK, Riverpark Drive at Mercury Boulevard, Newport News, VA 23607; (757) 886-7912; nnparks.com/parks_huntington.php. In addition to containing the largest public tennis facility in Virginia, with a beautiful new clubhouse overlooking some of the 20 lighted courts, this sprawling park has something for everyone: a well-maintained public rose garden (popular for weddings), baseball fields, a beach, a boat ramp for access to the James River, and Fort Fun—a 14,000-square-foot playground built on a bluff overlooking the James and featuring a state-of-the-art playground installed in 2011 with multiple slides, tunnels, climbing walls, fireman's poles, swings and much more. Take along a picnic lunch and some fishing poles or visit the swimming beach that is also part of the Huntington Park complex. Open from sunrise to sunset.

NEWPORT NEWS PARK, 13560 Jefferson Ave., Newport News, VA 23603; (757) 886-7912, (800) 203-8322; nnparks.com/parks_nn.php. This beautiful oasis at the northwestern end of the city has more than 7,700 acres of woodlands and 2 freshwater lakes. One of the largest municipal parks east of the Mississippi, it is home to a wide variety of wildlife—deer, fox, otter, raccoon, and beaver—making it a favorite destination for campers. Entrance to the park is free. Campsites, which include a picnic table, grill, access to heated restrooms, hot showers, laundry facilities, and water and electrical hookups, can be rented year-round. There is 24-hour registration, security, and a sewage dumping station.

The park has 20 miles of hiking trails, a 5-mile mountain bike trail, and bridle paths. Bicycles and helmets may be rented daily. For the angler, there are 2 reservoirs stocked with bass, pickerel, pike, bluegill, perch, and crappie. Boats are available for rent.

One of the highlights in the park is the 18-hole disc-golf course, one of the first of its kind in Virginia. The championship range will have you sailing your disc 5,450 yards, while the regulation, or white, course is 4,165 yards.

For history buffs, Dam No. 1, Confederate gun positions, and remaining Union trenches are evidence of the area's involvement in the 1862 Peninsula Campaign. The park's visitor center interprets the action that took place there and offers a free park map and literature on other pertinent sites nearby. Across from the Dam No. 1 Bridge is the park's Discovery Center, which displays flora and fauna exhibits as well as Civil War artifacts.

The park also hosts the annual **Fall Festival of Folklife** in October and is the site of Newport News **Celebration in Lights** during the holiday season. For more information on these and other nearby festivals, turn to our Annual Events chapter.

Hampton

GRANDVIEW NATURE PRESERVE, intersection of Beach Road and State Park Drive, Hampton, VA 23664; (757) 850-5134; visithampton.com/play/listing/grandview-nature-preserve. This 475-acre salt marsh has 2 miles of Chesapeake Bay beachfront, open for walking, beachcombing, and nature observation. It's off the beaten path. From I-64, take exit 263A to Mercury Boulevard (US 258). Turn left onto Fox Hill Road. Follow Fox Hill to Beach Road. Turn left again and you'll see the entrance. Open daily, year-round, from sunrise to sunset. Admission is free.

SANDY BOTTOM NATURE PARK, 1255 Big Bethel Rd., Hampton, VA 23666; (757) 825-4657; hampton.gov/sandybottom. This park contains more than 450 acres of woodland, 2 lakes, play and picnic areas, walking and interpretive trails, a wildlife area, nature center, paddleboats, and concessions. Built almost entirely by volunteers, this park has room for overnight guests, too. There also are 2 primitive group sites (popular with Boy Scout troops) and 4 tent cabins. The park also offers environmental education programs and special programming in astronomy, wildlife observation, and environmental field-testing. To get to the park, take exit 261A off I-64 and follow Hampton Roads Center Parkway to Big Bethel Road. The park entrance will be on your left. Open daily, sunrise to sunset, year-round (except Christmas Day). Admission is free.

If you want to get an angle on some outdoor fun, toss a line off one of the peninsula's many fishing piers. Depending on the time of year, you'll probably pull out spot, croaker, flounder, bluefish, or an occasional trout. No license is needed for fishing at any of these piers (it's included in the fee), and equipment rentals are available at most of them.

RECREATION

ABRAM FRINK JR. COMMUNITY CENTER, 8901 Pocahontas Trail, Williamsburg, VA 23185; (757) 887-5810; jamescitycountyva.gov/recreation/community-centers/frink-communitycenter.html The center includes a gymnasium, a multipurpose room with game tables and a large-screen TV, a glass-backed racquetball court, fitness room, table tennis and pool tables, 3 tennis courts, basketball courts, a sand volleyball court, soccer field, softball field, and a nature trail. The fitness room is equipped with Cybex equipment, dumbbells, a weight bench, and a pull-up dip station. Patron services include orientation on weight equipment, on-site registration for division-wide programs, and a wide variety of classes, such as karate, CPR, tennis, and oil painting.

The charge for nonresidents to use the facility for the day is $5 for adults and $2 for children. Open 4 to 9 p.m. Mon through Thurs (until 8 p.m. Fri). Closed Sat, Sun, and most holidays.

JAMES CITY COUNTY RECREATION CENTER, 5301 Longhill Rd., Williamsburg, VA 23188; (757) 259-4200; jamescitycountyva.gov/recreation/community-centers/james-city-jcwcc.html. This large facility has just about anything a person could want in recreation: a gymnasium with 2 basketball courts, 4 volleyball courts, a 2-lane indoor track, a swimming pool with 3 lap lanes, locker rooms with showers and saunas, racquetball courts, a whirlpool for 16 people, and a fitness room with free weights, 2 circuits of Cybex, and cardiovascular equipment. Trainers offer fitness assessments and personal fitness training.

There's a teen area equipped with TV and games, a craft room, a kiln and pottery wheels, and a dance and aerobics room.

The center offers senior activities through The Lounge, and rehabilitation and health education programs in conjunction with local hospitals. (See more about the center's services in the Retirement section.)

Although the center is primarily for area residents, visitors can use the facility for an $11 charge a day for adults, $4 for children ages 5 to 17. There are also nonresident annual and semiannual membership fees.

Open Mon through Fri, 6 a.m. to 9 p.m. (until 8 p.m. Fri); Sat 9 a.m. to 6 p.m.; Sun 1 to 6 p.m. Closed most holidays.

R. F. WILKINSON FAMILY YMCA, 301 Sentara Circle, Williamsburg, VA 23188; (757) 247-9622. This full-service fitness and child care facility provides exercise and dance classes, weight training, swim instruction, and lots more. State-licensed before- and afterschool care is available Mon through Fri for students ages 6 to 12. The Y also offers summer camp for children ages 5 to 12 from the end of June until mid-August. Anyone who holds a membership at another YMCA facility in Virginia is eligible to use this facility, part of the organization's new "Any Y is My Y" reciprocity program. Open 5:30 a.m. to 10 p.m. Mon through Thurs, until 9 p.m. Fri; 7 a.m. to 5 p.m. Sat; and 1 to 6 p.m. Sun.

WILLIAMSBURG INDOOR SPORTS COMPLEX, 5700 Warhill Trail, Williamsburg, VA 23188; (757) 253-1947; thewisc.com. This 50,000-square-foot indoor sports facility is privately owned but operated in partnership with James City County. The WISC, as it is known, offers opportunities to play just about any indoor sport you can think of, and some outdoor sports, too. There is a fitness center, and this is the site of The Zone, a children's play area. (See our full description in the Kidstuff chapter.) Summer camps for soccer (see more about soccer later in this chapter), in-line hockey, and field hockey are offered, as are classes in gymnastics, karate, yoga, and dance. There are no residency restrictions, but individuals must purchase a $20 annual membership ($30 for a family.) The fitness center opens most days at 6 a.m., and the number of activities throughout the day usually keeps the lights on here until 9 p.m. Check the website for information about specific sports activities.

ACTIVITIES

Biking

BIKE THE 'BURG, 515 York St., Williamsburg, VA 23185; (757) 570-7326; biketheburg.net. This full-service bike shop is the closest outfitter to the Historic Area, just east of Bassett Hall. Bike the 'Burg sells and repairs bikes and also rents bikes on a daily or a multiday basis. These devoted cyclists offer pickup and delivery on all service and repair. They carry electric bikes to rent or buy. Open 10 a.m. to 4 p.m. Wed through Fri; 9 a.m. to 4 p.m. Sat; noon to 4 p.m. Sun.

BIKES UNLIMITED, 230 Monticello Ave., Williamsburg, VA 23185; (757) 229-4620. This business offers complete biking services, including rentals by day and by week. Hours are 10 a.m. to 5 p.m. Tues through Sat, and noon to 4 p.m. Sun. Closed Mon.

CONTE'S, 4900 Courthouse St. (New Town), Williamsburg VA 23188; (757) 903-0702; contesbikes.com. A full-service bike shop with locations

Williamsburg offers many events for bike riders.
2017 Michael Ventura Photography

Close-up

Biking the 'Burg

Though the horse-drawn carriage is probably the most iconic image of non-automotive transportation in Williamsburg, the humble bicycle may be the most popular. Check the local listings of goings on around town any week in the *Virginia Gazette* and you will find Tuesday sunset rides that begin at Jamestown Settlement, Wednesday morning rides that set off from the Williamsburg Community Chapel on VA 5, and Friday morning rides at Chickahominy Riverfront Park. There are bike trails at New Quarter Park, Freedom Park, and York River State Park.

A favorite route for area cyclists is the 23-mile Colonial Parkway, which passes through various landscapes and provides wonderful views without the heavy traffic of local streets and highways.

Then there's the Virginia Capital Trail, a route that's on many a devoted cyclist's bucket list. This 52-mile paved path connects Virginia's first capital—Jamestown—with the current seat of its government—Richmond. For much of the trip, the path parallels VA 5, a Virginia Scenic Byway. You need not tackle the whole thing at once. Many of the historic plantations on Rte. 5 (see our accommodations chapter) now cater to weekend cyclists. If an overnight biking trip is too much to take on, the route is broken into digestible chunks for every ability level. One moderately strenuous ride is from the Jamestown Settlement trailhead to Chickahominy Riverfront Park in Charles City County—a there and back trek of about 14 miles. A great resource if you want to plan a cycling trip is the Virginia Capital Trail Foundation, virginiacapitaltrail.org. The website provides trail alerts, information about trail events, printable maps, and suggestions for lodging and dining.

If you want to cycle around the 'Burg, check out the website of the Williamsburg Area Bicyclists, a local bicycling advocacy group at wabonline.org. This club encourages bicycle use for recreation, fitness, and transportation, while also encouraging the development of facilities for bicycling on public lands. A calendar of rides is kept up to date on the website, which provides phone numbers for ride leaders. The club organizes more than 100 rides a year—at York River State Park, the Colonial Parkway, Jamestown, and around Williamsburg. Annual membership is $20. Riders are required to wear helmets for all rides.

If you need a bike, a bike rental, or a bike repair, there are several quality shops around town. There are also bicycle repair stations for self-repair at most trail access points.

throughout Virginia. Bicycles and accessories for sale from premium brands including Pinarello, BMC, Specialized, Cannondale, and Electra. Bike repair, rental and bike fitting are available. Conte's also accepts used bikes for trade-in. Open 11 a.m. to 7 p.m. weekdays; 10 a.m. to 6 p.m. Sat; and noon to 5 p.m. Sun.

TREK BICYCLES, 4640-5 Monticello Ave. (Monticello Marketplace Shopping Center), Williamsburg, VA 23188; (757) 229-0096; trekbikes.com/Williamsburg. This store stocks the latest in products from Trek and Bontrager but will provide service and tune-ups for any bike. They host "Get to Know Your Bike" nights and bike repair and maintenance classes. They sponsor cycling events, including Wednesdays on Your Wheel for kids and run a Facebook page geared toward female cyclists called BikeBeat Women's Ride Group. They will take your old bike as a trade-in including kid's bikes who need to size up. Trek Bicycles is also the closest repair shop to the Capital Trail. Open 11 a.m. to 6 p.m. Mon through Fri; 10 a.m. to 6 p.m. Sat, and noon to 5 p.m. Sun.

Bowling

AMF WILLIAMSBURG LANES, 5544 Olde Towne Rd., Williamsburg, VA 23188; (757) 565-3311; amf.com/williamsburglanes. No bowler is too young to play here. Novices pull up bumpers in the gutters so everyone has a good time—and a decent score at the end of a game. While the place is wildly popular and often crowded with league play, kids are welcome anytime. If you should experience a wait, visit the game room and snack bar. Visit the website to check on daily specials on both play and food. The bowling begins every weekday at 5 p.m and goes till 11 p.m.; Sat noon to midnight; Sun 2 p.m. to 10 p.m.

Fishing

A complete guide to fishing in the Historic Triangle's rivers, tributaries, lakes, ponds, wetlands, estuaries, and the Chesapeake Bay would require its own volume. Here we hit the highlights. If you're a die-hard angler, check with the **Department of Game and Inland Fisheries** in Richmond, (804) 367-1000, for a copy of its annual state fishing guide.

A fishing license is required for all those between the ages of 16 and 65. A freshwater/saltwater license is $40 a year for residents. A five-day, nonresident freshwater/saltwater license is $31; a one-day license for freshwater fishing is $8. Licenses are valid for the calendar year during which they are bought and are available at local bait-and-tackle shops, marinas, sporting goods counters of larger stores, and from county circuit-court clerks.

For more information on fishing licenses or for boat licenses, visit dgif.virginia.gov/fishing/regulations/licenses.asp.

> **i** Fishing is a year-round pursuit in the greater Williamsburg area. Even when popular fishing holes at area parks are closed, the bountiful James and York Rivers are always open for business. Of course, it's potluck what you catch, depending on the time of year.

LITTLE CREEK RESERVOIR PARK, 180 Lakeview Dr., Toano, VA 23168; (757) 259-5360. Located off Forge Road, this park is a fisherman's paradise, featuring year-round fishing and boating on a 996-acre reservoir, stocked with largemouth bass, bluegill, crappie, stripers, walleye, perch, pickerel, and a variety of sunfish and catfish. There is also a free fishing pier. Use of the boat ramps costs a nominal amount. In summer 2015, the park store was closed and boat rentals suspended due to the unavailability of a vendor to operate those services. Call the county for information about when these services will be reinstated. All fishermen must have a Virginia fishing license. This wonderful, practically secret lake is a bit hard to find for the new resident: From US 60 in Toano, take VA 610 (Forge Road) 2 miles to the first left, which is Lakeview Drive. Open daily 7 a.m. Mon through Fri and 6 a.m. Sat and Sun. The park closes daily at sunset.

POWHATAN CREEK PARK, 1831 Jamestown Rd., Williamsburg, VA 23185; (757) 259-5390 (parks dept.), (757) 592-1665 (park ranger). Boat launches in this park, which is part of the Chesapeake Gateways Network, provide access to the James River at Jamestown Island, with scenic views of Historic Jamestowne. Powhatan Creek is listed on the Natural Resources Inventory as the most biodiverse creek on the peninsula. Scenic views of tidal marshes and an abundance of wildlife highlight trips on this beautiful waterway. The facility consists of a small nonmotorized boat/canoe/kayak launch with gravel parking for up to 20 vehicles, as well as 5 observation/fishing piers. Fishing and boat launch access are available 24 hours a day. Open sunrise to sunset.

> **i** The temperate climate that makes outdoor life so enjoyable for humans also spawns a variety of tiny wildlife that can get you itching and scratching. This includes mosquitoes, ticks, and spiders, among others. Insiders will strongly urge you to use a bug repellent for comfort and safety when spending time outdoors.

WALLER MILL PARK, Airport Road (VA 645), Williamsburg, VA 23188; (757) 259-3778. For freshwater fishing, Waller Mill Park has one of the area's deepest lakes, known for large striped bass, crappie, largemouth bass, perch, pickerel, and channel catfish. There is no charge to fish from the pier. The fee to rent a boat is $5 per day per person; that charge includes fishing privileges. For more information on Waller Mill, see our earlier entry under Park Locations and Activities. Open sunrise to sunset.

YORK RIVER STATE PARK, 9801 York River Park Rd., Williamsburg, VA 23188; (757) 566-3036; dcr.virginia.gov/state-parks/york-river. The most scenic aspect of this park, located about 11 miles west of Williamsburg off I-64, might be the rich bounty below the surface of its waters, which includes 3 great fishing holes.

Freshwater anglers will find bluegill and largemouth bass in Woodstock Pond. A Virginia fishing license is required. Boats are available seasonally for rent on the pond, and only rental boats are allowed.

The York River, where catfish, spot, croaker, striper, and crabs are plentiful, is accessed at Croaker Landing. The landing has a boat-launch dock, a 360-foot fishing pier, parking, and restrooms. The pier is licensed so those fishing on the pier do not need their own saltwater license. Those fishing from boats and the shore, however, must have a Virginia saltwater fishing license. You can buy an annual pass for parking, boat launching, and pier fishing at the park or by calling (800) 933-PARK. Parking and launch-fishing-pier fees are required at all times.

Taskinas Creek, which has catfish and white perch, requires either a valid saltwater or freshwater Virginia fishing license. Canoes and kayaks are available for rent at the creek. (No motorboats are allowed in the creek.)

There is a parking fee of $5 per car, depending on when you visit. The park is open 8 a.m. to dusk.

Golf

The temperate weather allows golf courses in southern Virginia to stay open nearly year-round—a natural advantage that has helped Williamsburg become one of the premier golf destinations on the Eastern Seaboard. Another factor has been the annual splash of glamour provided by hosting LPGA tournaments at Kingsmill for nearly three decades.

Naturally, the courses in the area cater heavily to the communities with which they are associated, which includes a growing population of retirees. Though greens fees can be steep, there are bargains to be had, especially in the nonpeak months. It's even worth checking the sports pages of the *Virginia Gazette* for discount coupons.

In this chapter we give you an overview of the courses, including yardages (from the men's tees), special features, and driving directions for courses that are not in town. Reduced rates, based on time of year, time of day, and so on, are available at most of the courses, so greens fees can vary quite a bit. Carts are required at most courses, but the price is included in the greens fee. As elsewhere, soft spikes have become the rule here.

BRICKSHIRE GOLF CLUB, 5520 Virginia Park Dr., Providence Forge, VA 23140; (804) 966-7023; brickshiregolfclub.com. The popularity of this course can be explained in two words: player friendly. Wide, inviting fairways; artfully sculpted, true-rolling greens; and dramatic elevation changes mark the layout, designed by US Open champion Curtis Strange, who has replicated some of his favorite holes from around the world at this course, located in New Kent County between Richmond and Williamsburg. The 15th hole is a wickedly picturesque par 3; the 18th, a par 5 with panoramic views that has been called one of the best finishing holes in the mid-Atlantic. *Golf Digest* readers rate Brickshire four-and-a-half stars; *Golf Styles* named it one of the mid-Atlantic's "must play" courses. Now owned by the homeowners of the Brickshire development, local players say the course has never been in better shape.

Carts are not required but strongly suggested—the course is 7,291 yards. Greens fees vary seasonally, and discounts are offered to military, Virginia State Golf Association (VSGA) cardholders, and senior citizens, but expect to pay $65 on a summer weekend, and $50 during the week. Afternoon and off-season discounts—and a reward program for local golfers—will bring the price down quite a bit. Kids play free after 3 p.m. A clubhouse, pro shop, and restaurant round out the amenities.

The course is about 30 minutes west of Williamsburg; follow I-64 to exit 214 (Providence Forge). Take VA 155 south 0.5 mile to the course entrance.

COLONIAL HERITAGE GOLF CLUB, 6250 Arthur Hills Dr., Williamsburg, VA 23188; (757) 645-2030; colonialheritageclub.com. This artfully designed Arthur Hills masterpiece takes its cues from the landscape of its surroundings. Meandering through 175 acres of woodland, the 6,889-yard, par 72 course offers 12 sets of tees for all skill levels. Immaculately groomed greens, strategically placed bunkers, undulating fairways and carefully planned water features add up to a distinctive experience every round. The training center, complete with chipping greens and practice bunkers, is home to both the men's and women's teams from the College of William & Mary. Peak season greens fees top out at about $70. In the off-season, 18 rounds can cost as low as $30.

FORD'S COLONY COUNTRY CLUB, 240 Ford's Colony Dr., Williamsburg, VA 23188; (757) 258-4100; clubcorp.com/Clubs/Ford-s-Colony-Country-Club. Fifty-four holes of world-class golf, designed by Dan Maples, are set on verdant hills with water, water, everywhere. Choose from three 18-hole layouts—the Blackheath course plays 6,621 yards, and with rolling hills and water on 7 holes, it is a real challenge. The Marsh Hawk course is 18 holes over 6,650 yards; the Blue Heron course offers 18 holes over 6,266 yards.

Greens fees at Ford's Colony vary seasonally, so inquire about fees when calling for a tee time. Lessons are available, and guests of the Marriott Manor Club, a resort within the Ford's Colony development, can purchase golf packages at a discounted rate.

GOLDEN HORSESHOE GOLF CLUB, 401 S. England St., Williamsburg, VA 23185; (757) 220-7696; colonialwilliamsburg.org/locations/golden-horseshoe-golf-club-gold-course. Choose from 3 challenging courses here, including the Gold Course, first opened in 1963 and designed by Robert Trent Jones. In 1998, the course underwent a multimillion-dollar redesign by Jones's son, Rees, aimed at expanding the appeal for higher-handicap players and lengthening the course from the back tees. Nationally renowned, the course features numerous elevation changes, tight fairways, and plenty of water. Its signature hole, the par-3 16th, boasts the first island green ever built in America. Playing to a par of 71, the 6,817-yard layout's 5 closing holes are a test for any golfer. (Jack Nicklaus holds the course record of 67.)

The Golden Horseshoe—known locally as "the Shoe"—offers full clubhouse amenities, including a pro shop, locker rooms, and a lounge.

The Green course opened in 1991. Designed by Rees Jones, this is a 7,120-yard, par-72 course where mounds abound and the par-5 18th hole requires a 200-yard carry off the tee. More wide open than its sister course, this design still offers a stiff test for hackers of all levels. Like the Gold Course, the Green features a first-class clubhouse, pro shop, and restaurant.

The third course, named for colonial governor, Alexander Spotswood, was also designed in the 1960s by Trent Jones who oversaw the construction of the first 9 holes and then decided he didn't like. He went back to the drawing board and built the Gold Course. The Spotswood is not a true executive length (there are a few 4- and 5-par holes) but if you have only a few hours, this is your option.

KINGSMILL GOLF CLUB, 1010 Kingsmill Rd., Williamsburg, VA 23185; (757) 253-1703 (press 2 for golf); kingsmill.com. The 3 courses at this golf club have something to satisfy every golfer. **The River Course** is the crown jewel. Designed by the legendary Pete Dye, the par-72 5,001-yard course is both challenging and scenic. The design requires accuracy off the tee and precise shots into greens, which are well protected by strategically placed bunkers. Holes 16, 17, and 18 have spectacular river views.

The Plantation Course, par 72, is a 6,432-yard Arnold Palmer design. Undulating greens make for a putting challenge, and a couple of the par 4s will test you off the tee. Considered a challenging but fair layout, the Plantation Course has been ranked by *Golf Digest* as one of the top 50 courses for women.

Last, there is the **Woods Course,** designed by Tom Clark and two-time US Open champion Curtis Strange. East of the other courses, this 6,659-yard course features its own clubhouse with the amenities you would expect at an upscale resort.

Like the **Kingsmill Tennis Center** (see entry above), play on the courses here is restricted to resort guests or club members. Golf clinics are available to resort guests. One-, two-, and three-day Golf Academy programs are also available.

KISKIACK GOLF CLUB, 8104 Club Dr., Williamsburg, VA 23188; (757) 566-2200, kiskiackgc.com. This John LaFoy–designed course was carved from woodlands on a rolling terrain and is a favorite among local golfers—readers of the Virginia Gazette voted it "Best in Williamsburg" in 2017. Ten minutes west of Williamsburg, at the Croaker Road exit (exit 231B) on I-64, this 6,405-yard, par-72 layout is a treat. The par-3 11th hole, requiring a hefty carry over water, is the signature hole. Greens fees, including cart, top out at $69 on a summer weekend but the twilight rate can be had in the offseason for $39.

NEWPORT NEWS GOLF CLUB AT DEER RUN, Newport News Park, 901 Clubhouse Way, Newport News, VA 26308; (757) 886-7925; nngolfclub .com. Golfers looking for a budget day on the links often take advantage of Deer Run, a challenging 18-hole course located in an 7,700-acre park. (The city's Department of Parks and Recreation manages the course.) Whether you tackle Deer Run, Ed Ault's 7,206-yard wooded course, or opt for the middle-length Cardinal 6,645-yard course (suited to all levels of play), you can play for as little as $28 by booking online. (Peak time rates are $34 weekdays and $36 weekends.) There are senior, military, and student discounts, too. The club-house has a snack bar and restaurant, driving range, putting greens, and pro shop. The course is an easy 15-minute drive east on I-64. Take exit 250B, go straight through the light, and turn left at the golf club entrance, a mile down the road.

ROYAL NEW KENT GOLF CLUB, 10100 Kentland Trail, Providence Forge, VA 23140; (804) 966-7023; royalnewkent.com. This par-72 course, 2 miles south of Brickshire (see entry above), has been compared to Ballybunion and Royal County Down in Scotland, 2 of the world's greatest links courses. Among other things, it features stone walls, hidden greens, and blind fairways, giving this course a particularly natural setting. Greens fees with a cart top out at $95 for a weekend morning in summer. Discounts for afternoon and off-season play and for local golfers, senior, juniors, and military personnel are available. The course is about 30 minutes west of Williamsburg; follow I-64 to exit 214 (Providence Forge). Take Route VA 155 south 2.5 miles to the course entrance.

STONEHOUSE GOLF CLUB, 9700 Mill Pond Run, Toano, VA 23168; (757) 250-3399; stonehousegolfclub.com. This course, located 15 miles west of Williamsburg, is one of the most beautiful courses in the mid-Atlantic region. It features deep bunkering, awesome vistas, and undulating, fast greens comparable to Cypress Point in Pebble Beach, California. Some greens sit atop cliffs, while others meander along spring-fed creeks. The par-72 design measures 7,013 yards. Greens fees range from $60 in the winter to $75 on weekends in high season. Carts are required. The quickest route to the course is via I-64 West to exit 227. The entrance is 0.5 mile north on the right. An excellent restaurant, The Virginia Grill, serves lunch and dinner before or after your round.

WILLIAMSBURG NATIONAL GOLF CLUB, 3700 Centerville Rd., Williamsburg, VA 23188; (757) 258-9642; wngc.com. Located west of Williamsburg, partially within the Greensprings neighborhood, this semiprivate golf club offers two 18-hole courses—the Jamestown, designed by Jack Nicklaus's Golden Bear Associates, and the Yorktown, designed by Tom Clark. *Golf Digest* gave the courses here a four-star rating, and the Yorktown Course has been named one of the top 50 courses for women in America. Greens fees here range for $40 in the off-season to $89 on a summer morning. The 1607 Grille is open daily for lunch and dinner and for brunch Sat and Sun.

Horseback Riding

Horseback riding is a Virginia tradition dating back at least to George Washington, whose first real job was as a surveyor, exploring the then-uncharted wilds of the Old Dominion. The Historic Triangle has many stables that welcome children, who can take classes and, in some cases, sign up for summer riding camps. Generally, these places require children to be at least 6 or 7 years old. Some require that an adult accompany the young equestrian at all times; others provide adult supervision. Rules vary from place to place. Call ahead and find out what gear is required as well as days and hours of operation.

CARLTON FARMS, 3516 Mott Ln., Williamsburg, VA 23185; (757) 220-3553; carltonfarmsstables.com. Summer camps that offer instruction on horse care, riding safety and technique, and trail riding are offered throughout June and July. Riding lessons are available for all skill levels. Call 2 to 3 days in advance of your visit.

CEDAR VALLEY FARM, 2016 Forge Rd., Toano, VA 23168; (757) 566-2621. This full-service boarding and training facility offers lessons to beginner through advanced riders.

LAKEWOOD TRAILS, 2116-A Forge Rd., Toano, VA 23168; (757) 566-9633; lakewoodtrailrides.com. Small-group trail rides in the traditional English style of horseback riding are offered year-round, weather permitting. Riders must be at least 7 years old, and there is a 225-pound weight limit. Rides begin at the Stonehouse Stables (see full listing below), but reservations should be made by calling the number listed above.

STONEHOUSE STABLES, 2116-A Forge Rd., Toano, VA 23168; (757) 566-0666; stonehousestables.com. This full-service equestrian center offers lessons for beginners through advanced riders, and a full slate of summer camp programs.

Jogging and Hiking

Joggers will find that many area parks offer some kind of fitness path. Waller Mill Park offers 4 trails—its mile-long trail is one of the best—and the trail at the James City County Recreation Center is also very popular. Local runners recommend a jog along the Colonial Parkway as the best run around.

JAMES CITY COUNTY RECREATION CENTER, 5301 Longhill Rd., Williamsburg, VA 23188; (757) 259-4200. The center includes a 2-lane indoor track. The inside lane is reserved for walking and is also accessible to wheelchairs and canes; the outside lane is reserved for joggers and speed walking. The facility also has 2 miles of walking and bicycling paths on the grounds.

WALLER MILL PARK, Airport Road (VA 645), Williamsburg, VA 23188; (757) 259-3778. This park offers a wide range of trails for the jogger, walker, and bicyclist. All of them wind through a wooded setting. The mile-long Fitness Trail is especially popular because it features fitness stops along the way for different exercises. The other trails include the 1.5-mile Bayberry Nature Trail; the 3-mile Lookout Tower Trail; the 5.5-mile Dogwood Trail, which is used by joggers and bicyclists; and the 1-mile senior walking course.

For those looking for a pleasant outdoor walk, there are tons of choices. Three favorites:

BASSETT TRACE NATURE TRAIL, various starting points within the Historic Area. If you are driving to walk the trail, however, the best place to start is at either of CW's golf clubhouses, where there is ample parking. This 3.4-mile, moderately difficult trail meanders through the wooded area separating the Golden Horseshoe golf course from the Green course. Wear hiking shoes. The path is rough at times and hilly. There are stairs in 2 locations. The trail begins near Bassett Hall (which is not where you would park), the Williamsburg home of John D. Rockefeller. There are several ponds and small streams that are home to waterfowl and at one point you will see Mr. Rockefeller's boathouse. As the seasons change so do the sights of wildflowers, butterflies, deer, birds, and colorful leaves. If you park at one of the clubhouses, you can will yourself to finish with the promise of a refreshing beverage or a bite to eat. There is also parking for the CW Taverns near Bassett Hall. To find the Bassett Hall trail starting point from the Tavern lot on Francis Street turn onto Bucktrout Lane located near the Williamsburg Inn. Once on Bucktrout Lane, take your first left at the Williamsburg Inn tennis courts. Proceed down that road until it dead-ends at the parking lot located at the Providence Hall wing of the Williamsburg Inn. A sign labeled "Bassett Hall Woodland Trail" marks the starting point. Follow the circular orange blazes to stay on the trail.

GREENSPRINGS INTERPRETIVE TRAIL, 375 John Tyler Hwy. (behind Jamestown High School), Williamsburg, VA 23185; 757-259-5360. This 3.5-mile nature trail loops through a landscape of wetlands, and forest. Signs along the boardwalk offer information about the environment, historic events of the early colonists and Native Americans, and area wildlife. Over 200 species of birds have been documented on this site, which is part of the Virginia Birding Trail. The trail is dog friendly, but dogs must be leashed at all times. Deer are plentiful. Open daily from sunrise to sunset. Park at the tennis courts behind the school and follow the dirt road to the trailhead.

WILLIAM & MARY LOOP, various starting points depending on where you can find parking, mostly along Richmond Road. This 2.1-mile moderately easy walk takes you through the historic campus, beginning at the heart and soul of the campus, the Sir Christopher Wren Building, built in 1695. The Wren Building is the oldest building on a US college campus still in academic use. Walk through the building if it is open. Continue on the brick pathway to the left of the Sunken Garden through Old Campus with six academic buildings surrounding the Sunken Garden. Follow the walk Northward to the University Center, where walkers can join students during the school term for a quick bite to eat. The Crim Dell is next. The Crim Dell Bridge was voted the second most romantic spot on a college campus. Next you will see the Earl Gregg Swem Library, located in New Campus. Follow Ukrop Way to William and Mary Hall, the College's multipurpose arena. Continue down Gooch Drive to the William & Mary Alumni House, and to Zable Stadium at Cary Field where Tribe Football is played. Of course, after this long walk enjoy a cold beverage and something to eat at one of the "Deli" restaurants, across from Zable Stadium.

Pickleball

Like it has in the rest of the country, pickleball has exploded in popularity in Hampton Roads. A locally run website, pickleburg.com, is a great resource for finding out about local leagues, lessons, tournaments, even the proper way to serve.

Many local tennis courts have been retrofitted with tape marking pickleball court dimensions (although the local tennis players definitely object) but James City County has six dedicated pickleball courts at Veterans Park, and Williamsburg has adapted space at their recreation center for indoor play in the colder months.

JAMESTOWN HIGH SCHOOL, 3751 John Tyler Hwy., Williamsburg, VA 23185. There are 6 courts here, marked for dual tennis/pickleball use. There is no charge and no reservations are necessary but student use takes precedence when school is in session.

QUARTERPATH RECREATION CENTER, 202 Quarterpath Rd., Williamsburg, VA 23185; williamsburgva.gov/residents/facilities/quarterpath -recreation-center. There are 3 to 6 indoor courts here for open play, 5 days a week. Players pay $2 a day. The center also hosts tournaments that draw pickleburgers from across the region.

VETERANS PARK, 3793 Ironbound Rd., Williamsburg, VA 23185. James City County repurposed 6 tennis courts for dedicated pickleball play. The courts are available on a first-come, first-served basis, 7 a.m. to sunset daily. There is no fee. No chairs are allowed on court. There are bathrooms and water on-site.

Soccer

The sport of soccer is thriving here, with the number of youth soccer clubs on the increase.

JAMES CITY COUNTY PARKS AND RECREATION YOUTH SOCCER LEAGUE, 5249 Olde Towne Rd., Williamsburg, VA 23188; (757) 259-4200. Youth soccer leagues are offered in the spring and fall for boys and girls in grades one through nine. This program is for fun and educational purposes and is noncompetitive. Registration takes place in September. The Half-Pint soccer classes are offered for children ages 3 to 5.

WILLIAMSBURG INDOOR SPORTS COMPLEX, 5700 Warhill Trail, Williamsburg, VA 23188; (757) 253-1947; thewisc.com. The Colonial Football Club operates out of the Williamsburg Indoor Sports Complex (WISC). The sports complex offers numerous sports activities, including soccer. In the summer, there are adult soccer leagues, a development league, and a Little Rascals soccer program designed as an introduction to the sport. Check the website for information about specific programs.

YORK COUNTY PARKS AND RECREATION, 100 County Dr., York-town, VA 23690; (757) 890-3500. Boys and girls in kindergarten through 12th grade can play soccer in spring and fall programs. Practices take place at area elementary and middle schools and county parks. Registration begins at the end of Aug and Feb. Coach certification programs are also offered. A weather hotline at (757) 890-3501 keeps participants informed of weather cancellations.

Tennis

BACK CREEK PARK, 3000 Goodwin Neck Rd., Dandy, VA 23697; (757) 890-3850. This beautiful (if remote) 27-acre USTA award-winning facility, accessible year-round, features 6 lighted tennis courts. Fees are charged when the park is staffed—on weekends in the spring through late November. Court reservations are recommended and can be made one week in advance. To reserve a court or to rent the ball machine, call the park's staff at the number listed above. Court fees are $4 per hour before 5 p.m.; $8 per hour after 5 p.m. If staff is not on duty, courts are available for free by calling the parks depart-ment at (757) 890-3500 or the park to obtain lock combinations. Players can use the courts for free from the end of Nov through late Mar. Lessons are avail-able in the spring, summer, and fall.

CHARLES BROWN PARK, VA 238, Lackey, VA 23690; (757) 890-3500. This 10-acre park has 2 tennis courts open year-round. There is no fee for using these courts.

KIWANIS MUNICIPAL PARK, 125 Longhill Rd., Williamsburg, VA 23185; (757) 259-3760. Kiwanis Municipal Park has 7 hard-surface courts that are available, for free, when the city is not using them for youth tennis clinics led by the legendary coach Brent Hughes. Tennis lessons are offered in the spring, summer, and fall.

MCCORMACK-NAGELSEN TENNIS CENTER, 705 S. Henry St., Wil-liamsburg, VA 23185; (757) 221-7378; williamsburgtenniscenter.com. This gorgeous facility is home to the William & Mary men's and women's tennis teams, and the only place in town to play when the weather's bad. The complex offers 6 Har-Tru courts and locker rooms with changing facilities and showers.

Adult programs offered year-round include mixers and holiday socials. Instructional clinics, from beginners to advanced, are offered each week. Call the front desk if you want to sub in league play while you're in town; they keep a list. The center's tennis pros, Neely Zervakis and Mark Hildenbrand, are top-notch instructors if you need a lesson. There is a vibrant youth tennis program, and day-camp instruction during the summer and school holidays. During the pandemic, the facility was turned over for use by the law school. Call to ensure tennis is being played here again.

On the second floor is spectator seating for college matches and tournaments, and the Intercollegiate Tennis Association's Women's Tennis Hall of Fame, a collection of artifacts and memorabilia pertaining to collegiate women's tennis, and the players, coaches, and contributors who have influenced the sport. The Hall of Fame also functions as a library, archive, and research center for intercollegiate women's tennis.

QUARTERPATH PARK, 202 Quarterpath Rd., Williamsburg, VA 23185; (757) 259-3760. Three hard courts are available at no charge on a first-come, first-play basis.

Semiprivate Courts

KINGSMILL TENNIS CENTER, 931 Kingsmill Rd., Williamsburg, VA 23185; (757) 253-3945. This is arguably the most beautiful tennis facility in southeastern Virginia, offering 15 clay courts, including 2 lighted for evening play, but its access to the public has become limited due to a change in ownership and in the policies governing play. As of 2015, only tennis-center members and resort guests were eligible to play here, although the resort is for sale and that policy could change. Call the pro shop if you are interested in clay play—these are the best in Williamsburg. A player's lounge and locker facilities are located in the pro shop, which has a nice assortment of the latest tennis wear and equipment.

THE WILLIAMSBURG INN, 136 E. Francis St., Williamsburg, VA 23185; (757) 220-7794. Hotel guests have access to 8 immaculately maintained courts (6 Har-Tru and 2 cushioned hard courts). Annual memberships are available for area residents ($540 individual; $770 family). Lessons are available. There is a fully stocked pro shop offering Wilson products, ball machine rental, stringing, regripping, and matchmaking services. Open 8 a.m. to 6 p.m. from mid-Mar until mid-Dec.

BEACHES

Newport News

HUNTINGTON PARK BEACH, Riverpark Drive at Mercury Boulevard, Newport News, VA 23607; (757) 886-7912, (757) 888-3333. Newport News' public beach is located at the east end of the James River Bridge in the same park that is home to Fort Fun and the James River Fishing Pier (see Fishing, later in this chapter). Lifeguards are on duty daily during the summer, but at other times you're allowed to swim at your own risk. There's a snack bar with a deck and picnic tables, and restrooms are available at the lifeguard station.

Bring your volleyball; the beach has a court set up for play. Open sunrise to sunset.

Hampton

BUCKROE BEACH, North 1st St. (end of Pembroke Avenue), Hampton, VA 23664; (757) 727-8311 (general city of Hampton hotline); hampton.gov/Facilities/Facility/Details/Buckroe-Beach. This bay-front park has a gentle surf and sandy shore that are perfect for family frolicking and castle building. A paved boardwalk attracts strollers and cyclists, while an outdoor pavilion is the setting for occasional live entertainment. A bustling resort back in the 1930s, Buckroe Beach's fortunes declined when the 1957 opening of the Hampton Roads Bridge-Tunnel provided easier access to ocean attractions. In the late 1980s the city built Buckroe Park, complete with a playground, stage, picnic shelters, and public restrooms (open May 15 through Sept 15). Most Sundays in the summer there's live music at the pavilion from 6 to 9 p.m. Kayaks and paddleboats are available for rental.

The beach is located off exit 268 from I-64. Go east on Mallory Street to its end, then right on Pembroke Avenue. There's parking adjacent to the beach.

JAMES RIVER FISHING PIER, 2019 James River Bridge (access via Huntington Park), Newport News, VA 23607; (757) 247-0364. The first section of a brand new pier opened in 2015, replacing the old pier (a section of the former 2-lane James River Bridge, taken out of service when a 4-lane bridge opened in 1982). Now, the entire new structure is complete and it spans sixth-tenths of a mile, making it one of the longest fishing piers on the East Coast. The new pier also features LED lights, which will help anglers at night, when the croakers are biting. An on-site bait shop provides snacks, bait, and some tackle. Croaker and spot are caught year-round, while striped bass, flounder, grey trout and red drum are caught seasonally. If all that casting and reeling works up an appetite, the Crab Shack restaurant is located at the entrance to the pier and offers everything from soft shell crabs to shrimp. Anglers do not need a fishing license, but they do need to pay admission: $10 for adults, $8 for children ages 6 to 12 and seniors age 65 and older. The pier is open daily from 9 a.m. to 11 p.m. and 24 hours on Fri and Sat during the summer.

Day Trips

While Williamsburg is one of a kind, other pockets of Hampton Roads have plenty to offer the would-be wanderer. We've outlined some favorite adventures you can have simply by hopping behind the wheel. Whether you ferry across the James River to stroll along the historic streets of downtown Smithfield or brave the Hampton Roads Bridge-Tunnel for a day at the beach, these favorites are within 60 to 90 minutes of driving time. (Although we can't promise you won't run into traffic. Sorry.) We begin with the most picturesque way to leave Williamsburg: by boat.

JAMESTOWN-SCOTLAND FERRY, end of Jamestown Road, Williamsburg, VA 23185; (800) 823-3779; virginiadot.org/travel/ferry-jamestown .asp. This free, state-run service, the last of a once-thriving ferry industry in Hampton Roads, crosses the James River from Jamestown to Scotland Wharf in Surry County in Southside (many contend that the South doesn't really begin until one is below the James). For a large number of residents, this scenic ride is a twice-daily commute, either to the nuclear power plant in Surry or to jobs on the peninsula. For many others, especially on weekends in good weather, it's a favorite day trip.

You can reach the ferry by traveling either Jamestown Road or the Colonial Parkway to its end, near Jamestown Settlement. The schedule varies with the season and the time of day. Typically, in the summer you can hop aboard every half hour from 1 a.m.

While on the concrete dock waiting to board at the northeast end, you'll notice the 3 restored ships of Jamestown Settlement to your left: the *Susan Constant*, the *Godspeed*, and the *Discovery*. You don't get a better waterside view of all 3 ships than this; it's a prime opportunity to pull out the camera.

The trip takes a little less than 20 minutes from cast off to docking and offers beautiful views, especially on clear autumn days or during late-summer sunsets.

Once you have boarded one of the ferries of the fleet, you may leave your vehicle (being careful, of course, not to ding your neighbors' car doors—it's a tight fit) and enjoy the view from the railing or from bow or stern. There is a small cabin upstairs with water fountains and restrooms as well as good views, but there is no seating on most of the ferries.

The unique experience of riding a ferry is periodically threatened with extinction by studies that call for a replacement bridge spanning the river, either here or upstream. Each year approximately 936,000 vehicles use the ferry service.

There are 4 ferries in operation, departing at least once an hour 24 hours a day. Capacity varies from 28 to 70 cars.

SURRY COUNTY

After you're across the James and docked at Scotland Wharf, you'll drive off into Surry County. For decades, many people left the ferry and drove directly down VA 31 to the Edwards' **Virginia Ham Shoppe** for delicious ham or barbeque sandwiches.

If you aren't in immediate need of food, stop at **Smith's Fort Plantation**, right off VA 31 before you reach "downtown" Surry, or head east on VA 10 to **Bacon's Castle** or **Chippokes Plantation State Park**. A voyage across the James is a trip into a rural southern landscape that offers a view of what the peninsula used to be like. Miles of farmland and two-lane highways separate small, historic communities. Weathered tobacco barns, more tall than wide, occasionally are visible in fields where prized Virginia peanuts are now the major crop. It's a world away from generic fast food restaurants, hotel chains, and the sometimes-frantic pace of an established tourism industry.

Attractions

BACON'S CASTLE, 465 Bacon's Castle Trail (off Lake Powell Rd.), Surry, VA 23883; (757) 357-5976; preservationvirginia.org/visit/historic—properties/bacons—castle. One hundred years before the colonists started talking Revolution in Williamsburg, Nathaniel Bacon led the colony's first insurrection against Governor William Berkeley's rule. The struggle spread to Surry County, and, on September 18, 1676, Bacon's commander, William Rookings, captured this building, home to Major Arthur Allen, in a siege.

Allen built the house in 1665, and now, more than 340 years later, it is the oldest brick house in English North America. Architecturally, it is of extreme interest. Unlike its surviving, typically Georgian, contemporaries, the building has curving Flemish gables and triple chimney stacks. Its front and rear facades also are unusual in that they are broken midpoint by an entrance-and-porch tower in front and a corresponding stair tower in back. This gives the building a cruciform shape, the first house in the colony so designed. A formal garden has been excavated and restored, giving the whole estate a sense of antiquity and a peace that contrasts with its most famous historical event.

Open for tours, Fri and Sat 10 a.m. to 5 p.m., noon to 5 p.m. Sun, Mar through Dec; open 10 a.m. to 5 p.m. Mon, Memorial Day through Labor Day only. Closed in Jan and Feb.

Admission is $10 for adults, $9 for senior citizens, and $8 for students ages 6 to 18. A discount is available by buying a $12 ticket that affords entrance to both Bacon's Castle and Smith's Fort Plantation (see below).

CHIPPOKES PLANTATION STATE PARK, 695 Chippokes Park Rd., Surry, VA 23883; (757) 294-3728; dcr.virginia.gov/state-parks/chippokes plantation. The 1854 manor house within this state park is surrounded by formal gardens that contain one of the largest collections of crepe myrtles on the East Coast. This plantation, named after a Native American chief, has been continuously farmed for more than 370 years, which makes the model farm and the adjacent Farm and Forestry Museum a fitting part of the attractions here. There are biking and hiking trails, picnic shelters, and fishing. The Olympic-size swimming pool in a wooded setting is a unique summer treat. (The pool has a separate admission fee of $2–$4 depending on the age of the swimmer.) There's also lots of kid-friendly programming throughout the year—an Easter egg hunt, kid's fishing tournaments, bonfires on the beach, Halloween themed hayrides, and weekend festivals: the Steam and Gas Engine Show in June; the Pork, Peanut, and Pine Festival in July; and a Harvest Festival, all of which draw huge crowds from around the region for outdoor activities, food, and fun.

The park also has 32 campsites with water and electrical hookups, plus additional primitive campsites. Camping is open from Mar through Oct and costs $35–$40 (out-of-state guests pay a higher rate) a night for sites with water and electricity. If you prefer a less rugged stay, Chippokes also has 4 air conditioned cabins. It's a good idea to make plans well in advance if you want to camp. To reserve a spot, call (800) 933-PARK.

Admission to the park is $7. Because hours for both the manor and farm vary, it's best to consult the website listed above for precise information about operating hours during the time you plan to visit.

FORT BOYKIN HISTORIC PARK, 7410 Fort Boykin Trail (CR 673), Isle of Wight, VA 23430; (757) 357-2291; historicisleofwight.com/fort-boykin. Out in the country, along the banks of the James River, is the site of a fort that dates to the colonial era. Initially established in 1623, high on a bluff over the river so to spot any raiding parties that might be approaching, the current fort structure dates to the War of 1812. Shaped like a 7-point star, it's a well-preserved example of 19th-century military architecture and one that's played a role in every campaign fought on American soil. According to legend, the guns of Fort Boykin sunk 2 British men-of-war in 1813. A gazebo overlooks the river, and the park is located on a Virginia Birding and Wildlife Trail. The grounds are also home to the commonwealth's second oldest black walnut tree, which is an estimated 200 years old. A swimming beach frequented by locals was closed indefinitely in 2015 due to erosion caused by a recent nor'easter. Call the number above if you want to know if swimming has been reinstated. Otherwise, the fort is still a good choice for a picnic or a dose of history. Open daily 8 a.m. to dusk. Admission is free.

SMITH'S FORT PLANTATION, 217 Smith Fort Ln., Surry, VA 23383; (757) 294-3872; apva.org/smithsfort. The Smith in the name of this historic plantation is none other than Captain John Smith, who built a fort on high land at nearby Gray's Creek in 1609 as protection for Jamestown, directly across the river. The land has other famous connections as well, having been part of Chief Powhatan's wedding gifts to Pocahontas and John Rolfe. The building currently on the site was built in 1765 and is considered a fine example of a Georgian brick manor house with its typical one-and-a-half stories and central entrance.

Open for tours, Fri and Sat 10 a.m. to 5 p.m., noon to 5 p.m. Sun, Mar through Dec; open 10 a.m. to 5 p.m. Mon, Memorial Day through Labor Day only. Admission is $10 for adults, $9 for senior citizens, and $8 for students ages 6 to 18.

Restaurants

EDWARDS VIRGINIA HAM SHOPPE OF SURRY, 11381 Rolfe Hwy. (VA 31), Surry, VA 23883; (757) 294-3688; edwardsvaham.com; $. Not a restaurant, but you won't go away hungry from this retail shop, which sells Edwards' ham, a Virginia specialty. For three generations the Edwards family has cured hams in Surry County. At this outpost, they sell their specialty and other Virginia products, and there is a deli counter where you can get a sandwich—ham, turkey, barbecue, BLT, pimento and cheese—throughout the day. (The barbecue sandwich is delicious with slaw and hot sauce.) There's a cooler for drinks, and plenty of small snacks, candy, chips, and more to build an impromptu picnic. There's seating on the wood porch out front if your stomach is already grumbling.

Edwards' hams have a wide following. The company has its own catalog and also fills orders from merchandisers like Williams-Sonoma, Harry & David, Winterthur, and Neiman-Marcus—especially during the busy holiday months. Surry's most famous pork products were once endorsed by none other than celebrated chef Julia Child.

Open during the summer from 10 a.m. to 5 p.m. Mon through Sat; noon to 5 p.m. Sun. During the off-season, they close each day at 5 p.m. If you can't make it to Surry, check out **Edwards' Virginia Ham Shoppe of Williamsburg** at 5541C Richmond Rd. (757-220-6618); open daily 10 a.m. to 6 p.m. during the summer months.

SMITHFIELD

Speaking of ham, now that you're Southside, head to Smithfield in Isle of Wight County, home of the world-famous Smithfield ham. While ham has placed Smithfield on the map, the town actually grew up around the trade and commerce that flourished on the Pagan River. Its rich past provides Smithfield with much to tempt the day-tripper. The city's charming downtown is a

National Historic District, and many of the pre–Revolutionary War homes on Main and Church Streets have been winningly restored.

Smithfield is 18 miles east of Surry down VA 10. From the ferry, follow VA 31 (you don't have a choice) to VA 10, where you'll turn left. Follow VA 10 until you reach the stoplight, 17 miles or so away. Turn left and you'll be on Main Street.

SMITHFIELD AND ISLE OF WIGHT CONVENTION AND VISITORS BUREAU, 319 Main St., Smithfield, VA 23430; (757) 357-5182; genuinesmithfieldva.com. To start your visit, stop by this office for a historic walking tour map, which will direct you past dozens of gorgeous old houses. There are more than 65 structures on the tour, all within comfortable walking distance, including the Isle of Wight Courthouse, built in 1750 and one of only four remaining arcaded colonial courthouses. The visitor center has sample itineraries that fit a day trip or a weeklong stay. Personalized itineraries are also available from the friendly staff. Open 10 a.m. to 4 p.m. Mon through Sat; noon to 4 p.m. Sun. Closed Thanksgiving, Christmas, and New Year's Day.

ISLE OF WIGHT COUNTY MUSEUM, 103 Main St., Smithfield, VA 23430; (757) 356-1223; historicisleofwight.com/museum. This museum, housed in a former bank built in 1913, offers archaeological displays that highlight county history. But never mind that. On display here are the world's oldest ham, the world's largest ham, and the world's oldest peanut (dating to the 19th century). All this for just $2 (free for visitors 17 or younger), plus a nice introductory film that lays out the basics of Smithfield's colonial beginnings. If you can't make it in person watch the "Ham Cam" for live broadcasts at 12:05 p.m. every Tues and Thurs. Access the link from the website, listed above.

You won't need more than an hour to take all this in, and there's free parking in their lot so you can use this spot to launch a walking tour, or take in the shops and restaurants along Main Street. Open 10 a.m. to 4 p.m. Mon through Sat; noon to 4 p.m. Sun. Closed New Year's Day, Easter, Memorial Day, July 4, Labor Day, Thanksgiving, Christmas Eve, and Christmas Day.

SAINT LUKE'S CHURCH AND SHRINE, 14477 Benns Church Blvd. (VA10), Smithfield, VA 23430; (757) 357-3367; stlukesmuseum.org. Built in 1632 and nicknamed "Old Brick," this Episcopal church is the country's only original Gothic church and the oldest church in Virginia. The church features its original traceried windows, stepped gables, and a rare mid-17th-century communion table. Since 1957 Saint Luke's has been home to the oldest intact English organ in America. Constructed ca. 1630, the organ recently had its beautifully painted doors restored. Open 9:30 a.m. to 5 p.m. Thurs through Sat. Tours begin at the top of each hour. Admission is $8; discounts are available for educators, military AAA members, and senior citizens, and students.

SMITHFIELD LITTLE THEATRE, 210 N. Church St. (inside the Smithfield Center), Smithfield, VA 23430; (757) 357-7338; smithfieldlittletheatre .org. Check the theater's website to see if there's a show while you're in town. This delightful community theater (motto: "Hamming it up since 1962") has been packing the house for more than 50 years, offering year-round, high-quality, all-volunteer entertainment: musicals, full-length plays, a one-act play festival, and children's programming. Recent productions include Smithfield's take on many Broadway shows: *Hairspray, The Producers, SpamALot,* and *Thoroughly Modern Millie.* Refreshments are served in the lobby during shows for a donation to the theater's scholarship fund.

WHARF HILL BREWING COMPANY, 25 Main St., Smithfield, VA 23430; (757) 357-7100; wharfhillbrewing.com; $–$$. Long before it earned world renown for its ham, Smithfield was known for its bustling harbor. Steamboats unloaded their cargo and picked up hams, peanuts, and tobacco at the Pagan River docks, located at the spot where the last, steep block of Main Street met the waterfront, a section of town that came to be called Wharf Hill. With the steamboats gone by the dawn of the 20th century, that section of Main Street closest to the river became the heart of the Black business district. During segregation, when fraternal organizations didn't admit Black members, the all-Black "Improved Elks" owned a large building with multiple shopfronts on the south side of Main. They leased the ground floor to essential businesses: a barber, an undertaker, a pool hall, and a dentist's office. The second floor was where the Improved Elks met—and where the parties were held.

The latest tenant is the Wharf Hill Brewing Company. Though it opened in 2015, it already feels like a neighborhood institution. Part of that sense may stem from the decor: The interior is outfitted with refinished castoffs from historic structures all over Isle of Wight County. Beadboard from a two-room schoolhouse was repainted in muted rainbow colors to adorn the walls, and a dugout canoe retrieved from the bottom of Mill Swamp during a drought serves as wall art. Last call is announced by sounding the brass bell that once announced the arrival of the Old Dominion Steamboat at the docks.

Behind the bar, the brewery is pumping out its signature craft beer: Isle of Wheat Ale. It's slightly sweet (made with honey), but completely refreshing. The food is yummy pub grub with a twist: The Non-Won-Ton is a deep fried wrap containing barbecue and slaw; the Different Chicken Sandwich is a breast topped with provolone, bottomed with country ham, and served on a pretzel roll. The hand-breaded onion rings are massive (and delicious). The fried green tomatoes and coleslaw are scrumptious, too.

Live music every Wednesday draws a crowd, but the WHBC doesn't need entertainment to attract an audience. It's a perfect fit in a town that has long prided itself on knowing how to make visitors feel welcome. Open for lunch and dinner daily beginning at 11:30 a.m. The bar closes at 10 p.m.

WINDSOR CASTLE PARK, 301 Jericho Rd., Smithfield, VA 23430; (757) 365-4200; windsorcastlepark.com. Opened in 2010, this 208-acre riverside park sits on historic land and offers a unique way to experience Smithfield. Winding trails snake through woodlands and over pedestrian bridges that bring hikers close to the marshes on the banks of the Pagan River. It's hilly terrain—and a good challenge for runners. There's a picnic area, dog park, kayak/canoe launch (kayaks are available to rent), fishing pier, mountain bike path, scenic overlooks, and the historic manor house: Windsor Castle. The park sits on land bought in 1637 by Arthur Smith, an ancestor of the town's founder, Arthur Smith IV. Admission is free. There is ample parking on-site.

Restaurants

ANNA'S RISTORANTE PASTA VINO, 1810 S. Church St., Smithfield, VA 23430; (757) 357-4676; $–$$. There is a restaurant called "Anna's" in every single city in the 757 (some towns have more than one), but this is one of the better iterations. You can get pizza and takeout from a drive-through window, but the sit-down menu is vast with some delicious surprises, like the chicken piccata. Good wine list. Open daily for lunch and dinner.

SMITHFIELD GOURMET BAKERY AND CAFE, 218 Main St., Smithfield, VA 23430; (757) 357-0045; smithfieldgourmetbakery.com; $. This inviting eatery serves up tasty sandwiches and baked goods to an adoring public. All breads are baked fresh daily. The Piggly Wiggly is country ham on house-made sourdough; the Reuben comes between slices of fresh rye. Saving room for dessert is a must. Try the Royal Cookie (chocolate chips, macadamia nuts, coconut) or the lemon meringue pie. Actually, you can't go wrong with any of the cookies, pies, cinnamon rolls, muffins, or cheesecake. Open 8 a.m. to 5 p.m. Mon through Thurs; 8 a.m. to 8 p.m. Fri and Sat; 7 a.m. to 5 p.m. Sun.

SMITHFIELD ICE CREAM PARLOR, 208 Main St., Smithfield, VA 23430; (757) 357-6166; $. A Smithfield institution for more than 30 years, this old-fashioned ice cream shop sells subs, deli sandwiches, salads, and, of course, ice cream. Swivel on the counter stools while waiting for your banana split or scoop of chocolate chip mint. Open 10 a.m. to 7 p.m. Mon through Sat, 11 a.m. to 6 p.m. Sun.

THE SMITHFIELD INN & WILLIAM RAND TAVERN, 112 Main St., Smithfield, VA 23430; (757) 357-1752; smithfieldinn.com; $$–$$$. This elegant dining spot in the heart of downtown has been the best place to get something to eat in Smithfield since 1752. (That's not a misprint.) Fine food—seafood, pork, lamb, beef, and chicken—creatively prepared is served in an atmosphere of candlelight, flocked wallpaper, and crisp linens. A less expensive tavern menu is also available—try the BLT with fried green tomatoes. The tavern opens for lunch and dinner at 11:30 a.m. Mon through Sat. The dining room opens for lunch from 11:30 a.m. to 3 p.m., for dinner from 5:30 to 9 p.m. Tues through Sat, and 11:30 a.m. to 3 p.m. for Sunday brunch. Reservations are recommended.

SMITHFIELD STATION, 415 S. Church St., Smithfield, VA 23430; (757) 357-7700; smithfieldstation.com; $$. A popular destination for boaters, this restaurant, retail, and hotel complex sits at the foot of a small bridge overlooking the Pagan River (look for the huge decorated pig guarding the overflow parking lot) with docking for patrons on the riverfront itself. The restaurant serves lunch and dinner and specializes in seafood, pork, pasta, and daily specials. After your meal, stroll out on the deck that surrounds the restaurant and connects it to the marina. There's a mile of wraparound boardwalk. There's a separate pub, the IBX Bar, with a limited menu, daily food specials, and happy hour from 4 to 7 p.m. Sun through Fri. The restaurant is open daily 11 a.m. to 9:30 p.m. (10 p.m. on Fri and Sat). A breakfast buffet is served Sun from 8 a.m. to noon.

TASTE OF SMITHFIELD, 217 Main St., Smithfield, VA 23430; (757) 357-8950; $. Part restaurant and part gift shop, this establishment highlights the cuisine that makes Smithfield famous: row upon row of all manner of peanut (roasted, salted, with wasabi dust, chocolate covered, and one called the "milk chocolate peanut butter peanut"), Virginia wines, spiral ham and ham products, craft beer, and many, many decorative pigs, if you're in the market for one. The restaurant, with tables outside and at the front of the store plus some counter seats, serves pancakes, eggs, biscuits, and gravy beginning at 7 a.m., then switches to a menu of sandwiches, burgers (huge), house-made soups, ham biscuits, and barbecue for lunch and early dinner. Open 7 a.m. to 7 p.m. Mon through Thurs; until 8 p.m. on Fri and Sat; noon to 8 p.m. Sun.

NORFOLK

On the eastern edge of Hampton Roads fronting the world's largest natural harbor, Norfolk has been a sailors' city for nearly 400 years. Norfolk Naval Base is the world's largest navy base, and the numerous posts, bases, and businesses that support it have drawn thousands of men and women from around the nation to this city over the years. While Uncle Sam has always played a key role in the city's economy and demographics, Norfolk also serves as the region's financial hub: Within a two-block radius of downtown Norfolk are the Hampton Roads headquarters for all of the state's major banks. Norfolk is also home to the area's four dominant arts organizations: the Virginia Stage Company, the Virginia Symphony, the Virginia Opera, and Chrysler Hall.

The approach to Norfolk from the Historic Triangle is stunning by any criteria: I-64 moves out over the mouth of Hampton Roads on a bridge-tunnel that affords a breathtaking view of the harbor and the navy base on the far shore. To get downtown once you've crossed the water, follow I-64 to I-264 West. Exit at City Hall Avenue and you'll be on the east side of the downtown area, directly in front of McArthur Center, Norfolk's spiffiest mall.

The drive takes about an hour from Williamsburg, longer if traffic is backed up at the tunnel—and it frequently is during rush hour, on summer weekends, on holidays, and for absolutely no reason at all. Smart signs along the interstate warn travelers of potential delays well before the tunnel; an alternate route to Southside is via the Monitor-Merrimac Memorial Bridge-Tunnel, which dumps you into Norfolk on the western edge of the downtown, near the Ghent neighborhood.

There are special times of year when a trip to Norfolk has added interest. In late April through early May, the Virginia Arts Festival brings world-class music, dance, theater, and visual arts to multiple venues; the late April International Azalea Festival is staged amid the blossoms at Norfolk Botanical Garden; and, during the first weekend in June, you can join a crowd of thousands for Norfolk's annual Harborfest celebration, which brings music, food, and entertainment to the downtown waterfront for three days of fun in the sun. For more on the Virginia Arts Festival, turn to our Annual Events chapter.

NORFOLK CONVENTION & VISITORS BUREAU, 232 E. Main St., Norfolk, VA 23510; (757) 664-6620, (800) 368-3097; visitnorfolk.com. This is the best place to stop during weekday business hours for brochures and pamphlets, or call the number above and ask to have a visitor's guide sent to you. The bureau also operates a Visitor Information Center just off I-64. Take exit 273, the second exit after you come east through the Hampton Roads Bridge-Tunnel. The center offers brochures and a hotel reservation service; staff members there can answer all your questions. The center is open 8:30 a.m. to 5 p.m. Mon through Fri.

Attractions

Many of Norfolk's attractions are downtown, but along its western fringe is the Ghent neighborhood, where the downtown crowd, the artists, and the hipsters hang out. Colley Avenue, the main corridor in Ghent, is home to many small specialty shops, and some very good restaurants, and the Naro, a movie theater that specializes in the kind of films rarely shown at the cineplex. Norfolk is also home to the Harrison Opera House, the Scope, and Chrysler Hall, all of which stage big-name entertainment and productions, year-round. Due to the coronavirus pandemic, many of these venues were closed at the time of publication, so check their websites for updates on reopening plans and events.

THE CHRYSLER MUSEUM, 1 Memorial Place, Norfolk, VA 23510; (757) 664-6200; chrysler.org. The Chrysler is considered one of the top art museums in the country, with vast holdings that include works by Renoir, Matisse, and Gauguin, a superb collection of 19th-century sculpture, and art photography. The Chrysler also is world-renowned for its glass collection, which includes the work of Tiffany, Lalique, and other masters. A separate glass studio opened at 745 Duke St. (across from the museum grounds) in 2011, offering demonstrations, classes, visiting artists, and after-hours performances on the third Thursday of every month. The Chrysler brings many special exhibitions to Norfolk each year. The gorgeous building houses 60 galleries, a library, auditorium, gift shop, and restaurant.

Admission and parking are free; donations are appreciated. (Special visiting exhibitions may charge an entry fee; call for details or visit the website for more information.) Open 10 a.m. to 5 p.m. Tues through Sat; noon to 5 p.m. Sun.

DOUGLAS MACARTHUR MEMORIAL, 198 Bank St., Norfolk, VA 23510; (757) 441-2965; macarthurmemorial.org. This memorial honors the life and times of General Douglas MacArthur, as well as the men and women who served alongside him. The controversial general is entombed here, and his signature corncob pipe and the documents that ended the war with Japan are on display in the galleries. A 25-minute film featuring newsreel footage of MacArthur is shown in the theater, and the gift shop even displays the general's shiny 1950 Chrysler Crown Imperial limousine. Admission is free. Open 10 a.m. to 5 p.m. Wed through Sat, 11 a.m. to 5 p.m. Sun. Closed Mon and Tues.

HARBOR PARK, 150 Park Ave., Norfolk, VA 23510; (757) 622-2222; norfolktides.com. Just a long throw from downtown is Harbor Park, home base for the Norfolk Tides, a triple A farm team of the Baltimore Orioles. Designed by the same firm that built Camden Yards (the Baltimore Orioles' classic stadium), Harbor Park is a gem of a minor league facility, snuggled into a cozy urban corner with the Elizabeth River as its backdrop. Catch the boys of summer in action from early Apr through Labor Day for a fraction of what you'll pay to see them when they move up another level. Individual game tickets range from $11.75 to $17.75 (but there are deals to be had) and can be purchased at the ballpark or online through ticketmaster.com. Check their website for a game schedule.

MACARTHUR CENTER, 300 Monticello Ave., Norfolk, VA 23510; (757) 627-6000; shopmacarthur.com. Here are 3 levels of upscale shops, including more than 100 stores, 2 dozen places to eat, and a movie theater with 18 screens. In fact, a lot of people aren't shopping here. They're socializing, or letting their kids romp at the play area in the food court, or relaxing in one of the many conversational areas. Other amenities include valet parking, package carryout, complimentary strollers and wheelchairs, and 3 ATMs. If shopping is what you're after, the stores here include Nordstrom, Dillard's, Pottery Barn, Restoration Hardware, and Williams-Sonoma. Mall hours are 11 a.m. to 7 p.m. Mon through Sat, and noon to 6 p.m. on Sun. Parking is available in the attached garage for a fee.

NARO EXPANDED CINEMA, 1507 Colley Ave. (Ghent), Norfolk, VA 23510; (757) 625-6276; narocinema.com. Remember when every urban neighborhood had its own movie theater? This one still does. The Naro, founded in 1936, is a beloved institution in Ghent, having survived the multiplex era when just about every other small, independent theater succumbed. They did it by catering to the cineaste with programming that featured the art, foreign, and independent films nobody else was screening. In the Netflix era, they're feeling challenged again, but this movie theater might truly be the beating heart of Ghent—it'd be a tough place to let go. Every 2nd, 4th, and (if there is one) 5th Fri, the Naro shows *The Rocky Horror Picture Show* with a live cast at 11:30 p.m. Let your freak flag fly, people. The cafes and bars on either side of the Naro along Colley are where you'll find both Norfolk's downtown business crowd and its artistes after hours. At printing time the theater was still closed due to pandemic safety restrictions, but they offer private theater rentals and a great line-up of virtual screenings you can watch from the comfort of your home. A portion of these proceeds go to support the theater's operating costs until they can reopen to the public.

NAUTICUS, 1 Waterside Dr., Norfolk, VA 23510; (757) 664-1000; nauticus .org. This $52 million attraction opened in 1994 on the downtown waterfront, adjacent to Town Point Park. Combined with the USS *Wisconsin*—an 887-foot battleship that earned 5 combat stars during World War II, permanently docked in the next berth—this site has become a major attraction for downtown Norfolk. Visitors can go on board and take self-guided or audio tours of the historic ship's main deck.

The 120,000-square-foot science center was designed to have equal appeal for both adults and children with displays focusing on maritime commerce, the navy, exotic sea creatures, and the weather. Three theaters show films that help explain the maritime experience.

If you just want to eat at the Galley Restaurant or visit the gift shop, you can enter the museum's ground floor free. Access to the Hampton Roads Naval Museum, which moved from the Norfolk Naval Base to Nauticus, is also free, as is a tour of the *Wisconsin*'s deck. Admission to Nauticus is $15.95; children 3 and under are admitted free.

Open 10 a.m. to 5 p.m. Wed through Sat, and noon to 5 p.m. Sun. Closed Mon and Tues, as well as Thanksgiving, Christmas Eve, and Christmas Day. Parking is available in the municipal garage on Plume Street.

NAVAL STATION NORFOLK, 9079 Hampton Blvd., Norfolk, VA 23511; (757) 444-7955; cnic.navy.mil/regions/cnrma/installations/ns_norfolk.html. But why settle for just the museum experience of American military might? Naval Station Norfolk is the world's largest naval base, home port of 5 aircraft carriers (and 75 ships in all) and the US Navy's Atlantic Fleet command. The navy offers 45-minute guided tours, conducted by naval personnel. Schedules vary with the season. In the summer, they offer 9 tours a day, on the half hour, beginning at 10 a.m. The last tour begins at 2 p.m. Admission is $10 (ages 13 to 59), $5 for those over 60 or between 3 and 12. Active duty military and kids 2 and under are admitted free. At the time of publication, tours of the Naval Station were suspended due to coronavirus safety measures, so call or check the website for updates on whether visitors are allowed during the time of your visit.

NORFOLK BOTANICAL GARDEN, 6700 Azalea Garden Rd., Norfolk, VA 23518; (757) 441-5830; norfolkbotanicalgarden.org. This 155-acre garden began in 1938 as a Works Progress Administration (WPA) project. Today it boasts more than 12 miles of pathways and thousands of trees, shrubs, and flowering plants arranged in both formal and natural gardens. There are more than 20 themed gardens, including the 3.5-acre bicentennial rose garden, healing and herb gardens, and the fragrance garden for the visually impaired. The best time to go is in spring, when more than 250,000 azaleas are in bloom, but there's something to see just about any time of year. (Even during the winter months, you can enjoy camellias, witch hazel, wintersweet, colorful berries and a drive-thru Christmas lights show.) One of the best ways to view the gardens during the warm—weather months is by a 30-minute boat or tram ride. Admission to the gardens is $14 for adults, $12 for seniors, military, and children ages 3 to 17; free for children 2 and under. (Boat ride tickets are sold separately; tram ride is free with your paid admission to the garden.) Open 9 a.m. to 7 p.m. mid-Apr through mid-Oct and until 5 p.m. the rest of the year.

> **i** The tiger swallowtail is Old Dominion's state insect. This beautiful yellow-and-black butterfly, which feeds on buddleia, honeysuckle, bee balm, and sunflowers, is one of many that can be found in plentiful supply In the Bristow Butterfly Garden at Norfolk Botanical Garden.

THE NORVA, 317 Monticello Ave., Norfolk, VA 23510; (757) 627-4547; thenorva.com. Housed in a restored vaudeville theater that's nearly 100 years old, the Norva has a well-earned reputation for bringing cutting-edge and up-and-coming musicians to southeastern Virginia. Prince played here; so did James Brown. Long locally owned, the building was sold in 2014 to AEG Live, a sports and entertainment company based in Los Angeles. Local music fans hope this small-scale venue will continue to host big name acts.

Almost all shows are general admission; the main floor is generally left open, without seats, for standing and dancing. At those shows, there's limited table seating—first come, first served—on the main floor and the wraparound, second-floor balcony. Parking is available at a number of nearby garages, including the MacArthur Center mall. Tickets are available at the Norva's website or through ticketmaster.com.

VIRGINIA ZOO, 3500 Granby St., Norfolk, VA 23504; (757) 441-2374; virginiazoo.org. Situated on 53 acres along the Lafayette River, this lovely zoological park is home to more than 500 animals, including red pandas, zebras, rare Siberian tigers, primates, llamas, rhinos, and a pair of elephants who like to toss around tires and douse each other with water. The park takes special care to make its exhibits accessible to persons with disabilities. A 10-year, $15 million improvement plan resulted in a new entry and educational complex and the African Okavango River Delta exhibit. Special children's programs are offered year-round. Admission is $17.95 for 12 and up, $15.95 for senior citizens, $14.95 for children ages 2 to 11. All tickets must be purchased online. Last admittance is at 2 p.m. Open 10 a.m. to 4 p.m. daily.

Restaurants

Norfolk is a restaurant capital. Twice a year the downtown area hosts restaurant weeks with prix fixe menus and specials up and down Granby Street and the surrounding side streets. You can get pretty much anything your heart—and palate—desires; these are a few of our favorites, plus a word to the wise about a Norfolk institution.

DOUMAR'S CONES & BARBECUE, 1919 Monticello Ave., Norfolk, VA 23510; (757) 627-4163; doumars.com; $. Undoubtedly, if you tell someone you are traveling to Norfolk they will implore you to visit Doumar's, founded by Abe Doumar, who invented the ice cream cone in 1904 and died at age 92 in 2014. The restaurant's been at the same location since 1934. Guy Fieri has visited twice, and Garrison Keillor came by when he was taping *Prairie Home Company* at Chrysler Hall. In 1999, Doumar's was a James Beard Foundation Award winner, recognized as a "regional classic" whose food was "embedded in the fabric" of its community. Okay, but we've eaten here several times and not been impressed. A barbecue sandwich was so soggy it fell apart before it could be consumed. The fries were tasteless. Worst of all, at one of the only remaining Hampton Roads eateries that still has carhops, the service has been indifferent, bordering on surly. This is an institution, and the customer base still exists, but our current recommendation is go for dessert: The milk shakes in old-fashioned soda fountain glasses are superb, and the ice cream is a refreshing treat even on a cold day. Open 10 a.m. to 10 p.m. Mon through Thurs (until 12:30 a.m. Fri and Sat). Closed Sun.

RAJPUT INDIAN CUISINE, 742 W. 21st St., Norfolk, VA (757) 625-4634; rajputonline.com; $–$$. The name of this eatery refers both to royalty and to a region in western India. But the food here is surprisingly diverse, including seafood and vegetarian dishes, a tandoori mixed grill with chicken, lamb, fish, and shrimp, and a smattering of curry offerings. Open 11:30 a.m. to 3 p.m. (for lunch) and 4 to 10 p.m. (for dinner) every day except Tues (when they serve dinner only).

TOAST, 2406 Colonial Ave., Norfolk, VA 23517; toastplace.com; $. This funky new eatery, just across the tracks from Ghent, is a tasty bargain. Look at the neon sign and you'll know what to expect—that's not an *O* in the restaurant's name, it's a square slab of "old school white bread," the foundation for every dish they serve (except desserts—they're served on a brioche-style bread). All dishes are open-faced: Egg salad with kimchi and pecans, the BLATY (bacon, lettuce, avocado slaw, roasted tomato, and yolk), Taco Pig (carnitas with pickled peppers and onions), tuna melt, and the Curry Byrd (chicken with yellow curry butter and warm berry jam) are standouts. Two people can get out of here for under $25, and that includes a draft beer (or wine—the slightly carbonated rosé is on tap). Seating is at the bar, in booths, or walk through the kitchen to the enclosed patio, where you can sit by the herb garden or inside one of 2 shipping containers. It's like getting a great meal in somebody's well-outfitted garage. Park in the fenced-in lot or on 24th Street (*not* on Colonial). Open at 10 a.m. Wed through Sun, until 10 p.m. Wed and Thurs and 2 a.m., Fri and Sat. Starting at 3 p.m. Sun, "Toasted" programming goes into effect—a backyard party that goes until 10 p.m.

TODD JURICH'S BISTRO, 150 W. Main St., Ste. 100 (inside the Sun-Trust Building), Norfolk, VA 23510; (757) 622-3210; toddjurichsbistro.com; $$–$$$. This award-winning restaurant serves some of the most creative fare in town. Innovative creations by chef-owner Todd Jurich include crab cakes with Suffolk peanut slaw, flounder and lump crab Norfolk, meat loaf, salmon with local chard, and Kurobuta pork chops with bourbon–brown sugar peaches and sharp cheddar mac. Menus vary seasonally. Open 11:30 a.m. until 2 p.m. for lunch, 5 to 10 p.m. for dinner, Mon through Fri; 5:30 to 10 p.m. Sat.

VIRGINIA BEACH

If home is a landlocked region and the last time you saw the Atlantic Ocean was on a postcard sent to you by a vacationing friend, then by all means schedule a day trip to Virginia Beach. It isn't every day you get to dip your toes in the

Aerial view of Virginia Beach.
Mark E. Gibson/GettyImages

ocean, build a sandcastle, and sip a piña colada while watching the waves break on shore. A day at the beach might also be the perfect addition to your itinerary if you have small children. (Although we advise you to keep a very close eye on little ones. The surf may, on occasion, appear gentle, but the ocean's undertow is unpredictable.)

The route is fairly direct. Hop on I-64 and head east through the Hampton Roads Bridge-Tunnel to exit I-264 east toward Virginia Beach. Stay on the highway until it ends (it becomes 22nd Street). Continue until you intersect with Atlantic Avenue. The entire trip should take you about 90 minutes from Williamsburg.

There's parking—both free and metered, depending on how close you are to the water—on side streets all up and down the beach, but they fill up fast. There's also paid municipal parking in the 25th Street lot, or at the city's two parking garages at 19th Street and 31st Street. Parking will cost you between $2 and $10 a day, depending on how long you plan to stay and whether it's a weekday or a weekend.

Virginia Beach prides itself on being a family destination, and keeping it so is an ongoing multimillion dollar undertaking for the city that includes boardwalk upkeep, landscaping, and constant replenishing of sand to forestall beach erosion. The result is that the beach is one of the widest on the East Coast, and the widest it's been since perhaps as far back as 1700.

If you prefer to plan your visit around a special event, you're in luck. In mid-June the city hosts its annual Boardwalk Art Show and Festival, which brings close to 400 artists to the oceanfront to display and sell their work. In mid- to late September, the Neptune Festival salutes summer's end with free musical entertainment, a world famous sandcastle contest (really worth seeing), and a military air show. At Christmastime, the boardwalk is ablaze with more than 200 displays of 450,000 lights as part of Holiday Lights at the Beach.

Maybe just sticking one toe in the sand is enough for you, though. If so, Virginia Beach offers plenty of other things to do. Not even most Virginians realize that the largest city in Virginia is Virginia Beach. (The second largest is Norfolk, and the third is Chesapeake—it's no surprise the traffic is bad around here!)

VIRGINIA BEACH VISITORS CENTER, 2101 Parks Ave., Ste. 500, Virginia Beach, VA 23451; (757) 385-7873, (800) VA-BEACH (822-3224). If you'd like to find out exactly what this city on the ocean has to offer, call the toll-free number above or visit Virginia Beach's excellent website, which offers detailed information about distinct areas within this sprawling city. The central boardwalk area is where a lot of the action is—all the big hotels, tons of restaurants, water sports, and entertainment. (Lots of teenagers, too.) The Bay side has kinder, gentler waves that can be found on the north end of the beach in the waters of Chesapeake Bay. There are also accommodations and activities on Sandbridge Island, a peaceful oceanfront community 15 miles south of the resort area and home to the Back Bay National Wildlife Refuge. (See more below.) The visitor center is open daily 9 a.m. to 5 p.m., until 7 p.m. mid-June through Labor Day.

Attractions

ATLANTIC WATERFOWL HERITAGE MUSEUM AND DEWITT COTTAGE, 1113 Atlantic Ave., Virginia Beach, VA 23451; (757) 437-8432; awhm.org. The museum's 5 galleries feature artwork and decoy carvings, including some that date from the turn of the 19th century. Overlooking the ocean, the museum is located in the 1895 deWitt Cottage, the last remaining oceanfront cottage from the late 19th century. The museum is open Tues through Sat from 10 a.m. to 5 p.m., and Sun noon to 5 p.m. From Oct through Feb the museum is closed on Mon. A $2 donation per adult for admission is encouraged. Children age 16 and younger are free.

BACK BAY NATIONAL WILDLIFE REFUGE, 1324 Sandbridge Rd., Virginia Beach, VA 23456; (757) 301-7329; fws.gov/refuge/back_bay. It's all about the wildlife at this serene oasis, established in 1938 to provide a feeding and resting habitat for migratory birds along a critical segment of the Atlantic Flyway. As the population of Virginia Beach grew exponentially in the 1980s, the US Fish and Wildlife Service doubled the size of the refuge, to nearly 9,200 acres, to protect the watershed from development. A year-round birder's paradise—tundra swans, snow geese, and a large variety of ducks visit annually—the refuge's eight miles of scenic trails make it popular with hikers, too. It's also a place to spot loggerhead sea turtles, the endangered piping plover, brown pelicans, and bald eagles. Fresh- and saltwater fishing is allowed (state license required). Sunscreen, bug repellent, and water are essential during the summer months. No swimming and no pets are allowed. Entry fees vary depending on how you arrive—by foot or bike, $2; in a car, $5. Open daily dawn to dusk; the Visitor Contact Station is open 8 a.m. to 4 p.m. weekdays and 9 a.m. to 4 p.m. Sat and Sun. During the winter, the station does not open on Sun and it is closed on holidays except Memorial Day, July Fourth, and Labor Day.

EDGAR CAYCE'S ASSOCIATION FOR RESEARCH AND ENLIGHT-ENMENT (A.R.E.), 215 67th St., Virginia Beach, VA 23451; (757) 428-3588, (800) 333-4499; edgarcayce.org. Cayce died in 1945, but his work lives on at the Cayce Foundation headquarters on the oceanfront. Cayce was known as "the sleeping prophet," diagnosing and prescribing cures for medical ailments while in a trance. Each year, the A.R.E. hosts thousands of international visitors and researchers who have an interest in his holistic approach to healing. A free daily tour is offered at 2:30 p.m. An extrasensory perception (ESP) demonstration class takes place at 1 p.m. every Sat and Sun. There's also an informative film, a chance to walk the labyrinth, lectures on dreams and intuition, and a popular talk on reincarnation, given at 3:30 p.m. daily. A meditation room overlooks the ocean; there is also a meditation garden on the grounds. Open 10 a.m. to 7 p.m. Mon through Sat; noon to 5 p.m. Sun.

At the time of publication the headquarters had canceled their in-person events because of the pandemic, but they offer a number of virtual events and classes through their website.

FALSE CAPE STATE PARK, 4001 Sandpiper Rd., Virginia Beach, VA 23456; (757) 426-7128. Situated between Back Bay and the Atlantic Ocean, this park is one of the last undeveloped stretches of beach on the Eastern Seaboard. Its name stems from a case of mistaken identity. Sailors in the 1800s thought they had reached Cape Henry; only when their boats wrecked in the shallow waters of Back Bay did they realize their mistake. Shipwreck survivors founded one of the area's first communities, Wash Woods. Throughout the 19th century and into the 20th, the area was a haven for duck hunters—the park's Environmental Education Center is a converted hunt club. The park's 6 miles of beachfront extends to the North Carolina border. Guided kayak trips, primitive camping, and hiking and biking trails are available here, but the park is only accessible by foot, bicycle, tram, or boat; you can't get here by car. Campers usually boat over from Little Island City Park in Virginia Beach; hikers walk the trail or take the round-trip tram from Back Bay National Wildlife

Refuge, available April through October 31. (Between Nov 1 and Mar 31, access to the park is restricted to hiking or biking along the beach, by boat, or by reserving the park's beach transporter, the Terra-Gator.) Overnight guests must boat or canoe in, or hike or bike from the refuge (a 5- to 9-mile walk, depending on the campsite). Insect repellent is a must; biting flies and ticks are common in the summer. Beware of venomous eastern cottonmouth snakes. Bring your own water, and all trash must be carried out. Not recommended for young children, inexperienced campers, or the physically disabled. There is no electricity; pit toilets only. Open dawn to dusk. Admission is free.

FIRST LANDING STATE PARK, 2500 Shore Dr., Virginia Beach, VA 23451; (757) 412-2300 (on-site office), (800) 933-PARK (7275) (for campground and cabin reservations); dcr.virginia.gov/state-parks/first-landing. If you really want the complete colonial experience, visit this park, where in 1607 the English colonists first stepped ashore in the New World, before continuing on to Jamestown. Native Americans, 20th-century schooners, and modern cargo ships have all plied the waters here. Legend has it that Blackbeard hid in the narrows area of the park. The land—nearly 3,000 acres—was bought for $157,000 by the state in 1933. An all African American unit of the Civilian Conservation Corps built the park's trails and structures from 1933 to 1940. The park is both a National Natural Landmark and listed on the National Register of Historic Places. As Virginia's most-visited state park, it's an oasis within urban Virginia Beach. Nine hiking trails cover 20 miles. Interpreters conduct trail walks, or you can rent a bike from the Trail Center (in season).

There's 1.5 miles of sandy Chesapeake Bay beach frontage (but no lifeguards, and swimming at the Narrows area is not advised because of strong currents). Fishing and crabbing are popular (state saltwater fishing license required). Canoes, kayaks, and other watercraft may be rented at the boat ramp. The picnic area is equipped with drinking water, grills, tables, and restroom facilities. Campsites, with water and electricity hookups, and cabins are available, too. (The cabins go fast in the summer—reserve early.) One note: The park is used by the military for training. Occasionally there might be "unusual sights and loudness." The Trail Center, gift shop, snack bar, and Bay Store are open daily, in season. The park is open sunrise to sunset. Admission, per vehicle, is $10 Apr through Oct; $7 in the cooler months.

OLD CAPE HENRY LIGHTHOUSE, 583 Atlantic Ave. (Fort Story), Virginia Beach, VA 23459; (757) 422-9421; preservatiovirginia.org. The very first building the newly constituted US Congress funded was this lighthouse, built in 1792 (at the then-exorbitant cost of $17,500) to guide ships at the mouth of the Chesapeake Bay. It was George Washington's idea, and Alexander Hamilton oversaw its construction. How's that for a historic pedigree? The stone used in the structure came from the same Virginia quarry that supplied the White House, the Capitol, and Mount Vernon. One of the oldest surviving lighthouses in the US, it was taken out of service and replaced by a cast-iron beacon a little farther east in 1881. But you can still climb to the top (flip flops are strongly discouraged; the staircase is winding, steep, and narrow) and, if lucky, you may be treated to the sight of dolphins playing in the Atlantic. The lighthouse is on the grounds of Fort Story, a military base. Government-issued photo ID is required for entry for all visitors 16 years or older, and you must have proof of vehicle insurance and registration. Only visitors with an authorized government ID are allowed to drive directly to the lighthouse. All others will park at the gate and travel to the lighthouse via a shuttle.

General admission is $10 and includes access to the lighthouse's new visitor plaza, completed in 2019. The plaza showcases new interpretive signage and views of the Atlantic Ocean and Chesapeake Bay. There is a self-guided walking tour of historic points of interest, including a plaque commemorating the first landfall of colonists bound for Jamestown in 1607. There is a discount for seniors, military, AAA members, and children.

If you want to climb to the tippy toppy of the lighthouse, the admission charge is $14 (total) for adults but only a limited number of these tickets are sold each day and they regularly sell out. Buy them in advance on the Preservation Virginia website, listed above.

The lighthouse grounds are open from 10 a.m. to 5 p.m. beginning in mid-Mar through Oct, 10 a.m. to 4 p.m. the rest of the year. Closed Thanksgiving; Dec 24, 25, and 31; and Jan 1 and 2.

VETERANS UNITED HOME LOANS AMPHITHEATER, 3550 Cellar Door Way, Virginia Beach, VA 23456; (757) 368-3000; thefarmbureaulive .com. It's at least a 90-minute drive from Williamsburg to Virginia Beach when traffic cooperates, which it usually doesn't, given the tunnels between the two towns, but this amphitheater is a regular stop on the outdoor summer-tour schedule of many popular acts. There's seating under the pavilion or on the lawn, but go early if you're sitting on the grass and be prepared to brave whatever elements are in play at the time. The amphitheater has 7,500 reserved seats, with room for about 12,500 on the lawn. Two giant screens on either side of the stage provide a view for those in the back. Refreshments are available at every show. To purchase tickets visit the website listed above.

VIRGINIA AQUARIUM & MARINE SCIENCE CENTER, 717 General Booth Blvd., Virginia Beach, VA 23451; (757) 385-FISH (3474); virginia aquarium.com. An extremely popular destination for the entire family, this marine science museum draws crowds throughout the year, with dozens of hands-on exhibits in two separate buildings that are linked by a nature trail. The Bay & Ocean Pavilion traces water's journey through Virginia from rivers to the Chesapeake Bay to the ocean, introducing aquatic animals and plants.

Two touch pools allow up-close and personal time with creatures like the horseshoe crab or stingray. Visitors will see hundreds of fish, turtles, and sharks in 800,000 gallons worth of aquaria. In the Marsh Pavilion, river otters, sea horses, and snakes bring the explanation of this vital ecosystem to life. Walk outside on an elevated deck that contains an aviary with 55 different types of native Virginia birds. The Owls Creek Path links the two pavilions with a 10-minute walk through salt marsh and woodland preserve. Get a bird's-eye view of Owls Creek itself by climbing a 30-foot-tall observation tower, or stop at the various "curiosity carts" on the path, staffed by educators, for a hands-on examination of plants and artifacts. There's also a 3D theater showing Hollywood and IMAX features. This museum is actively involved in conservation programs and is home to the area's stranding program, which provides care for injured wildlife including dolphins, seals, fish, and coastal birds. Admission to the museum only is $24.95 for adults, $22.95 for seniors, and $19.95 for children, ages 3 to 11. Admission to the IMAX theater, dolphin-watching program, and the adventure park—an aerial trail (above the Owls Creek Path) of wooden platforms connected by challenge bridges and zip lines—all carry an additional fee. Open daily 9 a.m. to 5 p.m.

VIRGINIA BEACH SURF AND RESCUE MUSEUM, 2401 Atlantic Ave., Virginia Beach, VA 23451; (757) 422-1587; oldcoastguardstation.com. A former US Coast Guard Station built in 1903, this simple white clapboard structure operates as a museum honoring those who risked their lives to save sailors and other seafarers. A permanent display focuses on the impact of World Wars I and II on Virginia Beach. The TowerCam, a roof-mounted video camera, can zoom in on passing ships spied on the horizon. The camera transmits its pictures to a 27-inch television monitor, providing visitors with the same view crewmen had from the station tower almost a century ago. (You can see its transmission from the website listed above.) Admission is $1. Open Wed through Sat, 10 a.m. to 5 p.m. Closed Thanksgiving, Christmas Day, New Year's Eve, and New Year's Day.

VIRGINIA LEGENDS WALK, 1300 Atlantic Ave., Virginia Beach, VA 23451; va-legends.com. This outdoor monument between Atlantic and Pacific Avenues pays tribute to Virginians who have made significant contributions to the country and the world. Since the walk was dedicated in 1999 with 24 inductees, including Arthur Ashe, Pearl Bailey, Patsy Cline, Ella Fitzgerald, Patrick Henry, Thomas Jefferson, Douglas MacArthur, James Madison, George C. Marshall, Edgar Allan Poe, Bill "Bojangles" Robinson, Captain John Smith, Booker T. Washington, and Woodrow Wilson, another dozen or more legends have been added, including Katie Couric and Triple Crown–winner Secretariat. The plaques on the walk are lit from above so that they can be viewed at night.

Restaurants

All that splashing around in the ocean is sure to work up an appetite. While the beachfront has a well-rounded selection of restaurants for your dining pleasure, we've singled out a handful sure to please.

1608 CRAFTHOUSE, 1608 Pleasant House Rd., Virginia Beach, VA 23455; (757) 965-4510; 1608crafthouse.com; $$. The *Virginian Pilot*'s food critic proclaimed this new gastropub's hamburger the Best. Burger. Ever. And Delish.com declared 1608's version the "best bacon burger in Virginia." Naturally, we had to find out if they were right and . . . they were. The burger, a combination of ground chuck, short rib meat, and brisket, is stuffed with white American cheese, then crusted with crumbled applewood-smoked bacon. It's served on a brioche bun up to the task of staying firm while you consume this juiciest of burgers. (Ask for extra napkins.) This is an environmentally aware business that recycles its oyster shells and serves only those products that have been certified as "sensible seafood" by the Virginia Aquarium. Ninety percent of the craft brews they serve come from within a 250-mile radius, including many from the 757. With only 6 seats at the bar, 4 bar tables, and a nondescript dining room, the food deserves a better setting. Open daily 3 p.m. to close.

BEACH BULLY BAR-B-QUE, 601 19th St., Virginia Beach, VA 23451; (757) 422-4222; beachbully.com; $–$$. For some of the best open-pit barbecue in town—lunch or dinner—stop in at Beach Bully. Grab a beef platter or dig into half a chicken with 2 sides. The dress code is casual, so just come as you are after a day in the sun and the surf. Open daily for lunch and dinner at 10 a.m.

JUDY'S SICHUAN CUISINE, 328 Constitution Dr. (Pembroke Shops East), Virginia Beach, VA 23462; (757) 499-2810; $$. Named by Yahoo! as the "Best Chinese Restaurant" in Virginia (determined by Yelp data scientists who compiled a list based on customer reviews), others are learning what locals already know: The fare here is terrific. Try the chicken in chili oil or the tea-smoked duck, steamed dumplings, or sesame pancakes. Open daily for lunch and dinner at 11:30 a.m.

MANNINO'S, 3420 Atlantic Ave., Virginia Beach, 23462; (757) 390-2580; manninositalianbistro.com; $$. This locally owned restaurant was started by a family whose roots go back to Palermo, Italy. The award-winning lasagna is made from scratch with house-made noodles and mozzarella, fresh Parmesan, and three sauces: a Bolognese made with veal and beef, a ricotta béchamel, and a plum tomato sauce. In addition to a full menu of pasta and traditional Italian entrees, Mannino's she-crab soup is delectable. The oceanfront location is open daily 11 a.m. to 3:30 p.m. for lunch, 5 p.m. to midnight for dinner. There's a second location on Princess Anne Boulevard in the Kempsville area of Virginia Beach.

Annual Events

If you enjoy planning a vacation around a special event, a trip to the Historic Triangle offers plenty of options. While a summer excursion practically guarantees a jam-packed itinerary of historic tours, sun-soaked shopping, and theme park rowdiness, the other seasons can be just as glorious. And although the local festival season doesn't swing into high gear until April, you'll find a smattering of activities to choose from during the year's first quarter, a good time to visit if you don't like crowds.

If you schedule your visit during spring break or later, your choice of fun activities pretty much runs the gamut. From roller coaster thrills to craft beer festivals to lights and sounds of Christmas, the Williamsburg area gives you a diverse menu of events and activities from which to choose.

Below, we've listed the major celebrations that take place in and around the Williamsburg area. For those of you willing to drive a little farther for a good time, we've also included some of our favorite festivals elsewhere in Hampton Roads. Our annual events are listed month by month to make your vacation planning a little easier.

EVENT SCHEDULE

January

WORKING WOOD IN THE 18TH CENTURY, DeWitt Wallace Decorative Arts Museum, 301 S. Nassau St., Williamsburg, VA 23185; (800) 603-0948; colonialwilliamsburg.org. The annual Working Wood in the 18th Century conference is cosponsored by the Colonial Williamsburg Foundation and *Fine Woodworking* magazine. This program fills to capacity every year, so those interested are encouraged to register early. Call for specific registration information.

February

ANTIQUES FORUM, Williamsburg Lodge Conference Center, 310 S. England St., Williamsburg, VA 23185; (800) 603-0948; colonialwilliamsburg .org. This forum brings collectors and antiques experts together to share their knowledge in seminars, attend lectures given by Colonial Williamsburg's curators, take special tours, and socialize. Registration cost $650 (2019) but includes 4 continental breakfasts, three afternoon refreshment breaks, the opening and closing reception, dinner and Colonial Williamsburg admission; field trips and some lectures by distinguished scholars carry an additional fee. A discounted rate for museum professionals and students is available, as are a limited number of scholarships. Registration begins in November.

MID-ATLANTIC QUILT FESTIVAL WEEK, Hampton Roads Convention Center, 1610 Coliseum Dr., Hampton, VA 23666; (215) 862-5828 (Mancuso Show Management); quiltfest.com. February is the chilliest month of the year in Hampton Roads—the perfect time to get wrapped up in this major show focusing on quilts as an art form. Quilting, fiber arts, and wearable art are on display, and the event draws quilters and textile and fiber artists of all levels from a wide region to attend some of the workshops, lectures, and special activities offered.

PRESIDENTS' DAY WEEKEND, Colonial Williamsburg; (800) HISTORY (447-8679); colonialwilliamsburg.org. Programs throughout the weekend highlight the actions and experiences of three Virginians—George Washington, Thomas Jefferson, and James Madison—who all served as president of the US.

March
DAFFODIL FESTIVAL, 6509 Main St., Gloucester, VA 23061; (804) 693-2355 (parks and recreation dept.); daffodilfestivalva.org. Considered the opening event of the Hampton Roads festival season, this weekend-long celebration stems (no pun intended) from the town's long relationship with the early-season bloomer. Gloucester was once the daffodil capital of America—there are growers here who have been in the daffodil business for four generations. Held in late Mar or early Apr (depending on when Easter is), this free festival features food, arts and crafts, musical entertainment, and bus tours to Brent & Becky's Bulbs. There are children's events, games, historic displays, and the crowning of the Daffodil Festival Queen. Bring your pet along for the costumed "Mutt Show." To get to Gloucester, follow US 17 north from Yorktown over the Coleman Bridge.

2ND SUNDAY ART & MUSIC FESTIVAL, Downtown Williamsburg, VA. Nearly a hundred vendors offering photography, glass, woodcarving, pottery, textiles, and original art set up shop outdoors downtown on the second Sun of each month, Mar through Dec for this family friendly event. There's live music and performances by jugglers, mimes, yo-yo magicians, hula-hoop masters, student dance troupes and street theater. Amber Ox and the Precarious Beer Project run the beer garden. For more information, contact organizer Shirley Vermillion at 2ndsundayswb@gmail.com.

WOMEN'S HISTORY MONTH, Colonial Williamsburg; (800) HISTORY (447-8679); colonialwilliamsburg.org. Colonial Williamsburg celebrates the contributions of 18th-century women throughout the month. Tours, programs, and special presentations explore the various roles that our foremothers filled in the creation of a new country.

April

ART ON THE SQUARE, Duke of Gloucester St. (Merchants Square), Williamsburg, VA 23185; williamsburgjuniors.org/art-on-the-square. This uber-popular annual event is organized by the Junior Woman's Club to raise funds for local nonprofit arts organizations. The juried show regularly attracts 160 artists and craftspeople. The work on display is original, high quality handcrafted art in diverse media. Admission is free.

GARDEN SYMPOSIUM, DeWitt Wallace Museum, 301 S. Nassau St., Williamsburg, VA 23185; (800) 603-0948; colonialwilliamsburg.org. Colonial Williamsburg's 3-day crash course on cultivating a green thumb has been held for more than 70 years. If you want to know how to make your garden grow, join horticulturists and gardening enthusiasts for a host of lectures, tours, and master classes on garden design, sustainable garden practices, and plant choices. Advance registration is required.

HISTORIC GARDEN WEEK, (804) 644-7776 (Garden Club of Virginia); VAGardenweek.org. Sponsored by garden clubs throughout Virginia, this special week celebrating nature's beauty (and the decorating skills of a number of homeowners) is held the third week in Apr. On Tues of that week, the Williamsburg Garden Club sponsors its garden week tour of both the gardens and interiors of 4 or 5 homes in the Williamsburg area. In addition, a walking garden tour of portions of the Colonial Williamsburg gardens is offered. Because the chairperson of the local event changes annually, your best bet for more information is to contact the state Historic Garden Week headquarters at the number listed above or check the website for details.

MILITARY THROUGH THE AGES, Jamestown Settlement, 2110 Jamestown Rd., Williamsburg, VA 23185; (757) 253-5112, (888) 593-4682; jyf museums.org. This chronological display of military history has been held every Mar for 30-plus years, with reenactors in period dress demonstrating the evolution of weaponry and tactics from the Roman Legion in AD 64 through the Virginia Army National Guard in modern times. Musical performances include a Union Army regimental brass band from the 1860s and Ladies for Liberty, singing Andrews Sisters–style music of the World War II era. Cover your ears for the comparative artillery-firing demonstrations, with weapons ranging from a 17th-century swivel gun to a modern-day howitzer, and the cannon salute. The event also features a Sat children's parade and a Sun military pass in review.

VIRGINIA ARTS FESTIVAL, 440 Bank St. (Festival office), Norfolk, VA 23510; (757) 282-2822; vafest.com. An international lineup of artists in music, theater, and dance comes to venues throughout Hampton Roads for the Virginia Arts Festival, now in its third decade. Ballet and theater troupes, Broadway stars in cabaret settings, jazz greats, operetta, folk and chamber music, and the famed Virginia International Tattoo highlight 6 weeks of performances staged from Williamsburg to Virginia Beach. Patrons can create their own discount subscription package by choosing 3 or more events. The schedule is usually announced in Nov, and single tickets go on sale in Feb.

May

CHILDREN'S FESTIVAL OF FRIENDS, Newport News Park, 13560 Jefferson Ave., Newport News, VA 23603; (757) 926-1400; nnva.gov/851/Childrens-Festival-of-Friends. A popular 1-day festival for families with young children is held annually in early May. Children can meet their favorite book characters, see exotic animals, make crafts, play laser tag, or watch a kung fu performance. The festival features over 100 hands-on activities, including pony rides, a trackless train, rock-climbing wall, moon bounce, slide, obstacle course, science experiments, giant mural painting, and drumming. A special preschool play area filled with toys is available for the youngest festival guests. Admission is free, but there is a $5 fee to park.

CONFEDERATE ATTACK ON FORT POCAHONTAS AT WILSON'S WHARF, 13500 Sturgeon Point Rd. (off VA 5), Charles City County, VA 23030; (804) 829-9722; fortpocahontas.org. In an effort to preserve this once-forgotten fort, owned by the descendants of President John Tyler, reenactors meet each year for a 2-day event to restage the Civil War battle that took place here on May 24, 1864. It was the first major land-naval clash between the US Colored Troops and General Robert E. Lee's Army of Northern Virginia. The weekend events include a living-history encampment, an evening lantern tour, military demonstrations, and 2 battle reenactments. Sutlers—merchants dressed in period attire—offer plenty of wares for sale. Admission is $10 for adults, $8 for students per day, or $15 for adults and $10 for students for a 2-day pass. Discounts are available for groups of 10 or more.

JAMESTOWN DAY, Jamestown Settlement, 2110 Jamestown Rd., Williamsburg, VA 23185; (757) 253-5112, (888) 593-4682; jyfmuseums.org. At Jamestown Day—an event sponsored jointly by Jamestown Settlement and Historic Jamestowne—maritime demonstrations, military drills, and archaeology programs mark the 1607 anniversary of America's first permanent English colony. Separate admission charges apply to Jamestown Settlement and Historic Jamestowne. Free parking with a shuttle is available at both sites.

MEMORIAL DAY, Colonial Williamsburg, (800) HISTORY (447-8679); colonialwilliamsburg.org. A modern service honors military veterans who died while serving their country. Wreaths are placed at the Governor's Palace, Bruton Parish Church, and the French gravesite to honor those who died during the American Revolution and the Civil War. A procession with Fifes & Drums support begins at the Governor's Palace. A brief commemorative service with musket and cannon volleys takes place at the French gravesite.

June

GREEK FESTIVAL, Saints Constantine and Helen Greek Orthodox Church, 60 Traverse Rd., Newport News 23606; (757) 596-6151; newport newsgreekfestival.org. When more than 12,000 folks decide to have dinner at the same place, you know the food must be good. Join the crowd at this annual Hellenic festival for a few traditional favorites—moussaka, souvlaki, pastitsio, gyros, baked chicken, and rice pilaf—and enjoy the live entertainment. Stop at the *plaka* (marketplace), which sells everything from artwork and fine jewelry to Greek provisions such as phyllo, orzo, olives, and cheeses. Admission and parking are free. Meals are sold a la carte. The festival has become so popular that a smaller fall festival is now scheduled each Oct, held indoors at the Hellenic Community Center on the same grounds as the church.

HAMPTON JAZZ FESTIVAL, Hampton Coliseum, 1000 Coliseum, Hampton, VA 23666; (757) 838-4203 (Hampton Coliseum); hamptonjazz festival.com. This enduring festival (which started in 1968) is a major draw for fans of jazz, pop, the blues, soul, and R&B. The list of artists who have appeared here—including Aretha Franklin, Isaac Hayes, Stevie Wonder, B. B. King, Gladys Knight, and George Benson—reads like a roster from some soulful Hall of Fame. The festival typically is held in late June. For a full lineup, see the website after Apr 1 each year.

July

INDEPENDENCE DAY CELEBRATION, Main Street, Yorktown, VA 23690; (757) 890-3300; yorkcounty.gov/tourism/Events/July4th. Family-oriented festivities are the order of the day at Yorktown's Fourth of July celebration. Activities include a footrace, parade, arts and crafts, musical entertainment, and, of course, a magnificent display of fireworks. Satellite parking is provided away from the waterfront, but free buses will get you to the heart of the daylong festivities. The Yorktown Fourth of July Committee sponsors the free celebration.

INDEPENDENCE DAY FESTIVITIES, Colonial Williamsburg; (800) HISTORY (447-8679); colonialwilliamsburg.com/plan/calendar/fourth-july. Celebrate our nation's birthday in Williamsburg with the Fifes & Drums, militia parades, and Colonial Williamsburg's famous evening program of fireworks in the Historic Area. Admission is free.

LIBERTY CELEBRATION, American Revolution Museum, Yorktown, VA 23690; (757) 847-3156; jyfmuseums.org. Tactical drills, military exercises, and role-playing demonstrations salute America during the Fourth of July holiday. Visitors can see in museum galleries a rare broadside printing of America's Declaration of Independence dating to July 1776 and, during a special interpretive program, learn about the sacrifices of Americans who sought to be "free and independent" from Great Britain.

August

HAMPTON CUP REGATTA, Mill Creek, Hampton; hamptoncupregatta .com. The oldest and largest inboard hydroplane powerboat race in the US, the motto of these summer national championships is "Scaring fish out of their scales for 90 years." Eleven classes of boats, including the Grand Prix hydroplanes that are billed as the fastest piston—powered craft in the world, hit top speeds of 170 mph. There's also live entertainment and food. The races run for three days at Fort Monroe's Mill Creek. Admission is free, but get there early to grab a prime viewing spot.

September

CHICKAHOMINY FALL FESTIVAL AND POWWOW, Chickahominy Tribal Ground, 8200 Lott Cary Rd., Providence Forge, VA 23140; chickahominytribe.org/events/events.html. The Chickahominy tribe hosts its annual festival on its tribal ground nearby Charles City County in late September, featuring Native American dancing, singing, and drumming. There is an array of beautiful handmade Indian jewelry, pottery, and beadwork for sale, plus books, tapes, and food—fish sandwiches, chicken dinners, Indian fry bread. There is no admission fee, but donations are accepted. Special seating is provided for senior citizens; all others should bring their own lawn chairs or blankets. No pets.

October

AN OCCASION FOR THE ARTS Merchants Square, Duke of Gloucester Street, Williamsburg, VA 23185; aofta.org. Held annually during the first weekend in Oct, this is Williamsburg's premiere arts and music festival, a free celebration of visual and performing arts which boasts the oldest juried invitational art show in Virginia. In addition to the art on display, entertainers—magicians, musicians, dancers, mimes—perform on different stages, and "A Taste for Wine and Beer," offers visitors free samples of Virginia-made wine, beer, and cider.

First held in 1969, the festival has grown from a one-day event to a full weekend, open from 10 a.m. to 5 p.m., Sat and Sun. Unless the weather is bad for this outdoor event, the biggest challenge will be parking: 2019's event drew upward of 25,000 visitors. Arrive first thing in the morning or be prepared to walk a few blocks from outlying lots to the festival action.

FALL FESTIVAL OF FOLKLIFE, Newport News Park, 13560 Jefferson Ave., Newport News, VA 23603; (757) 926-1400; nnparks.com/festivals .php. This free event, held on the first full weekend in Oct, is billed as Southeast Virginia's biggest traditional craft show, featuring over 200 vendors. It's kid friendly, too. A children's area has stage shows, hands-on crafts, sheep shearing, candle making, and weaving demonstrations. There's also a folk dance stage, where spectators can see Native American, African, international, and square dancing presented in the round. This free event typically draws tens of thousands of people, warranting two bits of advice: Arrive early because on-site parking (which costs $10) can be an extended ordeal; and eat early, as lines at the food vendors get long, leaving you ravenous by the time you get a chance to dig into your pit-cooked steak sandwich and butterfly fries. No pets.

FAMILY FRIGHTS, Jamestown Settlement, 2110 Jamestown Rd., Williamsburg, VA 23185; (757) 253-4838, (888) 593-4682; jyfmuseums.org. *Halloween fun with a bit of history.*

POQUOSON SEAFOOD FESTIVAL, Poquoson Municipal Park, 830 Poquoson Ave., Poquoson, VA 23662; (757) 868-3580, (757) 868-3588; poquosonseafoodfestival.com. This 3-day festival is free (but you'll pay $5 to park) and features music, fireworks, dance exhibitions, arts and crafts, children's events, and, of course, plenty of seafood. Started in 1981, the event is a tribute to the working watermen and -women of Hampton Roads and has become a tradition in the region. Poquoson is a small town, southeast of Williamsburg and surrounded on three sides by the waters of the Chesapeake Bay. Take I-64 east to exit 256-B to VA 171 and follow signs for shuttle parking. If you think you'll get lucky and find a parking place at the festival site, follow VA 171 for 5 to 6 miles and follow signs to the parking area.

YORKTOWN VICTORY CELEBRATION, American Revolution Museum, 200 Water St., Yorktown, VA 23690; (757) 253-4838, (888) 593-4682; historyisfun.org. Military life and artillery demonstrations mark the anniversary of America's momentous Revolutionary War victory at Yorktown on October 19, 1781. To experience Continental Army life firsthand, visitors can enroll in "A School for the Soldier" to drill with wooden muskets and apply tactical skills in mock combat, as well as learn about soldiers' provisions and sleeping quarters. Special programs also held at Yorktown Battlefield and at Riverwalk Landing.

November

FOODS & FEASTS OF COLONIAL VIRGINIA, American Revolution Museum, 200 Water St., Yorktown, VA 23690; (757) 253-4838, (888) 593-4682; Jamestown Settlement, 2110 Jamestown Rd., Williamsburg, VA 23185; (757) 253-4838, (888) 593-4682; jyfmuseums.org. Colonial Virginia food ways are featured during this 3-day event, which begins each year the day after Thanksgiving. At Jamestown Settlement, learn how food was gathered, preserved, and prepared on land and at sea by Virginia's English colonists and Powhatan Indians. At the American Revolution Museum, learn about typical soldiers' fare during the war and trace the bounty of a 1780s farm from field to kitchen. Admission charges apply.

THANKSGIVING AT BERKELEY PLANTATION, 12602 Harrison Landing Rd., Charles City County, VA 23030; (804) 829-6018, (888) 466-6018; virginiathanksgivingfestival.org. In early Dec 1619, a company of Englishmen arrived to settle a grant of Virginia land known as the Berkeley Hundred. Their sponsor instructed that the day of their arrival be "a day of Thanksgiving." (This occurred, of course, more than a year before the pilgrims landed at Plymouth, Massachusetts in 1620.) Each year since 1958, the first Thanksgiving has been commemorated on the first Sun in Nov with this 1-day festival on the grounds of the plantation. Period interpreters stroll the grounds, offering instruction in colonial dance and games for children. A reenactment of the landing of the ship *Margaret* occurs midafternoon, with costumed historical interpreters portraying Captain Woodlief and his crew. The program ends with a friendship dance performed by the Chickahominy Tribal Dancers. Of course, there's food, too: Sandwiches, Brunswick stew, and other fare are available for purchase.

URBANNA OYSTER FESTIVAL, Virginia Avenue, Urbanna, VA 23175; (804) 758-0368; urbannaoysterfestival.com. Held the first full weekend in Nov in scenic Middlesex County, this festival's main attraction is oysters served raw, roasted, stewed, fried, or frittered. If you tire of oysters, you can sample the clam chowder, crab cakes, or steamed crabs. Parades, visiting tall ships, fine arts, an oyster-shucking contest, live music, children's events, ship tours, pony rides, and the crowning of the festival queen are all part of the two-day celebration, first organized in 1957. To get to this small, waterfront community from Williamsburg, take I-64 West to VA 33 East (exit 220). Follow it to US 17, where you will turn left and follow the signs for Urbanna. It's about an hour northeast of Williamsburg. The festival itself is pay-as-you-go for food but otherwise free. It'll cost you to park, though: $10 on Fri, $20 on Sat. The entire downtown area is closed to vehicular traffic during the festival, but there is a shuttle ($2) from the remote lots into town. An alternative is a $4 water taxi. Call (804) 366-1778 for information about pickup locations. No pets are allowed at the festival.

VETERANS DAY, Colonial Williamsburg's Historic Area; (800) HISTORY (447-8679); colonialwilliamsburg.org. All veterans of service in America's armed forces are invited to participate in the parade beginning at the Capitol. After processing to the Courthouse, there will be a ceremony honoring all American veterans.

December

CHRISTMAS EVE TREE LIGHTING CEREMONY, Market Square, Williamsburg, VA 23185; (800) HISTORY (447-8679); colonialwilliamsburg .org. Colonial Williamsburg and the Kiwanis Club of Williamsburg cosponsor the lighting of an evergreen at 5:30 p.m. on Christmas Eve at Market Square. A crowd of thousands gathers at the steps of the Courthouse on the Duke of Gloucester Street in the Historic Area. Guests will learn the story of the first Christmas tree in Williamsburg at the St. George Tucker House. The president of the Kiwanis Club of Williamsburg and the mayor of Williamsburg deliver holiday remarks.

GRAND ILLUMINATION, Colonial Williamsburg, Williamsburg, VA 23185; (800) HISTORY (447-8679); colonialwilliamsburg.org. On the first Sun in Dec, Colonial Williamsburg kicks off the Christmas season by lighting candles in hundreds of windows in Historic Area buildings. Cressets and bonfires also illuminate the evening. Locals come in droves (an estimated 30,000 attend), and visitors love this splendid and energetic Yuletide event, which includes performances by the Fifes & Drums; the firing of cannons; dancing, caroling, and carousing at four stages scattered throughout the restored area; and fireworks at three locations—the Governor's Palace, the Capitol, and the Powder Magazine. Candlelight tours are held, and 18th-century plays and concerts are performed; tickets are required for some events. Outdoor activities start at noon and are free to the public. Arrive early to avoid parking hassles, and bring a flashlight. When it comes to holiday programs, the Grand Illumination is the star atop the tree, so to speak.

LIBERTY ICE PAVILLION, West Duke of Gloucester St. (Historic Area), Williamsburg. This pop-up ice rink appears every year after Thanksgiving and until early Jan. Parking is available in the nearby hourly Merchants Square lots or in the paid parking garage on Henry Street. If you have a Colonial Williamsburg admission, park at the Visitor Center and catch a ride in one of the (heated) buses that will drop you off just down the street. Refreshments including hot cider, coffee, and more will be available for purchase only steps away from the ice. There is an admission charge which includes skate rental if you need them.

To Market, To Market

Saturday mornings are market days all around Hampton Roads. Williamsburg's Farmers Market opens at 8 a.m., traditionally on West Duke of Gloucester Street (check the website, williamsburgfarmers-market.com, for exact location since in 2020 most of DoG Street was taken over for al fresco dining during the pandemic). The Williamsburg market features more than 35 vendors selling produce, seafood, meat, cheese, honey, chocolate, peanuts, and more. There's usually live music, cooking demonstrations, activities for kids and lots of well-behaved pups.

In Yorktown, Market Day begins at 8 a.m. Saturday, rain or shine, April through October along the waterfront Riverwalk Landing. It's a lovely setting to shop for seasonal produce, baked goods, gourmet dog treats, handmade soaps, and candles.

Yorktown Market Days
York County Tourism

Though Yorktown brags that its farmers market was voted best in Hampton Roads, the town of Smithfield definitely disputes that title. Their market, behind the Bank of Southside Virginia at 115 Main St., is uber popular, drawing big crowds from 9 a.m. to noon, Saturdays April through October. On offer is locally grown produce, beef, pork, chicken, eggs, peanuts, plants, herbs, baked goods, coffee, cheese, honey, barbecue, wood-fired pizza, ham sandwiches, handcrafted items, and more. There's usually live music or other entertainment. Pets welcome. Once the growing season ends all three of these markets switch to showcasing holiday gifts on Saturday mornings in December. Those events usually include a special visit from Santa.

NEWPORT NEWS CELEBRATION IN LIGHTS, Newport News Park, 13560 Jefferson Ave., Newport News, VA 23603; (757) 926-1400; nngov .com/1762/Celebration-in-Lights. Remember when you were little and your parents would pile you in the car and drive up and down the neighborhood streets to look at all the sparkly (or maybe over-the-top) neighborhood Christmas displays? The city of Newport News offers a one-stop alternative with its annual Festival of Lights from Thanksgiving through New Year's. Two miles of animated scenes dazzle folks driving through Newport News Park. Cost is $10 per car.

YORKTOWN TREE LIGHTING FESTIVITIES, Historic Main Street, Yorktown, VA 23690; (757) 890-3300; yorkcounty.gov/tourism/Home.aspx. Typically held on the first Fri night in Dec, families are invited to hold candles aloft and walk down Main Street to participate in the annual holiday tree-lighting fun. There's caroling and background music by the Fifes & Drums of York Town. Light refreshments are served. There's even a guest appearance by jolly old Saint Nick himself. The lighted boat parade down the York River is typically held the following evening. Check the county's event listings at the website listed above for complete details.

Appendix:
Living Here

In this section we feature specific information for residents or those planning to relocate here. Topics include real estate, education, health care, and much more.

Relocation

The 2000s saw what can only be described as explosive growth in the Williamsburg area. Population nearly doubled; so did the median price of homes.

Several factors contributed—suburban development in the Lower Peninsula started sprawling north as available land ran out, but the major factor was a boom in relocations from retirees who cashed out of expensive homes in the Northeast US. They were lured by more affordable prices, lower taxes, and planned communities featuring resort-like amenities. It doesn't hurt that the mild weather allows one to play golf 10 to 11 months a year.

The result wasn't quite a bubble—but it was close. In 1999, the median price of a home in the Williamsburg area was a mere $156,000; by the 2015, it was $310,000. (A side note: Any discussion of growth in the area will use "Williamsburg" as shorthand—but very little of the growth actually has occurred within the city itself. Williamsburg is small, landlocked, and largely developed. So its population growth has been limited. The real growth occurred in the two suburban counties that ring the city, especially James City County, which arcs around Williamsburg from the south to the northeast. James City County's population has more than tripled from 1980 to today, from 22,000 to an estimated 72,500 in 2014.)

To the east, growth is constrained by the large government land holdings—the Naval Weapons Station and the CIA (oops! Sorry! The Defense Department—really!) base at Camp Peary. Still, significant growth also occurred on the available land near those installations. That area is colloquially known as upper York County to differentiate it from the rest of York on the other side of the government installations.

While recession slowed the pace of growth, construction had picked up again halfway through the decade of the 2010s. New apartments and townhomes are going up next to the (new) Riverside Hospital on the eastern portion of VA 199. The communities northwest of Williamsburg—Lightfoot and Toano—have seen luxury subdivisions replace horse pasture.

New construction in the suburban areas has been dominated by single-family subdivisions. They cover the range of the market—starter homes, middle-market family communities on 0.25-acre lots, and estate homes in master-planned country-club communities like Kingsmill, Governor's Land at Two Rivers, and Ford's Colony.

If you're thinking of relocating to the area, there are plenty of resources to consult. The real estate ads in the Saturday edition of the *Virginia Gazette* were long considered the best way to keep track of new listings, but nowadays nearly all the brokerages have excellent internet databases that contain all the homes

> ### Looking to Come to Williamsburg Frequently—But . . .
>
> don't want the expense and hassle of a second home? A boatload of time-share resorts have popped up in the area over the past few decades. Think about your decision carefully—plenty of consumer resources caution against buying time-shares because of lack of flexibility, a thin resale market, and sales tactics that can cross the line to high pressure.
>
> That said, for people who like visiting the same place at roughly the same time each year, time-shares can be more like home than a hotel. Among the local time-shares are Colonial Crossing, Diamond Resorts Greensprings Plantation, King's Creek, Marriott Manor Club at Ford's Colony, Powhatan Plantation, Westgate Historic Williamsburg, Williamsburg Plantation, Wyndham Williamsburg at Governor's Green, Wyndham Williamsburg at Kingsgate, and Wyndham Williamsburg at Patriots Place.

in the local multiple-listings service. The **Williamsburg Area Association of Realtors** is a good place to start (waarealtor.com). Zillow.com and Trulia.com are active in the market, aggregating on-sale properties and providing lots of useful data on individual communities.

There are also several new mixed-use developments (like New Town or the High Street project off Richmond Road near downtown) that have rental apartments, condominiums, or both. Condo listings are available from realtors. Apartment listings can be a bit tougher—there's no single great resource for them. A variety of free-distribution magazines contain listings, as do the *Gazette* and the *Daily Press*. Internet services like Apartments.com and Craigslist.com are useful, too.

NEIGHBORHOODS

Adam's Hunt

This subdivision off Centerville Road, about midway between US 60 and Longhill Road, features modest homes on good-size lots in heavily wooded, rolling terrain. The one- and two-story houses are in a mixture of styles. It is a good beginner neighborhood for people interested in getting into the single-family housing market.

Banbury Cross

About 5 miles west of Williamsburg, this lovely, sprawling neighborhood is accessible by I-64, exiting at VA 646 North. Large lots, mostly an acre or more, are the rule here. An abundance of natural woods with tall pines, oaks, and mountain laurel make this an ideal setting for those interested in living near town. Homes are large and colonial or transitional in style.

Baron Woods
Offered by Sash Digges, a prominent local builder, this property proved so popular that lots sold about as fast as they could be subdivided. The charming neighborhood features modest homes on small lots with many tall trees. It's on Ironbound Road, just north of VA 5 at Five Forks.

Berkeley's Green
Proving to be one of the area's most popular subdivisions, Berkeley's Green is off VA 5 and Greensprings Road. Tucked discreetly behind a facade of tall oaks and pines, this neighborhood features several carefully executed home designs, colonial as well as transitional.

Birchwood Park
Birchwood is one of Williamsburg's established neighborhoods, located off Route 199. Its modest homes, many of them ranch-style, have landscaped yards and established gardens. It is especially accessible to shopping and schools, as well as I-64.

Brandon Woods
Located on John Tyler Highway (VA 5) in Five Forks, this subdivision is characterized by rolling, wooded homesites on tree-lined streets and easy, quick access to shopping and services. Home styles are transitional and have either brick or "hardy plank" low-maintenance exteriors. These single-family detached homes are condominiums, which means the homeowner's association is responsible for all exterior maintenance, including roofs, and the upkeep of all common areas.

Canterbury Hills
An established, small neighborhood, this charming area boasts winding roads shaded by large, old trees, neatly tended yards, and larger, well-maintained homes. Off VA 5 and very accessible to the Williamsburg Crossing Shopping Center, it is bounded by Indigo Park and Mill Creek Landing.

Chanco's Grant
This neighborhood began as a two-street, starter-home subdivision with low-priced homes on small lots. It proved so popular that it has developed by leaps and bounds to include an abundance of attractive colonial-style homes on several well-tended streets. It is on Ironbound Road, midway between VA 5 and Jamestown Road, close to Clara Byrd Baker Elementary and convenient to shopping.

Chickahominy Haven

Chickahominy Haven started out as a recreational community with small summer homes tucked away on the river from which it gets its name. Now it boasts numerous year-round residents who have built a mix of large and small transitional or contemporary homes interspersed among the summer cottages. It's a drive back through the James City County woods to get there, but take Forge Road off US 60 West, keep bearing right, and wind your way to the river.

Cobble Creek

Located in York County, immediately off the Colonial Parkway and near Queens Lake, this community is close to shopping and convenient to I-64. Single-family homes are transitional in style, though some offer traditional colonial floor plans and exteriors. Some homes feature vaulted ceilings, kitchen islands, Jacuzzis, and other amenities. All have fireplaces. A choice of ravine lots or level tracts give this wooded community visual appeal.

Colonial Heritage

Located in the Lightfoot area west of Williamsburg, this sprawling 55+ community off Richmond Road offers "cottages, manors, and plantations" with a host of amenities specifically designed for active adults. Homes feature main-level living with spacious kitchens and great rooms for entertaining. The gated neighborhood has its own clubhouse, athletic center, dining room, indoor and outdoor swimming pools, golf course, tennis courts, walking and biking trails. Named one of the 50 Best Master-Planned Communities in America by *Where to Retire* magazine.

The Coves

Off South Henry Street, after it winds its way past the College of William & Mary's Marshall-Wythe School of Law, is this pristine little subdivision along two short lanes. Most homes here are masterpieces, custom-designed and meticulously maintained by their owners. Every once in a while, someone will put a lot up for sale in this extremely desirable area, but not very often—and they are pricey when they do become available. But its location—within walking distance of Colonial Williamsburg, Merchants Square, the college, and more—is ideal. It also offers easy access via VA 199 to I-64.

Cromwell Ridge

This condominium community is part of the Powhatan Secondary complex, situated just a short walk from the Monticello Marketplace. The three-bedroom condos here feature private garages, first-floor master suites, 9-foot ceilings on the first floor, and fireplaces.

Druid Hills

An established neighborhood off Jamestown Road, Druid Hills features a mix of large and small homes—two-story colonials as well as contemporary ranchers—on winding lanes shaded by old trees. Because of its proximity to the College of William & Mary, it is a popular choice for faculty and staff.

Fernbrook

Large, heavily wooded lots in James City County's Fernbrook development off Greensprings Road will appeal to families seeking to be within 10 minutes of the heart of Williamsburg. Colonial and transitional homes populate the area.

Fieldcrest

This upscale neighborhood offers luxurious living in a country setting. Large, new homes line its wide streets. Old, stately trees shade Greensprings Road as it leaves VA 5 and leads to the entrance of this lovely subdivision. Homes are primarily transitional in style and usually brick.

Ford's Colony

If you're looking for an elegant home in a gated community with golf, lighted tennis courts, and a country club, this expansive planned community is for you. The homes are large and luxurious; the condominiums, townhomes, and cluster homes are equally elegant. The two golf courses here are outstanding and will provide continual challenges. Ford's Colony is a gated community of 2,500 acres off Longhill Road, west of the Historic Area. Lots run in size from 0.3 acre to 0.5 acre.

Fox Ridge

Fox Ridge is off Centerville Road between Longhill Road and US 60. Charming, smaller homes are interspersed among tall trees, dogwoods, and mountain laurel on rolling hills.

The Governor's Land at Two Rivers

This is, without reservation, the most elegant subdivision in western James City County. Smaller than Kingsmill but no less impressive in its amenities and terrain, this subdivision offers large homesites, some along the river's edge. Off VA 5 at the confluence of the James and Chickahominy Rivers, it offers the last riverfront acreage in the county. A professional golf course, beach facilities, nature trails, a swimming pool, and tennis courts are in place, and the clubhouse offers all one could wish to complete the high quality of the neighborhood.

Graylin Woods

Understated is the best description of this charming, elegant, albeit small subdivision off VA 5 between VA 199 and Five Forks. Large, stately homes on modest, lovely wooded lots and rolling hills give this neighborhood charm and character.

Greensprings Plantation
The golf enthusiast looking for a home-based golfing community will find lots here with homes in the wooded hills adjacent to the Williamsburg National Golf Club, an 18-hole championship golf masterpiece designed by Jack Nicklaus's Golden Bear Associates. Additional amenities include a full-size pool, tennis courts, a recreational center, and two children's play areas.

Heritage Landing
This elegant subdivision off VA 5 west of Five Forks features large brick and wood custom homes on spacious lots. Rolling hills, winding lanes, and flowering trees and shrubs make this an exquisite venue just far enough out of town to make you feel like you're in the country.

Highland Park
This well-established in-town neighborhood bound by Henry Street, Route 60, and Chesapeake Avenue features small reasonably priced homes. It contains a city park, which includes a multistation playground, a half-court basketball court and a picnic shelter with grills. In 2020, Highland Park was chosen for a pilot program to improve broadband internet connectivity.

High Street
Apartments and town homes are part of the High Street Shops development off Richmond Road. Until Midtown Row, this was possibly the closest new construction to the Historic Area in decades, and super convenient to the College of William & Mary.

Holly Hills of Williamsburg
Upper-end new property within the city limits is hard to find. Holly Hills on Jamestown Road is located on nearly 300 acres of heavily wooded property just a mile from the Historic Area and the College of William & Mary. Homesites range in size from 0.4 to 2 acres. Strict architectural guidelines ensure that the appearance and value of properties will remain high. A separate small cluster of attached two-family brick townhomes called Holly Hills Carriage Homes has an entrance off Highway 199.

Hunter's Creek
This family-oriented subdivision is small but attractive with its modest colonial homes and well-tended gardens. Off US 60 west of Williamsburg on the edge of Toano, it offers easy access to I-64.

Indigo Park

One of the VA 5 area's earlier developments, Indigo Park has endured as a charming neighborhood of well-maintained, two-story ranch homes along rolling, winding lanes shaded by large, old trees. A family-oriented neighborhood with a private pool for residents, Indigo Park is within a 5-minute drive of Williamsburg Crossing Shopping Center and schools, as well as Williamsburg's Historic Area and other shopping areas.

Kingsmill on the James

One of Williamsburg's most prestigious neighborhoods, this multifaceted development of 2,900 acres includes everything from riverfront estates to tidy condos overlooking lush fairways on one of three world-class golf courses. Kingsmill residents enjoy on-site tennis, a spa, several superb restaurants, an outstanding recreation and conference center, a private marina, dry-dock facilities, and a riverside beach. Developed by the Anheuser-Busch Corporation, security is provided by the Kingsmill Police Department at limited-access entrances.

Kingspoint

This quiet, established neighborhood is tucked away at the foot of South Henry Street just across VA 199. Bounded by the Colonial Parkway on one side and College Creek on the other, it is a wide, tree-covered peninsula. Kingspoint offers quick access via VA 199 to other parts of James City County and the interstate. You'll find an eclectic mix of sizes, styles, and ages from '60s to new construction.

Kingswood

Conveniently located off Jamestown Road, about halfway between Merchants Square and the Jamestown Ferry, this idyllic, quiet neighborhood is the choice for those seeking convenience and solitude. Well-tended yards and an assortment of older contemporary and traditional homes line the area's streets and lanes. The neighborhood has a private pool that is open for a fee each summer to guests from nearby developments as well.

Kristiansand

The Norwegian name pays tribute to the town of Norge, which is adjacent to this small subdivision. Off US 60 West, it is just down the road from the Williamsburg Pottery Factory. It offers quick and easy access to I-64.

Lake Toano

If you don't mind driving about 15 minutes west of Williamsburg along US 60 West, you can find this subdivision situated in a heavily wooded area surrounding a quiet reservoir in the Toano area. Large and small homes, both contemporary and traditional, line the streets and cul-de-sacs that make up this country neighborhood. It is just minutes from the I-64 exit for Toano.

Landfall at Jamestown
Talk about a lush setting! This upscale subdivision is located on prime real estate, off Jamestown Road, about 0.5 mile from the James River. Some lots sit amid meandering streams and creeks; others front the James River. New construction includes transitional and contemporary as well as traditional colonial design, most with brick exterior.

Longhill Gate
Located on Longhill Road just before the entrance to Ford's Colony, these attached homes range in size from moderate to fairly large. Sidewalks, manicured landscapes, and winding streets are indicative of the low-key family ambience that sets the tone of this charming neighborhood.

The Meadows
Looks are deceiving as you approach this small community of small- to moderate-size homes, between Strawberry Plains and Ironbound Roads. At the back edge of a wide-open field, the streets of this neighborhood dip and wind, curve and wander. Neatly kept yards and pristine houses characterize this subdivision, halfway between downtown Williamsburg and Jamestown via Sandy Point Road.

Midtown Row
This new apartment complex is part of Midtown Row, a renovated, mixed-use development at the intersection of Monticello Avenue and Richmond Road, within walking distance of the College of William & Mary. Specifically designed to ease a severe housing shortage for graduate students at W&M, the complex is offering study lounges, a bistro and on-site sports bar, fitness room and "resort-style" pool and hot tubs. Opening summer 2021.

Mill Creek Landing
Without a doubt, this elegant subdivision of custom-built homes (nearly all of them brick) situated around a 7-acre fish-stocked pond is one of the area's best kept secrets. Limited in size, it is off VA 5 and Stanley Drive. It offers a country setting less than 2 miles from Williamsburg's Historic Area, with easy access to schools, Williamsburg Crossing Shopping Center (which is within walking distance), and I-64.

Mirror Lake Estates
About 15 minutes west of the Historic Area, this inviting neighborhood features small, moderate, and larger starter homes. It can be reached via Richmond Road or from I-64, which is less than 1 mile from the entrance of the subdivision.

New Town

A "New Urbanism" community at the intersection of Ironbound Road and Monticello Avenue, New Town offers apartments, townhomes, and condominiums in blended residential neighborhoods within easy walking distance of restaurants, offices, a 12-plex cinema, and shops.

North Cove

Off VA 646 in York County, this large-lot subdivision features rolling hills, large homes, lots of trees, and quick access to I-64. About 10 minutes west of Williamsburg, it is a charming setting that seems far removed from the bustle of downtown. It is also near York River State Park and a public boat ramp on the York River. You'll find homes in brick, cedar, and stucco.

Peleg's Point

Conveniently located off Neck-O-Land Road in James City County, this neighborhood features larger homes, many brick, in colonial, transitional, and contemporary styles. It is only a few miles from downtown Williamsburg but offers proximity to the James River and Colonial Parkway.

Piney Creek Estates

Two of the area's most renowned builders, Ronald T. Curtis and Joel S. Sheppard, offer homeowners a prime city address within a mile of the James City County Recreation Center and Kiwanis Park. It's a short drive from all area attractions and shopping.

Poplar Hall

About 8 miles east of downtown Williamsburg, this meandering neighborhood is tucked discreetly away from the traffic of US 60 East, off of which it is located. This subdivision offers a variety of sizes and styles and boasts both older and new homes. It is midway between two I-64 interchanges and is just minutes from Busch Gardens and the Anheuser-Busch brewery.

Port Anne

One of the last subdivisions in the city where you can still purchase land and build a custom house, this neighborhood is for the discerning homeowner in search of an idyllic setting above College Creek. Large, custom-designed homes on smaller lots provide the perfect place to settle down in style. A clubhouse, tennis courts, and pool are among other amenities. It offers quick access to I-64 and is within biking and walking distance of the city's Historic Area.

Powhatan Crossing
This small but charming subdivision is just east of VA 5 at Five Forks. It features affordable, small to moderately sized homes along a cozy lane that stretches into the woodlands. Residents enjoy easy access to downtown Williamsburg or I-64 via VA 5.

Powhatan Place
Located near Monticello Marketplace off News Road, this three-bedroom luxury townhome community offers excellent location and all amenities. Two floor plans are offered. The 2,700-square-foot end units feature first-floor master suites. The 2,500-square-foot interior units feature master bedrooms with spacious his/her master baths. All units feature gas heat and hot water, as well as gas log fireplaces, single-car garages, and laundry rooms.

Powhatan Secondary of Williamsburg
On the site of the early 17th-century Powhatan Plantation off Ironbound Road at Veterans Park, this popular subdivision offers wooded homesites and custom-built homes in a mix of contemporary and traditional styles. The community includes 45 acres of recreational land and lakes.

Powhatan Shores
Boaters may want to consider this charming family neighborhood where most lots have private access via a creek to the James River. It is just a few minutes from the city's Historic Area and is close to VA 199 and I-64.

Quarterpath Village
Still under construction in 2021, this new development featuring attached townhomes, apartments, and luxury senior living is located on the same secluded campus as the new Riverside Doctor's Hospital, off US 60 and just minutes from I-64, Colonial Williamsburg, and the College of William & Mary. Though much of the surrounding acreage is undeveloped (and for sale), a Harris Teeter supermarket is less than a mile away, and the exclusive Kingsmill community is just across a wooded area and VA 199 from this subdivision.

Queens Lake
This stately, established neighborhood, bounded by Queens Creek and the Colonial Parkway, is one of the most prestigious neighborhoods in the greater Williamsburg area. Tennis courts, a pool, a recreation center, and a marina are among the amenities. Some of the area's loveliest homes are situated on the rolling, wooded lanes. It offers country living just minutes from I-64, Colonial Williamsburg, and area schools.

Queenswood

Off Hubbard Lane, this family-oriented neighborhood features newer homes on moderate-size lots away from the activity of downtown Williamsburg and major roads. Ranches and two—story colonials are the norm here. It is within minutes of Colonial Parkway, James York Plaza Shopping Center, and VA 143, which leads to I-64.

Richmond Hill

This is a small, high-end neighborhood within the city limits very close to the Historic Area. All brick homes are Federal architectural designs similar to those on Richmond's Monument Avenue. Indoor tennis (at W&M's McCormack-Nagelsen Tennis Center) and the shopping and dining of Colonial Williamsburg are all within walking distance.

Rolling Woods

Lovely homes with brick, vinyl, and cedar exteriors tucked away under stately oaks and pines make this hilly subdivision much sought after. Off Lake Powell Road in James City County, it offers seclusion just minutes from VA 199 and I-64.

Seasons Trace

One of the most popular planned communities in the area is this neighborhood with its neatly maintained townhomes, condos, cluster homes, and small private homes. Off Longhill Road, adjacent to Lafayette High School and across the road from the Windsor Forest subdivision, Seasons Trace features winding lanes and a pond stocked with fish and populated with ducks. Other amenities include a pool, tennis courts, a basketball court, and dry-dock storage for boats and RVs.

Settler's Mill

Off Jamestown Road approximately halfway between VA 199 and Jamestown, Settler's Mill is located in a heavily wooded area, with a lake, ponds, and rolling hills. It is a joint venture of four of the most prestigious names in residential building and development in the area: Larry McCardle, Sterling Nichols, Joel Sheppard, and Ron Curtis. Homes feature a variety of traditional and transitional styles.

Skimino Hills

Developed in the late 1970s and early 1980s, this large subdivision is situated on gently rolling hills in western York County. Off I-64 at VA 646, it offers large lots with trees and lush growths of mountain laurel and dogwood. A mix of large and small contemporary and traditional homes lines narrow streets.

Skimino Landing Estates

Large lots—from an acre up—and lots of trees, including hardwoods, characterize this subdivision in upper York County. The neighborhood features a boat ramp with access to the York River. Construction reflects a mix of styles, many transitional, most with brick facades.

Skipwith Farms

This was the City of Williamsburg's first real subdivision, built in the 1950s and '60s, and it features modest single- and two-story homes. Few areas are more centrally located or offer easier access to shopping, recreation, and area schools. It is off Richmond Road, less than 3 miles from the heart of the city's Historic Area.

St. George's Hundred

One of the area's most popular, family-oriented neighborhoods, St. George's is off VA 5 about 5 miles west of Williamsburg. Charming homes, mostly colonial style, line the streets. Established decades ago, this neighborhood continues to grow. In addition to its easy access to area shopping and schools, it features a recreation area with picnic tables, basketball courts, and a softball field.

Stonehouse

Located along the I-64 corridor in both James City and New Kent Counties is Stonehouse, a 5,700-acre development that offers homeowners an all-digital residential community in a beautiful natural setting. A joint venture of the real estate divisions of Dominion Resources Inc. and Chesapeake Corporation, Stonehouse is offering large single-family homes, golf villa, patio homes, and town houses. The project includes lots ranging in size from 0.3 acre to more than 1 acre. Stonehouse homeowners have access to a variety of technological services, from digital TV with more than 200 audio and video channels to state-of-the-art security systems and high-speed internet service. The community is being developed on a 25-year plan. More than 50 percent of the property will remain in its natural state.

The Vineyards at Jockey's Neck

Nestled next to the Williamsburg Winery, this subdivision of large, stately homes is one of Williamsburg's most prestigious addresses. Larger houses are the rule, but there are a few areas offering smaller, exquisitely constructed dwellings. Many are tucked away discreetly among old shade trees. Breezes from the nearby James River and proximity to both Jamestown Road and the Colonial Parkway make this a much-sought-after location. Two lakes and 86 acres of green space with walking trails, playgrounds, swimming pool, and tennis courts enhance the lovely, natural setting.

Westgate at Williamsburg

Located off US 60 just west of the Premium Outlets, this condominium complex is convenient to Williamsburg and I-64. Placed along quiet streets, the charming two- and three-bedroom condos here are large, measuring about 1,600 square feet. They feature natural gas heat and water, vaulted ceilings, walk-in closets, and lofts. Some have gas fireplaces and sunrooms. The community also offers owners use of a pool and cabana.

Westmoreland

Off Olde Towne Road near its intersection with Longhill Road, this small development currently has 15 single-family lots on richly wooded property developed by the Hornsby family (relations of musician Bruce Hornsby). Convenient access to shopping and amenities on the Richmond Road side of town, proximity to the Historic Area (a 10-minute drive), and convenient access to I-64 are strong advantages to this neighborhood.

Westray Downs

Rolling hills, winding lanes, and charming homes characterize this relatively new neighborhood off VA 5 in James City County. Ranch-style homes, traditional two-story homes, and some charming colonial-style homes add interest to the landscape. It is minutes from the county's Law Enforcement Center and Fire Station on VA 5 and offers quick, easy access to Williamsburg Crossing Shopping Center, Five Forks, the Jamestown Ferry, and I-64 via VA 199.

Windsor Forest

This upscale subdivision in James City County is off Longhill Road, and features large homes—some contemporary, most traditional colonial-style. Nearby are the county recreation center and lots of shopping. There is easy access to I-64 via Airport Road, and the city's Historic Area is just a few miles away.

The Woods

This handsome subdivision features large, stately homes situated on rolling hills amid lush woods and tall, old oaks and pines. Off Jamestown Road and within a brisk walking distance of the city's Historic Area, this fine subdivision offers easy access to just about everything, including I-64 via Route 199.

Yorkshire

This small neighborhood of lovely homes is conveniently located off Jamestown Road near the VA 199 intersection. Large custom homes are located on quiet meandering streets and cul-de-sacs set inside rolling hills and woodlands. The neighborhood is less than a mile from the city's Historic Area and is located within the city limits.

REAL ESTATE COMPANIES

BERKSHIRE HATHAWAY HOME SERVICES/TOWNE REALTY, 4135 Ironbound Rd., Williamsburg, VA 23188; (757) 253-5686; bhhstownerealty .com.

CENTURY 21 NACHMAN REALTY, 1101 Richmond Rd., Williamsburg, VA 23185; (757) 220-8205; century21nachman.com.

HORNSBY REAL ESTATE, 4732 Longhill Rd., Ste. 1101, Williamsburg, VA 23188; (757) 565-0100; realhornsby.com.

HOWARD HANNA/WILLIAM E. WOOD REAL ESTATE SERVICES, 724 Thimble Shoals Blvd., Ste. A, Newport News, VA 23606 (757) 229-0550; howardhanna.com.

KINGSMILL REALTY, 100 Kingsmill Rd., Williamsburg VA 23185; (800) 392-0026; kingsmillrealestate.com. Other companies represent properties in Kingsmill, but this is the community's on-site real estate agency, which usually has the best information about which properties are coming on the market in all of Kingsmill's neighborhoods.

LIZ MOORE & ASSOCIATES, 5350 Discovery Park Blvd., Williamsburg, VA 23188; (757) 645-4106; lizmoore.com.

LONG & FOSTER REALTORS, 5234 Monticello Ave., Ste. 110 (New Town), Williamsburg, VA 23188; (757) 229-4400; williamsburg.lnfre.com.

RE/MAX ALL AMERICAN, 1246-A Richmond Rd., Williamsburg, VA 23185; remax.com.

TWIDDY REALTY, 4808 Courthouse St., Ste. 104 (New Town), Williamsburg, VA 23188; (757) 220-4663; twiddyrealty.com.

WILLIAMSBURG REALTY INC., 5231 Monticello Ave., Ste. A (New Town), Williamsburg, VA 23188; (757) 291-1717; williamsburgrealtyofva .com.

RELOCATION

Retirement

The Historic Triangle continues to grow in popularity as a retirement destination, drawing older Americans from across the nation. The mild climate is a significant draw. We enjoy four distinct seasons, but wintry weather doesn't usually begin in earnest until January and by late February, the high school tennis teams are practicing outside. It snows, but it doesn't stick for long.

Colorful redbud and dogwood are harbingers of spring, which often arrives early-March. Summers can be sultry, but mild weather can last through October, and fall weather can last through December, making the impending winter easier to take.

People retiring from military service in Hampton Roads are familiar with the area, and many settle here. The cost of living is lower than other parts of the country, particularly the Northeast. Recreational opportunities are numerous. Local health care options are many and good. And, as a college town, Williamsburg offers a broad spectrum of generally inexpensive cultural activities senior citizens are invited to enjoy.

Perhaps the most important contact point for seniors here is The Lounge (formerly the Historic Triangle Senior Center), located in the James City County Recreation Center. The center, open to those age 50 and older, is the site of many regularly scheduled monthly events, and the starting point for varied day trips. The center also offers Wellness Days programs, which focus on such themes as maintaining good health through smart physical activity, risk factors for coronary artery disease, and what to expect when you undergo joint replacement surgery. The center also offers free blood pressure and glucose screenings. Call (757) 259-4187 for scheduled dates and times.

Senior residents are eligible for annual **Good Neighbor passes** from Colonial Williamsburg. These $20 tickets entitle them to admission, bus service, and shopping discounts in Colonial Williamsburg's properties. Senior residents of York County, James City County, and Williamsburg are also entitled to free admission to Jamestown Settlement and the American Revolution Museum (formerly the Yorktown Victory Center). Proof of address is required.

SERVICES

COMPUTER LITERACY TRAINING, The Lounge, James City County Recreation Center, 5301 Longhill Rd., Williamsburg, VA 23188; (757) 259-4187; jamescitycountyva.gov/recreation/community-centers/TheLounge. Volunteer instructors will assist seniors, provide access to computers for practice, or arrange a self-paced course between the instructor and the pupil.

MEALS ON WHEELS, Williamsburg Baptist Church, 227 Richmond Rd., Williamsburg, VA 23185; (757) 229-9250. This volunteer group serves local seniors a nutritionally balanced, hot meal Mon through Fri. Recipients are charged on the basis of their ability to pay. Anyone in need should call the number listed above. The program serves all who meet its criteria, not just the elderly.

PENINSULA AGENCY ON AGING (PAA), 739 Thimble Shoals Blvd., Suite 1006, Newport News, VA 23606; (757) 873-0541; paainc.org. The central source of information on services for senior citizens throughout the entire area, this office provides services and programs covering needs such as housing, health, income or financial aid, community services, adult day care, legal services, nutrition and meal programs, transportation, recreation, in-home support, and social services. The staff will make an appropriate referral for the closest service that meets your needs.

RIVERSIDE ADULT DAY SERVICES, 1010 Old Denbigh Blvd., Newport News, VA 23602; (757) 875-2033; riversideonline.com/continuing_care/adult-daycare.cfm. This organization provides a structured environment for seniors from 7:30 a.m. to 5:30 p.m. Mon through Fri. While this group caters to seniors with physical limitations and mental disorders such as Alzheimer's disease, the center is open to all interested seniors, including those in good health. Although there is no transportation provided to the center, Medicaid patients can make use of the "Medicaid cab."

Activities

Active seniors interested in participating in social, civic, and special-interest activities don't have to look very far. The College of William & Mary sponsors concert series, theater productions, exhibits, and gallery talks, usually for a small admission fee or no charge at all. We describe some of these in The Arts chapter. What follows is a list of some of the more active clubs and programs in this area.

RETIREMENT

OSHER LIFELONG LEARNING INSTITUTE (formerly The Christopher Wren Association for Lifelong Learning), College of William & Mary, Williamsburg, VA 23185; (757) 221-1506; wm.edu/osher. No report on retired living in the Historic Triangle would be complete without mention of this continuing education program, begun at the College of William & Mary in 1991. Any Williamsburg area resident over 50 is welcome to take part. Don't worry; there are no grades or tests.

The institute, founded by retired college professors Ruth and the late Wayne Kernodle, is peer-run and peer-taught. By tapping the area's reservoir of retired persons with expertise in art, literature, history, social sciences, and other fields, the program is able to offer courses on government, comparative religions, photography, music, and many other subjects. The enrollment fee is $135 per semester. That fee allows members to take up to eight courses over a 12- to 15-week semester.

In addition, the association sponsors the Town & Gown brownbag luncheon-and-lecture series, held weekly at William & Mary's Campus Center. This program attracts many area retirees, who gather to hear speakers from near and far give informal talks after a catered luncheon on topics of sometimes general, sometimes specialized, interest. The series is open only to regular and associate members (who pay a $50 fee and may attend the luncheons, social events, and day trips, which carry an additional fee. Associate members are eligible to enroll in classes).

A full schedule of course offerings and additional information is available by visiting the website listed above.

SENIOR CENTER OF YORK, 5314 George Washington Hwy., Yorktown, VA 23692; (757) 890-3444; yorkcounty.gov/727/Senior-Center-of-York. This center offers activities for citizens ages 55 and up. Seniors can participate in quilting, dominoes, bridge, line dancing, and computer classes but participants are asked to register online for events they plan to attend. Drop-ins are not permitted. A free monthly calendar, available at the center, lists scheduled activities and events, including special senior citizen trips. Open 9 a.m. to 4:30 p.m. Mon through Fri.

> **i** Retired military officers and their families can keep abreast of what's happening through the Virginia Peninsula Chapter of the Retired Officers Association. This organization puts out a monthly newsletter, holds local chapter meetings, and enjoys social events. To learn more about this special group, call (800) 234-6622.

RESIDENTIAL LIVING

While many seniors choose to live in conventional neighborhoods, others prefer the more exclusive, secure, or convenient atmosphere of the retirement community. Currently, Williamsburg offers many options for retirees in search of a community lifestyle.

BROOKDALE WILLIAMSBURG, 3800 Treyburn Dr., Williamsburg, VA 23185; (757) 561-2137; brookdale.com. This well-maintained senior community (formerly known as Chambrel) is located on a 56-acre site in James City County. Active seniors can choose from a number of lifestyle options, including apartments or cottage homes. All units feature washers and dryers, and many have screened porches.

In addition, assisted living is available in both efficiencies and full-size garden apartment arrangements. Brandon House and York Manor are the special-care needs sections offering services tailored to the specific requirements of each resident.

The Village Center includes a dining room, library, swimming pool, and wellness center. Residents can take advantage of scheduled transportation, social and cultural events, and walking trails in natural woodlands. Several shopping areas, Colonial Williamsburg, the College of William & Mary, and many golf courses are nearby.

COLONIAL HERITAGE, 7015 Statesmen, Williamsburg, VA 23188; (757) 542-9981; lennar.com/New-Homes/Virginia/Williamsburg/Williamsburg/Colonial-Heritage. Located in the Lightfoot area west of Williamsburg, this sprawling 55+ community off Richmond Road offers "cottages, manors and plantations" with a host of amenities specifically designed for active adults. Homes feature main-level living with spacious kitchens and great rooms for entertaining. The gated neighborhood has its own clubhouse, athletic center, dining room, indoor and outdoor swimming pools, golf course, tennis courts, walking and biking trails. Named one of the 50 Best Master-Planned Communities in America by *Where to Retire* magazine.

COMMONWEALTH SENIOR LIVING, 236 Commons Way, Williamsburg, VA 23185; (757) 814-2961; commonwealthSL.com. Includes independent and assisted living and memory care.

CONSULATE HEALTH CARE AT WILLIAMSBURG, 1811 Jamestown Rd., Williamsburg, VA 23185; (757) 229-9991; centers.consulatehealth care .com/ll/US/VA/Williamsburg/1811-Jamestown-Rd. This senior nursing-care facility is staffed by health professionals who provide care in a homelike setting. The center offers 3 levels of care: intermediate, skilled, and Alzheimer's. Residents are accepted for both short- and long-term stays. On-site services include comprehensive rehabilitative services as well as physical therapy, occupational therapy, and speech-language pathology. It also offers daily recreational therapy, beauty/barber services, cable TV, and a code alert security system.

DOMINION VILLAGE, 4132 Longhill Rd., Williamsburg, VA 23188; (757) 258-3444; fivestarseniorliving.com. Many seniors in need of long-term, assisted living care opt for this facility, located about 5 miles from the city's Historic Area across Longhill Road from the entrance to Ford's Colony. It provides permanent and short-term residence options in private and semiprivate rooms.

Dominion Village offers 3 levels of care, ranging from minimal to more extensive assistance with activities of daily living. It also offers a secure, positive atmosphere for residents with Alzheimer's disease or dementia. The monthly fee covers meals; afternoon and evening snacks; around-the-clock nursing care; assistance with bathing, dressing, and personal care as needed; medications monitored by the nursing staff; daily activities, programs, and monthly outings; church services; housekeeping and linen services; cable TV; and all utilities except telephone. Amenities include a dining room; living room; cozy sitting areas; an activity room for crafts, art, reading, and conversation; an outdoor garden patio for cookouts; and an emergency call system in each room.

The Bridge to Discovery is a special-care unit designed for those with Alzheimer's, dementia, or related disorders.

ENVOY OF WILLIAMSBURG, 1235 S. Mount Vernon Ave., Williamsburg, VA 23185; (757) 229-4121; centers.consulatehealth care.com/ll/US/VA/Williamsburg/1235-S-Mt-Vernon-Ave. This 130-bed, skilled nursing center opened in Williamsburg in 1976 but is now owned by Consulate Health Care. This facility has 8 private rooms and 61 semiprivate rooms. Services include long-term and skilled nursing and respite care, as well as physical, occupational, respiratory, and speech therapies. Services and amenities include a dining program tailored to each resident's dietary needs, a rehab gym, garden and patio, a beauty/barber shop, a library, pastoral support, and transportation services. An extensive volunteer program brings in church groups, civic groups, students, and local entertainment on a regular basis. This center offers an enclosed courtyard for those residents who wish to spend time outdoors in nice weather.

PATRIOTS COLONY, 6000 Patriots Colony Dr., Williamsburg, VA 23188; (757) 220-9000, (800) 716-9000; patriotscolony.com. Retired military officers, federal civil service employees, and their spouses can investigate this gated, continuing-care retirement community with private villas, apartments, and freestanding homes. Located adjacent to the Greensprings Plantation National Historic Site on historic VA 5 west of Williamsburg, Patriots Colony offers a community center for 55+ that features fine dining, a fitness and wellness center, and recreational areas. Other amenities include a community greenhouse, pool, and tennis courts. In addition to independent living facilities, the community partners with Riverside Health System to offer assisted living, assisted living for residents with Alzheimer's disease and other dementia, and a convalescent care center. While the independent living community is open to retired officers of the seven uniformed services and retired federal civil service employees only, the assisted living and convalescent care centers are open to everyone.

VERENA AT THE RESERVE, 121 Reserve Way, Williamsurg, VA 23185; (757) 345-2995; trueconnectioncommunities.com/senior-living-communities-virginia/verena-at-the-reserve-senior-living/. This tree-filled campus offers independent living for seniors within a close-knit community of residents, family and staff. Part of the True Connection Communities of senior living properties, the focus here is on ease of living—somebody else takes care of routine maintenance and repairs—which frees up residents to make the most of retirement. Frequent outings to nearby shopping centers, historic destinations, and local restaurants are complimented by a wide variety of on-site activities including billiards, poker, and monthly museum talks.

WILLIAMSBURG LANDING, 5700 Williamsburg Landing Dr., Williamsburg, VA 23185; (757) 565-6505, (800) 554-5517; williamsburglanding .com. At this well-manicured community, seniors can choose home or apartment independent living and take advantage of health services that range from a minimal wellness program to licensed nursing home care. The gated community offers around-the-clock security, housekeeping, all interior and exterior building maintenance, one meal per day, and shuttle bus service to doctors' offices and special events in town. The Landing also offers on-site banking, shopping, library, computer room, woodworking shop, billiards, health spa, outdoor pool, tennis court, and more.

Situated on 135 woodland acres adjacent to VA 199 and College Creek, this long-term care facility offers social, recreational, and cultural activities such as concerts, tours, physical fitness classes, and events presented in conjunction with the College of William & Mary. Outpatient clinic services include care by physicians and registered nurses.

The independent living units are a mixture of cluster homes and apartments. A monthly service fee covers meals, utilities, and other items. Those who need to move temporarily or permanently into the Woodhaven Hall health care complex can choose private or semiprivate care. The Landing is a pet-friendly community, but there are some restrictions—call for detailed information.

WINDSORMEADE, 3900 Windsor Hall Dr., Williamsburg, VA 23185; (757) 941-3615; windsormeade.org. This active senior living community offers a continuum of care ranging from independent living in villa homes to assisted living, skilled nursing, and memory care options. Located just off VA

199 and minutes from the Historic area, WindsorMeade is also very close to Monticello Marketplace, a large shopping complex with groceries, retail stores and restaurants.

Education

COLLEGE OF WILLIAM & MARY, 116 Jamestown Rd., Williamsburg, VA 23185; (757) 221-4000; wm.edu. Located in the heart of Williamsburg, W&M is one of the finest universities in America and is the second oldest institution of higher learning in the US. (Harvard is the oldest.) King William III and Queen Mary II granted the charter in 1693. Although many out-of-state visitors assume William & Mary is a private school, it is actually a state school, though often referred to as a "public ivy." William & Mary offers its students the diverse resources of a large institution within the community atmosphere of a smaller town.

The campus is at the western end of Duke of Gloucester Street between Jamestown and Richmond Roads, a landmark known locally as Confusion Corner. Near this intersection you'll find the Sir Christopher Wren Building, which typically has served as the starting point for any self-guided walking tour. It is well worth spending a few hours of your stay in Williamsburg to survey the gracious campus of this school, whose earliest alumni, Thomas Jefferson among them, were the first leaders of our nation.

As you approach the Wren Building, you'll notice the brick wall surrounding the triangular College Yard, which also holds two other pre–Revolutionary War structures: the President's House and The Brafferton, formerly an Indian school. The Crown chartered the college in 1693 in response to a petition from Virginia's General Assembly; bricks weren't laid for the Wren Building (originally known as "The College") until 2 years later, making it the oldest academic building in continuous use in the US.

For several years the building served as temporary headquarters to Virginia's colonial government. Then in 1705 and again in 1859, fires destroyed portions of the building, which was twice rebuilt by using the remaining foundation and walls. Alas, in 1862, federal soldiers set the building afire again. Despite such damage, the original exterior walls survived to be restored during the 1920s and '30s, and what the Wren Building visitors see now has the appearance of the pre–1859 fire structure. Today the Wren houses faculty offices. Visitors also will see early classrooms, the 1732 chapel—under which noted Virginians such as Sir John Randolph and Lord Botetourt are buried—and the Great Hall, where the Burgesses assembled.

North of the Wren Building in the College Yard is the President's House, built in the early 1730s. Besides serving as a home to such famous college presidents as James Madison and James Blair, it also housed British general Cornwallis before he decamped to Yorktown and surrendered to the Revolutionary army led by Washington. The building is still in use as a residence for College of William & Mary presidents.

The third and smallest structure facing the College Yard is The Brafferton, now used for offices, but originally an Indian school. The Brafferton was built in 1723 with funds provided by an English scientist determined to bring Christianity to Native Americans, who were forced to attend a training school in Williamsburg. Apparently, the young boys were not at all happy about living in town, learning English, or wearing uniforms, and they longed for their villages and tribes. A William & Mary myth holds that one of these students can sometimes be seen running across campus at night, as if trying to regain his freedom.

You can stroll in the Sunken Garden west of the Wren Building or cross the shady Crim Dell Bridge over a small pond. Other buildings worth noting on campus include Phi Beta Kappa Memorial Hall, which is undergoing a major renovation, the Earl Gregg Swem Library, and the Muscarelle Museum of Art.

Its long history, appealing campus, and strong national reputation for topnotch academics have made admission to William & Mary highly competitive. A record number of applicants—nearly 15,000—sought admission to the class of 2024, competing for 1,525 spots.

For information on campus tours for prospective students call (757) 221-4223 or check the website.

CHRISTOPHER NEWPORT UNIVERSITY, 1 University Place, Newport News, VA 23606; (757) 594-7000; cnu.edu. Once a satellite campus of the College of William & Mary, CNU split from the larger college in the 1980s and since has developed a distinct identity of its own. Located on a 260-acre campus about 25 miles southeast of Williamsburg in Newport News, this four-year institution offers undergraduate and graduate programs to 5,000 students

> **i** One of the best-kept secrets in Williamsburg is the Earl Gregg Swem Library at the College of William & Mary. The public is welcome to use the materials found here, including copies of most major American newspapers. In addition, you'll find more than one million books, even more microforms, and a half million items in the government publications collection. A branch of Aroma's coffee shop is located within the library. For more information call (757) 221-4636 or visit swem.wm.edu.

in business, science, technology, education, government, and the performing arts. Once known primarily as a commuter school, the campus has undergone a massive transformation in the past 20 years, adding a state-of-the-art sports and convocation facility, a new library, additional campus housing, the Ferguson Center for the Arts (a performance venue designed by the architectural firm founded by I. M. Pei), and the most recent addition, a new art museum slated to be completed by 2021. Local wags have suggested the school mascot should be changed from the Captains (for Christopher Newport) to the Bulldozers, because construction of all these new facilities remade the Warwick Boulevard corridor (US 60), along which the university is situated, into a demolition zone for more than a decade.

CNU's intercollegiate sports program includes NCAA Division III contests in 18 sports including a 12-time national championship women's track and perennial nationally ranked men's basketball team.

HAMPTON UNIVERSITY, 100 E. Queen St., Hampton, VA 23668; (757) 727-5000; hamptonu.edu. Privately supported Hampton University opened its doors on Apr 1, 1868, as the Hampton Normal and Agricultural Institute. It had a few buildings on 120 acres of land, little equipment, 2 teachers (who earned $15 a month), 15 students, and a dormitory retrofitted from a converted hospital barracks. In 2010, the man who gave the commencement address was President Barack Obama. You've come a long way, Hampton U.

General Samuel Chapman founded the school with a plan to educate newly emancipated African Americans. Today Hampton University is one of the most popular Black colleges in America, boasting an undergraduate enrollment of more than 3,600 students.

Hampton has a $280 million endowment, state-of-the-art facilities, a distinguished faculty, and an innovative curriculum. It offers a variety of programs including especially strong ones in science, engineering, pharmacy, business (including an MBA degree), architecture, and nursing.

Hampton offers a strong athletic program as well with 14 sports, including a men's and women's sailing team.

The university, which stresses the importance of leadership, also reaches out to the community with its A Plus (A+) Summer Program for Pre-College Students. The month-long program for 13- to 15-year-olds offers everything from mentoring and mathematics to art and scuba diving.

Listed among famous graduates is Booker T. Washington, class of 1875, who took what he learned here south, where he founded Tuskegee Institute. Other grads include Spencer Christian (class of '70 and former weatherman on ABC's *Good Morning America*), Ms. Frankie Freeman (class of '37 and former US Civil Rights Commissioner), and Vanessa D. Gilmore (class of '77 and a federal judge in Texas).

The **Hampton University Museum** (detailed in the attractions section of our Newport News and Hampton chapter) is worth seeing. And no visit to Hampton University would be complete without a stop at the Emancipation Oak—a massive shade tree on the northeast side of the campus. It was under this tree in 1863 that Hampton's Black community—people who the law then prohibited from attending school—gathered to hear the first southern reading of President Abraham Lincoln's Emancipation Proclamation.

THOMAS NELSON COMMUNITY COLLEGE, 99 Thomas Nelson Dr., Hampton, VA 23666; (757) 825-2700; 4601 Opportunity Way, Williamsburg, VA 23188; (757) 253-4300; tncc.edu. Thomas Nelson was a signer of the Declaration of Independence. The community college that bears his name was established in 1968, granting associate degrees, including many which are transferable to 4-year colleges.

A satellite campus opened in Williamsburg in 1999 to provide service to residents in the Williamsburg–James City County–York County area after having offered a limited schedule of evening classes at various locations in the area for 30 years. The campus provides one-stop admissions, registration, academic assessment, counseling, and book ordering, so students do not have to go to the Hampton campus, about 30 miles away, for any services. The new location allows TNCC to offer classes at the Historic Triangle location on both day and evening schedules. Students also are able to enroll in a growing number of distance learning courses the college now offers via television and the internet.

Like the campus in Hampton, the Historic Triangle operation provides a full range of workforce training, economic development, and employment skills to its community.

Another benefit of Historic Triangle campus is dual enrollment arranged through the high schools, allowing students in certified high school courses to take those courses for college credit. Senior citizens may take courses at TNCC on a space-available basis without paying tuition under a program the college offers.

ELEMENTARY AND SECONDARY EDUCATION

Two public school systems serve the Williamsburg area's kids: The **Williamsburg–James City County Public Schools** division is a unified system that serves the majority of students in the area from kindergarten through high school. The **York County school system** serves the balance of students from families living in the northern and eastern portions of the Historic Triangle.

Williamsburg-James City County Public Schools

Williamsburg–James City County operates 16 schools: 3 high schools, 4 middle schools, and 9 elementary schools, serving more than 11,000 students.

Students are assigned to schools through a districting formula that is revisited regularly to ensure enrollment balance for each school.

A seven-member school board governs the system, which is run by a superintendent and staff. The five representatives of James City County are elected, while the two city representatives are appointed to the school board. All public meetings of the school board are televised on the W-JCC Schools cable channel.

The system is fully networked and computerized, with each school sporting a website of its own. More important, interested individuals can access information on anything from curriculum, the school calendar, block scheduling, sporting events, and programming by visiting wjccschools.org. Here you can learn about everything from the teacher evaluation process to the division's Strategic Plan, with links to each school website and allied organizations such as the PTA (Parent Teacher Association).

Options for high school students include advanced placement courses, vocational education, technology education, business, practical nursing, and fine arts sequences. The school district's graduation rate is about 97 percent. Approximately 90 percent of its graduates go on to some form of higher education.

Student services include special education, psychological services, substance abuse prevention, health services, school social work services, adult education, and dropout prevention.

An important component of local public education is the Williamsburg–James City County Education Association, an active advocate for high quality public education. It supports rigorous standards and seeks to develop, maintain, and strengthen meaningful partnerships between parents, the community, and educators. It is a local affiliate of the Virginia Education Association and the National Education Association. WJCEA is governed by an executive board, which is elected each year by the membership.

For information or registration, call the administration, located at 117 Ironbound Rd., Williamsburg, at (757) 603-6400.

York County Public Schools

The York County school system is a large division that covers a vast area. It includes the territory bounded by Hampton on the southeast and Newport News and James City on the western and northern perimeters, and several military installations such as Cheatham Annex, the Yorktown Coast Guard Station, and Yorktown Weapons Station.

The system operates 19 schools, including 4 high schools, 4 middle schools, 10 elementary schools and one charter school. It is a large system, governed by a five-member school board and run by a superintendent and staff. One member represents each of the county's five election districts. The board meets monthly, usually on the fourth Monday of each month, for its regular meeting. The public is welcome to attend; the meetings are also televised on local cable television.

Known for academic excellence, the York schools' division has achieved 100 percent accreditation by the Southern Association of Colleges and Schools and is a seven-time winner of the "What Parents Want" award given by *School-Match* magazine.

While there are more than 12,750 students who attend York public schools, the vast majority of them live outside of the greater Williamsburg area. Residents of upper York County near Williamsburg enjoy a zoning plan designed to let children attend the schools that are closest to their homes. This plan routes students of Waller Mill and Magruder Elementary Schools to Queens Lake Middle School and Bruton High School.

The system is computer networked, and the division has a large, easily accessible website at yorkcountyschools.org. On the site, you can learn about each school and the vast array of special programs the division offers. This includes such special programs as adult education, gifted education, the Governor's School, the honors program, New Horizons, NJROTC, the York County School of the Arts, the TV Broadcast Center, the Lifelong Learning Center, special education, and vocational education programs.

For information or registration, call the school board office, located at 302 Dare Rd., at (757) 898-0300 or check yorkcountyschools.org.

Private Schools

HAMPTON ROADS ACADEMY, 739 Academy Ln., Newport News, VA 23602; (757) 884-9100; hra.org. Founded in 1959, Hampton Roads Academy, or HRA as it's referred to locally, has an enrollment of more than 500 students, many who commute from the Greater Williamsburg area. There is an upper and a lower school. From its inception HRA has stood for excellence in college preparatory education and has earned the designation as a "Blue Ribbon School" from the US Department of Education. Hampton Roads Academy is fully accredited by the Virginia Association of Independent Schools. HRA appeals to a wide cross section of students because of its commitment to athletics, arts, and music programs; small class size; active Honor Council and honor code; and reputation for sending 100 percent of its graduates to four-year colleges and universities.

WALSINGHAM ACADEMY, 1100 Jamestown Rd., Williamsburg, VA 23185; (757) 229-2642; walsingham.org. Established in 1948 and directed by the Sisters of Mercy in partnership with a lay faculty, Walsingham is committed to the education and development of the whole person through a caring, value-centered, high-standard curriculum, emphasizing responsible leadership in an increasingly complex world. This independent, coeducational institution offers an elementary as well as a college-preparatory high school, and while it is a Catholic academy, it is open to students of various faiths. Its spirit of ecumenism and a strong sense of community, which provides an environment of friendship, care, and concern, characterize life at Walsingham. The academy stresses academic distinction and self-discipline, encouraging all to rise to their fullest potential. The Mercy heritage of compassion and service is reflected in the school's outreach programs, which extend to the larger community of town, nation, and world. Nearly all of Walsingham's graduates move on to colleges and universities. Enrollment is limited.

WILLIAMSBURG CHRISTIAN ACADEMY, 101 School House Ln., Williamsburg, VA 23188; (757) 220-1978; williamsburgchristian.org. Opened in 1978, this school is an independent, interdenominational Christian school with no church affiliation. After outgrowing several former locations (beginning with the founder's dining room), the school built its own 65,000-square-foot facility in the Stonehouse development west of Williamsburg in 2004. New additions to the school have enabled it to increase enrollment and expand on the variety and scope of programs offered students. The school accepts students from 4-year-old preschoolers through 12th graders.

Health Care

The Williamsburg area has become known for things other than tourism in the past 20 years—as a bedroom community for both Richmond and Hampton Roads, and as a mecca for second-homeowners and early retirees (could be that "play golf 11 months a year" thing).

Those factors have combined to nearly double the region's population, and in Williamsburg, specifically, there are two main groups: college students and retirees. It's all the retirees that have led to growth in health care facilities in the area. Two competing groups—Norfolk-based Sentara Health care and Newport News–based Riverside Health Systems—have competed for years to become the dominant system in the area, building or planning a range of new facilities—specialty physician offices, outpatient surgery and treatment centers, and not one but two full-service hospitals.

As a result, the Williamsburg area offers practically every medical service available in major metro areas.

In 2006, Sentara opened its Williamsburg Regional Medical Center on a 120-acre medical campus off Mooretown Road in York County. The $96.4 million facility has 145 acute-care beds and is surrounded by an outpatient care center, physician offices, and other ancillary services. It replaced the Williamsburg Community Hospital, originally built in 1961, near the William & Mary campus.

Riverside countered with Doctors Hospital—a $72 million, 40-bed facility near the junction of US 60 and VA 199, not far from Kingsmill and Busch Gardens, opened in May 2013.

HOSPITALS

RIVERSIDE DOCTOR'S HOSPITAL, 1500 Commonwealth Ave., Williamsburg, VA 23185; (757) 585-2200; riversideonline.com/rdhw. Williamsburg's newest hospital opened in 2013: a $72 million, 2-story, 100,000-square-foot facility on a secluded campus at the intersection of VA 199 and US 60. Doctor's Hospital has 40 private rooms, 33 medical/surgical suites, 7 ICU rooms, and a full-service emergency department with 12 private patient rooms. The ground floor of the new hospital has a lobby/public area, cafe, meditation room, and community education/conference space. A lifelong health center focuses on simplifying the transition from inpatient acute care to settings outside the hospital.

SENTARA WILLIAMSBURG REGIONAL MEDICAL CENTER, 100 Sentara Circle, Williamsburg, VA 23188; (757) 984-6000; sentara.com/williamsburg. This hospital opened in 2006, bringing much-needed modern technology to the hospital landscape in Williamsburg. A certified primary stroke center, the facility has 145 beds and offers a full range of medical care from emergency heart procedures to obstetrics care.

URGENT HEALTH CARE

Minor, but in need of immediate attention, medical issues—cuts that may require stitches, injuries, or sudden serious illness—can be handled at these urgent care centers. All offer a variety of diagnostic tools, including X-rays, and can see patients without appointments.

FIRST MED OF WILLIAMSBURG, 312 2nd St., Williamsburg, VA 23185; (757) 229-4141. On the side of the city closest to Busch Gardens and Water Country USA, this clinic is open 9 a.m. to 4 p.m. Mon through Fri.

M.D. EXPRESS URGENT CARE, 120 Monticello Ave., Williamsburg, VA 23188; (757) 564-3627. Part of the Riverside Health group, this facility near the intersection of the US 60 Bypass and Richmond Road, is open daily 9 a.m. to 9 p.m., except Thanksgiving and Christmas.

VELOCITY URGENT CARE, 4374 New Town Ave., Ste. 100, Williamsburg, VA 23188; (757) 704-4943. This facility, affiliated with Sentara hospital, opened in 2008 in the New Town mixed-use development. Open daily 8 a.m. to 8 p.m.

WILLIAMSBURG URGENT CARE, 5239 Monticello Ave., Ste. 3, Williamsburg, VA 23188; (757) 279-2999. It's part of the Settlers Market shopping center—look for the Fresh Market as you approach. Open 7 a.m. to 7 p.m. Mon through Fri; 8 a.m. to 2 p.m. Sat and Sun.

Media

Williamsburg's location smack between two metro areas leaves it in an odd position: It can get radio and TV from both—but has relatively few sources of truly local information. Here's a quick review of the media sources available to visitors and newcomers.

NEWSPAPERS

DAILY PRESS, 703 Mariners Row, Newport News, VA 23606; (757) 247-4800, (757) 247-4600; dailypress.com. After nearly 50 years in a low-slung building a few blocks from Newport News shipyard but close to nothing else, the *Daily Press* moved its headquarters to City Center, the mixed-use development in the more centrally located Oyster Point neighborhood of Newport News in 2014. Founded in 1896, the newspaper is published daily (for now), serving the Peninsula and Gloucester and Isle of Wight Counties. It's owned by Tribune Company, owner of the *Chicago Tribune.* The newspaper has a small team of reporters assigned to cover Williamsburg and York County and is widely circulated through the Historic Triangle.

FLAT HAT, College of William & Mary, Campus Center, PO Box 8795, Williamsburg, VA 23187; (757) 221-3283; flathat.wm.edu. The *Flat Hat,* the college's student paper, is published Tuesday and Friday during the regular academic year. It is completely student-run, with no faculty adviser. Its name and its motto—*Stabilitas et fides*—is derived from the Flat Hat Club, the nation's first secret society, founded at the college in 1750, whose members included Thomas Jefferson. The paper expounds on events from the student perspective and upcoming performances, lectures, and programs presented by faculty, students, national performing troupes, and artists, as well as by local organizations.

VIRGINIA GAZETTE, 216 Ironbound Rd., Williamsburg, VA 23188; (757) 220-1736; vagazette.com. The *Virginia Gazette* publishes on Wed and Sat, covering only local news. The paper, like the town, also takes its history very seriously: The *Gazette* was first published in 1736, and styles itself as America's oldest nondaily newspaper. The paper is regarded as a public forum where readers comment freely and regularly on everything from local politics to their experiences as visitors. (The anonymous comments in the Last Word section, typically published on the back page, can range from amusing to downright scurrilous.) While it has the same ownership as the *Daily Press,* the papers have separate newsrooms and content.

The *Gazette* it is a gold mine for information on attractions, local restaurants, places to stay, special events during your stay, and news about the real estate market.

WILLIAMSBURG-YORKTOWNDAILY.COM, 4732 Longhill Rd., Ste. 2201, Williamsburg, VA 23188; (757) 565-1079; wydaily.com. We could get all philosophical with questions about whether a newspaper is a newspaper if it's not published on paper, but the people running this web-only news outlet believe that "you can do without the paper; you can't do without the news." To wit, *WY Daily* publishes (online only) a flow of continuously updated, professionally produced news stories, as they become available, about the goings-on in Williamsburg and James City and York Counties.

Tom Davis, owner of 2 local radio stations, launched the site in 2008 to provide another source of local news.

MAGAZINES

COASTAL VIRGINIA MAGAZINE, 1264 Perimeter Pkwy., Virginia Beach, VA 23454; (757) 422-8979; coastalvirginiamag.com. This glossy regional magazine (formerly known as *Hampton Roads Magazine*) covers features, dining, arts, and entertainment throughout Hampton Roads, with a particular focus on Norfolk and Virginia Beach. Williamsburg restaurants and entertainment are frequently featured. It's available on newsstands throughout the region, and is published 8 times a year by the same company that now produces *The Official Williamsburg/Jamestown/Yorktown Visitors Guide.*

WILLIAMSBURG MAGAZINE, 216 Ironbound Rd., Williamsburg, VA 23188; (757) 220-1736; williamsburgmag.com. The monthly *Williamsburg Magazine,* published by the *Virginia Gazette,* is designed for tourists and those relocating to the area. It includes a variety of feature stories about the region and its attractions and lists of upcoming events, and it's a great source for coupons and special offers from regional merchants. It is free and widely distributed at news racks, stores, hotels, and tourist attractions.

RADIO STATIONS

Three radio stations are based in Williamsburg, but because of its proximity to both the Hampton Roads and Richmond media markets, more than two dozen are available. We'll touch on the local stations in depth, and list the others by their program format.

WBQK, 107.9 FM, "All news 102."

WCWM, 90.9 FM, web.wm.edu/so/wcwm. College radio in all its glory: an eclectic mix running from indie rock to techno and hip-hop. The station also programs a variety of locally produced news and public affairs shows.

WTYD, 92.3 FM, The Tide, tideradio.com. "The Tide" is the primary locally programmed FM serving Williamsburg. It plays what it likes to call "hand-picked music"—a blend of contemporary and older rock, blues and folk, reminiscent of free-form FM stations from the early 1970s. It wears its localness on its sleeve—primary owner Tom Davis moved to the region when he bought the station, and lined up a group of local investors (including musician Bruce Hornsby). The station also covers local news in a way most radio groups don't anymore, and uses its news updates to power a news website, WYDaily.com.

WXGM, 99.1 FM, XTRA 99.1, Gloucester. While not technically a Williamsburg station (it's actually headquartered in Gloucester, across the York River), this station includes the Historic Triangle in its target audience. It plays "today's hits and yesterday's favorites."

WMBG, 740 AM. This locally owned AM plays "golden oldies"—nostalgic music from the 1930s through the 1950s. It has relatively low power, especially at night, making reception tricky.

Elsewhere on the dial, you can find these types of music and programming (this isn't a complete list, but it attempts to cover the stations with the best signal into Williamsburg and the most popular programming styles).

NOTE: Most stations carry the same traffic reports from an outside provider; but the State Department of Transportation offers updated traffic alerts at 1680 AM.

Adult contemporary/R&B
WKJM, 99.3/105.7 FM, Kiss-FM, Richmond
WKUS, 105.3 FM, 105.3 Kiss-FM, Norfolk

Adult contemporary/soft rock
WTVR, 98.1 FM, Lite 98, Richmond
WVBW, 92.9 FM, The Wave, Norfolk
WWDE, 101.3 FM, 2WD, Norfolk

Christian
WAUQ, 89.7 FM, Richmond
WRJR, 1010 AM, Norfolk

Classical
WHRO, 90.3 FM, Norfolk

Classic rock/classic hits
WAFX, 106.9 FM, The Fox, Norfolk
WKLR, 96.5 FM, 96-5 KLR, Richmond
WNOB, 93.7 FM, Bob FM, Norfolk
WWLB, 98.9 FM, 98-9 Liberty, Richmond

Contemporary Christian/inspirational
WGH-AM, 1310 AM, Star 1310

Contemporary hits/Top 40
WBTJ, 106.5 FM, The Beat, Richmond
WCDX, 92.1 FM, iPower 92-1, Richmond
WMXB, 103.7 FM, Mix 103-7, Richmond
WNVZ, 104.5 FM, Z104, Norfolk
WOWI, 102.9 FM, 103 Jamz, Norfolk
WPTE, 94.9 FM, The Point, Norfolk
WRVQ, 94.5 FM, Q94, Richmond
WVHT, 100.5 FM, Hot 100.5, Norfolk
WVKL, 95.7 FM, 95-7 R&B, Norfolk

Country
WGH, 97.3 FM, 97-3 The Eagle, Norfolk
WKHK, 95.3 FM, K-95, Richmond
WUSH, 106.1 FM, US106, Norfolk

Modern rock
WDYL, 100.9 FM, Y-101, Richmond
WNOR, 98.7 FM, FM99, Norfolk
WROX, 96.1 FM, 96X, Norfolk
WRXL, 102.1 FM, The X, Richmond

National Public Radio/public affairs
WCVE, 88.9 FM, Richmond
WHRV, 89.5 FM, Norfolk

News/talk
WLEE, 990 AM, Richmond
WNIS, 790 AM, Norfolk
WRVA, 1140 AM, Richmond
WTAR, 850 AM, Norfolk

WTPS, 1240 AM, Richmond

Smooth jazz
WJCD, 107.7 GM, Smooth Jazz 107.7, Norfolk

Spanish language
WTOX, 1480 AM, La Equis
WVNZ, 1320 AM, Selecta 1320
WVXX, 1050 AM, Selecta 1050

Sports/talk
WRNL, 910 AM, Richmond's Fox Sports, Richmond
WVSP, 94.1 FM, 94.1 ESPN, Norfolk
WXGI, 950 AM, ESPN 950, Richmond
WXTG, 102.1 FM and 1490 AM, The Game, Norfolk/Hampton

TELEVISION STATIONS

As with radio, residents of Williamsburg and the surrounding area can pick up television stations from both Norfolk and Richmond. (The dominant local cable-TV provider, Cox Cable, only carries the Norfolk stations, however.)

WTKR Channel 3 (CBS), Norfolk
WSKY Channel 4 (Independent), Norfolk
WTVR Channel 6 (CBS), Richmond
WRIC Channel 8 (ABC), Richmond
WAVY Channel 10 (NBC), Norfolk
WWBT Channel 12 (NBC), Richmond
WVEC Channel 13 (ABC), Norfolk
WHRO Channel 15 (PBS), Norfolk
WCVE Channel 23 (PBS), Richmond
WGNT Channel 27 (UPN), Norfolk
WTVZ Channel 33 (MyNetwork), Norfolk
WRLH Channel 35 (FOX), Richmond
WVBT Channel 43 (FOX), Norfolk
WZTD Channel 45 (Telemundo), Richmond
WUPV Channel 47 (CW), Richmond
WPXV Channel 49 (Ion), Virginia Beach

Index